CULTURAL FRONT

GENERAL EDITOR: MICHAEL BÉRUBÉ

MODERNISM, INC.
BODY, MEMORY, CAPITAL

EDITED BY

JANI SCANDURA AND MICHAEL THURSTON

NEW YORK UNIVERSITY PRESS
NEW YORK AND LONDON

NEW YORK UNIVERSITY PRESS
New York and London

Library of Congress Cataloging-in-Publication Data
Modernism, inc. : body, memory, capital / edited by
Jani Scandura and Michael Thurston.
p.   cm. — (Cultural front)
Includes bibliographical references and index.
ISBN 0-8147-8136-5 (acid-free paper) —
ISBN 0-8147-8137-3 (pbk. : acid-free paper)
1. American literature—20th century—History and criticism.
2. Modernism (Literature)—United States. 3. Literature and
society—United States—History—20th century. 4. Art and
society—United States—History—20th century. 5. United
States—Civilization—20th century. 6. Art, Modern—20th
century—United States. 7. Modernism (Art)—United States.
8. Art, American.   I. Scandura, Jani. II. Thurston, Michael, 1965–
III. Cultural front (Series)
PS228.M63 M63 2001
810.9'112—dc21   2001000738

New York University Press books are printed on acid-free paper
and their binding materials are chosen for strength and durability.

Manufactured in the United States of America
10 9 8 7 6 5 4 3 2 1

CONTENTS

ACKNOWLEDGMENTS

W e met one night in 1996 at an MLA party and stood in the corner for a long time, talking and bonding in our mutual frustration over the formalist and anti-theoretical bent that still seemed to dominate critical work on modernism. (This was before the new vogue in modernisms had come to the fore.) Where did the United States fit into all this? What about cultural studies? And why did American studies and modernist studies still seem at odds? This book found its genesis then and in the long e-mails that followed. Like all anthologies, *Modernism, Inc.,* had a bumpy birth; during its production, we weathered a dissertation defense, the writing of single-authored books, four jobs, and four moves between us. Our debts to others are large. We would most like to thank our contributors, many of whom stuck with us patiently over a number of years. We would also like to thank Michael Bérubé, the editor of the Cultural Fronts series, for believing in the book and supporting its publication; Eric Zinner, who is as smart, supportive, and patient an editor as one could ever hope for; and Despina Papazoglou Gimbel, Cecilia Feilla, and Emily Park at New York University Press. Grateful acknowledgment is made to Columbia University Press for permission to print William Maxwell's "Kitchen Mechanics and Parlor Nationalists: Andy Razaf, Black Bolshevism and Harlem's Renaissance," which appeared in a slightly revised form as Chapter One in *New Negro, Old Left: African-American Writing and Communism Between the Wars* (Columbia UP 1999); to the University of Michigan Press for permission to print David Nicholls' essay, "Jean Toomer's *Cane,* Modernization, and the Spectral Folk" a version of which appeared as Chapter Two of *Conjuring the Folk: Forms of Modernity in African America* (U of Michigan P 2000); and to Johns Hopkins University Press for permission to print Maria Damon's essay, an earlier version of which appeared as "Gertrude Stein, Jewish Social Scientists and the 'Jewish Question'" in *Modern Fiction Studies* 42:3 (1996), 489–506. © Purdue Research Foundation. We are also grateful to Yale University, the Whitney Humanities Center, the University of Minnesota, the McKnight Foundation, and the Merge Research Institute for support; to Cary Nelson, who introduced us and gave us helpful advice during the production of the volume; and to Rebecca Scherr, who secured many of the permissions, found copies of photographs, and generally helped keep things running smoothly during the editing process. Tom Augst, Maria Damon, Paula Rabinowitz, Rita Raley, Susan Rosenbaum, Karen Till, and members of the "Postmodern Modernisms" seminar at the October 2000 Modernist Studies Association conference gave us generous feedback on the writing of the introduction. Bruce Braun, Geoff Eley, Simon Gikandi, Jean Leverich, Marjorie Levinson, Erin O'Connor, Susan Rosenbaum, Carroll Smith-Rosenberg, Karla Taylor, Patricia Yaeger, and the librarians and curators at the Nevada Historical Society and the University of Nevada-Reno advised on the research and writing of an earlier version of the Reno essay. And, finally, Lisa Stowe-Thurston helped us technologically and psychically throughout a long production process.

INTRODUCTION

AMERICA AND THE PHANTOM MODERN

Jani Scandura and Michael Thurston

> enie menie minie moe plenty other pine boxes stacked up there con-
> taining what they'd scraped up of Richard Roe
>   and other person or persons unknown. Only one can go. How did they
> pick John Doe?
>   Make sure he ain't a dinge, boys.
>   make sure he ain't a guinea or a kike,
>   how can you tell a guy's a hundredpercent when all you've got's a gun-
> nysack full of bones, bronze buttons stamped with the screaming eagle
> and a pair of roll puttees?
>   . . . and the gagging chloride and the puky dirtstench of the yearold dead.
>   —John Dos Passos, *Nineteen Nineteen*

John Kennedy (the son, not the father) was killed while we were completing
this project. As a result, these essays will always be haunted by his image: the
toddler saluting his father's coffin; the curly-headed hunk in graduation garb; the
self-assured editor, his ice-princess wife on his arm, fighting in Central Park, kiss-
ing at the White House, battling paparazzi. He was dubbed an "American prince,"
but his greatest feat was to be somewhat average—though significantly richer than
most and, let's face it, more attractive. His death, it was said, marked the end of an
era, if not of JFK's Camelot, at least the memory of it. But it was the absence of
Kennedy's body that consumed us. As the days progressed and the corpse was not
found, news stations began recording the building of a makeshift monument outside the Kennedys' Tribeca loft. A panorama of posters and flowers and stuffed

teddy bears piled up on the sidewalk, spilled out past police barricades and into the crowds in the streets. The rows of people who lined up to leave artifacts became artifacts themselves in a kind of Situationist performance of mourning. In the end, it felt voyeuristic, an appropriation of sorts to watch the spectacle of the search, the memorial service, and the burial at sea.[1] And the ad hoc monument, incomplete without onlookers, came to signify both an appropriation of loss and a substitution for some unspeakable lack.[2]

The collective obsession with Kennedy's death recalled the recent, more subdued search for another young man. But not, it turns out, because his body was missing. In the spring of 1998 the remains of the Vietnam War's Unknown Soldier were disinterred from their crypt in Arlington National Cemetery and subjected to DNA tests.[3] Suddenly, unexpectedly, the Unknown Soldier had a name: Air Force First Lieutenant Michael Joseph Blassie, listed as missing in action since 1972. His body, ritualistically selected and buried ("enie menie minie moe") like those from the two world wars, was supposed to stand in for all the missing dead, for any man and every man lost in battle. Still, the selection of the corpse was suspicious.[4] For a war fought disproportionately by men of color without means, the body that stood for Everyman was white and middle-class. The Unknown body, reclaimed from metaphor, became metaphor: this time to suggest that there is no one who can stand in for any man or every man (or woman), no possibility of collective identity, only identifiable bodies, mangled beyond recognition. Yet the means through which Blassie's body was particularized were also the means through which it was exhumed from historical and cultural particularity and made generic. A body is just so much matter with a DNA code. It is said that Blassie will be the last of the Unknowns, a last relic of modernism, an homage to the fraternity of loss embedded in twentieth-century macro-warfare.[5] The Vietnam Unknown's tomb will remain empty as a kind of memorial gap and implicit salute to medical—and military—technology.

But the body as matter, despite the ritualistic veneer, really was never the point. The Tomb of the Unknowns has always only been about the fact of the crypt itself. In her book *Dismembering the Male: Men's Bodies, Britain, and the Great War,* Joanna Bourke points out that writings about the British World War I Unknown Warrior, the first Unknown Soldier entombed in 1920, were less concerned with the soldier himself than with the unknown grave.[6] The body of the Unknown Warrior was planned for bereaved families and for politicians under pressure, Bourke argues, not for the living servicemen "who had risked their bodies" and "were incapable of persuading themselves that the anonymous body could statistically ever 'actually be' the body of the beloved."[7] The absence of the body, of a body, in the Vietnam War's memorial crypt reveals only that the tomb was empty all along.

Now fallen celebrities have become the unknowns of our age. We eat their beautiful bodies, regurgitating, only to chew on them again and again.[8] Our rumination is marked not so much by a "refusal to mourn" as by a refusal to stop mourning, a refusal to let go of the whole and unfragmented image and the market drive that perpetuates this refusal. (Princess Diana, three years after her death, still regularly appears on the cover of *People*.) This is an era of death after dark, of "unnatural" histories and bodies buried invisibly. We ingest the junk food of simulacra: video clips of dismembered dummies and actors dripping with Red Dye No. 3. These make poor substitutes for the bodies we know are out there—in Kosovo, in Sierra Leone, and on dim-lit Detroit streets. We—perhaps Euro-Americans, or middle-class intellectuals, or media junkies in the CNN age—imprint the image with the aura of the original and permanent, and incorporate into it what we cannot see but desire to see: the corpses in their grotesque brutality, unspeakably bloody, bloated, and mangled. Impermanent. Vulnerable. Charred remains.[9] We seek out and resist those bodies in decay and changing colors, as Hemingway described, "from white to yellow, to yellow-green, to black."[10]

These unseen corpses become an allegory for all we have not been permitted to see, but have been induced to desire to see and thereby possess: the "nothing of the secret," to borrow from Jean Baudrillard, that produces celebrity in the first place.[11] The cult value of the dead celebrity, like that of the Unknown Soldier, relies on the unknowability of the corpse. (It is not insignificant that Kennedy was burned and not buried or that his dead parents were entombed not far from the Unknown's crypt.)[12] Instead, we substitute places for bodies, making places artifacts—the condo at Bundy, the tunnel in Paris, the Tribeca loft. These are our Tombs of the Unknowns. They encrypt not so much anonymous corpses as named absences—the emptiness of the corpse as sign and the hollowness of the image that we have buried and refuse to bury with the corpse.

Two bodies then. John Doe and John-John. One an unknown body that wasn't unknown; one a known body that wasn't known. Both reclaimed from the grave. Haunted, these bodies haunt us in their absence with the inherited words and sorrows and sins of father(s) they never knew. We no longer need the body as an object to allegorize that which we would not could not bury, we are too busy serving as gatekeepers for the entombed secrets of generations already past. A century and a half after Emerson's *Nature*, it is still and again a "retrospective age." But we are left without even the bones of our ancestors with which to toy. We live instead in an era of phantoms, formations of the "unconscious that have never been conscious," and of crypts that are not of our making.[13]

And so it is with the modern—and with *Modernism, Inc.* The essays in this collection are all in some way about crypts, those "secret vaults" within the subject, within history, that hide repressed traumas and forbidden pleasures and "the hiding of that hiding."[14] As a whole, they suggest that the empty crypts of our present serve as allegories for the "awareness-unawareness" of the shames of the past in the present, of the modern in the postmodern.[15] The relationship between modernity and postmodernity, between modernism and postmodernism, becomes one that can no longer be formulated through paradigms of rupture,[16] recurrence,[17] continuation,[18] dissolution,[19] or concentration,[20] but instead reveals itself as a complex and constant process of imbrication and inheritance, repression and memory, resistance and phantasmatic return.[21] Modernity is postmodernity's ghost. Its unspeakable secrets have come back to haunt us through phantoms of our own design. And we—postmoderns—are compelled to perform the phantasmatic ventriloquism of the stranger within.

NATION

This is a collection, then, that looks at our ghosts—and at the tombs from which they're derived. Of these, perhaps the phantom by which we are most profoundly haunted is "America." Certainly, as a conceptual term and ontology—or one might say *hauntology*—"America" occupies a privileged position within the discourses of modernity.[22] More than simply referring to a nation-state or states or a geological formation, America may be seen as an allegory for modernity itself, or, at the least, for "a disenchanted modernity," serving elsewhere (mainly in Europe) as "a catalyst for [twentieth-century debates] on modernity and modernization."[23]

It could be argued, in fact, that if "America" is not *the* grand narrative of modernity, certainly it is one of them. It was in America that many of the signs of modern life—jazz, skyscrapers, automobiles—were born or seemed most at home. And it was to America that many of the technologies of modernism—Fordist mass production, corporate capitalism, the Hollywood studio system—were attributed. Moreover, it is through America that many, though certainly not all, of the atrocities of modernity have been mediated and Media-tied. (Consider, for instance, the commodification and Disneyfication of Holocaust memory and the collective forgetting of Hiroshima transposed onto the beatific image of the mushroom cloud).

Although most of the essays in this collection are primarily concerned with North American modernisms and modernity, we are not suggesting that "America" refers solely to the United States or even to the North America, but to the whole of the so-called "New World" that constitutes the Americas, North, Central, and South. As Perry Anderson notes, "we owe the coinage of 'modernism' as an aesthetic movement to a Nicaraguan poet, writing in a Guatemalan journal, of a literary encounter in Peru."[24] Indeed, the terms modernism and postmodernism themselves incorporate (remember-forget) their own Latin American inheritances.

To speak of American modernism and modernity, in other words, is not to locate aesthetic and social formations within the boundaries of a national discourse, but to consider those cultural symbols, modes of production, social organizations, and processes of subject formation associated with "Americanism" and "Americanization." If we cannot avoid an implicit reference to the United States it is because the United States-as-America might be seen to signify the modern in its purest form. For the United States-as-America is, as Jean Baudrillard remarks, the "original version of modernity," a place that lives in the "perpetual present of signs."[25] Moreover, implicit in Bill Brown's suggestion that "modernism can be understood as the aesthetic of globalization" are the specters of United States industrial expansiveness and the imperialist prowess of global English (read: American).[26] (What other nation would have the audacity to call itself *US*.) The United States-as-America is in fact encrypted within the High Modernist aesthetic dream of wholeness in fragmentation—an aesthetic that might be described, as was Gertrude Stein's prose, "like the United States viewed from an airplane."[27]

Nor is it an accident that when Benedict Anderson speaks of the remembering-forgetting that is constitutive of the later nationalisms of the nineteenth century, he uses the United States as an example. Nations, he argues, hold together by "having to 'have already forgotten'" those threats to its cohesion, "those tragedies of which one unceasingly needs to be 'reminded.'" In the United States, modernist nationalism might be said to have been possible only after the 1861–65 conflict had been reinscribed in cultural memory as a "great 'civil' war between 'brothers' rather than between—as surely they briefly were—two sovereign nation-states."[28] And this requires both a temporal distance from the material events and the remembered-forgetting of psychological incorporation on a national scale, at least in terms of official memory.

The modern does not so much imply an erasure of the past, therefore, as an encryptment of certain uncomfortable narratives. Indeed, the suggestion that progressive modernity throws itself to the future is itself a denial of the obsessive attention that modern cultures paid to "looking back" to Darwinian origins, nostalgic folk histories, and the childhood wounds of oedipal dramas. Still, modernist nostalgia was not marked so much by a longing for a past, as by a desire for not having had one.[29] America was imagined and imagined itself as having no past and therefore seemed to be less subject to the malaise of nostalgia that marked European modernisms.

In touting its eternal youth, America might more properly be seen as melancholic, encrypting its own history in a narrative of a perpetual process and present. America was always "becoming" and therefore always new—and re-newed. Ann Douglas points out that it was not until the 1930s that Americans began to use the term "United States" to refer to their nation, rather than the more unified monolith, "America."[30] This is not simply due to an acknowledg-ment of "possible divisions among separate parts of the national self" and a recognition of the limits of American power, as Douglas suggests, but to a kind of return of the repressed: It alludes to the deep instability encrypted in all dis-courses of modern nation building.[31] The Birth of the Nation is and must be founded on rupture itself. The shift in terminology also served to rescue the na-tion from the discursive grab bag called "America" and thereby not only dis-tanced the nation from a conceptual collapse into modernity, but preserved progressive modernity from the taint of depression—and the Depression—that embroiled American culture. Modernity thus incorporated America and was in-corporated by America, with its concomitant legacies of embodiment, memory, and capital.

MEMORY

We speak of incorporation in a specific sense. Incorporation is a dialectical term. It is connected etymologically to the *corpus,* the body and materiality, but it also anticipates an erasure of matter. To incorporate, according to the *Oxford English Dictionary,* means not simply "to put one thing into another so as to form one body or an integral whole," it also suggests the ineffable and that which is "with-out body or substance," incorporeal, un-embodied. Thus, to incorporate requires a kind of amnesia, a forgetting of any originary separation or distinction between two bodies or terms. The incorporated body is not a hybrid that (potentially at least) recognizes the distinct origins of its parts, but a "uniform," "thoroughly blended" mixture. To incorporate is to integrate separate elements so thoroughly that traces of what had previously been separated, indeed, the very fact of separa-tion, is erased. It is that line of erasure that implies both modernity—if imagined as a break from the past and a perpetual propulsion into the future—and Americanness, which celebrates the eternal youth of the nation, its heterogeneity, and the individualism of its citizens, and which denies its own possession of his-tory and its commitment to conformity, assimilation, homogenization, and Anglo-fication. When President McKinley initiated his "overseas crusades to spread the blessings of 'our deeply incorporated civilization'" at the turn of the twentieth century, he spoke truer words than he realized.[32]

It is the amnesia constitutive of incorporation—and its concomitant vio-lence—that compelled Ferenczi and Freud to distinguish *incorporation*, the process by which one refuses to mourn, from *introjection*, the inclusive process of "healthy mourning."[33] Unlike *introjection*, a "casting inside" in which the self is redefined by bringing the object of loss into the ego, preserving it in conscious memory, the "fantasy of incorporation reveals a gap within the psyche; it points to something that is missing just where introjection should have occurred."[34] Nicolas Abraham and Maria Torok suggest that this refusal to mourn the lost object made manifest in a fantasy of incorporation is the root of melancholy.[35] *Incorporation* involves what Maria Torok calls "preservative repression," in which "an already fulfilled desire lays buried—equally incapable of rising or of disintegrating." One brings the lost object into the self and encrypts it—buries it alive—refusing to mourn the loss, denying that anything ever was lost, that the self might ever have to transform as a result. Thus, as the architect Mark Wigley points out,

> The logic of incorporation turns out to be that of the parasite, the foreigner occupying the domestic interior and unable to be expelled from it, by being thrown up and out, without ruining the space. . . . The uncanniness of the parasite is that it "is never simply alien to and separable from the body to which it has been transplanted or which it already haunts."[36]

In this context, modern American culture may be read as embedded in an economy of repression and melancholy in which difference and difficulty must be incorporated for the foundation to hold. Dramatically transformed due to the influx of some 25 million immigrants to the United States between 1880 and 1924,[37] modern America was reconstructed through a simultaneous remembering and forgetting of the Other within. Debates about Americanization, assimilation, and nativism continually negotiated the boundary of "foreignness," through a complex economy of embodiment and cultural memory with consumer capitalism as the determining glue.

In *Our America*, Walter Benn Michaels argues that in the early twentieth century, "American" came to designate "not a set of social and economic conditions but an identity that exists prior to and independent of those conditions."[38] According to Michaels, debates about nativism and Americanization were largely debates over family ties.[39] Certainly, discourses of embodiment underwrote squabbles about Americanization. For instance, in his 1914 nativist tract Edward A. Ross proposed the social philosophy of the melting pot, in which "external differences" between groups of people are made to disappear by "a fusion of blood" and the transformation "by the miracle of assimilation of Jews, Slavs, Poles, Frenchmen, Germans, Hindus, Scandinavians and so on" into WASPs. "It is fair to say that the blood now being injected into the veins of our people is 'sub-common,'" writes Ross, adopting not simply a familial metaphor, but an ominously erotic one: the disembodied penis runs amok, spreading

"Caliban's" seed throughout the "normal population."[40] Michaels points out that critics of nativism likewise privileged discourses of the body in order to articulate their positions. Although Horace Kallen's response to Ross in his 1915 essay in the *Nation* presents a more complex picture of the process of assimilation, for example, he nonetheless relies on a Cartesian split between the internal subject, in which the immigrant's "ancestral blazings" are housed, and the external body that performs an "Americanization" dependent on visible cues: seeming to "adopt the American [read Anglo-Saxon] variety of English speech, American clothes and manners, the American attitude in politics."[41] Interactions between immigrants of different ancestry served not to meld them—or melt them—together, but instead produced an awareness of the "categorical difference[s]," indeed the imposition of categorization itself by modern American culture. "At the present time," Kallen argues, "there seems to be no dominant American mind other than the industrial and theological. The spirit of the land is inarticulate, not a voice but a chorus of many voices each singing a rather different tune."[42]

CORPORATION

The language of embodiment and capital was, in fact, more deeply intertwined in debates about modern national identity than even Michaels allows. Horace Kallen's early twentieth-century reading of Americanization as consciously and conspicuously "external" resists the socialization that Pierre Bourdieu argues is produced when relations of order are internalized as "self evident." For Bourdieu, "the *sense* of limits implies *forgetting* the limits."[43] When the rules and categories of social order are successfully remembered by the body, they may be, must be contemporaneously forgotten by the brain. Or, conversely, what the mind incorporates, the body remembers. Kallen posits American culture as a struggle for new limits. "Americans of British stock still are prevailingly the artists and thinkers of the land," he admits, "but they work without common vision or ideals. They have no *ethos* any more. The older tradition has passed from a life into a memory, and the newer one, so far has an Anglo-Saxon base, holding its own beside more and more formidable competitors."[44] (The successive tightening of immigration restrictions during the first half of the century may be seen as a way of reducing such competition, a re-membering of those limiting "rules of the game.")[45]

Laudatory though his critique may be, in relying on a distinct divide between the inside and outside, between body and memory, Kallen had already missed the point. To be Americanized meant to be modernized—and not simply because you acquired the appropriate external signs by becoming a consumer of mass-produced goods, but also (and this was the sticky point for

Kallen) because you internalized the notion that exteriority produced who you were. The modern American was, literally, the clothes that he wore. "As a basic lesson in *modernization,* immigrant and migrant workers learned to be 'presentable,'" writes Stuart Ewen, "to rely on tools of presentation while navigating the treacherous waters of everyday life. True moderns were learning to internalize the dictum of Bishop Berkeley, that 'to be is to be perceived.'"[46]

The shift to a "commodity construction of identity"[47] occurred earlier and was perhaps more trenchant in American culture than elsewhere. It was made possible by what Alan Trachtenberg calls the "incorporation of America" in the late nineteenth century, the hegemonization of that "system of corporate life" that Charles Francis Adams Jr. declared in 1869 was "a new power, for which our language contains no name."[48] In the early twentieth century, the "merger movement" that transformed small, private companies into monopolistic giants reached its apex, such that the *corpus* of the company seemed to displace the *corpus* of the nation. By 1904, Trachtenberg writes, three hundred industrial corporations controlled more than 40 percent of American manufacturing. By 1929 "the two hundred largest corporations held 48 percent of all corporate assets . . . and 58 percent of net capital assets such as land, buildings, and machinery."[49]

As Trachtenberg makes clear, the "incorporation" of America refers less to the changes in practices of production than to the range of cognitive and cultural transformations enabled by them. Corporations perpetuated new conceptions of the body-as-machine through the introduction and application of Taylor's *Principles of Scientific Management* to the assembly lines, binding the *corpus* of the nation to the corporation as the worker's body built the machinery of capital. Corporations also perpetuated transformations in the creation and dissemination of culture and information, bringing to a crisis point the tensions between mass culture and high art that Andreas Huyssen sees as being constitutive of the modernist "great divide."[50] The domination of what Max Horkheimer and Theodor Adorno call the "culture industry"—which included the new newspaper and magazine empires built by Henry Luce and Randolph Hearst and the Hollywood mega-studios—changed forever the way Americans viewed the world and themselves.[51]

CULTURE

Not surprisingly, the central impetus of *Modernism, Inc.* is to make sense of some of these cultural and cognitive transformations and to analyze our critical understanding of them. Our title makes a backhanded reference to John Crowe Ransom's 1937 polemic, "Criticism, Inc.," in which Ransom advocates a newly professional criticism that distinguishes itself both from the belletristic and historical scholarship then dominant in American literary studies and from the aggressively politicized reading strategies of Marxist or proletarian critics outside the universities.[52] Such a criticism, Ransom argues, must acknowledge the bipolar character of literary discourse, taking into account both the text's content, its gesture to the universal, and its form, the set of artifices and devices that thwart this gesture and render the text stubbornly individual. For the properly *professional* critic, form is what matters, not content. It is the critic's technical knowledge of formal devices that enables him (and it is always *him* for Ransom) to see that any access to the universal can come paradoxically only through all those things about a text that militate against its absorption into the universal—those bits and pieces of technique that grant the text its enabling irrelevance. While belletrists seek to dissolve the unique literary text into a bland, undifferentiated Culture, while historians seek to sink it in the turbulent waters of its time, while moralists discard its form in favor of its ethical prescriptions, and while Marxists wire it up to the machinery of dialectical materialism, Ransom declares that professional criticism (Criticism, Inc.) will save the text by turning it back on itself. For Ransom, the professional critic should not waste his time on polemical, mass-produced, and vernacular works that were also emerging during the period. Nor should he foray across disciplines or concern himself much with the multiplicitous worlds outside the linguistic text. Instead, he should seek the universal embodied in prosodic and tropic invention.

Ransom, like most of the critics who lauded or condemned his approach, emphasized the first term in his title, *criticism*. Yet it is the second term that deserves more attention. We hope, through the essays included in this collection, to read and reread what is written in that *Inc.* Bad puns aside, Inc. spills; its multiple significance marks the historically particular discourses of embodiment, subjectivity, aesthetics, and economics. Therefore, we have organized the essays in *Modernism, Inc.* along a continuum of the matrix of meanings of *incorporation* as a paradigm through which America, modernism, and modernity may be redefined. Part 1 is concerned with how bodies and matter—and "bodies *that* matter"[53]—figure within the urban and technological spaces of modernity. The essays in Part 2 turn inward to consider cultural memory and forgetting in their analyses of the individual and collective effects of traumas inflicted by and upon modern Americans, mediated through them. Part 3 considers the legacies of the economic and social turbulence embedded in the machinery of capitalism and the modernist corporatization of America.

It is with some self-conscious irony that *Modernism, Inc.* sets its sights on contributing to an academic trend that is attempting to make modernism new again, a gesture that can only be labeled neomodernist, as Paula Rabinowitz observes in her essay included here on the "Great Lady Painters." Certainly, we are indebted to those revisionary modernisms of the past several years that have attempted to recover a history of "making it new" that was a good deal more complex than had heretofore been articulated.[54] But this collection is less interested in identifying the narratives of individuals and artists who were underrepresented in a pluralistic sense, than it is with the epistemological questions that undergird those gestures. In this we are particularly influenced by Cary Nelson's astute observation in *Repression and Recovery: Modern American Poetry and the Politics of Cultural Memory, 1910–1945* that "what and who we are now is already in part a result of what we no longer know we have forgotten."[55] In these essays, then, modernism, as the aesthetic articulation of modernity, comes to signify less a quest for the new than for those secrets of hindsight that that pursuit necessarily entails.[56]

The essays in *Modernism, Inc.* generally are more concerned with the mobile, populist "low modernisms," what Marshall Berman calls "modernism in the streets," than with those materials with which Ransom was preoccupied.[57] This tendency derives in part from the fact that the essays are concerned with those histories, forms, objects, and memories of which we are aware-unaware. If high modernism and its critics imagined "wholeness in fragmentation" on the level of formal aesthetics, mass culture literalized the fantasy. Bill Brown has argued that early science fiction, for instance, was "fundamentally prosthetic, imaginatively repairing the damaged body, the fragmented body, the separated head and hand. The monumental male these texts produce is a body without scars, a body on which history is not written but erased, a body without memory, a national body with no nation."[58] Yet, as we have suggested, it is not so much the "great divide" between the high and the low that preoccupies us here as it is the technologies of cultural memory and forgetting, production and consumption, encryptment and disinterment. *Modernism Inc.* constitutes a kind of meta-unburial—a digging up and investigation of what we imagine we were not supposed to have seen.

NOTES

1. There is no way around it: to discuss Kennedy's death is to be complicit in appropriating an event so deeply private—remember the photos of his sister's face after the memorial service—to ignore it is to suppress understanding. Yet the event, like Kennedy's body, could not help but produce an excess of signification.

2. Of course, the young Kennedy's body had always been one we knew we could desire—were compelled to desire—but couldn't have. (His father's body, by contrast, was narrated as a body that everyone could—and did—have indiscriminately.)

3. The monument contrasts ironically with the Vietnam Veteran's Memorial, in which even the spectators are mourned—their ghostly reflections slide across the stone-etched names of the lost.
4. The notion of a "collective" body being found in the Unknown Soldier was always suspect—as the opening Dos Passos citation demonstrates.
5. The Vietnam Unknown, buried during the Reagan administration, was always already an outdated symbol, a nostalgic attempt by the Republican Right to reclaim modernity and a potent revision of the Vietnam Veteran's Memorial, which made the postmodern gesture of maintaining the gap while leaving nothing out—and no one uncomplicitous, not even the spectators.
6. See Joanna Bourke, *Dismembering the Male: Men's Bodies, Britain, and the Great War* (Chicago: Chicago University Press, 1996). World War I made the problem of finding and identifying the bodies of missing soldiers formidable. Under political pressure and after great controversy, in October 1920, King George V agreed to have the body of an unidentified British soldier, "An Unknown Warrior," disinterred from the battlefields in France and ritualistically buried in Westminster Abbey. A few months later, the Americans followed suit. Joanna Bourke argues that "the modesty of death during battle made the need to honor the dead servicemen after war by a majestic display more urgent."
7. Bourke 249–50.
8. The familiar "we" marks the problematic and familial collective both assumed and produced by a global media that constructs traumatic material events as always out-there-and-elsewhere even in their immediacy. It is a "we" of collective impossibility: you cannot watch it if you are part of it, you are not part of it until you watch it.
9. Jacques Derrida argues that mourning always consists in

> attempting to ontologize remains, to make them present, in the first place by *identifying* the bodily remains and by *localizing* the dead. . . . One has to know. *One has to know it. One has to have knowledge* [Il faut le savoir]. Now, to know is to know who and where, to know whose body it really is and what place it occupies—for it must stay in its place. In a safe place. Nothing could be worse, for the work of mourning, than confusion or doubt: one has to know who is buried where— and it is necessary (to know—to make certain) that, in what remains of him, he remain there.

The lost bodies both initiate an incomplete mourning and are its sign. See Jacques Derrida, *Specters of Marx: The State of the Debt, the Work of Mourning, and the New International,* trans. Peggy Kamuf (New York: Routledge, 1994), 8.
10. Ernest Hemingway, "A Natural History of the Dead," in *Death in the Afternoon* (New York: Simon and Schuster, 1996), 137.

11. See Jean Baudrillard, "On Seduction," in *Selected Writings,* ed. Mark Poster (Palo Alto: Stanford University Press), 1988).

12. A year after Kennedy's death, the supermarket rags proclaimed scandalously that the Kennedy family hushed up this unspeakable fact: the bodies were so badly disfigured as to be virtually unidentifiable. Without an understanding of the allegorical significance of Kennedy's body, that this should make news, even in the *National Enquirer* or *Star*, seems incomprehensible. After all, they had plunged to their deaths in a plane crash.

13. We draw here on the work of Nicolas Abraham and Maria Torok. "Phantoms," according to Abraham in his critique of Freud, are not the "effect of unsuccessful mourning," of incorporation or the carrying of a tomb within the self, but of the objectification of an inherited tomb, the "gaps left within us by the secrets of others." See particularly Nicolas Abraham, "Notes on the Phantom: A Complement to Freud's Metapsychology," and Nicolas Abraham and Maria Torok, "The Topography of Reality: Sketching a Metapsychology of Secrets," in Nicolas Abraham and Maria Torok, *The Shell and the Kernel,* vol. 1, trans. Nicholas Rand (Chicago: University of Chicago Press, 1994), 171–76, 157–61.

14. Here we draw specifically on Abraham and Torok's psychoanalytic topography and on Mark Wigley's reevaluation of the terms of their study in *Derrida's Haunt: The Architecture of Deconstruction* (Cambridge: MIT Press, 1993), 141–47.

15. As Hayden White, Dominick LaCapra, Eric Santner, and others have argued, the history and experience of modernity are inherently traumatic, marked as they are, to paraphrase Walter Benjamin, by the "shock" of the new. While most recent work on modernity and trauma has focused on the Holocaust as the apotheosis of traumatic modernity, the possibility that the totality of modernity may be read through a paradigm of traumatic confrontation and memory opens up a new and dynamic relationship between modernity and postmodernity that exceeds the continuity versus rupture debates (see below). This paradigm would include and embody Paul Gilroy's construction of the "Black Atlantic" as well as Houston Baker's recent suggestions that American modernism might best be read as burgeoning in the postbellum period of the American Civil War rather than against the backdrop of World War I. See, in particular, Paul Gilroy, *The Black Atlantic: Modernity and Double Consciousness* (Cambridge: Harvard University Press, 1993). On the relationship between trauma and modernity I refer here largely to Dominick LaCapra's analysis of this position, given in a recent lecture, "Writing History, Writing Trauma," at the Humanities Institute, University of Minnesota, October 1999. See also Eric L. Santner, *Stranded Objects: Mourning, Memory, and Film in Postwar Germany* (Ithaca: Cornell University Press, 1993); Dominick LaCapra, *Representing the Holocaust: History, Theory, Trauma* (Ithaca: Cornell University Press, 1996); Dominick

LaCapra, *History and Memory after Auschwitz* (Ithaca: Cornell University Press, 1998); Saul Friedländer, ed., *Probing the Limits of Representation: Nazism and the "Final Solution"* (Cambridge: Harvard University Press, 1992); Michael Rothberg, "After Adorno: Culture in the Wake of Catastrophe," *New German Critique* 72 (fall 1997): 45–81. See also Walter Kalaidjian's essay on the poetic representations of the Armenian genocide, included in this collection.

16. In the famous debate of the 1980s, the French poststructuralists, particularly Jean Baudrillard and Jean-François Lyotard, were critiqued by Habermas for their sustained and complete rejection of all rationalist Enlightenment legacies. They suggest that postmodernity is marked by the collapse of metanarrative as a legitimizing force.

17. In *The Postmodern Condition*, an attack on Enlightenment intellectual and political traditions, Lyotard argues that postmodernism is a recurring stage within the modern. Like Lyotard, we are suggesting that the relationship between the modern and postmodern is imbricated in a complex and nonlinear way. But the nature of that relationship is distinct, taking into account material history as well as aesthetic formation. See Jean-François Lyotard, *The Postmodern Condition: A Report on Knowledge,* trans. Geoff Bennington and Brian Massumi (Minneapolis: University of Minnesota Press, 1993).

18. Linda Hutcheon also posits a mobile conception of postmodernism, though in reference to its conflicted political nature, arguing that "postmodern texts paradoxically point to the opaque nature of their representational strategies and at the same time to their complicity with the notion of the transparency of representation—a complicity shared, of course, by anyone who pretends even to describe their 'de-doxifying' tactics." See Linda Hutcheon, *The Politics of Postmodernism* (London: Routledge, 1989), 18.

19. Attempting to bridge the gap between the French poststructuralists and Habermas, Andreas Huyssen argues that postmodernism continues various projects of the modernist avant-garde that challenged the high modernist strategy of excluding mass culture from high art. See Andreas Huyssen, *After the Great Divide: Modernism, Mass Culture, Postmodernism* (Bloomington: Indiana University Press, 1986). Fredric Jameson's conception of postmodernism as the "cultural logic of late capitalism" may be seen as an extension of this view, though Huyssen and Jameson diverge in their conception of mass culture, particularly the ways postmodernism renegotiates the relationship between popular and mass culture and high culture. See Fredric Jameson, *Postmodernism, or The Cultural Logic of Late Capitalism* (Durham: Duke University Press, 1991). See also Fredric Jameson, *The Cultural Turn: Selected Writings on the Postmodern, 1983–1998* (London: Verso, 1998).

20. Jürgen Habermas argues in a series of famous essays, and particularly in the lectures that make up *The Philosophical Discourse of Modernity,* that post-

modernity is marked by the liquefication of modernity's rationalist project. See Jürgen Habermas, *The Philosophical Discourse of Modernity,* trans. Frederick C. Lawrence (Cambridge: MIT Press, 1992).

21. In their introduction to their edited collection, *Modernity and Identity,* Scott Lash and Jonathan Friedman argue that for Sharon Zukin, postmodernization is "fully the conquest of space by time," and thus, "hypermodernization." See Scott Lash and Jonathan Friedman, "Subjectivity and Modernity's Other," in *Modernity and Identity* (Oxford: Blackwell, 1992), 21.

22. Marshall Berman begins to gesture toward something like this when he argues that "modernists can never be done with the past: they must go on forever haunted by it, digging up its ghosts, recreating it even as they remake their world and themselves" (346). Yet Berman disputes any theories that seek to distinguish the postmodern from the modern. He argues that what was seen as "post-modern" in the 1970s was a modernism "distinguished by its desire and power to remember." For Berman, postmodernity's denial of its own modernity is self-delusional and politically regressive. See Marshall Berman, *All That Is Solid Melts into Air: The Experience of Modernity* (New York: Penguin, 1988), 346–47. Derrida's coinage of *hauntology* refers to what he calls the "staging for the end of history." More powerful than an ontology, this logic of haunting would "harbor within itself, but like circumscribed places or particular effects, eschatology or teleology themselves." See Derrida, *Specters of Marx,* 10.

23. Miriam Bratu Hansen, "America, Paris, the Alps: Kracauer (and Benjamin) on Cinema and Modernity," in *Cinema and the Invention of Modern Life,* ed. Leo Charney and Vanessa R. Schwartz (Berkeley: University of California Press, 1995), 367.

24. Perry Anderson, *The Origins of Postmodernity* (London: Verso, 1998), 3–4. We are indebted to Wendy Eberle-Sinatra for pointing this out to us in a seminar paper for the Modernist Studies Association conference in October 2000.

25. Jean Baudrillard, *America,* trans. Chris Turner (London: Verso, 1988), 76.

26. Bill Brown, "Science Fiction, the World's Fair, and the Prosthetics of Empire, 1910–1915," in *Cultures of United States Imperialism,* ed. Amy Kaplan and Donald E. Pease (Durham: Duke University Press, 1993), 139–40.

27. William Carlos Williams, *Selected Essays* (New York: New Directions, 1954) 116, 119, quoted in Brown.

28. See Benedict Anderson, *Imagined Communities: Reflections on the Origin and Spread of Nationalism* (London: Verso, 1991), 201.

29. One could argue, in contradiction to Berman above, that this too is one of the things that distinguish the modern from the postmodern.

30. This is, of course, not strictly true since the term "United States" shows up in much of the literature that debated nativism and pluralism. Nonetheless, Douglas's point is an interesting one.

31. Ann Douglas, *Terrible Honesty: Mongrel Manhattan in the 1920s* (New York: Farrar, Straus and Giroux, 1995), 3.

32. Alan Trachtenberg, *The Incorporation of America: Culture and Society in the Gilded Age* (New York: Hill and Wang, 1982), 231–32.

33. Jacques Derrida, "*Fors*: The Anglish Words of Nicolas Abraham and Maria Torok," trans. Barbara Johnson, in Nicolas Abraham and Maria Torok, *The Wolf Man's Magic Word: A Cryptonymy* (Minneapolis: University of Minnesota Press, 1986), xvi.

34. See Abraham and Torok, *The Shell and the Kernel,* 127.

35. Abraham and Torok, *The Shell and the Kernel,* 99–164.

36. Wigley 179.

37. James R. Barrett, "Americanization from the Bottom Up: Immigration and the Remaking of the Working Class in the United States, 1880–1930," in *Discovering America: Essays on the Search for an Identity,* ed. David Thelen and Frederick E. Hoxie (Urbana: University of Illinois Press, 1994), 163.

38. See Walter Benn Michaels, *Our America: Nativism, Modernism, Pluralism* (Durham: Duke University Press, 1995), 8–9.

39. Michaels 6–8.

40. Edward A. Ross, "American Blood and Immigrant Blood," in *The Old World and the New: The Significance of Past and Present Immigration to the American People* (New York: Century, 1914), reprinted in *Contested Values: Democracy and Diversity in American Culture,* ed. Michael Kammen (New York: St. Martin's Press, 1995), 117–20.

41. Horace M. Kallen, "Democracy versus the Melting Pot," *Nation* 100 (February 18 and 25, 1915), reprinted in Kammen 121–28.

42. Kallen 123.

43. Pierre Bourdieu, *Distinction: A Social Critique of the Judgement of Taste,* trans. Richard Nice (Cambridge: Harvard University Press, 1984), 471, original emphasis.

44. Kallen 123.

45. Immigration was first restricted by what Walter Benn Michaels calls the 1908 "gentleman's agreement" between Theodore Roosevelt and the Japanese government, which restricted Asian immigration, then with the 1921 immigration law, which limited European immigration, and finally with the Johnson-Reed Immigration Act of 1924, which restricted all immigration to the United States. See Michaels 8, 144. For more on the specific legislation that limited the immigration of Asians to the United States, see also Lisa Lowe, *Immigrant Acts: On Asian American Cultural Politics* (Durham: Duke University Press, 1996).

46. Stuart Ewen, *All Consuming Images: The Politics of Style in Contemporary Culture* (New York: Basic Books, 1988), 76.

47. We borrow the term from Jonathan Friedman, "Narcissism, Roots, and Postmodernity," in Lash and Friedman 361.

48. Adams quoted in Trachtenberg 3.

49. Trachtenberg 4.

50. See note 19.

51. Max Horkheimer and Theodor W. Adorno, "The Culture Industry: Enlightenment as Mass Deception," in *Dialectic of Enlightenment,* trans. John Cumming (New York: Continuum, 1993), 120–67.

52. John Crowe Ransom, "Criticism, Inc.," *Twentieth Century Literacy,* ed. David Lodge (1937; rpt. London: Longman, 1972).

53. See Judith Butler's analysis of materiality, melancholia, and subjectivity in *Bodies That Matter: On the Discursive Limits of "Sex"* (New York: Routledge, 1993).

54. Some of these revisionary modernisms include Houston A. Baker Jr., *Modernism and the Harlem Renaissance* (Chicago: University of Chicago Press, 1987); Shari Benstock, *Women of the Left Bank: Paris, 1900–1940* (Austin: University of Texas Press, 1986); Joseph Boone, *Libidinal Currents: Sexuality and the Shaping of Modernism* (Chicago: University of Chicago Press, 1998); Erin Carlston, *Thinking Fascism: Sapphic Modernism and Fascist Modernity* (Stanford: Stanford University Press, 1998); Laura Doyle, *Bordering the Body: The Racial Matrix of Modern Fiction and Culture* (New York: Oxford University Press, 1994); Rita Felski, *The Gender of Modernity* (Cambridge: Harvard University Press, 1995); Anthony L. Geist and José B. Monléon, eds., *Modernism and Its Margins: Reinscribing Cultural Modernity from Spain and Latin America* (Ann Arbor: University of Michigan Press, 1999); Simon Gikandi, *Writing in Limbo: Modernism and Caribbean Literature* (Ithaca: Cornell University Press, 1992); Walter Kalaidjian, *American Culture between the Wars: Revisionary Modernism and Postmodern Critique* (New York: Columbia University Press, 1993); Michael North, *The Dialect of Modernism: Race, Language, and Twentieth-Century Literature* (New York: Oxford University Press, 1994); Paula Rabinowitz, *Labor and Desire: Women's Revolutionary Fiction in Depression America* (Chapel Hill: University of North Carolina Press, 1991); Bonnie Kime Scott, *Refiguring Modernism* (Bloomington: Indiana University Press, 1995).

55. Cary Nelson, *Repression and Recovery: Modern American Poetry and the Politics of Cultural Memory, 1910–1945* (Madison: University of Wisconsin Press, 1989), 3.

56. This is, of course, what Walter Benjamin suggests in his allegory of the angel of history who "sees one single catastrophe which keeps piling wreckage upon wreckage and hurls it in front of his feet." See Walter Benjamin, "Theses on the Philosophy of History," in *Illuminations: Essays and Reflections,* ed. Hannah Arendt, trans. Harry Zohn (New York: Schocken Books, 1969), 257.

57. See Berman 131–71. See also Lash and Friedman 3.

58. Brown 155.

BODY

incorporate
v. [f. late L. *incorporāt-*, ppl. stem of *incorporāre* to embody, include, f. *in-* (IN⁻²) + *corporāre* to form into a body, CORPORATE v.]:
I. *trans.*
1. To combine or unite into one body or uniform substance; to mix or blend thoroughly together (a number of different things or one thing *with* another).
2. To put into or include in the body or substance of something else; to put (one thing) in or into another so as to form one body or integral whole; to embody, include.
a. (*sb.*) *rare.* [ad. rare L. *incorporāt-us* not embodied, f. in- (IN⁻³) + *corporātus* CORPORATE]:
1. Without body or material substance; incorporeal, unembodied.
2. 'Not incorporated; not existing as a corporation; as an incorporate banking association or other society.' (Webster, 1864).
—Oxford English Dictionary (1976)

The essays in part 1 are concerned with how issues of embodiment and materiality figure within and construct the historical, cultural, spatial, and psychological manifestations of modernity. In "Machine Dreams," a haunting analysis of the daydreams of a drunk lying down on a train track, the anthropologist Kathleen Stewart meditates on the train as metaphor and metonym for a surreal and corporeal modernity in which desire is indistinguishable from dread. Both Janet Lyon and Marlon Ross discuss the performative mechanisms through which African American artists attempted to negotiate a gendered and racialized modernity. Janet Lyon investigates Josephine Baker's synecdochic relation to the institutions of Parisian modernism and white racialized modernity in "Josephine Baker's Hothouse." Lyon argues that Baker reinvents the modernist salon and her own role as salon hostess to resignify race under the signs of sexuality, consumption, and parody. In doing so, she produces a complex and performative partnership between herself and the white, cosmopolitan Europeans who patronized her Parisian bistro, Chez Josephine.

Marlon Ross complicates prevailing critical constructions of the New Negro in "Trespassing the Colorline," an analysis of William Pickens's second-generation response to Booker T. Washington's accommodationist "balancing act" that had kept the colorline intact. Ross argues that Pickens's radical New Negro "rubs shoulders with modernity" through aggressive acts of "racial trespassing"—emblematized by the bodily confrontation of black men with white adversaries on the Jim Crow railroad car. Negotiating the conflicted sphere of masculinity during the Progressive Era, the racial trespasser performed an aggressive kind of racial passing—one that sought confrontation and exposure. He put his own body at risk—and sought to be displayed at risk—in an attempt to rupture the colorline and claim a right to spatial and economic mobility. Yet Ross also exposes the problematic of a New Negro agenda of race advancement through intrusion, imposition, and insemination, arguing that these rely on an ambivalently gendered paradigm of masculine competition embedded in the white mythologies of American global expansionism.

Julia Walker approaches Eugene O'Neill's play *The Hairy Ape* in the context of technological changes in communication and through institutions of literary and speech studies in the first decades of the twentieth century. Negating his play's theatricality by ironically inscribing the actor's body in the text, O'Neill not only gained critical acclaim as a literary artist, but also exploited the fragmentation wrought by new communication technologies.

MACHINE DREAMS

Kathleen Stewart

aurie Anderson had a performance exhibit at the Soho Guggenheim called *Your Fortune, $1*. A spooky white plastic owl perched on a stool in a darkened corner of the museum droned on and on in a computer-synthesized voice that was at once eerily mechanical and sensuously grainy. It transfixed me in a stream of two-bit advice, trenchant commentary, and stray advertising lingo. Then it said something, I swear, I had already been anxiously chanting to myself all day (or all my life). It said, "Sometimes when you hear someone scream it goes in one ear and out the other. Sometimes it passes right into the middle of your brain and gets stuck there."

One minute you're in the realm of sheer circulation, drifting in a flood of Hallmark greeting-card schlock. Then, in the same minute, something plucked out of the random wanderings of circulating sound bites hits you with a shocking recognition that seems to bring you to your senses. That's modernism for you. In its simultaneous disenchantment and reenchantment of the world, there is both anaesthesia and shock, boredom and exhilaration, distraction and the lyrical pause we call meaning.[1] Far from a stable clarity of vision, or reason, modernity is like seeing double. One eye sees its object as "just there to be used as the white screen on to which society projects its cinema," while the other eye catches a glimpse of something so real and powerful that the forces that constructed it fade to the point of invisibility.[2] On the one hand there is a kind of sobering up, a cruel lucidity not incompatible with blindness, as a flood of images, discourses, and ideologies inundate us with news that is neutralized by its own sheer quantity. On the other hand, a mobile psyche invents itself as a private, compressed interiority, projecting a vision of unrealized will and desire capable of transforming the world.[3] The fetish registers the animation of objects in circulation[4] and a fantasy desire to know everything and to experience everything simultaneously initiates the world of the daydream.

Modernity looks through powerfully naturalized constructs in the effort to gain access to things in themselves. As Latour has argued, it is not fundamentally the simple realization of humanism, the secularization of society, and the mechanization of the world, but "the conjoined production of these three pairings of transcendence and immanence."[5] Its invented dualisms of thought and matter, science and religion, machine and dream produce their own excess or remainder in the very claim to "mobilize nature, objectify the soul, and feel the spiritual presence of God, even while firmly maintaining that Nature escapes us, that Society is our own work, and that God no longer intervenes."[6] For Benjamin, modernity is the world dominated by its phantasmagorias. The bourgeois dream world inscribes a collective equivalent to individual desire in public forms and forces; architectures, fashions, the detritus of earlier forms, and even the weather become collective objects of ambivalence and dream-like disfigurations laden with vital social energy. A form of cultural critique that privileges nonrational forms of "working through" mimics their prolific social production, fashioning a dialectical image through the use of dream elements in waking.[7]

THE TRAIN WAILS WHILE WE SLEEP

When the owl spoke to me of screams that go in one ear and out the other or pass right into the middle of your brain and get stuck there, I went home and wrote down a story that begins with a haunted question and opens onto a harsh, metallic landscape of machine dreams. The haunted question: Do you ever wake up in the morning, or in the middle of the night, with a sense of sudden dread? Do you scan your dreamy brain for the memory of what you've done or a premonition of what's coming? For some of us, this is just what morning has become—a grievous mourning caught in the repetition of half-known shocks. The harsh, metallic landscape: Austin, Texas (or Anywhere, U.S.A.).

I have a big iron bed lodged against long, wide windows that open onto the back deck. Tropical breezes waft over me in the night, carrying the sweet and fetid smells of kumquat trees and mimosa blossoms. In the dawn there are wild bird cries—mourning doves and grackles and parrots that once escaped their pet cages and now breed in the trees. At certain hours in the still of the night, the train cries in the near distance. The night pulses with the high lonesome sound of haunted nostalgic machine dreams roaming the landscape.

When I have guests I give them the iron bed and they wake up talking about the bed and the wailing train as if they feel pleased to be set down in some kind of American Heartland. But I am only too happy to lay myself down a pallet on the living room floor and fall into a deep sleep with only the smell of old ashes from the fireplace. Because I know why the train sings. A story told to me has lodged itself in the middle of my brain and I keep it to myself.

The story has it that the train cries for a homeless drunk named Bobby, who laid himself down on the tracks one night and passed out as if he, too, could lay down a pallet and escape from his ghosts. He and his old lady had been down at the Wednesday night free concert on the river, where street people become self-appointed hosts for the night. Some dance wildly in front of the stage and between the blankets laid out on the grass. Some laugh a little too loudly or give people unwanted directions and advice. It's like it's their fifteen minutes of fame. Down by the river in the gathering dark, glamour flows contagiously from the band on stage, touches spellbound bodies and reaches out to the neon skyline reflecting in the dark, glassy expanse of the river. There are graceful moments: a dance gesture, a wide open smile, a sudden upsurge of generosity, the startled feeling of pariahs who suddenly feel at home in public. There are crashes too: people falling down drunk in front of the stage, the vomiting, a man huddled and pale, too sick to party tonight, flashes of hope and ease dashed on the rocks of familiar fury, frustration, humiliation, grief. People making spectacles of themselves. At the end of the night there are always fights.

That night, Bobby and his old lady got into it. Bobby stomped off and ended up at the train tracks, licking his wounds in the abjection of his own night airs. Nearby there was an encampment of street people—a tent city of ragged belongings and campfires. But Bobby went off alone and laid himself down on the tracks. Picture the pull of the high, lonesome sound in the distance for a drunk taking stock and wallowing in a booze-soaked moment of reprieve. The romance of the whistling train draws close, promising simple contact and a sudden inclusion in the warm winds of history. The train holds machine dreams of tactility: the rumbling weight of power incarnate, the childhood drama of the penny laid on the tracks, the surge of passion that tempts fate and lunges toward an end.

Bobby cozied up to the tracks as if the train's promise could chase away the ghosts that would flash up like sparks at the blink of an eye and linger on the insides of his eyelids like a TV you can't turn off when it gets ugly. Checking out. Then, in the middle of the long train passing over him he raised his head, awakening. Otherwise, they say, the train would have passed right over him. But who can sleep while a train passes overhead? Or when your eyelids are a spectral screen?

Now the train screams out a warning when it approaches that place on the tracks not far from my iron bed. It often wakes me. Or it lodges in my sleep and comes as an unknown shock of anxiety in the morning. So I'm only too happy to give my visitors the big iron bed so *they* can hear the train cry, *not me*. I don't tell them Bobby's story because I figure it would only fester in them the way it festers in me. Or worse, they'd forget it in the blink of an eye. In one ear and out the other.

The screech of the night train brings me back to the sleepless nights at my grandmother's place after my grandfather died screaming in his bed as his poisoned liver turned his skin green and then black. Those were nights of grim anxiety, listening to the dull, droning hum of tires on the highway. It reminds me, too, of the night a drunk in West Virginia lay on the tracks and the coal train took off his legs at midthigh and he died before anyone noticed he was there. Later, my neighbor and his buddies would sit on the stumps of my woodpile passing around mayonnaise bottles full of the clear liquid moonshine they made and drank in the moonlight. They'd swap drunk talk about going down into it until they'd see Jesus and demons and "*Man!* you wouldn't *believe* it!"

Sometimes the train breaks into the light of day, like when I'm stopped at the railroad crossing on the way to the office. The scene of cars and trucks waiting by the tracks fills me with the wild and fecund daydreams of the American modernist imaginary. One day a boxcar full of Mexican illegals drifted slowly by and the men waved and smiled at us like this was their fifteen minutes of fame and we were the welcoming audience. Or there were the times in the coal camps in West Virginia when the coal trains would block the only road out of the holler, sometimes for hours, you never knew how long it would be. Waiting, we would get out and lean on the trucks, gazing into the scene as we talked. Sometimes a confident claim would begin to circulate that someday someone was gonna get a pile of dynamite, blow the train in half, and clear the road for good. An arresting image.

KATHLEEN STEWART

There is both abjection and exuberance in these daydreams weighted with promise and threat. Something in the exuberant waving of the new immigrants, the explosive claims in the coal camps, or Bobby lying down to sleep on the tracks calls up Benjamin's dialectics of intoxication.[8] Surging between life and dream, and haunted by the rough vitality of sensory memories that return with a shock, they take us to the realm of delirium, daydream, and grandiose gesture not as ideal states of consciousness or agency but as afflicted, weighted moments of desire. They gesture to the reckless hope that a severed body or tracks blasted apart might actually interrupt the world in its course, might puncture the heart of a heartless world or sing it to a restless sleep.[9]

THE TRAIN OF MACHINE DREAMS

The train is both a primary metaphor of modernity and its metonym,[10] or what Kracauer called an encrypted historico-metaphysical figure.[11] It shares an iron substance with the thing it symbolizes, rubbing shoulders with it and exchanging sparks. The drunk lying down on the tracks surges toward its solid matter as the real repository of dreams. The train is the machine dream of the concrete ending, or the primal object on which the mind can stare itself out to a completed mourning. But it is also the haunting reminder that there is always something more, or something else, released in the very moment when the virtual transmogrifies into the actual. It speeds by and is gone, yet it culls our attention to it in its very passing, holding the promise and threat of a stopping even as it hurtles past and dual temptations to hop the train of machine dreams or to feel its impact as a literal shock of recognition. In one ear and out the other. Or the penetrating scream.

Encrypting the drama of enlightenment in an iron form, the train wavers between utopian possibility and apocalyptic threat. Promoted as the direct engine of progress and the ultimate embodiment of a technological sublime, it entered public culture with early railroad advertising of panoramic vistas of trains cutting through wild scenes of raw nature and folkloric figures of man and machine like John Henry and Casey Jones.[12] It worked its way into childhood imaginaries and nostalgic longings in the figures of the little train who thought it could, the songs of wailing trains carrying outlaws and abject heroes home to a final resting place under the green, green grass of home, and the bucolic scene of the miniature train set up in the attic. Yet from the start, the railroad also carried an undercurrent of menace or fear.[13] From the early neurasthenia of railroad travelers, to the thrilling spectacle of train wrecks staged at county fairs,[14] to the terrified reaction of silent film audiences at the sight of gigantic trains pulling into a station,[15] the train became the image of the machine grown to monstrous proportions; it was the machine that killed everything in its path, the ruthless power of an unstoppable economy, the threat of apocalyptic collapse in a world running out of control.

The train marked the childhood of a new mass public, christening both rationalized systems and daydreams of fortune, fame, and fancy. It gave birth to the value of circulation itself, where whatever is part of circulation is healthy, progressive, and constructive and whatever tries to detach from it or falls to the wayside is threatening or somehow "other."[16] It launched the simultaneous modernist dreads of being left behind or being caught up and crushed. Then the mobility of the train went deeper, penetrating the "self image" of the modern subject itself. Split between the well-tempered self at home in the regulated life of rationalized systems and the free fall of mobile desires, the modern subject is a suggestible subject. Linked to shifting objects of desire, it is nomadic and prolific.[17] At one moment it might dream of suturing itself to the train of progress for a smooth ride down the rails of life. Then, at the next moment, it might long for reenchantment, or the freedom of the open road, or it might give itself over to a fantasy of submission—of being run over and assaulted, penetrated.[18] But whatever the fantasy is, the subject becomes filled by a suggestive image, stopped in its tracks and mesmerized by the impact of the image itself and the magic of metamorphosis in which transcendence meets immanence and daydream becomes, for a moment, an iron substance.[19]

The modern subject has the double vision of a mobile psyche drawn into circulation and waiting for a moment of impact that exposes rather than masks disintegration[20] and brings the powers and pleasures that traverse the social order to a point of maximal corporeal saturation.[21] At the first sight of the trains in silent film, the audiences ran for their lives. Now drunks lie down on the tracks of the real thing. Both are states of excitement in which desire is indistinguishable from dread, respite literally "finds itself" in a state of shock, and the gaze is seized, touched, and put in contact with appearance[22] as if through the magic of a machine dream.

NOTES

1. See Lauren Berlant, "The Face of America and the State of Emergency," in *The Queen of America Goes to Washington City* (Durham: Duke University Press, 1997), 175–221; Susan Buck-Morss, "Aesthetics and Anaesthetics: Walter Benjamin's Artwork Essay Reconsidered," *New Formations* 20 (1993): 123–43; Marilyn Ivy, "Have You Seen Me? Recovering the Inner Child in Late Twentieth-Century America," *Social Text* 37 (1993): 227–52; and Michael Rogin, "Make My Day!" Spectacle as Amnesia in Imperial Politics,"

in *Discovering Difference*, ed. Christoph Lohman (Bloomington: Indiana University Press, 1993).

2. Bruno Latour, *We Have Never Been Modern* (New York: Harvester Wheatsheaf, 1991), 53.

3. See Susan Stewart, *On Longing: Narratives of the Miniature, the Gigantic, the Souvenir, the Collection* (Baltimore: Johns Hopkins University Press, 1984); and Anthony Cascardi, *The Subject of Modernity* (Cambridge: Cambridge University Press, 1992).

4. Jonathan Beller, "Cinema, Capital of the Twentieth Century," *Postmodern Culture* 4, 3 (1994).

5. Latour, *We Have Never Been Modern*, 34.

6. Latour, *We Have Never Been Modern*, 34.

7. See Susan Buck-Morss, "Dream World of Mass Culture," in *The Dialectics of Seeing: Walter Benjamin and the Arcades Project* (Cambridge: MIT Press, 1991), 253–86; and Margaret Cohen, *Profane Illumination: Walter Benjamin and the Paris of the Surrealist Revolution* (Berkeley: University of California Press, 1993).

8. Walter Benjamin, "Surrealism: The Last Snapshot of the European Intelligentsia," in *Reflections*, ed. P. Demetz (New York: Harcourt Brace Jovanovich, 1978).

9. Marcus Bullock, "Bad Company: On the Theory of Literary Modernity and Melancholy in Walter Benjamin and Julia Kristeva," *boundary 2* 22, 3 (1995): 74.

10. I thank Vincent Raphael for this point.

11. Siegfried Kracauer, *Mass Ornament* (Cambridge: Cambridge University Press, 1995).

12. Wolfgang Schivelbusch, *The Railway Journey: The Industrialization of Time and Space in the Nineteenth Century* (Berkeley: University of California Press, 1986); Leo Marx, *The Machine in the Garden: Technology and the Pastoral Ideal in America* (New York: Oxford University Press, 1964); David E. Nye, *American Technological Sublime* (Cambridge: MIT Press, 1994).

13. Schivelbusch, *The Railway Journey*, 10.

14. Lynn Kirby, "Male Hysteria and Early Cinema," *Camera Obscura* 17 (1991).

15. Tom Gunning, "An Aesthetic of Astonishment: Early Film and the (In)Credulous Spectator," in *Film Theory and Criticism*, ed. Leo Braudy and Marshall Cohen (New York: Oxford University Press, 1999) 818–32; Lynn Kirby, *Parallel Tracks: The Railroad and Silent Cinema* (Durham: Duke University Press, 1997).

16. See Kathleen Stewart, *A Space on the Side of the Road: Cultural Poetics in an "Other" America* (Princeton: Princeton University Press, 1996).

17. Elizabeth Grosz, *Volatile Bodies* (Bloomington: Indiana University Press, 1994).

18. Kirby, "Male Hysteria and Early Cinema," 122.

19. See Steven Shaviro, *The Cinematic Body* (Minneapolis: University of Minnesota Press, 1993); Gunning, "An Aesthetic of Astonishment"; and Ben Singer, "Modernity, Hyperstimulus, and the Rise of Popular Sensationalism," in *Cinema and the Invention of Modern Life*, ed. Leo Charney and Vanessa Schwartz (Berkeley: University of California Press, 1995).
20. Gunning, "An Aesthetic of Astonishment," 832.
21. Shaviro, *The Cinematic Body*, 261.
22. Shaviro, *The Cinematic Body*, 75.

2

JOSEPHINE BAKER'S HOTHOUSE

Janet Lyon

Josephine Baker has always been treated as an enigmatic figure by cultural critics, not least because her biography pulls together threads from so many areas of inquiry staked out by cultural studies: she was an African American woman born into the country's worst phase of institutionalized racism. She was also a millionaire, a star, and an exile in modernist Paris whose career involved the staging of race and sexuality and colonialism. Born into brutal poverty in East St. Louis in 1906, witness to the horrific East St. Louis race riots at the age of eleven, she married at thirteen, worked her way into a string of all-black musical reviews at fifteen, and at nineteen sailed for Paris, where she starred sensationally in *La Revue nègre* on the stage of the Théâtre des Champs-Élysées. Her fame in Paris began with dance: she won instant attention for her outrageous improvisational autochoreography, her limber and distinctly non-European rhythm, her self-conscious physical comedy, and her fabulous body. Gradually she cultivated her thin singing voice to the pitch of a cabaret chanteuse, learned French, and, until her death at sixty-nine, lived multiple lives as fashion icon, cabaret owner, sex symbol, nightclub singer, international star, Montmartre denizen, French citizen and Resistance patriot, adoptive mother of twelve children, gay idol, civil rights advocate, comeback queen. Not surprisingly, the kaleidoscopic nature of her public life has left a fractured composite portrait. Arising in pieces out of numerous biographies and autobiographies, "Josephine Baker" never coheres into a stable historical identity.[1]

Partly this lack of coherence is textual. Critical commentary on Baker is of necessity based on the self-interested testimonies of fellow performers, friends, and lovers, as well as on Baker's own notoriously confabulated accounts. But the incoherence surrounding Baker runs much deeper than inconsistency, insofar as it generates questions that get asked over and over in critical writings: was Josephine Baker a dupe of consumerism, a shill for lewd cabaret culture, a willingly exploited performer of some French notion of primitivism? Was she a shrewd businesswoman capitalizing on white modernism, a makeover artist riding the wave of the modern premium on racial novelty? Or was she a performance artist, a surrealist renegade, an avant-gardiste self-consciously engaging in racial forms of *détournement* and sexual forms of *épater*?

The problem with such questions, however, is that they assume a kind of cultural empiricism that obscures Baker's key relation to two sets of institutions that helped to produce her public identity. It will be the aim of this essay to discuss her synecdochic relation to those institutions, which may be identified, first, as the institutions of modernism—especially Parisian modernism—through which Baker became famous; and second, the social and political institutions of white Western modernity, whose racial contradictions, I would insist, are largely the source of a prevailing reception of Baker-as-enigma. Baker was born "in 1906, in the twentieth century," as she quipped to those invested in the myth of Baker-as-primitive.[2] She was a product of that most modern of countries, where the scars of progress were deepest—where the uneven implementations of modernity's institutions left African Americans "struggling in the eddies of the fifteenth century," in Du Bois's famous words.[3] Her particular brand of fame was uniquely tied to the twentieth-century color line described by Du Bois, to its manifestations in the shifting discourses of race, primitivism, and sexuality that characterized modernist culture and inflected the nationalist core of U.S. modernity. And like other African Americans hailed by modernism, especially those in Harlem and Paris, Baker had to negotiate a bizarrely labile relation between formal modernist aesthetics and the incoherent racial ideology of the dominant institutions of modernity.

Baker's early successes in the United States, first on the T.O.B.A. performance troupe circuit and then in black musicals booked into white theater districts, were sharply circumscribed by American racism, and would have remained so had she not expatriated.[4] White Broadway tolerated black performers only so long as they acted "black"; as Eubie Blake put it, "people who went to a colored show expected only fast dancing and Negroid humor."[5] By the same logic, white theater depended for its intelligibility on a distinct and separate black genre of performance. This relationship is exemplified in a theater critic's complaint that one of the musical numbers in *Shuffle Along* (the Sisley and Noble production in which Baker danced chorus) was racially unmarked—devoid of minstrelsy—and therefore "pretentious" (quoted in *JC* 61). And while, as Baker herself noted, "black folks were all the rage in New York" in the twenties,[6] that "rage" was carefully controlled, heavily specularized, and culturally intelligible as a "safe" staging of a modern/primitive dialectic.[7]

Baker's arrival in Paris in 1925 was marked for her by the palpable absence of the quotidian racism of U.S. life; in this respect her introduction to Paris replayed the initial (and initially euphoric) experiences of the African American soldiers stationed in France during World War I, and the black jazz musicians who established a community in Montmartre at war's end. "I felt liberated in Paris," Baker later recalled. "People didn't stare at me. But," she added, "when I heard an American accent in the street, I became afraid."[8] Baker's fear of U.S. racist contagion suggests that the mere absence of the aura of racism did not afford her the luxury of a pure, detached cosmopolitanism. Rather, it exposed the sedimentation of racialism in French culture, which was itself subject to the inflections of racism. Tzvetan Todorov distinguishes racialism from racism by characterizing the latter as a "behavior, usually a manifestation of hatred or contempt" based on otherness. Racialism, by contrast, is "a matter of ideology, a doctrine concerning human races," which may issue in racism but is of interest (at least to Todorov) principally for the historically shifting configuration of its arguments.[9] Upon its nineteenth-century reconfiguration as a disinterested discipline of natural science, racialism easily became an instrument of French colonialism, at once identifying race empirically and justifying Western aggression developmentally. But I would also suggest that, when patterned into the fabric of cosmopolitanism, racialism helped to condition and qualify the self-congratulatory French truism of the 1920s—that, in Janet Flanner's words, "Paris has never drawn a color line."[10] For while racialism in France did not issue in a particularly pernicious or pervasive form of racism as it did in the United States, it nevertheless produced a racialized horizon of expectation that conditioned the reception of African Americans in Paris.

Tyler Stovall's discussion of the "dual nature" of African American culture in Paris in the 1920s may help to illuminate this horizon of expectation. The African component of its dual nature, as understood by Parisian intellectuals and artists, was a valorized primitivism associated with an imported species of "African" culture, which offered a foil of "lush, naive sensuality" when seen against the hideous methodical slaughter of the recent European war.[11] Such primitivism undergirded the choreography of the dance for which Baker became instantly (in)famous: the *Dance Sauvage*, in which a nearly nude Baker, decorated with feathers and partnered by a muscular "savage," danced to riotous rhythms on an exotic set. At her first appearance onstage during the piece's premiere, according to one observer, "a scream of salutation spread through the theatre," as if in recognition of Baker's magically modern animation of the primitive.[12] The second, American component of African American culture in Paris, according to Stovall, was modern mass culture itself, associated explicitly with the U.S. entertainment industry, and thrilling in the seductive promise it held out for new forms of imaginary social identification. This aspect of American culture was epitomized for Parisians by black jazz and dance, which was, in turn, epitomized by Josephine Baker's dancing.

Stovall maintains that the "dual nature of African American culture ensured that its representatives would be twice as welcome in the City of Light" (*PN* 33), and he convincingly extends his reading to Baker's reception in Paris. At the same time it must be noted that the welcome afforded by this duality only partially palliated the fraught metaphysical duality of racialized experience that Du Bois had famously described fifteen years earlier: the African American "always feels his twoness—an American, a Negro; two souls, two thoughts, two unreconciled strivings; two warring ideals in one dark body."[13] Such double consciousness, however modern in its intelligibility and however modernist in the cultural uses to which it might be put,[14] attests forcefully to the asymptotic relation between "progress" and racial justice in the United States. To be African American, whether in Paris or in Pittsburgh, was to be "a problem," and even if one were not the same *kind* of problem in Paris as in Pittsburgh, one's racialization remained problematic.[15]

In her astute study of Josephine Baker in Berlin, Nancy Nenno emphasizes what seems to be the paradoxical force of this duality. Quoting from the diary of Count Harry Kessler, who admiringly described the African American performers of *Negerrevue* as products of both "the jungle and the skyscraper . . . Ultramodern and ultraprimitive," Nenno develops the constellation more closely around the specularized figure of Baker.[16] "As a black American woman," she argues, "Josephine Baker's body represented the confluence of both the black body and the feminine, the primitive and the modern."[17] Indeed, for Baker's audience, such a confluence had the desired effect of telescoping modernism's favorite fetishes into one figure. But then again, such confluences register as paradoxical—indeed, they register as "confluences"—only under a cultural perspective that holds "the primitive" and "the modern" in mutual exclusivity. Certainly this was not the case for audiences in Paris (or Berlin, for that matter), for whom primitivism was a defining if somewhat blurry aesthetic of modernism, conceptually developed and employed as an organic refutation of instrumental modernity. Moreover, the primitivism embodied in Baker's most provocative stage persona—the persona of the exotic tropical native existing just beyond the reach of colonial interpellation—engaged thoroughly with French intellectual paradigms of liberal racialism. If, as Victor Segalen wrote in the 1910s, exoticism was "the fundamental law of the intensity of sensation, of the exaltation of feeling," and if, as he asserted, "diversity [was] the source of all energy,"[18] then exaggerated contact with racial difference would not only fuel the "modern" experience so prized by the intellectuals and artists of modernism, but would also help to foster cosmopolitan self-consciousness. And cosmopolitanism was at a premium in Paris in the twenties, especially insofar as it was— somewhat paradoxically—prized as a "national" French quality. Paris's liberal reception of Baker as an immensely talented African American stage star was marked by a very public and self-satisfied display of racial tolerance, and few opportunities were missed to contrast this aspect of Parisian cosmopolitanism with the infamous bigotry of American national culture.[19] There was, in short, an element of nationalistic quid pro quo in Paris's reception of Josephine Baker: for while parochial racist Americans in Paris suddenly seemed capable of buying out the city on the strength of their bloated stock market, this one aspect of the metropole's character—its tolerant cosmopolitanism—was not for sale.

From this perspective it is possible to offer a précis of Baker's relation to her audience during her first few years in Paris: in her shows with *La Revue nègre,* and later at the Folies-Bergère, she was an African American woman performing the implicitly parodic role of a primitive African woman for a white European audience. For its part, the audience was performing a disidentification (or a self-differentiation) from white racist American audiences even as it was participating in an ironized colonialist tableau. This complicated performative partnership between Baker and her audiences was formed around the ideals of a developing modernist cosmopolitanism, the modernist component of which reveled in scandalous iconoclasm, and the cosmopolitan component of which valorized and cultivated the self-reflexive experience of otherness.[20]

The performances of Baker and her audiences were complicated by an additional—and, for the purposes of my argument, a crucial—component of modernist cosmopolitanism. A year after Baker took Paris by storm—a year that included tours, product promotions, unending publicity, and singing lessons—she opened her own cabaret, Chez Josephine. Located in Montmartre, the black expatriate quarter of Paris known for its jazz and its raucous, bad-boy atmosphere, the club was a small, unassuming place where Baker arrived every night after her Folies-Bergère show, staged an entourage-driven entrance dressed in gorgeous evening wear, changed into clothes suitable for dancing, and danced for as long as it suited her—usually until dawn. Of course, there is nothing particularly unusual about a performer endorsing or buying or inhabiting a nightclub. Nor was it particularly unusual in Montmartre in the 1920s. Baker was preceded in her nightclub venture by two other popular African American figures, the brilliant Florence Embry Jones (of Chez Florence) and Baker's own mentor, Bricktop (of Bricktop's). But what I want to argue, in a twofold way, is, first, that Baker's stewardship of Chez Josephine effectively set her up in the role of a modernist hostess. With the term "hostess" I mean to invoke the tradition of hostessing associated with the institution of the cultural salon, which forms a series of nodal points in the development of modernity. And by calling Baker a modernist hostess, I mean to link her club to other modernist salons of the period, salons run by the likes of Mabel Dodge and A'Lelia Walker in New York, Violet Hunt in London, and Natalie Clifford Barney and Gertrude Stein in Paris. The second part of my argument is that Baker radically reinflects the role of the modernist hostess. At Chez Josephine, the private salon becomes a public site of cosmopolitanism and commerce, where Baker stages her own conversation with modernity under the signs of race, sexuality, consumption, and parody.

What exactly comprises the "salon tradition"? From one perspective, we may think of the salon as the private, class-marked precursor to the public coffeehouse, with all that the institution of the coffeehouse implies. If the coffeehouse has been enshrined in Enlightenment narratives as the structure that enabled forms of (male, white) public consensus upon which depended the development of modern, nonabsolutist institutions of government and commerce, so its sister the salon played a more formally staged role in modernity's history. With its origins in fifteenth-century class-based *politesse*, the bourgeois salon of the seventeenth, eighteenth, nineteenth, and twentieth centuries acted as a contained, private site wherein circulated the scripts of reasoned disagreement, individualism within collectivity, cosmopolitan tolerance, and all the sweetness and light of culture. The hostess, usually a woman of social standing, was distinguished by her abilities to facilitate conversation and to polish manners, to make her guests feel welcome, to provide a structure within which the incrementally progressive alchemy of enlightenment might occur.

From another perspective, we may understand the salon as a site of social power operating outside the immediate orbit of institutional state apparatuses. In this regard it may be thought of as a zone of what de Certeau termed "local authority," an "area of free play on a checkerboard that analyzes and classifies identity."[21] By valuing conversation over pedantry, particular experience over absolute values of truth, sociability over domesticity, debate over aggression, the salon could stand in as a kind of hand-painted miniature of the communicative ethic valued (but whose practice was deferred) by the post-Enlightenment ruling class. It provided a forum for the enactment of ideal speech situations while firmly controlling the directions that that speech might take. If salonnières and salon attenders fancied themselves freely dancing on the leading edge of culture, their dance was nevertheless imbricated in a closed grid of identity.

To cast Chez Josephine as a salon involves a revision of previous conceptions of the European salon tradition. Baker's "hospitality," after all, was based in a money-making bistro where the hostess charged exorbitant prices for champagne and snacks;[22] and far from being an articulate conversationalist, the hostess was barely conversant in French during the year of her first club's existence.[23] The revision I propose requires a reinterpretation of the issues of embodiment and race in the history of institutions of modernity like the salon. Typically these issues have been bracketed in standard accounts of modernity, leaving the impression, in the words of Paul Gilroy, "that an all-encompassing modernity effects everyone in a uniform and essentially similar way."[24] Conversely, their bracketing has rendered largely unintelligible the cultural work done by traditions of the black Atlantic as well as by subcultural formations within modernity. I would instead like to illuminate the unacknowledged cultural work performed by Baker through the phenomenal if transient success of her club, which functioned, in many ways, like a modernist salon. If the salon is known to us historically as an institution instrumental in the development of modern cosmopolitanism, the salons of modernism took the cultivation of cosmopolitanism in the direction of the aesthetics of "the shocking new," promulgating— in the case of Stein's salon, for example—a collective visual aesthetic rooted in the act of scrutinizing Stein's large collection of controversially antirepresentational post-Impressionist paintings. In Mabel Dodge's Greenwich Village salon an aesthetic of collective political activism dominated discussion and produced a variety of faux-radical performances. And at around the same time any number of London "evenings" were devoted to the actual crafting of radical new styles of literature and art.

At Chez Josephine the double function of pushing the borders of the cosmopolitan into the aggressive realm of "the new" occurred in yet a different register. This club was in a sense a workshop of modern music and dance—a crowded, intimate, uncensored joint where audiences learned the idiom of full-tilt twenties jazz and experienced an intensely physical form of improvisational dance. To put this more explicitly: Chez Josephine was, from an aesthetic perspective, a laboratory of embodied experimentalism—a concept dear to modernists—wherein its extraordinary hostess synthesized two traditional arts, music and dance, into one astonishing new form—astonishing, at least, to its white European audience, for whom the experience of black Atlantic artisanship was largely unavailable. Baker seemed to be, as one French review put it, "not a woman . . . not a dancer, but something extravagant and furtive like the music itself—[she was] the ectoplasm, if you will, of all the surrounding sounds" (*MJB* 23). Like all good hostesses, Baker insisted on her audience's participation in the experiment—not through the traditional salon milieu of vigorous conversation, but through physical, embodied contact and passional involvement. She "danced with the fat ladies," as she put it, and "petted men's bald heads and plucked their whiskers" (*MJB* 116), pushing them into a language of African American musical phrases even as she recognized the futility of "translat[ing] black songs" to a white European audience that "would like to impose neat rhythms" on them (*MJB* 128–29). Acting as a conduit between racialized cultures while avoiding both the elitism and the abjectness usually associated with that role, Baker drew a crowd from "the four corners of Europe" who arrived "to see for themselves the Orient and the two Americas."[25] What they saw instead of the anticipated spectacle of colonial display (on view in her theater shows) was a performance of modern culture on black terms—terms that were beyond explication or the spectators' full comprehension.[26]

In this regard, Baker's club may also be understood as an institution thoroughly in keeping with the avant-garde cabarets that flourished in Montmartre a generation earlier. At Les Quat'z'Arts and Le Chat Noir had gathered the Incohérents and the Hydropathes, artistic groups dedicated to radical aesthetic innovation, which they achieved collectively through regular salon-like meetings that issued in artistic shows, balls, and performances. Targeting middle-class taste and centrist sensibility, these artists aimed to *épater la bourgeoisie* by experimenting with, among other things, monochrome painting, minimalist music, cartoon lithography, shadow theater, and parodic song. As was the case with Baker's club, bourgeois audiences in the cabarets were repelled and enchanted and eventually came in huge numbers—in a "throng of emblazoned carriages"—to see their values flouted in the cabarets' thematics of grossness, incivility, violence, and parody.[27] The most famous production of the period is Jarry's *Père Ubu* (1896), which was performed by actors and puppets in a long theatrical run. Many Montmartre cabaret productions shared *Père Ubu's* antibourgeois techniques, while others concentrated on the parody of received forms and genres.[28] In particular, the cabaret song frequently came in for defor-mation: for every warbling, sentimental song performed in the Montmartre cabarets, ten were sung with twisted lyrics and a mocking delivery.

Baker had become famous for her cross-eyed, knock-kneed delivery of the sentimental song early in her career; that act had begun during her U.S. chorus-line days, described by Phyllis Rose: "She clowned outrageously, unable to stop herself. She crossed her eyes. Her feet tripped over each other while the other girls were kicking neatly in step. The effect of her performance was to mock the very idea of a chorus line, a row of people mechanically repeating the same ges-tures" (*JC* 57). But when Baker clowned solo in a cabaret in Montmartre, one important effect was to link her performance to earlier forms of avant-garde an-tibourgeois improvisation. Significantly, her use of her body as an instrument of both comedy (in a specific tradition of African American theater) and music (as a jazz dancer) added something entirely new to the experimental mix: it intro-duced and foregrounded a racialized thematic that had been only implicit in earlier Montmartre productions. In the previous generation, race had been used to anchor the subject positions of the white dissenting artists who formed that avant-garde community: their parodies and sketches were peppered with black characters notable only for their bewildered stupidity. Jews figured in some of their nationalistic polemics as caricatured threats to the integrity and indepen-dence of the artists' community.[29] Racism and anti-Semitism, in other words, were foundational negative discourses in the particular brand of avant-gardism produced in fin-de-siècle Montmartre. When Rodolphe Salis declared, in 1883, that Montmartre was "the modern capital of *l'ésprit*," he might have added that *l'ésprit* resembled a white man's empire.[30]

Part of the shock value of Baker's cabaret performances derived directly from the frank incorporation of race into the ambience of her club-salon. Baker's per-formances were largely *about* race as a patterning of representations in twenti-eth-century Europe: she mixed black orchestra, black dancer, black music, black rhythm, black chic, black idiom, black patter, and a black chef with white cus-tomers, white voyeurism, white (non-)rhythm, white money, white incompre-hension, white cosmopolitanism. In her club, a resignification of the concept of race evolved out of extensive, nonsequential performances replete with audi-ence participation, so that it became possible to conceive of race not as an ex-tant set of properties, not as an empirical map, but rather as a by-product of the collision of African American performers and white European audiences. Baker chaffed her audience's backward racialism, its insistence on reducing "tropical," "exotic," "African," "African American," "Negro," and "black" to a monolithic epistemological category of "race" and its concomitant inability to see "white European" as a similar (and similarly erroneous) epistemological category. In

Baker's club, the white audience was "white" principally by virtue of the forms of its cultural illiteracy: stupefied by jazz (also notoriously bad at dancing to black jazz) and spellbound by Baker's shifting racialized personae, the audience in essence paid Baker to translate, educate, and enlighten them out of a hegemonic and parochial white perspective. The new conversation of the cosmopolitan elite was the conversation about race, however politically circumscribed its borders may have been; and while Josephine Baker the Folies performer was often reified as a specularized object in a conventional *tableau vivant* of race, Josephine Baker the modern hostess brilliantly reopened the race conversation over and over again.[31]

From the moment of her entrance into the club—her "light sealskin-brown" body "swathed in a blue tulle frock with a bodice of blue snakeskin," as *Vogue* reported it one night (*JC* 112)—Baker flaunted a unique form of cultural expertise, the very possession of which magnified her audience's relative cultural impoverishment. Her multiple performances—from the gorgeous paragon of Parisian *haute couture,* to the contortionist dancer whose body made sense of unfathomable music, to the joking, flirting master of ceremonies, to the dance instructor who brought her menagerie of pets along with her white students onto the dance floor—ultimately exfoliated the story of race that had been a subtext in dominant accounts of Western culture and a supporting narrative in French colonialism. She was a modern woman who lived within and beyond racial stereotype, not because of some magically induced transubstantiation, but because the stereotype itself could contain neither the vivid intersubjectivity of Baker and her band nor the particularity of her historical success. The Parisian impulse to understand Baker as a cipher existing beyond the civilizing forces of modernity contained a remarkable disavowal: for in fact Baker's club performances were geared to attenuating the savageness of her uncivilized audience. Baker herself had remarked on the "savagery" of the midnight crowds in Montmartre, and the explanation that she gave for opening her own club was that she wanted to escape the "savages" in other Montmartre venues "who gobble you up with their eyes" (*MJB* 116–17). In her own club she could control the terms of her spectacle, maintain the distance between performance and reality so often blurred by racist audiences, and establish her agency in relation to "white men," those "very curious beings" (*MJB* 117) who habitually mistook her physical genius for sexual availability.

The "curious beings" who mystified Baker—the white men who responded with such force to her influence on Parisian culture—in fact fought out a cultural sparring match around her performing body.[32] Rose quotes at length from two influential reviews that more or less anchored the positions of the warring sides. In *Le Figaro*, French Academy member Robert de Flers called *La Revue nègre* "a lamentable transatlantic exhibitionism which makes us revert to the ape in less time than it took us to descend from it" (*JC* 32). In reply, the art dealer Paul Guillaume posted an impressive list of modern European artists whose genius depended on the "primitive" qualities of African art (Picasso, Matisse, Apollinaire, Cocteau, Breton, etc.), and pronounced that "we who think we have a soul will blush at the poverty of our spiritual state before the superiority of blacks who have four souls, one in the head, one in the nose and throat, the shadow, and one in the blood" (*JC* 45).

As these passages suggest, the initial controversy over Baker had very little to do with Baker herself, who was neither an ape, nor African, nor possessed of a soul in her nose. The racialized struggle for the voice of French cultural authority was, rather, massed, as it often is, around issues of nationalism and national identity and directed more particularly in this case (though perhaps not so obviously) toward the dilemma typically posed to the state by the opacity of avant-garde tactics and theory. Simply put, the performances of an African American theater company challenged the classical aesthetic of wholeness and harmony, offering instead a heap of broken images. But the racism of de Flers's polemic indicates that *La Revue nègre*'s performance represented more than just a clash between Ancients and Moderns. Rose surmises that "the *Revue Nègre*'s popularity signaled to de Flers the beginning of black cultural hegemony and thus, to him, the end of civilization" (*JC* 33). Since black culture was absolutely unintelligible to de Flers—since, indeed, "black culture" was for him an oxymoron inadmissible under any terms to the epistemological reach of a nation-securing institution like the French Academy—it posed the same threat to national culture as was posed both by popular culture and by strands of the avant-garde. It is appropriate, then, that the artists listed by Guillaume in his response to de Flers were experimentalists whose work crossed over into political critique. The techniques developed through their work—the radical altering of dimensionality, the undermining of logical discursivity, the subversion of allegory—had for a generation ballasted new forms of avant-garde collectivity and epistemology. Indeed, Gertrude Stein's salon was structured around the appreciation of just these revolutionary techniques; it was not lost on her French academic critics that the tutelage she offered was delivered in the studio of a middle-class Jewish American expatriate lesbian whose own "poetry" defied understanding and aimed to unravel the syntax of rationality and empiricism. In the same year that Baker performed at Chez Josephine, 1926–27, surrealists were advancing their program of irrational aesthetics, with the aim of displacing the obstacles to the liberatory unconscious put in the way by "civilization." For them, art was to be discovered by mistake, through Baudelairean shock, along psychic detours and in uncontrollable vortices of passion. *L'amour fou*—mad love, which Breton associated with prerational and nondeterministic surrender—was, for surrealists, one of the purest precipitants of psychic (and, therefore, political) liberation.[33]

In several important respects, Josephine Baker's dance qua dance followed the anti-representational contours of avant-garde projects, as had the work of some of the American dancers in Paris who preceded her arrival, particularly Isadora Duncan. Twenty years earlier, Duncan had advocated the breaking of classical dance syntax through style and choreography. Eschewing sets, "disrespectfully" improvising her compositions to canonical classical music, and wearing nothing more than a loose-fitting toga, Duncan had shattered Parisian reserve and garnered for herself thousands of wild-eyed admirers who spoke of her performances in the language of primitivist apotheosis. A testimony by Elie Faure exemplifies the cadence of these tributes:

> From deep within us, when she danced, there arose a flood that swept away from the recesses of our soul all the filth which had been piled up there by those, who, for twenty centuries, had bequeathed to us their critique, their ethics, and their judgements. . . . When we eagerly watched her we rediscovered that primitive purity which, every two or three thousand years, reappears from the depth of the abyss of our worn-out conscience to restore to us again a holy animality.[34]

Primitive purity and holy animality were, of course, the same terms used to describe the qualities of Baker's dancing sixteen years later (just as they had been used to describe William "Juba" Lane's dancing in London in 1848); but these were precisely the qualities that revolted Baker's critics.[35] Whereas Duncan's "primitive purity" was interpreted as a return to an uncorrupted Greek ethos, Baker's threatened, according to her critics, to cast her audience into a cycle of modern degeneration.

At this point we are obviously deep into the conflicted idiom of racialized colonialism, and it is an idiom that helps to explain (though not fully) the difference in reception experienced by the two American dancers in Paris. But I wish for the moment to press a further point about the rage created by Baker's dance, both in her wrathful critics and in her raving fans. What, we may ask, constituted "the primitive" in Baker's (as opposed to Duncan's) dance style? Certainly not just the extraordinary sense of rhythm with which she directed every part of her body, and certainly not just the audience's (unearned) sense of the easy synecdochalism of Baker's raced body. In Hans Ulrich Gumbrecht's discussion of Baker's dancing, which draws on Harry Kessler's observation that "Baker danced with extreme grotesqueness and purity of style . . . for hours, apparently without getting tired, always finding new forms," Gumbrecht pauses over the idea that Baker's dance might have been viewed as, in his words, "a pure surface phenomenon, consisting of endless varieties of form."[36] He goes on to note the contrast between this style of "dancing as body rhythm" with the more formally established "dancing as expression" epitomized for him by Mary Wigman and the school of *Ausdruckstanz*.[37] Indeed, Gumbrecht's thesis that Baker's fascination derived in part from her performance of rhythm as "pure surface phenomenon" helps to make sense of the confusion and conflict surrounding her reception in Paris. It also helps to make sense of the performative bond formed between Baker and her club/salon audiences. As a "surface phenomenon" existing well outside the realm of the expressionist model of dance— a model first popularized by Isadora Duncan, it should be noted—Baker's dance necessarily resisted the interpretative act. This is to say that, whereas Duncan created movements that aimed to "represent" (in a symbolist vocabulary) Ionian columns and the chora of tragedy, Baker's dancing subverted the impulsive referentiality fostered by expressionism. Hers was an improvisational performance of rhythm, formal only insofar as it possessed a barely recognizable body syntax ("back arched, haunches protruding, arms entwined" [*JC* 31]) that structured her movements. This meant that it was unavailable to the interpretive modes of formal complexity and imagist depth so singularly (and, by this time, so institutionally) valorized by modernism. Baker the dancer, seemingly a product of modernism and certainly an object of the racialist modernist imaginary, worked beyond the boundaries of modern aesthetics in a rhizomatic mode that perhaps warrants a Deleuzean reading.[38]

Baker also flouted the interpretive paradigms of colonialism. For if her dancing could not be read as an expression of a "deep core" of race—if her rhythmic "wildness" did not "mean" anything other than an inexhaustible improvisational ability—then her figure could not coherently anchor the binarism of wildness and civilization on which colonial ideology depended. We may here recall Hayden White's argument that "wildness" and "savagery" are part of "a set of culturally self-authenticating devices" that "are used not merely to designate a specific condition or state of being but also to confirm the value of their dialectical antitheses."[39] Given the racialist horizon of expectation of Paris in the twenties, it is no wonder that Baker threw her reviewers into paroxysms, which they resolved only imperfectly in the language of metaphor and hyperbole. For Baker could not be used effectually as a figure for nationalistic colonial conservatism ("she shows us that we must bring our light to them"), nor could she be used as a figure for cosmopolitan colonial humanism ("she shows us that they must bring their light to us"). Her club audiences, imperfectly prepared for the lessons of otherness, were utterly unprepared for this deconstruction of racialism.

But it was precisely in the gap between the interpretive yearnings of modernism and the ontological ephemerality of race that Baker's cosmopolitan "salon" cohered. "Cosmopolitanism," writes Amanda Anderson, "is characteristically elaborated within an experience of cultural multiplicity and at least limited self-reflexivity, and against a specific form of parochialism."[40] The specific forms of parochialism in this case were, first, American racism, and second, the parochialism by which the French construed cosmopolitanism as a particularly French attribute. The self-reflexivity, as I have argued, took the form of performances of race and racial tolerance. The experience of cultural multiplicity was orchestrated by Baker the hostess (though it was also delimited by the institutional confines of the "free play" zone of Montmartre). It was a radically new form of multiplicity, one that tacitly repudiated the condescending conception of otherness derived from French Revolutionary ideology, according to which *egalité* was a property to be granted by the metropole. Instead, the cultural multiplicity experienced in Baker's club—the otherness within which cosmopolitanism was elaborated—took the form of embodied identification. It emerged as a uniquely physical property catalyzed by music and dance. Otherness, in other words, was comprised of both the dancer and her audience, bound together in a historical moment. The improvisational participation that prevailed at Chez Josephine seems to have created a path of intimacy that largely evaded the double threat of political relativism and racialist essentialism.

Baker described this intimacy from the perspective of the dancer: "Watch me when I dance in the middle of you," she wrote to her public. "It is like that that I must dance, not against a backdrop but in the middle of a circle of clapping people forming around me, in the middle of men and women, on the same level, the same light, side by side" (*MJB* 118). Not against a set piece or on someone else's stage or in some other culture's narrative, but in the middle of a circle of people with their hands on the music. What she's talking about are the sociopolitical possibilities produced by her performances—possibilities for her, different possibilities for her audiences. This kind of improvisational, intersubjective contact creates joy for Baker, even jouissance, through the medium of dance, shaped as it is, in this club and this city, by the conversation of race. Implicit in her comments are the questions of equality and specularity and economic footing so often obscured by modernism's infatuation with black *objets d'art*. But this is about as textual as Baker gets; for Baker at Chez Josephine, riotous dance is its own end. Maurice Wallace has written that "to dance is to expand the repertoire of human representation, to pursue with one's body the extreme limits of self-knowledge";[41] at Chez Josephine, this experience seems to have occurred en masse. We may recognize the cultural multiplicity to which Anderson's précis of cosmopolitanism refers at Chez Josephine's intersecting circles of racialized cultures and cultural aesthetics.

Baker's hostessing was geared to her own pleasure and profit, as she said again and again. That pleasure derived as much from shaking it to great music as it did from the novelty of leveling, for once, the racial playing field in performance and in business. But just as important, for the purposes of my argument, Baker's hostessing was squarely based in what I would call *xenos*. Her guests were aliens, strangers, who were treated as equals despite their uncomprehending limitations. They left her salon confused and altered by this surprising new script of modernity, and while undoubtedly their disorientation was temporary and wholly reversible, the script still possesses the capacity for surprise, and its accompanying music and movement have resonated in ways for which contemporary cultural critics have yet to account.

NOTES

I wish to thank Elizabeth Majerus for inspired research assistance, and Michael Bérubé and Bill Maxwell for the expertise and insights they contributed to this essay.

1. For accounts and discussions of Baker's life, see Josephine Baker, *Les Mémoires de Joséphine Baker*, collected and adapted by Marcel Sauvage (Paris: KRA, 1927); Stephen Papich, *Remembering Josephine* (Indianapolis: Bobbs-Merrill, 1976); Josephine Baker and Jo Bouillon, *Josephine,* trans. Mariana Fitzpatrick (New York: Harper and Row, 1977); Lynn Haney, *Naked at the Feast: A Biography of Josephine Baker* (New York: Dodd, Mead, 1981); Bryan Hammond and Patrick O'Connor, *Josephine Baker* (London: Jonathan Cape, 1988); Phyllis Rose, *Jazz Cleopatra: Josephine Baker in Her Time* (New York: Vintage, 1989); Jean-Claude Baker and Chris Chase, *Josephine: The Hungry Heart* (New York: Random House, 1993).
2. Quoted in Haney, *Naked at the Feast*, 88.
3. W. E. B. Du Bois, *The Souls of Black Folk,* intro. Randall Kenan (1903; New York: Signet, 1995), 221.
4. T.O.B.A. (Tough On Black Asses) was a Southern performance troupe during the 1920s.
5. Quoted in Rose, *Jazz Cleopatra,* 61; hereafter cited in text and abbreviated *JC.*
6. Baker, *Les Mémoires de Joséphine Baker,* 37; hereafter cited in text and abbreviated *MJB.*
7. See, e.g., Ann Douglas, *Terrible Honesty: Mongrel Manhattan in the 1920s* (New York: Farrar, Straus, Giroux, 1995), 105–7.
8. Henry Louis Gates, Jr., "An Interview with Josephine Baker and James Baldwin" [1973], *Southern Review* 21:3 (summer 1985): 597. See Tyler Stovall's historical account of the sense of freedom felt by African Americans in Paris in *Paris Noir: African Americans in the City of Light* (Boston: Houghton Mifflin, 1996), chapters 1 and 2.

9. Tzvetan Todorov, *On Human Diversity: Nationalism, Racism, and Exoticism in French Thought*, trans. Catherine Porter (Cambridge: Harvard University Press, 1993), 90. Todorov characterizes the intellectual history of French racialism as an Enlightenment "movement of ideas" (91) developed in France by the likes of Buffon, Voltaire, Renan, Gobineau, and Le Bon. His book chronicles the debates in French racialist history that pit monogenesis against polygenesis, universalism against particularism, natural against human, and progressivism against determinism.

10. Ventriloquized by Janet Flanner, *Paris Was Yesterday: 1925–1939*, ed. Irving Drutman (New York: Harcourt Brace Jovanovich, 1972), 3.

11. Stovall, *Paris Noir*, 31; hereafter abbreviated *PN*.

12. Flanner, *Paris Was Yesterday*, xx.

13. Du Bois, *Souls of Black Folk*, 45.

14. Baudelaire's inaugural discussions of what we now characterize as modernism arise out of his fascination with doubleness, the *Doppelgänger*, and the double consciousness produced by modern urban specularity. See, e.g., "The Painter of Modern Life," in *"The Painter of Modern Life" and Other Essays* (London: Phaidon, 1995), especially the aphoristic "My Heart Laid Bare" (18).

15. Du Bois, *Souls of Black Folk*, 43: "[Whites] approach me in a half-hesitant sort of way, eye me curiously or compassionately, and then, instead of saying directly, How does it feel to be a problem? they say, I know an excellent colored man in my town . . ." Howard Winant suggests that Du Bois's identification of "the problem" must now be understood in a paradigm of "universal racial dualism." "Racial Dualism at Century's End," in *The House That Race Built: Black Americans, U.S. Terrain*, ed. Wahneema Lubiano (New York: Pantheon, 1997), 87.

16. Nancy Nenno, "Femininity, the Primitive, and Modern Urban Space: Josephine Baker in Berlin," in *Women in the Metropolis: Gender and Modernity in Weimar Culture*, ed. Katharina Von Ankum (Berkeley: University of California Press, 1997), 154–55.

17. Nenno, "Femininity, the Primitive, and Modern Urban Space," 149.

18. Quoted in Todorov, *On Human Diversity*, 326. For an example of modernist valorizations of "energy," see the manifestos by Ezra Pound in *BLAST* 1, ed. Wyndham Lewis (London, 1914).

19. Such "tolerance" was an undisguised strategic plank in contemporary French colonial discourse, wherein nationalism was deployed to parse "good" French colonial ideology from the "bad" versions of the competitors. David Spurr argues that

> where Kipling sought to shift a portion of the white man's burden onto other powers, apologists for the French empire came to see that high calling as preeminently their own: Albert Sarraut thus writes in 1931 that "France, to her honor, was the first to under-

stand the human worth of the backward races, and the sacred obligation to respect and increase that worth."

The Rhetoric of Empire: Colonial Discourse in Journalism, Travel Writing, and Imperial Administration (Durham: Duke University Press, 1993), 120.

20. My use of the term "performance" here is meant to invoke not a Butlerian citationality that parodies and destabilizes identity, but rather an acute consciousness, on the part of all the actors (and audiences), of their roles in this new drama unfolding around twentieth-century racialism. Although the drama itself entailed parodic forms of colonialism and racializing, the performances to which I allude—especially the audience's disidentification from U.S. racism—tended to consolidate rather than destabilize identity formations. A symptom of this drama may be viewed in Parisian journalists' struggles to capture what it was they were witnessing in the racialized fads spawned by Baker—the "tanned-up" skin, slicked-down hair, the rage for jazz dancing, her endorsement of a driving school (which in itself constituted a repudiation of the "type" of premodern black embraced by modernist primitivism). Public records and private journals alike pulsed with idiomatic screams about Baker and wild animals, Baker and sleek sophistication, Baker and mass consumption.

21. Michel de Certeau, *The Practice of Everyday Life*, trans. Steven Rendall (Berkeley: University of California Press, 1984), 106.

22. I do not mean to suggest that all salon-like gatherings necessarily involved the *gratis* provision of food and drink or assurances of structured or serious conversation. On the contrary, the salons of the Harlem Renaissance and of Greenwich Village in these same years often resembled rent parties or potluck bistros. See *Greenwich Village: Culture and Counterculture*, ed. Rick Beard and Leslie Cohen Berlowitz (New Brunswick: Rutgers University Press, 1993); David Levering Lewis, *When Harlem Was in Vogue* (New York: Oxford University Press, 1982), chap. 6.

23. Baker opened subsequent clubs in Berlin, Harlem, and, again, Paris as "tie-ins" to her scheduled tour stops. My argument is concerned solely with her first club.

24. Paul Gilroy, *The Black Atlantic: Modernity and Double Consciousness* (Cambridge: Harvard University Press, 1993), 46.

25. Review quoted by Marcel Sauvage in his introductory comments to *Mémoires de Joséphine Baker*, 34.

26. The difference between Baker's performances in her own cabaret and in other theatrical venues must be marked. Her scripted and choreographed performances in theaters and film productions in the twenties and early thirties usually drew explicitly on conventional, stereotypical narratives of race and colonialism, while her club performances concentrated on the improvisational performance of contemporary jazz dancing and music. For descriptions of the

former, see T. Denean Sharpley-Whiting, *Black Venus: Sexualized Savages, Primal Fears, and Primitive Narratives in French* (Durham: Duke University Press, 1999), 105–18; and especially the excellent overviews provided in Karen C. C. Dalton and Henry Louis Gates Jr., "Josephine Baker and Paul Colin: African American Dance Seen through Parisian Eyes," *Critical Inquiry* 24 (summer 1998): 903–34.

27. Phillip Dennis Cate, "The Spirit of Montmartre," in *The Spirit of Montmartre: Cabarets, Humor, and the Avant-Garde, 1875–1905,* ed. Phillip Dennis Cate and Mary Shaw (New Brunswick: Rutgers University Press, 1996), 36.

28. See Cate, "The Spirit of Montmartre," 1–93; and Daniel Grojnowski, "Hydropathes and Company," in *The Spirit of Montmartre,* ed. Cate and Shaw, 95–109.

29. See Cate, "The Spirit of Montmartre," 38, 55. Note, however, that this racial thematic was partially reversed by subsequent avant-gardists, particularly self-exiled dadaists in Zurich. Stovall points out that in 1916 dadaists "staged several *soirées nègres,* public theatrical events that prominently displayed blacks as comic figures in a critique of European racism and Western civilization in general." *Paris Noir,* 69.

30. Grojnowski, "Hydropathes and Company," 111.

31. For a sense of the reduced version of this conversation as it circulated in political cartoons of the period, see the excellent sampling provided by Stovall, *Paris Noir.* Most of these cartoons depict some version of the rancid indignation of white American tourists upon encountering the free fraternizing of races in Paris.

32. Janet Flanner astutely described this force as "the acute response of the white masculine public in the capital of hedonism of all Europe—Paris." *Paris Was Yesterday,* 3.

33. Mad love was epitomized by Breton in the eponymous character of his novel/journal *Nadja* (1927). And while it is tempting to see similarities between Nadja and Baker—both are frankly sexual, unconventional, impulsive, non-normative figures—there is a world of difference between the fragile, abject Nadja, who seems at times to be no more than a figure of Breton's imagination, and the robust, self-directing agency of the very real Josephine Baker. Baker seems to have been pestered regularly by Bretonian dreamers who couldn't understand that she preferred to go home alone to bed after a long night of dancing. See *MJB,* 117–18.

34. Allan Ross Macdougall, *Isadora: A Revolutionary in Art and Love* (New York: Thomas Nelson and Sons, 1960), 124–25.

35. See Maurice Wallace, "The Autobiography of an Ex-Snow Queen: Dance, Desire, and the Black Masculine in Melvin Dixon's *Vanishing Rooms,*" in *Novel Gazing: Queer Readings in Fiction,* ed. Eve Kosofsky Sedgwick (Durham: Duke University Press, 1997), 379–80, for an account of this African American dancer's celebrity.

36. Hans Ulrich Gumbrecht, *In 1926: Living at the Edge of Time* (Cambridge: Harvard University Press, 1997), 67.

37. Gumbrecht, *In 1926*, 70.

38. For example, it would be easy to characterize the relation between Baker and her club audience as an "assemblage" of desire, the self-generating product of a field of highly charged contact.

39. Hayden White, *Tropics of Discourse: Essays in Cultural Criticism* (Baltimore: Johns Hopkins University Press, 1978), 151.

40. Amanda Anderson, "Cosmopolitanism, Universalism, and the Divided Legacies of Modernity," in *Cosmopolitics: Thinking and Feeling beyond the Nation*, ed. Bruce Robbins and Pheng Cheah (Minneapolis: University of Minnesota Press, 1998), 272.

41. Wallace, "The Autobiography of an Ex-Snow Queen," 382.

3

TRESPASSING THE COLORLINE

AGGRESSIVE MOBILITY AND SEXUAL TRANSGRESSION IN THE CONSTRUCTION OF NEW NEGRO MODERNITY

Marlon B. Ross

The new spirit which has produced the New Negro bids fair to transform the whole race. America faces a new race that has awakened, and in the realization of its strength has girt its loins to run the race with other men.
                                                                    —E. Franklin Frazier

The modern concept of the New Negro emerges in the post-Reconstruction period in response to the intensification and dissemination of Jim Crow strictures, which follow upon the heels of African Americans as they migrate cityward and/or northward in the hope of finding a larger scope for physical, social, and economic mobility. Rather than trusting the "New South," frequently referred to by New Negro writers as a re-enslaved region, the New Negroes picture themselves as making their own more authentic newness against the grain of conditions gripping the South—and increasingly the nation itself—in the muck of an enslaving past. Although New Negro strategies are historically and ideologically multiform because they are constantly being tested and contested by the New Negroes themselves as well as by white patrons and antagonists, those New Negroes who image themselves as radically progressive invariably employ one strategy from their vast armory: what we might call *racial trespassing*, the contrary of the more frequently studied phenomenon of racial passing. Through this strategy of intrusive mobility, figuring on-the-go black bodies as too motivated and energetic to be kept in place by legalized race codes, New Negroes also stake their claim to United States citizenship as a global enterprise signaling a country whose ambitions are too large to be contained within its national boundaries. New Negroes therefore frequently represent their right to mobility by resorting to the same national myths other citizens use to justify and motivate an imperialistically expansive U.S. culture: the self-made entrepreneur, the lone frontiersman or cowboy, the New World immigrant, the urban reformer, the go-to-it muscled laborer, the sophisticated cosmopolitan, and the know-how inventor.

This breed of radical New Negro puts his or her body on the colorline, makes a literal and metaphorical weapon of the body itself, in order to claim an absolute freedom of mobility. Given the legal, political, social, and economic import of the segregation of the railroad system toward the end of the nineteenth century, not surprisingly New Negro writers often represent colorline trespassing as climaxing in a showdown on a Jim Crow railcar, thus exploiting the railroad as the ultimate symbol of the nation's global might, technological know-how, civilizing progress, cross-continental mobility, and promise of reunification after Civil War and Reconstruction.[1] New Negroes set out to exploit the "physical presence" of rail power as an opportunity for reshaping the signification of their own black bodies as an advance guard of modernity. Finding in physical mobility the enabling embodiment of other kinds of movement—class ascent, professional development, wealth accumulation, social reform, and advancement in higher education—New Negroes rewrite the iconography of the black body itself to effect the bodily intrusion they see as the sole means to personal and collective uplift. The energetic force of the black body is indicated in its very composition and stance—the serious countenance of the face, the concentrated intentness of the eyes, the upward bearing of the head, the alert posture of the limbs.

If the unfettered black body confronting white adversaries on a Jim Crow railcar is the climactic image of radical New Negro discourse, then the specter that haunts this discourse is the lynched black body. The dream of modernity borne by an energetic, aggressive, stalwart, focused body of mobility is everywhere hedged in by a nightmare of savage reversion, in which the flexible, mobile black body is haltered on a limb or torn to pieces by a mob. Lynching not only represents the potential entrenchment in a primitive condition analogous to chattel captivity, wherein the black body is trapped as the national emblem for lethargy, docility, immobility, and vulnerability to arbitrary torture; it also betokens the disfiguring and disembodying maligning of racial character and features through fixed typecasting to deny African Americans bodily versatility and integrity as whole persons.[2]

It is against this implacable image and reality of racial degradation through lynching that New Negro imagery becomes immersed in a counterdiscourse of conventionally masculine bodily aggression. Embedded in the New Negro iconography of bodily intrusion, disarming weaponry, nationalist enterprise, aggressive frontiersmanship, imperialist expansion, and cross-racial violence are gender expectations whose operation is racially encoded. To be a modern, straight-up, quick-thinking, forward-looking U.S. citizen ready to compete in the new century is to carry the self—to boast, stare down, and swagger, for instance—in ways commonly seen as off-limits not only to women but also to nonwhite men. In other words, the signs of self-confident modernity are marked on the body in ways normally defined not only as white but also as masculine.[3] Focusing especially on the work of William Pickens, this essay examines the gender, sexual, racial, ideological, and rhetorical implications of racial trespassing as the physical vehicle of New Negroes' attempts to overcome and overturn the dominant status of an embodied white masculinity that had come to emblematize modern progress.[4]

If it is to be more than simple linguistic inflation, "newness" requires action, news-making political activity, and constant image building and rebuilding. "Newness" requires that the black body itself be put at risk—and that it be *displayed* as being put at risk. Even Booker T. Washington, whose accommodationist agenda helps to disseminate the idea of the New Negro at the turn of the century, engages in this display of the at-risk black body in order to assert his "Bookerite" brand of newness and renewal.[5] The cues to Booker T. Washington's grand new experiments exist, for instance, not only in his well-known institution building but also in minute changes borne in and worn on the body of blackness itself. Washington is very much aware that apprehensive whites are eager to read the smallest signs of "newness" on black bodies so that they can discipline and punish those who cross taboo lines of conduct, lines defined explicitly by race and silently by gender.

Though rhetorically he presents himself and his protégés as humble, ordinary, and contentedly mired in the muck of menial Black Belt labor, Washington *does* portray his own body, and those of his colleagues and students, in upwardly mobile terms whenever *visual* representations of his enterprise are at stake. When he presents himself and his colleagues as "new" in the myriad photographs in the anthology *A New Negro for a New Century* (1900), they are photographed in their fancy military uniforms, captain of industry suits, and lady's high society dresses.[6] While this sort of attire accords with Washington's idea that the best proof of worthiness for citizenship is the visual documentation of the race's loyal, humble labor and gradual accumulation of material wealth, this fancy clothing also jeopardizes his rhetorical notion that Bookerite New Negroes have no sociopolitical ambitions beyond their circumscribed place within the current racial scheme. "To publicly present one's self . . . not as a field hand," Kevin K. Gaines writes, "but as successful, dignified, and neatly attired, constituted a transgressive refusal to occupy the subordinate status prescribed for African American men and women."[7] The bold stares, haughty bearing, and bourgeois clothing of the Bookerite New Negroes in *A New Negro for a New Century* belie the notion that Washington's accommodation necessitates the avoidance of all "manly" risk to the body. Instead, these corporeal signs reveal how such accommodation captures the essence of economic modernity by displaying the bold entrepreneurship practiced by *individual* New Negro leaders who can maneuver into the productively ascending middle class without upsetting the larger racial hierarchy. For Washington's New Negroes, this creates the need for a balancing act between displaying the upward mobility of individual bodies and downplaying the collective black body's potential for uppity sociopolitical demands as full-fledged citizens.

When William Pickens tries to wrench this "new" epithet from the hands of Washington's generation, he dramatizes the risks to the body that he has taken and would be willing to take in order to deserve the appellation. Rather than a balancing act that keeps the colorline intact, Pickens's radical New Negro strategy focuses on how the black body itself necessarily imbalances that line in every conceivable way. In his radical polemic, *The New Negro: His Political, Civil, and Mental Status; and Related Essays* (1916), Pickens makes black bodies volatile agents of modern progress despite their ongoing entrenchment in immobilizing experiences like sharecropping, illiteracy, (self-)segregation, lynching, and subsistence-level survival at the marginal bottoms. Despite his claim of constant mixing of blood among arbitrary racial groupings, Pickens keeps the races intact—rather than viewing them as amalgamated into new races, one single race, or no races at all. The dynamism in Pickens's history occurs, instead, in the constantly changing *status* of the races in relation to one another. Pickens's polemic shifts the emphasis in dominant culture away from history as a stable, gradual progress among hierarchically fixed races to history as a volatile interruption of race-tribes on the go, constantly jockeying for global power in a fast-paced race toward an abstract finish line called "the modern." Precocious at the start, the race of black men gets overtaken by "the virile and aggressive people who grew up in Europe."[8] Just as the "energetic" Europeans were to advance by assimilating Egyptian civilization, however, so the African is now rising again as

a result of "his" having assimilated colonizing European civilization in the New World: "He stands to-day on the threshold of a renaissance of civilization and culture after four hundred years of interruption by captivity, slavery and oppression."[9]

Like much of the discourse of this period, Pickens assumes the contemporary framework of a U.S. capitalist economy, where individual men with varying resources based on their racial heritage must compete for labor and profit.[10] Although the text appears to be about a global history of tribal race wars, it is really about the capitalist warfare at work in America's northern urban centers. Previously asleep amidst this manly competition for the rights of the advance guard, the black race is now awakening to do combat: "And they are now awakening to the truth that they must advance along all lines to make their advancement secure, that they must 'straighten out their front,' as they say in the European war."[11] This bellicose metaphor of violent bodily *invasion*, blacks "straighten[ing] out their front" to penetrate and conquer modernity, is repeatedly conflated with images of more pacified bodily mixing as both racial (i.e., social) integration and biological miscegenation in New Negro discourse. Driving these conflicting metaphors are ambivalences about both the meaning of *race* as a sign on which to hinge the notion of an advancing *culture* and the posture of masculine aggression as a sign on which to hinge the potential for race solidarity, integrity, and empowerment. Pickens's text reveals the extent to which the New Negro agenda of race advancement through intrusion, imposition, and insemination rests on an ambivalently gendered paradigm of masculine competition, conquest, and warfare.

What should not be overlooked here in the logic of this race dynamism is the implicit valuation of two sexual characteristics normally seen as recessive, primitive, and uncivilized: promiscuous miscegenation and the gendering of the black race as an unstable sexual (com)position. Pickens celebrates indiscriminate sexual mixing as a subtle metaphor for racial cosmopolitanism, as he casts the gender-sexual status of any race as historically unstable. At one moment the African race is the manly ravisher, penetrating and inseminating the passive Europeans; at another moment the Europeans become the sexual, and thus cultural, aggressors, having their way with pacified and passive Africans. A race is not permanently typed as either masculine or unmasculine, aggressive or passive, inseminating or inseminated; instead its position as top or bottom and its composition as manly invader or unmanned boy are constantly renegotiated in the give-and-take of the race toward modernity.

Strangely, Pickens figures all races as male, each at different stages of anatomical development at different moments in the race's history.[12] When invaded and pacified, then, a race is not exactly feminized or emasculated; it is, more precisely, stripped *temporarily* of manhood, a process and state for which we do not have a satisfactory vocabulary. By no means has Pickens, in deviating from the standard account of Darwinist racial competition, toppled the masculine structures and values that enable his narrative of world civilization to cohere. Ironically, he exploits gender deviation figuratively, and perhaps unwittingly, to enable a future in which the African race, through the manly powers of unpredictable dis/insemination, can be on top again.

By writing *The New Negro*, Pickens nonetheless affirms and displays his own New Negro manhood against the charge of racial emasculation as a physical sign of racial enervation. New Negroes associate economic degradation, social abjection, and cultural backwardness—all emblems of unmanly passivity—with entrapment in the rural Deep South under the aegis of Washington's "old Negro" strategy of accommodation. As an advertisement of his radical New Negro identity, *The New Negro* squarely places Pickens in the aggressive anti-Bookerite camp as a man willing to bid for New Negro leadership through racial trespassing in the cosmopolitan North, rather than accommodating himself to Jim Crow strictures in the lagging South. Against the Bookerite idea that blacks patiently should consolidate for gradual economic development in the "wastelands" of the Black Belt, Pickens announces his faith in the renaissance of African civilization through the scattered contact and consolidated massing that can be achieved only in fast-paced cities. Lambasting loyalty to the Black Belt as a site for gradual progress as a sort of immobilizing fixation, Pickens suggests that "[t]hese views consider the Negro in his relation to white people *only as a commodity*."[13] Instead of the well-scrubbed, well-mannered uniform body of self-sacrificing rural teachers, family farmers, and small-time entrepreneurs envisioned by Bookerite policies, Pickens's "new" vision captures the self-interest of a varied, versatile, and energetic mass body, rubbing shoulders with modernity and assimilating civilization by infiltrating its metropolitan centers as self-promoting free agents of change rather than as objectified commodities exploited for the progress of others.

In the urban context, all boundaries—between white and black, urbanity and primitivism, power and dispossession, image and reality—become relative, unstable, penetrable, up for grabs. The first step in seizing a racial destiny is for a race to be seen in the spotlight of modernity, the arena in which the future of civilization is fought over, negotiated, claimed, and reclaimed. The first trespassing tactic that Pickens proposes and enacts in *The New Negro*, therefore, is a modern advertising campaign in which the New Negro gains control of the circulation of his own image in the urban media (publishing houses, magazines, newspapers, advertising concerns, and sociological studies). The shaping of racial self-interest depends on the marketing of a versatile self-image: "But along with the great advance which the Negro can be expected to make in the United States in the next fifty years, every few years should see a book up to date on the general subject of 'The Renaissance of the Negro Race' or 'The New Negro.'"[14] Because modern mass media are always seeking to exploit and expand into ever-new markets, they create an unprecedented opening in which urbanizing African Americans can reshape themselves as a viable market, thus enhancing their value as economic free agents and overcoming their customary status as commodified, and thus *fixed*, objects of anachronistic feudal labor.

Updating his 1911 autobiography, *The Heir of Slaves*, Pickens titles the 1923 version *Bursting Bonds: The Autobiography of a "New Negro"* to indicate the sort of self-marketing of bodily aggression ("bursting bonds") that he wants to elicit in opposition to the focus on lineal continuity ("heir of slaves"). As William Andrews has pointed out, Pickens's narrator views all of life as a masculine "contest."[15] As opposed to Washington's *Up from Slavery*, Pickens borrows from the myth of the Wild West as a training ground for the modern great man, Roosevelt's self-fashioning myth of the rough-riding "strenuous life."[16] Pickens's series of lawless frontier adventures rewrites this myth in terms of the New Negro's preparation for modern life in the city, the racial jungle of whiter civilization. Even though Pickens initially thinks that he is headed for command of a black college in Washington's footsteps, his representation of his ascent to such a position—and ultimately his rejection of it as too passive/pacific—differs markedly from that of the Wizard of Tuskegee.[17] His most formative experiences, like Washington's, come in learning to work for and with whites at menial tasks, but unlike Washington's cooperative housekeeping lessons from female Yankee missionaries, Pickens stresses his rivalrous encounters in "uncivilized" outdoor contests with rough men who always have an unfair advantage, especially savagely cruel white southern men from the bottom to the top of the class scale.

Trespassing on white turf entails, on the one hand, standing one's ground in hand-to-hand combat with those who seek to impede the progress of the race, and on the other hand, an increasing sophistication in modern media—public speeches, mass book publication, a syndicated column for the Associated Negro Press,[18] and leadership in a cross-racial, overtly political organization willing to exploit the most modern advocacy techniques, the NAACP. Uplift can be effected only through a paradoxical combination of direct, open, manly competition with whites and cosmopolitan, urbane dis/insemination among them. In both cases, Pickens celebrates intrusive directness; he applauds the bluntness of primitive aggression and the boldness of self-advertising through sophisticated manipulation of mass media.

In order to exploit the opportunity for race building afforded by the modern

city, race leaders ironically must lodge their bid to modernity in primordial features that lie just on the other side of putatively natural male instinct. As Gail
Bederman has shown, turn-of-the-century white U.S. leaders desired to retain a
primitive masculine power while casting civilization as the act of moving beyond and ruling over "primitive" behavior. This paradox fuels much of the anxiety over a loss of national manhood during the Progressive Era.[19] Like "whiter"
race leaders of his time, Pickens has to balance virility as the source of progressive race power over against refinement as the consequence of civilizing
progress, but his racial situation further complicates the logic in this balancing
act. Beyond the reaffirmation of the kinds of masculine claims being made by
ruling whiter men, Pickens has the further task of legitimating, at the most
basic level, the black race's (meaning the black man's) right to claim a place in
the contest determining who will rule during the next stint of civilization in the
ongoing race toward modernity. Pickens sees the savage fights that take place in
the southern bottoms, western frontiers, and urban factories as rites of passage
that shape the muscularity, stamina, agility, and cunning of the young man des-
tined for militant leadership in the urban centers, where these natural attributes
can be transformed into the physical and mental dexterity of street smarts.
These rough sites can just as easily doom him to subsistence living in these marginal, backwards spheres, however, *if* he exploits them merely to survive rather
than using them to keep his eyes keenly trained on the advance guard of sophisticated accomplishment in a leading metropolis. In *Bursting Bonds*, Pickens represents his body as literally endangered in each of these sites, and he adeptly carries himself—literally positions his body—to manage these bottom margins in
order quickly to maneuver himself beyond them.

Bursting Bonds charts Pickens's rise as a New Negro through bonded rivalries
with white men who unwittingly toughen him and prepare him for uplift. We
might call such bonded rivalries *homoracial* to indicate Pickens's aspiration toward
a normative homosocial act, in which superior white men legitimate one another's
power by competing and bonding with one another while excluding women, gender nonconformists, and racialized others from the arena of competition. When
Pickens meets Dink Jeter, his antagonist in an early factory episode, many years
after their original conflict, the encounter demonstrates how Pickens's virile, cool,
straight-up attitude toward adversaries pays off in turning racial enemies into
eventual allies and savage competition into high aspiration. "This fellow, who had
done his uttermost to kill or maim me when I was a child, now put his arms about
me, hugged me dramatically and called out to the bewildered railroad hands: 'See
this boy! I been knowin' him all his life,—this the bes' boy in the whole worl'."[20]
This macho hugging across race represents the assertiveness of manhood, its claim
to be a transcendent standard, adjudicating and bridging men's accomplishments

beyond color, geography, and class. Not only does the passage highlight the embrace between this whiter savage-machine and the black man who has advanced beyond him; it also stresses the way Pickens's own willingness to be embraced by his former enemy can emerge only against a backdrop of other black men still entrapped by the whims of the whiter savage-machine.

> This chance meeting with "Dink" Jeter was a test for the sentiment which I had expressed years before, when I thought he was dead: that I could never feel hatred or resentment toward the man, and that as I looked back, he seemed to be one of my appointed teachers who trained me in the art of vigilant self-defense. (72)

The "art of vigilant self-defense" constitutes the magic bullet in Pickens's armory. Because he has had to survive on the bottom margins, he can aggressively anticipate the worst that whiter male competition at the top has to offer. This basic training at the internecine front is not the aim of Pickens's ambition, but rather its modus operandi.

When Pickens journeys to the frontier to do railroad work with his father as a way of getting money to attend Talladega College, he again proves his mettle against older, bigger, stronger, rougher, whiter men. "The bulk of the laborers and camp-followers were of the scum of humanity, white and black; there were rough, coarse men and undesirable *women*" (27, emphasis added). Like his earlier test in a southern city, this stint on the western frontier confirms his Darwinian worldview: "There was no law in that wilderness but the law of the jungle. I had seen the foreman chasing white men with a revolver, as one might chase rabbits" (29). One expects to see a foreman do such a thing to his black workers, but the frontier experience of a railroad camp reinforces the idea of both the immediate salience and ultimate irrelevance of race (and anatomical sex) in this jungle. It is against the backdrop of such whiter savagery that Pickens is able to spotlight his versatile, mobile body as trespassing into the center of modernity. As in all of the autobiography's episodes, the narrator's mettle is duly recognized by a white man who helps to deliver him from that phase of the struggle.

> On my first day at concrete-mixing the men laughed and swore that I could not last till noon, but would "white-eye." That term was applied to the actions of the sufferer because his eyeballs rolled in a peculiar manner, showing the white, when he became overheated and fell upon the ground. I did last till noon; and then the foreman, a stocky German of the coarsest possible nature who had kept a half amused eye on

me all the morning, expecting to have some fun when I should "white-eye," was so touched by the determination with which I stuck till noon that he gave me lighter work. (28)

In this passage, we can see clearly how literal bodily cues, however minuscule, signal for himself and others both a threat to and an affirmation of Pickens's bid to be physically marked for quick-paced modern progress.

Pickens's refusal to white-eye may be taken as a pun, indicating the ocular motion that precedes fainting as well as the "coon" stereotype of the black man whose eyes bulge in a moment of superstitious fear. In either case, the white-eye jeopardizes Pickens's claim to the manly directness required for modern progress. This constitutes a double jeopardy, given how fainting would place him as ladylike in tandem with the prefiguration of black men as already unmanly in their feminine physical weaknesses and superstitious fears. Furthermore, to "white-eye" is to lose sight of the situation at hand in the game of hunter and hunted. It is to lose the agility and alertness of always being aware of the potential danger in one's jungle surroundings. By literally keeping his self-aware gaze, his "art of vigilant self-defense," Pickens also assures that the whiter eye of his boss will be impressed when gazing upon him. The foreman "sizes" him up so quickly because Pickens exudes so glaringly the virtues of a virile nature. The supervisor can literally see Pickens's manly mettle in the young man's refusal to faint like a lady and/or a black man.

Ironically, however, Pickens's "better position" takes him away from the more masculine tasks that have supposedly served to bring out and strengthen his manliness. From hard labor on the construction crew to "lighter work" in the kitchen, this upward move both capsulizes and threatens to capsize the focused, speedy trajectory of Pickens's illustration of New Negro manhood. The goal is to get to the less coarsely masculine place in culture—the seat of learning, the furnished parlor, the executive's office—and yet making it there depends on how well one can compete on the turf of the coarsely masculine.

Unlike Washington's celebration of obedient housekeeping, Pickens sees his stint in the kitchen as a very temporary status. He does not want to contaminate the tenor of his ambition or the course of his career or the definition of his racial role with the charges of emasculation and provincial backwardness that taint Washington's cultural influence. Immediately following the passage above, he associates this "lighter work" in the kitchen with Bookerite bathing and moral habits:

At nights I had only vitality enough left to bathe in the green waters of the bayou and lie down to rest in my tent. On Sundays I read two

57

borrowed books, one of them being "Uncle Tom's Cabin." Most of the men gambled all day Sundays and caroused till late at night. My better habits soon gave me superior strength and endurance and I could tire the toughest rival. This seemed wonderful to the men. They seemed to think that I was a strange fellow. They did not reckon on the habits of life. (28)

Pickens's bathing ritual, sentimental reading, sexual abstention, and other spin-sterish habits at the camp are clearly *not* moral ends in themselves. Just as Washington's housekeeping rituals are intended to mark his body as a civilizing object lesson to be gazed on and emulated even as they single him out as an exceptional example of racial progress, Pickens's solitary habits serve more clearly to demarcate his singular masculine stance as the toughest of all rivals while offering to his black (male) readers a heuristic example of cool quick thinking. Though viewed as a "strange fellow" for refusing the sexual carousing, gambling, and other gestures of masculine camaraderie, he achieves, miraculously to these coarse men, a greater status as male rival while retaining his refining aspirations. Pickens's ascent to sophisticated Yankee culture, symbolized here by his reading Stowe and in the final chapter of the first volume by his success in oratory at Yale, will not diminish his instinctual manliness. In fact, because manliness will remain the only attribute he can rely on in competing with the spoiled white men of privilege in the North, his manhood is paradoxically enhanced as he rises into the polished corridors of polite society.

Ultimately, Pickens indicates that being *out of place* means aggressively taking opportunities in places where black people are neither expected nor initially desired—foreseeing a potential for the race's self-empowerment as a massive consolidation *out of place*. This self-promoting invasion of supposedly white territory constitutes racial trespassing, for it is a more aggressive kind of racial passing: just crossing over as though one belongs, as though one will blend into the white crowd. But, of course, as opposed to the passing person, the trespasser knows and, to some extent, desires spectacular confrontation around the hyper-visibility of the solitary black body, rather than an erasure of that body's linkages to an oppressive racial history. Ironically, then, once Pickens arrives in a northern city (Chicago), desiring racial consolidation out of place, he ends up having to make opportunities for solitary trespassing, for being out of place alone. "I redoubled my determination and easily passed by all the huge temptations of a great city. On Sundays I attended Moody's church and the city Young Men's Christian Association. It appeared strange to me that out of 40,000 Negroes I saw no other one at this Young Men's Christian Association during the whole summer" (36). Rather than assuming the colorline can determine where he doesn't belong, Pickens instead exploits the anonymity, alienation, and hordes of the great city to test and contest racial limits, always aware that he may have to defend his right to be where he is. In this sense, Chicago prepares him for New Negro life, just as the ironworks prepare him for Yale: "[T]he ironwork gave me superior physical strength, which is a good part of any preparation for college. At night I read Carlyle and Emerson, Latin and German, in anticipation of work at Yale" (35–36). Pickens's disposition to anticipate his competition again takes the form of triple preparation: clean living and Yankee Christian temperance in the Bookerite mold, bonded to physical endurance and mental cunning from the folk-mass; the two together are enhanced by concentration on arrogant mastery of the highest classics of European learning filtered through a perspective celebrated as distinctively *African* American, as advocated by Talented Tenth scholars like Alain Locke and W. E. B. Du Bois.

Pickens's success at Yale hinges on anticipating this assimilative, confrontational synthesis, resulting in a necessary audacity, arrogance, and masculine bravado when trespassing amidst the civilization of his alleged betters. He understands that, given others' "*lack of expectation*" for his success, he has to conduct himself so as to cause others to "*expect more of the American Negro*," which means constantly expecting more of himself (39, emphases in original). When Pickens sets out to win the Yale oratory contest, he announces his intention, rather than keeping it secret, and goes so far as to give up extra work at his job in anticipation of winning the cash award. Against Bookerite humility and Du Boisian anguished passion and regret, Pickens's New Negro preempts the arrogance of the privileged whiter man and turns it into the New Negro notion of "cool."

This strategy constitutes a sort of passive aggression at the core of Pickens's notion of New Negro modernity. For Washington, modern progress meant a wily segregation of his own two faces, the accommodating house servant for the race in public and the ruthless powerbroker of black interest in private. Du Bois in *Souls of Black Folk* had theorized the advance toward modernity as the power to resolve in the new century the double consciousness created for blacks by their past and current relation to the colorline. For Du Bois, this modern doubleness was not a calculated political compromise but rather a deeply felt, genuine angst of modern psychic dislocation. Revising these writers, Pickens publicizes the relation between his unbridled individual ambition and his binding service to the race as a forthright badge of arrival. For Pickens, double consciousness is nothing to be embarrassed about or to anguish over; it is, instead, a weapon in knowing oneself and one's enemies. When confronted with an imposition, he does not back down, no matter how big the opponent. His bravura is intended to set him apart not only from the dominant black male images of the previous generations but also from those potential whiter patrons who might mistake him for an old-fashioned Negro rather than a New Man.

In Pickens's view, the black man's achievement of his manhood will bring about eventually the collective success of the race. That manhood is full manhood only when it advertises and markets itself, when it can preen in its display of manly achievement as a measure of success. The standard for measuring both manhood and success is determined, then, not so much by a bonding relation to the black race that is to be consolidated, as by a rivalrous relation to the superior men in the dominant race, who serve as the acknowledged norm. For it is not the norm itself that is being contested but instead who can qualify to fulfill that norm. Pickens wants to demonstrate the impact of his manhood on both whites and blacks. He wants to show that he has sized up the situation, and does not fear to shoot straight from the hip in a wide variety of matters from the faulty patronage of white teachers and administrators at black schools to black men's betrayal of their obligation to the race, from white fascination with black sexuality to white chicanery in trying to cheat black people out of money.

This is why so much of *Bursting Bonds* focuses on literal sizing-ups, shoot-outs, and showdowns between Pickens and whiter bad men with lesser blacks looking on. Rafia Zafar has pointed to the solitary persona unaided by fellow African Americans that Frederick Douglass creates for himself in his earliest autobiography as a kind of masculine pose that projects a self-sufficient hero to a largely white audience.[21] Something similar can be said about Pickens's projection of the defiant, solitary New Negro in *Bursting Bonds*, except that, unlike Douglass, Pickens is also responding to the, by his time, established tradition of black autobiography, especially the giants preceding him, Douglass, Washington, and Du Bois. In all the showdowns Pickens chooses to focus on, he portrays himself as alone against a stronger foe, or against several men with the authority of law and the force of weapons and numbers on their side. In this way, he follows minutely the structure of the Wild West myth, at the expense of the racial consolidation he theorizes in *The New Negro*. To stand together with other black men and women would seem to diminish his manhood, as it is normally defined in dominant U.S. culture, by undermining his territorial claims of never imitating any authority beyond the self.

But because the body of the New Negro specimen always also serves as synecdoche for the race, Pickens is very much aware of the need for black others to legitimate his actions. This is why all his showdowns are staged before a live audience. Of course, in this way, these scenes further enact the Wild West myth of the lone man acting to protect others. These others in need of his protection become spectators to the showdown, either in sympathy with him or ironically with his enemy, but they cannot act with him or for themselves. Their paralysis enables the alert and agile mobility of his heroic black body. Such scenes are palpably haunted by the punishing violence of the white mob seeking to paralyze manly black action; unlike a white mob, however, the black onlookers, even as they outnumber the whites, in their stupor and fear fail to become a punishing lynching mob in support of their black hero.

The structure of racial trespassing demands this logic of manly exceptionality against a double background of endangering white mob and paralyzed black collectivity. There is only one instance where Pickens does represent his New Negro stand-down as bolstered by a lesser black other, but he nowhere depicts himself bonding equally with another strong black figure. In the Jim Crow railcar episode, he is aided by a Pullman porter.

> I called the porter and told him to make down my berth so that I could retire. As I ascended the ladder, I told him in a low voice to apprise me of any hostile movements towards me, so that I might wake up and do my duty. I was surprised and pleased to hear him reply in a loud voice, that rang of indirect defiance: "I'll do it—you bet I will!" (69)

As Gaines suggests, the porter often represents the old-fashioned Negro:

> The porter came to symbolize to white travelers the company's service and luxury, as well as its institutionalization of black subordination, reinforcing white passengers' assumptions of class privilege and authority. For the porters, low wages, harsh working conditions, and constant confrontations with Jim Crow customs and patronizing, if not abusive, passengers made the job all too reminiscent of slavery.[22]

Pickens approaches this porter knowing that readers will hold these expectations. At the same time, however, the porter paradoxically represents a new enterprising figure who commands a relatively large salary, compared with the work of most black men; who has the freedom of constant travel; who gets to trespass through otherwise segregated railcars; who is identified with the high-speed modernity of the train; and who represents the best potential for autonomous union organizing and a form of manly racial consolidation. In other words, the porter is both literally and symbolically a threshold figure for Pickens, for the porter's constant crossing of the colorline into otherwise segregated railcars can represent either backwards accommodation or a form of radical New Negro trespassing into the machinery of modern white power.

Pickens's defiance has a salutary effect on the porter. Pickens is "surprised" by the "loud" support, expecting the porter to protect himself by returning the whispered command with a whispered reply. Unlike Pickens's own defiance, however, the porter's is characterized as "indirect," though it would seem that in endangering his job and his life, it is a consequent indirectness. Pickens's narrative proceeds with a paragraph of eulogy that seems to contradict the original surprise at the porter's "indirect defiance" and to replace it with the more progressive connotations of portering:

> I learned later that he had kept his eye and ear on the whole situation and had resolved to sacrifice his job and any thing else to stand with me, if it came to that.—Your Pullman porter is a wonderful being. He understands. Nobody ever fools the porter. (69)

In other words, the porter is a true in-the-know urbanite, a man who cannot be conned by the most street-smart blacks and whites. This paean, while it praises the sizing-up ability of often maligned porters, also serves to validate Pickens's own "straight-up" capacity for natural leadership. The porter is eager to stand with Pickens because he knows that he is a real man, one who will not back down when it comes to the final draw. As the only episode in the autobiography where consolidation between black strangers is depicted, this bond carries a great deal of weight for the narrative. Through it, Pickens suggests the potential for a mass consolidation among black people that remains just beyond the purview of the narrative, largely because a narrative so steeped in self-made "straight-out" masculinity cannot afford to go too far in that direction without jeopardizing its own mythic frame.

In his chapter on the tour of Europe, Pickens addresses the gender repercussions of his trespassing though a different sort of black masculine bonding, this time with a black man (Jack Johnson) for whose body Pickens's is mistaken by mob-hungry whites. Pickens takes to Europe, the heart of advanced civilization, his self-testing of modernity on the cool nerves of a manhood nurtured at the savage bottoms and wild margins. The rigidity of Pickens's masculine pose dictates a formulaic rigidity in relation to his sweetheart and wife unimaginable even in the puritanical *Up from Slavery*. Clearly, when Pickens curtails the presence of black women and feminine roles in the narrative, it is not because he wants to treat matters of romance and sexuality with a gingerly touch. As is borne out with the proliferation of romance and overt sexual themes in later New Negro narratives, the ideology of radical New Negrodom fosters not less but greater attention to such matters.

Pickens himself provides an audacious taunt in this sexual realm, but one that seems elliptical to readers seven decades after the event. What are we to make of the fact that Pickens takes with him on his European tour not only Mrs. Pickens but also "Mrs. Flora E. Avery, our friend of Galesburg, Illinois, and an unapologetic friend of Negro education and advancement" (53)? From a party of one, the new situation escalates into "an ideal tourist party" of three. Pickens knows that despite the squeaky-clean respectability of his wife, his white patroness, and himself, white strangers all over Europe, especially U.S. citizens, will immediately espy bigamy, adultery, fornication, prostitution, triangulated sex, and other manner of deviant sexual behavior. Of course, trumping all these other sexually deviant practices is the idea that Pickens is engaging in miscegenation with one (or both) of the apparently white women whom he is escorting around Europe.

Pickens delights in getting a rise out of fellow travelers from the U.S. by appearing as a black man invading the best places in Europe with a white woman on each arm.

> Strange truth it is, that whenever any person tried to insult us, we knew at once that he or she was not one of our potential "enemies" but one of our fellow-patriots. Often we would never have been able to discover his identity and our relation to him, if only he had been able to control his feelings. . . . And those who made the biggest scenes, proved, on investigation, to be from the section of the United States where they are *most used to colored folk*, where from infancy they sit in the laps and eat out of the hands of black people. If a fellow was from Mississippi, where he had slept in the bed and suckled at the breast of a black nurse, he made the biggest fuss of anybody. Some of it was ludicrous. We had great fun. (55, emphasis in original)

With World War I looming, Pickens is able to spot the true "potential enemy" in his fellow U.S. residents, not in some German or Italian foe. By italicizing the familiarity and intimacy of relations between black and white in the South (*"most used to colored folks"*), Pickens makes it obvious that the threesome is taking great pleasure in playing on U.S. whites' assumptions that a racially gender-mixed party has to have a taboo sexual interest. Pickens stresses how the spectacle is self-consciously staged as a ludicrous game that he must play as a black man. It is southern whites, however, who make "the biggest scenes." Pickens uses the transportable U.S. colorline to highlight its sexual undertow, and to suggest that he has utter disregard for its dangerous motions. He encourages us to imagine humorous showdowns between Mississippi gentlemen and himself before an astonished audience of white Europeans more advanced—that is, more modern—than the absurd southern whites, as the white southerners seek to protect the honor of the two white-appearing women whom the scoundrel Pickens has managed to seduce. The double standard of these gentlemen is brought down to the most graphic level, as sleeping in bed with and suckling the breast of a black nurse too easily translates into the frequent sexual dalliances and rapes white gentlemen have perpetrated on black women.

In case his readers miss this graphic point, Pickens boldly throws it in their face with even greater aggression. "In that summer Jack Johnson was just running away from the American police, so in Belgium and Naples they took me for him.—A black person, a white-colored person, and a white person together make a combination fit for any experience" (55). No reader of the time would fail to recognize this sexual taunt, given that Jack Johnson's sexual-racial indiscretions and crimes are as widely known as Booker T. Washington's industrious discretions and bathings. Because Johnson is the baddest black man of the time, known for facing down white bullies in the boxing ring, he is an apt alter ego for Pickens's own narrative. When Pickens alludes to Johnson, the allusion becomes loaded with the evidences and rumors of Johnson's capacious sexual appetite in scandals of bigamy, adultery, prostitution, multiple sex partners, attendance at homosexual drag balls, suicidal passions on the part of mesmerized white lovers, and so forth. We realize, as his contemporary readers would have, that Pickens's threesome is "a combination fit for any experience" because only the lurid imagination of scandalized U.S. whites is capable of projecting the sex of black men to a size so much larger than life. Pickens is doing then in a rhetorical-metaphorical way what Jack Johnson had done literally, wrapping his penis to enlarge it in the knowledge that it would fit the gargantuan size imagined by white spectators.[23] For a narrative so obsessively concerned with sizing up men's hidden weapons, it seems only fitting that Pickens should take pleasure in parading around Europe in the figure of the phallus-wielding giant, Jack Johnson.

In expressing this odd sort of racial consolidation with the much maligned and criminalized Jack Johnson, Pickens ultimately casts himself as a criminal outlaw to the U.S. state, mostly because of his gargantuan success within that country's unfair rules of manly gamesmanship. This jaunty alliance with the most famous black man of his time does not overcome, however, the complicated ambivalences that attend the narrative format and ideological form of *Bursting Bonds*. Bringing together Jack Johnson, the epitome of black phallic aggression, and the Pullman porter, the epitome of black male accommodation, into his coalition enables Pickens to forecast the New Negro as a wide-ranging phenomenon, unpredictable in his open assaults and unstoppable in his transmigrations across the globe at iron-horse speeds.

NOTES

1. On the rise of American railroads as the "earliest giant corporations," which "offered means of exercising unexampled ruthlessness of economic power," see Alan Trachtenberg, *The Incorporation of America* (New York: Hill and Wang, 1982), 57.

2. About this reactionary aspect of New Negro identification, Henry Louis Gates Jr. writes, "A paradox of this sort of self-willed beginning is that its 'success' depends fundamentally upon self-negation, a turning away from the 'Old Negro' and the labyrinthine memory of black enslavement and toward the register of a 'New Negro,' an irresistible spontaneously generated black and sufficient self." "The Trope of the New Negro and the Reconstruction of the Image of the Black," *Representations* 24 (fall 1988): 129–55, 132. As will be evident below, I disagree with Gates, however, that this paradox is an act that derives from the "non-place of language" (132).

3. This does not mean that women cannot or do not participate in New Negro activity and discourse. As is evident in the life and work of Ida B. Wells-Barnett, for instance, women could take on this conventionally masculine aura, although not without some self-conscious risks seen as a threat to proper womanhood. As we'll see in the following analysis of William Pickens, African American men must likewise negotiate a masculine identity seen as intrinsic to modern know-how and thus to New Negro progress but at odds with the gender expectations for African American men as prescribed by dominant culture.

4. Very influential in the early history of the National Association for the Advancement of Colored People (NAACP), William Pickens (1881–1954) is now largely (and unfortunately) forgotten in the annals of African American and U.S. history. He burst on the scene in 1903, when he won a Yale oratory contest while a student there. He then returned to the South to teach at Talladega College in Alabama, where as a student he had first attracted the attention of white patrons before moving on to Yale. Later becoming the national field secretary for the NAACP, Pickens is credited with helping to enlarge the membership of the organization through his exceptional oratorical skills. In addition to publishing *The New Negro: His Political, Civil, and Mental Status; and Related Essays* (1916; New York: AMS Press, 1969), two autobiographical volumes, and a novella/short story collection called *Vengeance of the Gods: And Three Other Stories of Real American Color Line Life* (1922; Freeport, NY: Books for Libraries Press, 1972), he was a popular syndicated columnist for black newspapers at the height of the black press's influence.

5. "Bookerite" here is used merely to identify Washington's patron network, rhetorical ploys, and social, economic, and political strategies of accommodation—not intended here in the pejorative sense with which it is frequently associated.

6. Booker T. Washington, *A New Negro for A New Century: An Accurate and Up-to-Date Record of the Upward Struggles of the Negro Race* (Chicago: American Publishing House, 1900; reprint, Miami: Mnemosyne, 1969).

7. Kevin K. Gaines, *Uplifting the Race: Black Leadership, Politics, and Culture in the Twentieth Century* (Chapel Hill: University of North Carolina Press, 1996), 53. On the importance of clothing as black migrants urbanized themselves, see Carole Marks, *Farewell—We're Good and Gone: The Great Black Migration* (Bloomington: Indiana University Press, 1989), 102–9.

8. William Pickens, *The New Negro*, 10.

9. Pickens, *The New Negro*, 14.

10. E. Anthony Rotundo instructively points out that this image of the competitive workplace is partly myth, given the extent to which the work of these middle-class white male managers of capitalism depended on business contacts, male sociability, loyalty, conviviality, and trust. *American Manhood: Transformations in Masculinity from the Revolution to the Modern Era* (New York: Basic, 1993), 196–205.

11. Pickens, *The New Negro*, 15.

12. Pickens's insistence on gendering the collective body of the African race masculine goes against the grain of dominant scientific and sociological discourse of the time. Only two years after Pickens's *New Negro*, for instance, Robert E. Park, the influential Chicago sociologist and former publicity chief for Washington, publishes his "Education in Its Relation to the Conflict and Fusion of Cultures," wherein he notoriously identifies the African as "the lady of the races." Reprinted in Park, *Race and Culture: Essays in the Sociology of Contemporary Man* (Glencoe, NY: Free Press, 1950), 280.

13. Pickens, *The New Negro*, 161 (emphasis added).

14. Pickens, *The New Negro*, 15.

15. William L. Andrews, introduction to *Bursting Bonds: The Autobiography of a "New Negro,"* by William Pickens (1923; Bloomington: Indiana University Press, 1991), xi–xxviii, xix.

16. On Teddy Roosevelt's influence in shaping this idea of the frontier as manly preparation for the civilizing mission, see Michael Kimmel, *Manhood in the Making: A Cultural History* (New York: Free Press, 1996), 181–88; and Gail Bederman, *Manliness and Civilization: A Cultural History of Gender and Race in the United States, 1880–1917* (Chicago: University of Chicago Press, 1995), 170–215.

17. The general influence of Washington's *Up from Slavery* on Pickens's *Bursting Bonds* was recognized early in what little scholarship there is on the latter autobiography. See, for instance, Rebecca Chalmers Barton, *Witnesses for Freedom: Negro Americans in Autobiography* (New York: Harper, 1948), 27. More recently, Sheldon Avery has done the most extensive work on Washington's influence on Pickens; see *Up from Washington: William Pickens and the Negro Struggle for Equality, 1900–1954* (Newark: University of Delaware Press, 1989).

18. Avery notes that the Associated Negro Press was the "largest and most successful black news-gathering service in America." *Up from Washington,* 55.

19. Bederman, *Manliness and Civilization,* 185–86. Also see Rotundo, *American Manhood,* 247–83; and Kimmel, *Manhood in the Making,* 157–88.

20. Pickens, *Bursting Bonds,* 72. Hereafter cited in text.

21. Rafia Zafar, "Franklinian Douglass: The Afro-American as the Representative Man," in *Frederick Douglass: New Literary and Historical Essays,* ed. Eric J. Sundquist (Cambridge: Cambridge University Press, 1990), 99–117, 112.

22. Gaines, *Uplifting the Race,* 15.

23. On Johnson's penis-wrapping practice, see Randy Roberts, *Papa Jack: Jack Johnson and the Era of White Hopes* (New York: Free Press/Macmillan, 1983), 74, 140.

4

BODIES, VOICES, WORDS

MODERN DRAMA AND THE PROBLEM OF THE LITERARY

Julia A. Walker

With the wide-scale implementation of telegraph, telephone, phonograph, radio, and silent film technologies at the turn of the twentieth century, the felt experience of communication radically altered. When a pattern of electrical impulses could be sent across the continent and decoded in a matter of seconds, when the grain of the voice could be heard apart from the immediate physical presence of the speaker, when meaningful gestures were presented by bodies removed in both space and time, the messages transmitted through these new technologies must have seemed strange because so unexpectedly removed from the moment of their communicative intent. The act of communication—once experienced as a relatively integrated process—was rent apart; the communicative experience shivered into various splintered elements.

The first half of my title—bodies, voices, words—is meant to evoke the radical dissociation of these elements as experienced by communicants in this moment of rapid technological change. However familiar print had made the word, all of these elements were exposed anew to the analytical gaze of philosophers, linguists, orators, poets, and dramatists. Newly separable, they posed the problem of where exactly meaning lay: did it reside in or as a function of words alone, or did it include performative features such as gesticulation, intonation, and inflection? At the turn of the century several theories were advanced, each revealing its own anxiety about the impact of modernization on the human experience of communication. From oratorical theorists who expanded "speech" to include all forms of communication issuing from the body, to poetic theorists who privileged the word, such debates were part of the cultural milieu that gave shape to literary modernism. In fact, as I argue in the first half of this essay, an influential version of modernism defined the literary in specifically antiperformative terms.[1]

As indicated by the second half of my title, however, this particular conception of the literary posed a vexing problem for the drama, especially at a time when it was under increasing pressure to enhance its status as a literary genre. Taking Eugene O'Neill's play *The Hairy Ape* (1922) as my example, I show how this work offers its own uneasy resolution to contemporary debates over meaning's place within the fragmented experience of modernity. Capitulating to the antiperformative bias in order to secure his reputation as a "literary" dramatist, O'Neill paradoxically developed a new dramatic technique that gave rise to an important phase of American theatrical modernism.

O'Neill, of course, is one of the few American dramatists to be recognized for the specifically literary merit of his plays. However, in her recent book, *American Drama: The Bastard Art*, Susan Harris Smith argues that O'Neill's *exceptionalism* is due less to the uniqueness of his talent than to a lingering bias against drama within the literary-critical establishment.[2] Tracing the discursive history of this bias, Smith shows how it reveals a whole host of anxieties attending the legitimation of American culture, especially literature and the discipline of literary criticism. Although one of the implications of her argument is to redress this bias and reclaim a space for drama within the study of American literature, I would like to retrain her focus to explore how the category of the literary itself came to be based on an antiperformative foundation.

In short, I argue that a specific historical formation of the category of the literary developed under the pressures of modernity in such a way as to locate meaning—that which had become fractured in the development of communicative technologies—in the word alone. And I attribute this particular formation of the literary to T. S. Eliot, in whose early critical work I detect an antiperformative bias. This may seem like an odd statement to make, given that Eliot is generally recognized to be one of the most dramatically informed of the modern poets, layering multiple voices in his poems, writing dramatic criticism, and composing several plays. Yet in his early critical work, Eliot's conception of the drama is peculiarly antiseptic in the way it isolates the text from its performative context.[3] Consider his well-known 1919 essay "Hamlet and His Problems," in which Eliot criticizes Shakespeare's play for the inability of its central character to give adequate verbal expression to the emotions motivating his dialogue. Note that for Eliot it is not a matter of an actor's interpretation of Hamlet's emotional expressivity that is the problem; rather it is the author's construction of his character in words. Coining his famous critical term "objective correlative," Eliot criticizes Shakespeare for his inability to objectify in language the correlating emotion that propels his character to speak.[4]

Though the term itself is indebted to George Santayana's notion of "correlate objects," Eliot appears to borrow the substance of his critique from Friedrich Nietzsche, who, in book 17 of *The Birth of Tragedy*, similarly cites the inadequacy of the play's language to fully account for its action.[5] But where Nietzsche saw Shakespeare's play as merely another example of tragedy's post-Euripidean decline (where music—the source of Dionysiac ecstasy—had ceded its place to language—the vehicle of Apollonian reason), Eliot diagnosed the play's "problem" in quite another way. Where, for Nietzsche, the play's meaning could not be reduced to its language, for Eliot, it must be.

More than a simple difference of opinion, Nietzsche's under- and Eliot's overvaluation of language in the making of a drama's meaning suggest the existence of a now obscure context in which the stakes of such a debate were once easily seen. That context—which was so obvious in its moment as to need no name—was, I believe, the "expressive culture movement," a broad-based popular movement at the turn of the twentieth century that taught that a work of art was not fully realized until expressed through the body in performance.[6] Encompassing poetry, drama, music, and dance, the expressive culture movement was in fact international (drawing on the theories of the French vocal instructor François Delsarte and the Swiss movement theorist Emile Jaques-Dalcroze, among others).[7] However, in the United States its popularity tended to center around the practice of oral interpretation as theorized by the speech educators Lewis B. Monroe and S. S. Curry.

Monroe, a professor of oratory at Boston University, sought to rehabilitate his field at a time when the American university was being restructured according to the model of a German research institution. Hoping to provide it with a firmer intellectual foundation, Monroe wed oratorical study to the theories of

American Transcendentalism, arguing that, unlike elocution, which focused solely on vocal technique, oral interpretation allowed for orator and auditor alike to commune with the universal spirit that had "spoken" through the poet.[8] After Monroe's unexpected death in 1879, Curry put his theories into writing, expanding on them to such an extent that he decided to christen this new field of study "expression" in order to distinguish it from "elocution," its discredited forebear. To further establish expression as an intellectual course of study, Curry shifted the emphasis from disciplining the voice and body to training the mind, formalizing a method of close reading that focused on the subjective impressions a literary work evoked in the mind of the interpreter. Essentially a program of textual explication, Curry's "think-the-thought" method anticipated that of the New Critics by emphasizing attention to such features as figurative language, meter, and the significance of line length.[9]

First conceptualizing the meaning of the work as a whole, Curry's interpreter then had to concentrate on the various figures and images that produced that conception and, using the expressive means of his/her entire body, communicate that meaning to the audience. These expressive means included the three primary "languages" of the body: verbal (the conventionalized symbols of language), vocal (e.g., tone-color and inflection, which register emotion), and pantomimic (gesture and bodily comportment). Only through the unified and effective use of these three languages could the interpreter arouse the sympathetic identification of auditors so as to make the conceptualization that had manifested itself to him/her manifest itself to them.[10]

The problem with Curry's method—as Santayana, for one, pointed out—was that this method of interpretation was premised on the pathetic fallacy, that tendency of assuming that things in the natural world are imbued with human feeling, not to mention the affective fallacy (which had yet to be so named). In his essay "The Elements and Function of Poetry" (1900), Santayana implicitly challenges the assumptions underlying Curry's method. While he acknowledges that emotions are the stuff out of which poetry is made, he goes on to insist that poetry does not present us with an unmediated experience of them as they occur in the natural world; rather, it presents us with emotions that have been transformed first in the poet's imagination. The key to the poet's success, Santayana avers, lies in his/her ability to find the "correlative object" by which that emotion may be expressed.[11]

"Expression," he contends,

> is a misleading term which suggests that something previously known
> is rendered or imitated; whereas the expression is itself an original fact,

the values of which are then [mistakenly] referred to the thing expressed, much as the honours of a Chinese mandarin are attributed retroactively to his parents. So the charm which a poet, by his art of combining images and shades of emotion, casts over a scene or an action, is attached to the principal actor in it, who gets the benefit of the setting furnished him by a well-stocked mind.[12]

In other words, expression—as theorized by Curry—not only misattributes to the poem the poet's skill, but effectively denies poetic agency by suggesting that the poet is simply a conduit of some larger universal truth, which he/she merely inscribes on the page.

As a student at Harvard in the first decade of the twentieth century, Eliot certainly would have known about expression and the expressive culture movement. Not only was he at its geographical ground zero, but, as a student of Santayana, he would have been aware of his critique. After all, it is from Santayana that he derives his famous notion of the "objective correlative," and it is around this phrase that he constellates his concerns over language and its ability to fully express the author's meaning.

For Eliot, it would seem, Curry's emphasis on the integration of the three languages of the body does not take into adequate account the importance of the significatory work performed by the poet on the verbal level. Although Curry did allow that "verbal expression . . . is the most complete and adequate means of revealing ideas," he maintained that it is not adequate unto itself; vocal and pantomimic languages complete the expression by introducing nuances that can augment or even reverse the presumed meaning of a verbal utterance.[13] With this context in mind, then, we can see how Eliot's insistence on the primacy of verbal signification may have been a reaction to Curry's theory of expression. Nor is it difficult to imagine how his conception of the literary took on an antiperformative bias, given Curry's distinction between the writer, who merely "arranges his ideas and endeavors to embody thought in words," and the speaker, whose "co-ordination of all the living languages of his personality" required superior skill. In "The Possibility of a Poetic Drama," in *The Sacred Wood* (1920), Eliot reverses Curry's scale of valuation, claiming that the greatest obstacle to the creation of a poetic drama is the fact of performance and the need for actors to perform it: "The interest of a performer is almost certain to be centred in himself: a very slight acquaintance with actors and musicians will testify. The performer is interested not in form but in opportunities for virtuosity or in the communication of his 'personality.'"[14] With statements such as this, is it any wonder then that Eliot sought to fix meaning on the level of verbal signification alone? Is it any wonder that his conception of the literary—a conception that forms a basis of Anglo-American literary modernism and lies at the heart of New Critical practice—bears within it an antiperformative bias?[15]

That an antiperformative bias is at the core of Eliotic modernism is less surprising than that it exists in the work of one of the American theatre's leading dramatists, Eugene O'Neill. Yet O'Neill too liked to denounce actors, insisting in a 1925 playbill that, until the theatre nurtured "a new quality of depth of feeling and comprehensive scope of technique in actors and actresses," the best he could do with his plays was simply to "write 'em and leave 'em."[16] Though not unknown to us now, such writerly pride was unusual at a time when the cultural field was changing and the playwright's position had yet to be secured.

At the turn of the century, what had been primarily an actor's theatre—a showcase for highlighting the actor's physical and interpretive skills—was deemed (by O'Neill among others) a *playwright's* theatre—a staging ground for self-consciously literary plays. Consequently playwrights, once considered mere "hacks" for the stage, were beginning to be recognized as legitimate authors in their own right. And the dramatic playscript, once a blueprint for the creation of a work of art, became the work of art itself—a Platonic ideal whose artistic, cultural, and symbolic value exceeded that of any particular realization of it on stage.

As decisive as this shift seems now, it was, in its moment, uncertain and slow to come. Thus, O'Neill's remarks above may have been less boastful than talismanic. As we'll see, O'Neill appears to have harbored some anxieties about his literary credentials, especially in the early part of his career. Even a Pulitzer Prize in 1920 was not enough to secure his tie to the theatre, which, more often than not, stood to high culture as its definitive "low" other. Given his sensitivity to the theatre's benighted status, then, we should not be surprised to find an antiperformative bias in much of O'Neill's work. But, as I show in my reading of his 1922 play *The Hairy Ape*, this bias is effectively dismantled by the play's experimental form. Although critics persistently misattribute it to German expressionism, I show how *The Hairy Ape*'s formal design ultimately derives from Curry's theory of expression.

The Hairy Ape dramatizes the life of a ship's stoker, Yank, whose worldview is founded on a celebration of the virtues of speed and strength—virtues that place him at the top of a superficially Darwinian world order in which the strongest not only survive but rule. "Who d'yuh tink's runnin' dis game," he shouts to the unseen engineer blowing the whistle for him to work, "me or you?"[17] This world order is turned upside down, however, when Yank is insulted by Mildred Douglas, a steel heiress, who is horrified by his brutal appearance, likening him to a filthy beast just before she faints. Yank initially wants to respond to the insult with physical violence but is waylaid by his shipmate Long who wishes to tutor him in the subject of class struggle and raise his class consciousness. Frustrated by Yank's inability to understand Mildred's insult in anything but personal terms, however, Long eventually gives up, leaving Yank in a state of utter confusion. After a stint in jail, Yank becomes convinced that his belief that "might makes right" is shared by the IWW and seeks to join their brotherhood. They, however, are wary of his terroristic rhetoric and, thinking him a Pinkerton spy, cast him back out on the street alone. Finally, in an attempt to see the beast that Mildred saw in him, Yank goes to the zoo, where he encounters a caged gorilla. As he gropes toward an understanding of his situation, Yank explains to the gorilla, "She wasn't wise dat I was in a cage, too—worser'n yours—sure—a damn sight—'cause you got some chanct to bust loose—but me— (*He grows confused*)." Finally, giving in to the gorilla's fatal embrace, Yank surrenders his original worldview in which only the strongest survive.[18]

On one level, the play clearly deals with the theme of alienation: Yank's identification with the product of his labor—speed and steel—is disrupted by the appearance of Mildred and the knowledge she brings that his labor is ultimately not his own. But on another level, the play seems to abstract and depoliticize the problem of alienation by figuring it in philosophical rather than economic terms. Yank's alienation is a spiritual one. The rhythms of industry have so restructured his life that he can no longer integrate himself back into society, let alone nature; sadly, he finds that he cannot "belong." This understanding of Yank's problem as primarily spiritual was first advanced by O'Neill himself in an interview printed in the *New York Herald Tribune* in November 1924. Here, O'Neill claimed that Yank "was a symbol of man who has lost his old harmony with nature, the harmony which he used to have as an animal and has not yet acquired in a spiritual way."[19] O'Neill's conception of alienation as a loss of "harmony with nature" is clearly reminiscent of Curry's theories of expression and their quasi-philosophical basis in American Transcendentalism. Indeed, one of the reasons for the movement's popularity was the way it tapped into many Americans' fears about modernization. Suggesting that the pounding repetitions of industry and the technological transformation of urban space had altered the body's natural rhythms and alienated humankind from the spiritual universe, the expressive culture movement offered what was essentially a program of de-alienation. Its proponents taught that, by participating in the performing arts, the body could be released from bad habits of breathing, speaking, gesture, and movement, and thus restored to a state of communion with the natural world.

As we've seen, Curry believed that such spiritual harmony could be achieved through a perfect coordination of vocal, pantomimic, and verbal expression.

Thus, a playwright wishing to represent a character in a state of disharmony might arrange these three languages in counterpoint. This, in fact, is exactly what O'Neill does with Yank. Pulling apart the layers of verbal, vocal, and pantomimic language in his play, O'Neill calls for his actors to speak their lines in voices that mock the words they speak and to strike poses whose meanings they cannot possibly realize. For example, stage directions call for Yank's buddies to make fun of him as he tries to think, shouting, "Think!" in a "brazen, metallic" bark, "as if their throats were phonograph horns."[20] Here and elsewhere, the script undermines the referential function of the word by calling for it to be given an ironic vocal inflection. This mocking tone is repeated when one of Yank's buddies facetiously suggests that Yank's problem is having fallen in love—"Love!" It continues again when Long suggests Yank take his case before the law—"Law!"—that they have the power to change governments—"Governments!"—and that they're equal before God—"God!"[21] By having these characters speak in voices that are "brazen" and have a "metallic quality," O'Neill suggests that they too are mass-produced, transformed by the rhythms of industry. But what is more, the radical dissociation of verbal and vocal expression severs the presumed connection between the ideational content of their speech and the material apparatus used to express it, further dramatizing his theme of spiritual disharmony.

O'Neill similarly disrupts the relationship between verbal and pantomimic expression when he has Yank assume the posture of Rodin's *The Thinker*. As we have seen, Yank is stunted in his ability to think. Thus, modeled in soot if not in bronze, Yank's pose is meant to ironically inscribe him as a purely material and sensuous being. This pose recurs in scenes 6, 7, and 8—each time registering the inability of the pose to realize what it is meant to represent. And if his audience holds out hope that Yank will in fact become the thinker that he "apes," O'Neill not only dashes their hopes but mocks them when, in the final scene, not Yank but the gorilla assumes *The Thinker*'s pose.[22]

Understood as the story of an alienated man who's lost his harmony with nature, the play achieves its dramatic effectiveness through the separation of verbal, vocal, and pantomimic modes of signification. But what are we to make of the fact that, of Curry's three languages, O'Neill counterpoints only two (vocal and pantomimic) against the third (verbal) rather than each against the other? Given that the first two are associated with the body and the third with the mind, the play's formal structure would seem to further encode the Hegelian dialectic of matter and spirit. Such a reading is supported by the play's treatment of alienation as a spiritual rather than economic problem, and allows us to make sense of the play's otherwise ambiguous ending. After the gorilla's fatal embrace, O'Neill's stage directions tell us that Yank "slips in a heap on the floor and dies. The monkeys set up a chattering whimpering wail. And, perhaps the Hairy Ape at last belongs."[23] Only in death, it would seem, can Yank's alienation be overcome; only by casting off his body can his spirit reunite with nature.

But insofar as the body—associated with vocal and pantomimic forms of expression—is represented as something to be cast off, and the mind or spirit—associated with verbal expression—is represented as having conditionally achieved transcendence, the play also invites us to read it symptomatically. That is, it invites us to read it as an attempt to aesthetically resolve the tensions posed by the problematic of the text/performance split. Figuring the theatre as the body, and literature as mind or spirit, O'Neill's play suggests that drama can achieve literary status only by casting off its associations with the theatre. Thus, he ironically inscribes the conventional languages of performance (vocal inflection and gesture) in order to affirm the play's status as a literary text. After all, we should remember that in this moment of uncertainty, the drama had yet to emerge as a fully recognized literary artform. For playwrights who were also developing literary reputations in fiction and poetry (such as Susan Glaspell or Edna St. Vincent Millay), the drama's "subliterary" status may not have caused much concern.[24] But for those such as O'Neill whose literary reputations depended solely on their dramatic writings, the genre's questionable status was a source of great anxiety.

As Joel Pfister has pointed out, O'Neill appears to have tried to allay this anxiety by consciously figuring himself as a professional author early in his career. Examining several photographs of O'Neill at his desk with pen in hand, Pfister argues that they helped establish the playwright's reputation as a serious literary artist by representing him as a writer of "deep" psychological truths.[25] Thus, insofar as O'Neill may have felt the need to shore up his reputation as an author, we may wish to read the play as a *fantasm*, or what Fredric Jameson refers to as an unconscious fantasy master narrative, in which real contradictions are resolved through imaginary means.[26] So, for example, O'Neill's desire to "belong" to the literary world—a world in which authors possess greater symbolic capital than do "hacks" for the stage—finds expression in the content of the play, even as it is negated in its formal design. That is, while O'Neill deploys the codes of the theatre against themselves (in order to write himself into the position of literary author), he paradoxically insists on the play's theatricality. After all, this is a play that inscribes the conditions of its own performance. In this way, O'Neill imaginatively resolves the contradiction between his literary and theatrical desires. Such a reading is not as far-fetched as it may seem; O'Neill himself once claimed that the play was a sort of "unconscious autobiography."[27] Thus we might read Yank as a figure for O'Neill, who, in casting off the body of the theatre, is able to ascend to a higher (read "literary") plane.

JULIA A. WALKER

Refusing Eliot's edict that meaning resided in the word alone, O'Neill drew on all three of Curry's "languages": verbal, vocal, and pantomimic. But where Curry insists that meaning is a function of their perfect coordination, O'Neill counterposes these languages to suggest that meaning is produced out of the human struggle to fit them—and the experiences they express—into some sort of sense-making pattern. This is why, for all his literary ambition, O'Neill never forsook the theatrical medium of his work: it allowed him to situate meaning within a fully corporeal experience of the world. Ironically inscribing the actor's voice and gesture in the dramatic text, O'Neill not only created a drama that met the standards of literary high modernism, but, in turning expression into expressionism, raised the curtain on American theatrical modernism.

NOTES

1. In using the terms "performative" and "antiperformative," I am not necessarily invoking the specific definition outlined by J. L. Austin in *How to Do Things with Words*. Rather, I use the term in the more general sense of having to do with a context of (mostly but not only theatrical) performance.
2. Susan Harris Smith, *American Drama: The Bastard Art* (Cambridge: Cambridge University Press, 1997).
3. For example, in "Seneca in Elizabethan Translation," Eliot links "playability" to metrical form, arguing that Elizabethan translations of Seneca's plays inspired the development of blank verse and the renaissance of English drama. Even his admiration for the music hall entertainer Marie Lloyd (in his essay of her name) is premised on a text/performance split; while he praises her sympathetic engagement with her audience, he does not address her ability to interpret the materials she performs. See *Selected Essays* (1932; reprint, London: Faber and Faber, 1949). Many thanks to my colleague Jed Esty for directing my attention to these important essays.
4. T. S. Eliot, "Hamlet and His Problems," in *Selected Essays: 1917–1932* (New York: Harcourt, Brace, 1932), 268.
5. Friedrich Nietzsche, *The Complete Works of Friedrich Nietzsche, The First Complete and Authorised English Translation*, vol. 1, *The Birth of Tragedy or Hellenism and Pessimism*, ed. Oscar Levy, trans. Wm. A. Haussman (Edinburgh: T. N. Foulis, 1910), 129. The full passage reads as follows:

> The history of the rise of Greek tragedy now tells us with luminous precision that the tragic art of the Greeks was really born of the spirit of music: with which conception we believe we have done justice for the first time to the original and most astonishing significance of the chorus. At the same time, however, we must admit that the import of tragic myth as set forth above never became transparent with

sufficient lucidity to the Greek poets, let alone the Greek philosophers; their heroes speak, as it were, more superficially than they act;
the myth does not at all find its adequate objectification in the spoken
word. The structure of the scenes and the conspicuous images reveal a
deeper wisdom than the poet himself can put into words and concepts: the same being also observed in Shakespeare, whose Hamlet, for
instance, in an analogous manner talks more superficially than he acts,
so that the previously mentioned lesson of Hamlet is to be gathered
not from his words, but from a more profound contemplation and
survey of the whole.

6. As Santayana once explained to Daniel Cory, the issues that prompted his
   critical intervention into poetic theory "were very much 'in the air' at the
   turn of the century." See Daniel Cory, *Santayana: The Later Years: A Portrait
   with Letters* (New York: George Braziller, 1963), 17; also quoted in Joel
   Porte's introduction to *Interpretations of Poetry and Religion,* by George Santayana (1900; Cambridge: MIT Press, 1989), xxv.
7. Although he does not discuss the expressive culture movement per se,
   Harold Segal gives an excellent account of the international milieu that gave
   rise to it and what he refers to more generally as "the physical imperative" in
   modernism. See Harold B. Segal, *Body Ascendant: Modernism and the Physical Imperative* (Baltimore: Johns Hopkins University Press, 1998).
8. In 1872 Boston University became the first American university to offer a
   school of oratory. Franklin Sargent claimed that Lewis B. Monroe was the
   first to bring Transcendentalism to bear on American theories of elocution.
   See Edyth Renshaw, "Five Private Schools of Speech," in *The History of
   Speech Education in America,* ed. Karl Wallace (New York: Appleton-Cen-
   tury-Crofts, 1954), 302.
9. S. S. Curry, *Imagination and Dramatic Instinct* (Boston: Expression Company, 1896), 112. For Curry's method of reading figurative language, see
   Curry, *Imagination,* 112; for his elucidation of meter and the significance of
   line length, see S. S. Curry, *The Foundations of Expression* (Boston: Expression Company, 1907), 234. For a critical account of Curry's "think-the-
   thought" method, see Mary Margaret Robb, "The Elocutionary Movement
   and Its Chief Figures," in Wallace, *The History of Speech Education in America,* 193–96.
10. S. S. Curry, *The Province of Expression* (Boston: School of Expression,
    1891), 58.
11. See George Santayana, "The Elements and Function of Poetry," in *Interpre-
    tations of Poetry and Religion,* 165. Here Santayana speaks of the poet's need
    to find "correlative objects" adequate to the emotion he/she wishes to ex-
    press: "The substance of poetry is, after all, emotion. . . . The various forms
    of love and hate are only possible in society, and to imagine occasions in

which these feelings may manifest all their inward vitality is the poet's function. . . . The glorious emotions with which he bubbles over must at all hazards find or feign their correlative objects."

12. Santayana 158.

13. Curry, *Province of Expression,* 52–54.

14. T. S. Eliot, "The Possibility of a Poetic Drama," in *The Sacred Wood* (London: Methuen, 1920), 69.

15. See, for example, Cleanth Brooks, "The Heresy of Paraphrase," in *The Well Wrought Urn: Studies in the Structure of Poetry* (New York: Harcourt Brace, 1947), 186–87. Here he invokes a similarly disembodied notion of drama as an analogy for the structure of poetic form.

16. Quoted in Arthur Gelb and Barbara Gelb, *O'Neill,* 3d ed. (New York: Harper and Row, 1973), 587.

17. Eugene O'Neill, *The Hairy Ape,* in *Complete Plays, 1920–1931* (New York: Literary Classics of the United States, 1988), 136.

18. O'Neill 161.

19. Quoted in Barrett H. Clark, *Eugene O'Neill: The Man and His Plays* (1926; rev. ed., New York: Dover, 1947), 84.

20. O'Neill 139.

21. O'Neill 139–40.

22. Travis Bogard argues that

> The Rodin sculpture held for O'Neill an evolutionary significance appropriate to the play—brutish man attempting to puzzle out the truth of his existence and perhaps to better it, mind triumphing over brute force. Rodin's bronze, however, is far from pessimistic, and considering the course Yank is to follow, question may be raised as to the appropriateness of its ironic use here. Under any circumstances, deletion of the pose would not materially damage the scenes. What is important is that Yank should think, not that he should quote Rodin.

See Travis Bogard, *Contour in Time: The Plays of Eugene O'Neill* (New York: Oxford University Press, 1972), 246–47. As I hope my argument here makes clear, O'Neill's use of the pose *is* important; its deletion *would* materially damage the scenes.

23. O'Neill 163.

24. Smith identifies several fallacious assumptions that have led to drama's marginalization: that it is "emotional rather than intellectual, subliterary rather than literary, theatrical rather than dramatic, and derivative rather than indigenous" (47).

25. See Joel Pfister, *Staging Depth: Eugene O'Neill and the Politics of Psychological Discourse* (Chapel Hill: University of North Carolina Press, 1995), 6. As

Pfister argues, "It was precisely O'Neill's psychological and aesthetic 'depth' that demonstrated the American theatre was capable of producing recognizably 'literary' material."

26. Fredric Jameson, *The Political Unconscious: Narrative as a Socially Symbolic Act* (Ithaca: Cornell University Press, 1981), 180.

27. Gelb and Gelb 488.

MEMORY

Like a commemorative monument, the incorporated object betokens the place, the date, and the circumstances in which desires were banished from introjection: they stand like tombs in the life of the ego.
            —Maria Torok, "The Illness of Mourning"

The essays in part 2 suggest that if modernity may be read as traumatic, the traces of those traumas of migration, transformation, and terror reveal themselves quietly—in cryptic aesthetic forms, narrative leakages, and phantasmatic imagery. Daniel Rosenberg's essay, "No One Is Buried in the Hoover Dam," addresses the complex tension between the architectural design and material construction of the Hoover Dam and its discursive construction in oral history and in film representations of mortified bodies, spectacular deaths, and impossible burials. Designed as a kind of sublime monument to technology, modernity, and American cultural incorporation, the Hoover Dam springs discursive and symbolic leaks into the historical and particular through oral tales and unlicensed concrete inscriptions that speak about race and labor, bodily pain and death.

In "The Edge of Modernism: Genocide and the Poetics of Traumatic Memory," an exploration of the relationship between trauma and literary representation, Walter Kalaidjian explores the transhistorical and cross-generational discursive responses to the 1915 Armenian genocide, the twentieth century's first case of state-administered genocide. Figured largely through leakages in the "numbed silence" of literary modernism, the trauma of genocide is phantasmatically revisited and renegotiated in contemporary Armenian American survival literature in a linguistic act of mourning. For Kalaidjian, poetry is a discourse of phantoms that offers a "redemptive supplement to the dead letter of historical narrative." And postmodern poetics reveal the traces of the traumatic force of genocide stricken from modernist memory.

The trauma of genocide, this time the Jewish Holocaust, also underwrites Maria Damon's essay, "'Is the Identity There Anywhere': Writing, Social Science, and Ethnicity in Gertrude Stein and Certain Others." Responding to critics' discomfort in negotiating Stein's complex relationship to Jewish identity, Damon reads Stein's work against the backdrop of the self-hating racism of the Jewish social scientist Otto Weininger. Without disputing Weininger's influence on Stein, Damon suggests that Stein's language experiments "eviscerate" the truth claims of modernist reason and liberal morality that were clung to by scientists such as Weininger. Indeed, Stein's Jewishness reveals itself as a language practice. "Stein creates makeshift homelands," writes Damon, "in books composed of language that itself is not stable, but portable, mobile, motile, [and which] enacts the instability that necessarily informs a Jewish notion of home." Stein's wartime writing practice, like that of other secularized Jews in 1930s Europe such as Walter Benjamin, enacts the melancholic underside of displacement and instability, due, Damon claims, not to a thwarted faith in origins, but to a "thwarted desire . . . to explore—through memory and language—the processes of memory, language, and human being itself."

In "Jean Toomer's *Cane*, Modernization, and the Spectral Folk," David G. Nicholls argues that *Cane* is an ambivalent text that seeks out the interstices of modern spatiality and temporality. The book slips between the binaries of rural/urban, South/North, agrarian/industrial, premodern/modern, political/economic, folk songs/city culture to nostalgically celebrate the fecundity of the southern farm and the promise of economic autonomy and political modernity, while proclaiming the doom of the agricultural South under modernization. Nostalgic for the cultural wealth of African American folk songs and—in the abstract—for the southern agrarian folk culture, Toomer constructs the southern folk as specters who haunt the modernized landscape and find spiritual comfort by consuming spirits in a kind of literal incorporation of the ghost. Yet it is their evanescence, Nicholls argues, that enables Toomer's southern folk mobility through time and space. The essay itself suggests that it is haunted by a ghost all its own: that of Toomer himself, the absent genius, who left the literary life in quest of the spiritual one, and who, as an early poster boy of the New Negro Renaissance, turned his back on his African American heritage as well as on literary modernism and produced a novel that itself has a spectral presence within the discourse of the Harlem Renaissance, for it instigated even in refusing the nostalgic appropriation of southern folk culture by Harlem Renaissance writers.

In investigating the reception of the Korean American writer Younghill Kang's 1937 novel *East Goes West: The Making of an Oriental Yankee* and of Kang himself by his editor Max Perkins and within contemporary Asian American studies, Walter K. Lew argues that the critical paradigms that have processed Kang fall into the totalizing traps of modernist discourses on race, nativism, and assimilation. Lew articulates instead Kang's more complex narrative strategy of "transplantation," the grafting together of "culturally disparate narratives" into a polysemy that is complex enough to resist both a complete assimilation into a hostile American culture and a futile attachment to a homeland in the grasp of Japanese imperialist rule.

5

NO ONE IS BURIED IN HOOVER DAM

Daniel Rosenberg

The most frequently asked question of tour guides at Hoover Dam is how many people are buried in the dam. Visitors are surprised to learn that the answer is none. People like to believe in tall tales, legends and myths, and this seems to be the one for Hoover Dam. The story of workers being buried in the dam has been around for a very long time, it originated when Hoover Dam was being built in the 1930's. Tourists would come and watch the dam being built, and they felt compelled to humanize the dam by concocting wild stories about its builders and the hair-raising dangers they faced. One of these stories was the myth of men buried alive in the concrete. But this is just a story.

—U.S. Bureau of Reclamation

There is a technical story they tell about the Hoover Dam. Historians tell it. Reporters tell it. And the Bureau of Reclamation honors it as a point of faith. No one is buried in the Hoover Dam.[1]

A variety of proofs are offered up. The concrete was poured in this and that way. No one could ever have fallen in. Everyone who ever did fall in was pulled out. And even if he wasn't, someone got back to him later. Once someone's boots were found in the dam. But it turned out to be a joke. It was just some boots.[2]

As one architectural historian explains it, "The often told tale of workers buried in the concrete during construction is apocryphal; the tolerances of the concrete could never stand such a messy water-filled object."[3]

But the story springs up over and over, as if it had a life of its own. Tour guides find themselves parrying the question so often that they lead off tours with a denial. The dam is supposed to be the site where American humanity conquered nature. In order for the dam to be what it is supposed to be, it must first not be a tomb.

The dam killed. There is no question about that. It killed in diverse and gruesome ways. Some workers fell from cliffs, some from the dam. Many were struck by falling tools or pipes. Some had accidents with air guns, others with explosives, still others were hit by trucks or swinging cables. A handful were electrocuted. During the first summer of construction, fourteen died from dehydration.[4] The first recorded fatality at the dam was a man by the name of J. G. Tierney, a surveyor for the U.S. Bureau of Reclamation. He died in 1922. The last recorded death was that of Patrick W. Tierney of the U.S. Bureau of Reclamation. He died in 1935, thirteen years to the day after his father. Between 1922 and 1935, 114 people lost their lives at the dam site. None of them are buried in the dam.

There are numerous specific instances of workers not buried in the dam. On November 8, 1933, for example, W. A. Jameson had the bad luck to find himself in front of a hundred tons of falling concrete. In an instant, he was swept from the side of the dam and crushed on the canyon floor. Searchers worked for hours, finding nothing more than "an ugly mound of wet concrete studded with gagged fragments of lumber and pipe." It took most of a day of digging and untangling before Jameson's shattered corpse was finally recovered. W. A. Jameson is not buried in the dam.[5]

Despite the fact that he was a very good candidate for it, Ike Johnson isn't buried in the dam either. On the night of January 3, 1934, he and Happy Pitts were standing on a form waiting for a twenty-ton bucket of concrete. The bucket arrived, but before they could begin unloading it, a cable broke, knocking the two of them off into space. It didn't take long to find Happy's body. He had fallen 150 feet straight down. Ike, on the other hand, seemed to have gone up in thin air. For a time, workers searched the canyon floor with no success, when finally someone noticed "a tiny flicker of flame halfway up the towering face of the dam." When workers arrived, they found Ike "reposing on his back on a narrow catwalk, holding a lighted match aloft like a fallen Goddess of Liberty." According to witnesses,

> He was one mass of concrete from head to foot. He couldn't talk, or see, or hear. But when he was finally cleaned up a bit, to the surprise of everyone, he didn't have a single broken bone. His eyes were sore from the lime in the cement, and he was battered and bruised, but otherwise he was as good as new. How he got where he was, or why he wasn't killed, nobody to this day can explain, least of all Ike himself.[6]

At the dam, everything technical can be explained. The puzzle is how to sort out the stories left in "gagged fragments" at the foot of this great machine.

The big dam killed, but, as if by force of will, it resisted mixing with the men whose lives it took. The stories are strikingly similar: mortified bodies, spectacular deaths, and the impossibility of burial. "One cannot work on the edge of Hades and expect to observe the same niceties as prevail elsewhere," explained the companies that built the dam in a report offered to Congress. Workers, they said, adopted the "fatalistic attitude that when their time came they would just as soon 'take it standing' as asleep in bed, and they jocularly referred to the ambulances standing always in readiness, as 'the sawbones' meat wagons.'"[7] But according to a union newspaper, workers also had a more ominous saying: "Build a dam, kill a man."[8] When a laborer was maimed or killed at the site, buddies would drag his body to the Arizona side of the project, where the death and dismemberment benefits were better than in Nevada.[9]

The first thing you learn when you arrive at the dam is that no one is buried there. A strange fact that tells as much about the dam as any technical datum. There are no workers buried in the dam, but their stories are buried there (incompletely).

The Hoover Dam presents itself as the modernist monument par excellence: "a system of plain surfaces," union of form and function, radiant white concrete climbing forty stories up the rough walls of the Black Canyon.[10] The builders and the politicians who made the dam imagined that they were making something so big that it would transcend time. Something universal. A modern pyramid. Seventh engineering wonder of the world. And they traced these ambitions into its surfaces. Its visual design emphasizes "pure engineering" over and against illusion and ornament. In the words of a contemporary poet, the dam demonstrates "power in absolute control, freed as a gift, a pure creative act."[11]

And the dam is awesome. Built in less than four years in the withering heat of the desert, at its inauguration in 1935 it was the tallest and heaviest dam in the world. Out of the famously dangerous and unpredictable Colorado River, it created the world's biggest reservoir and a hydroelectric plant capable of producing more power than any other facility then in operation.[12] To this day, it remains an icon of American technological ambition.

From the earliest days, tourists flocked to the Black Canyon to gaze down at the construction site. In 1934 and 1935 alone, 750,000 tourists came to witness it.[13] Some arrived on special streamlined trains chartered by Union Pacific. Others drove for "hours and hours along narrow dirt roads through the high emptiness of Nevada" in order to see it. But, according to an English visitor, the dam was a spectacle "worth travelling weeks to see."[14]

DANIEL ROSENBERG

FIG. 5.1. There was no shortage of talk about death at the dam. A sign at the entrance to the construction site took the long view. Courtesy of the Bancroft Library, University of California, Berkeley. Henry J. Kaiser Photographic Collection.

Even then, before its completion, the dam was stupefying. From the perspective of the viewer at the canyon's edge, workers looked like scurrying ants. According to one historian, when visitors arrived at the dam for the first time, "There was usually a long moment of silence, a moment when [they] groped for something appropriate to say, something that expressed proper awe and reverence for the dazzling, half-formed monstrosity they saw. The dam defied description; it defied belief."[15]

Put another way, it commanded a kind of suspension of disbelief. And the many films and pamphlets and radio programs that the government devoted to it only emphasized the point.[16] Indeed, when the Second World War "made it necessary to withdraw from the public the privilege of inspecting Boulder Dam and its great power plant," the Department of the Interior produced a radio program called "Man Is a Giant" to "vicariously gratify" the "forbidden thrill of visiting the structure."[17] Hearst Metrotone and International Newsreel did their part, filming a biplane circling over the dam and the Mormon Tabernacle Choir singing hymns atop it.[18] But the dam is so big that in these newsreels it falls almost entirely outside the frame. In Hitchcock's 1942 *Saboteur,* too, the dam is enacted as if in a radio play, through the "oohs" and "aahs" of our heroes gazing at it through a spyglass.[19]

To an English visitor in 1935, looking at the dam under construction was like watching a science fiction movie. "It is like the beginning of a new world," wrote J. B. Priestley, "that world we catch a glimpse of in one of the later sequences of [H. G.] Wells' film, *Things to Come,* a world of giant machines and titanic communal enterprises. Here in this Western American wilderness, the new man, the man of the future has done something, and what he has done takes your breath away."[20] The dam overwhelms us with the magnitude of our own technological power. In the first moment of encounter, it leaves us breathless. Popular representations of the dam frequently hinge on this moment. In the film *Desert Bloom,* for example, the paranoia of the conspiracy theorist played by Jon Voight is dimmed only by alcohol or the sight of the dam. Just as in *Saboteur,* the camera dwells on the stupefied viewer.[21]

But there is more than one kind of breathlessness. If the dam has the power to make us dumb, it also has the power to exhaust us with words. Words swirl around it, overflowing its sluices, turning its turbines, exploding through its penstocks. As if from the great reservoir behind, the dam can release a massive linguistic flow:

> Fly away, Modesty! Avaunt, Shame! Diffidence, be dispelled! My cheek is as blushless as a brass pan. In this article I shall deal in nothing but superlatives, because positives and comparatives fall short. The meekest whisper will be a megaphoned roar. It is the story of . . . the greatest undertaking ever planned for human hands. If this seems boastfulness, bring up the competitors. Earmark the date. Name the rivals. By comparison with the dam—the enormous, stupendous, Cyclopean dam . . . —the pyramid of Cheops is a rockpile in the desert. The Panama Canal shrinks. The Suez Canal is a mere trickle of water. The Assuan dam . . . is little more than a shovel and wheelbarrow affair. The Washington monument is a milepost. All very well for yesterday, of course. The Boulder Dam is for tomorrow. I am breathless.[22]

At times, like the Holy Spirit in a Pentecostal church, the dam fills us up with words. Seven hundred twenty-six feet from the riverbed to the top of the structure, four and a half million cubic yards of concrete poured, nine-hundred seventy-five thousand horsepower, thirty-two million acre feet of water stored.[23] It is a language of angels. How else to explain the scene in *Viva Las Vegas* in which, to the amazement of Elvis Presley, an airborne and bikini-clad Ann-Margret bursts forth into a recitation of technical facts about the dam?[24]

From a distance, the Hoover Dam seems a pure luminosity. Wordless, plain, and immense, in daylight it appears to rise whole from the Colorado and to open until it joins the sky. The approaches by road are carefully choreographed

FIG. 5.2. The dizzying array of astronomical, cosmological, and historical inscriptions on the dam. Courtesy of the Bureau of Reclamation, United States Department of the Interior. Photographer Cliff Segerblom (1940).

to achieve this effect. As you drive—and you must drive—you get glimpses, then views, and finally you descend fully into the canyon. In the words of one commentator,

> The experience, especially the first glimpse of the dam from one of the hairpin turns in the road zigzagging down through the red and black cliffs, seldom fails to elicit a visceral response. The sight is unearthly, particularly at night, when recessed lamps illuminate the expanse of the concrete and the tailrace below in a blaze of dazzling golden light.[25]

But up close the dam defies expectations. When you make it to the structure itself, you find that the Hoover Dam leaks . . . discourse. The closer you get to it, the louder it gets. The architects of the project made it their goal to leave the dam plain. But they were unable to contain themselves.

As if mad with language, they flooded the surface of the dam with cosmological installations and explanations. Words run all over it. There are statues,

NO ONE IS BURIED IN HOOVER DAM

bas-reliefs, plaques, and signs. And at the center of all this, there is a zodiac and a star map. Dozens of lines of text on astronomy and spectroscopy are inlaid in stylized brass letters on the black diorite plaza, along with a timeline preserving for "future men" the dates of the construction of the Pyramids, the birth of Christ, and the "split second" of the dam's dedication "in the year 1935 of Our Era, on September 30, and at 8:56, 2.25 seconds in the evening of that day, as calculated from the center of our Sun, or the center of the Ecliptic."[26] The inscriptions continue in a kind of delirium of technical precision:

> The sidereal year is now 365.2563360 mean Solar days; 3.258 sidereal years are required for light to travel one parsec at the rate of 186,300 miles per second. Our Sun has an absolute magnitude of +4.9; the most luminous star, S. Doradus, a value of -8.9 (320,000 times as bright as our Sun); and the least luminous star, Wolf, 359, a value of +16.5 (1/50,000 the brightness of our sun).[27]

Local legend has it that there are only five people in the whole world who can understand the rest of the inscription.[28] But if the astronomical formulas on the dam are not quite so impenetrable as that, the legend about them does capture something of the mystery conveyed by this strange place and these strange linguistic artifacts. At the dam, language begets language. Rumor seeps through the spaces between hard words.

Another local legend maintains that the dam is ultimately not for "men" at all, that the dam builders were expecting extraterrestrial visitors when they laid down their star map and dedicated the dam to "future peoples" and "future minds" and to the extension of knowledge concerning "other worlds in space."[29] As one visitor recalled,

> I walked across the marble star map that traces a sidereal revolution of the equinox and fixes forever, the Reclamation man had told me, for all time and for all people who can read the stars, the date the dam was dedicated. The star map was, he had said, for when we are all gone and the dam is not. . . . Of course that was the image I had seen always, seen it without quite realizing what I saw, a dynamo finally free of man, splendid at last in its absolute isolation, releasing water and transmitting power to a world where no one is.[30]

The dam has the power to make us think in millennial terms, of vast stretches of time and space, of silences awesome and sublime. Indeed, the celestial map and calendar atop it are made to be accurate for the next fourteen thousand

FIG. 5.3. Terrazzo floor in visitors' gallery. Engineering as a universal language. Courtesy of the Bureau of Reclamation, United States Department of the Interior. Photographer Paul Bond (1936).

years, until the time that Vega becomes our polestar. The dam is supposed to communicate to the ages and to the universe. In the words of the designers, it speaks a language that "even a Martian could understand."[31]

But for all of its pretensions to universality and science-fiction appeal, the dam is unmistakably an artifact of its time. In retrospect it almost seems as if the designers were pointing to this when they decided to mark in stone the moment of the dedication of the dam as a "split second on the face of the universal clock." People who attended the event remember that it didn't come off quite as simply as the text on the dam would suggest.

On the day of the planned dedication, President Roosevelt and his escort arrived at the dam on schedule. But shortly before Roosevelt was supposed to launch the dam on national radio, it was realized that his planners had not adjusted their schedules to Pacific Standard Time. A debate ensued over when to give the speech. According to one of the construction engineers, the secretary of the interior insisted on continuing on Washington time. "We don't care about the 20,000 people" coming in person to see the dam dedicated, he is reported to have said. "We're talking about the 20 million who are going to listen to us on the radio."[32] And so, hours ahead of most of the local crowd, Roosevelt gave his speech.

NO ONE IS BURIED IN HOOVER DAM

Squinting fiercely at the desert sun, standing on a platform jerry-rigged to mask his crutch, Roosevelt read his prepared statement. It was dam-speak of the purest variety, made for the radio. "I came, I saw and I was conquered," he said, to what masses had been able to assemble.[33] Extraterrestrial visitors will not be notified that the "split second" petrified on the face of the Hoover Dam needs to be recalibrated to Western time.

In fact, the much vaunted permanence of the dam is part of its script and show.[34] The construction of the Hoover Dam commenced in 1930, less than four years after the completion of the Los Angeles Aqueduct and the ruination of the Owens Valley at the hands of the Los Angeles Department of Water and Power. And it was less than two years after the spectacular and fatal failure of the Saint Francis Dam, built and managed by the same department.[35] The first of these cases gave the lie to the millennial visions of the water authorities; the second made them look downright apocalyptic.

The story of the economic and social disaster wrought by the Los Angeles Aqueduct is now well known. It resembles a thousand other stories of official expropriation: carefully calculated official lies, bureaucratic manipulation of legal specifics, and in the end the deployment of private and public forces to put down popular insurrection. It also resembles a thousand other stories in its final pointlessness. Owens Valley would not have been such a tragedy after all if it had served the needs of Los Angeles in some compelling way. But the water that was taken was barely a drop in the bucket of Los Angeles. Planners had known all along that in order to deal with projected urban water demands the Colorado would have to be tapped. And in short order.[36]

In the second case, the supposed permanence of modern concrete dams was put seriously into question. When the Saint Francis Dam outside Los Angeles failed apparently without warning at 11:56 P.M. on March 12, 1928, it caused one of the worst peacetime catastrophes in American history. In only a few minutes, more than 450 people were killed. According to investigative reports, the failure of the Saint Francis Dam did not reflect on the safety of other concrete dams; it was caused by poor surveying at the site. Ironically, the City of Los Angeles did its best to cover this up. In court, William Mulholland, the storied head of Water and Power, even entered into evidence a strand of rope caulking from the dam, claiming that it was the remnant of the fuse of a terrorist bomb. This did nothing to reassure the public. It did help to establish the founding conspiracy myth of Los Angeles so memorably amplified in Roman Polanski's *Chinatown*.[37]

The builders of the Hoover Dam were keenly aware of the need to quell public concern over dam safety. In this respect, the construction of the dam

FIG. 5.4. The Winged Figures of the Republic atop the dam. In the cosmology of the dam, the fleshy body of the worker metamorphoses into winged metal. Courtesy of the Bureau of Reclamation, United States Department of the Interior. Photographer R. C. Middleton (1959).

Nadean Voss remembers that Oskar Hansen, the sculptor who created the winged figures, told her that he could have used her husband, Dave, as a model. What would it mean to serve as a model for the transcendence of the human form? Dunar and McBride, *Building Hoover Dam,* 282.

was as much an event of political theater as it was of engineering practice. The U.S. Bureau of Reclamation published hundreds of images of the dam in venues of all sorts. But it discouraged the release of images that might suggest dangers associated with the project.[38] Indeed, to this day, it is very difficult to come by images of construction problems or industrial accidents at the dam. They are almost entirely absent from federal government records. The idea of the permanent dam is as much the result of carefully produced images as it is of carefully poured concrete.[39]

The designers of the dam were fascinated by the idea that technology itself might be a kind of universal language. The design of the dam expresses this ambition in a hundred ways. Responding to questions about his work, one of the designers of the dam compared himself to Gertrude Stein. Making monuments of this sort, he explained, is not really so much building as it is revealing.[40] The work of art expresses things in their concreteness. A dam is a dam, as Stein might say. And if any dam ever was, it was the Hoover Dam.

But the dam is even more reminiscent of Stein than this would suggest. It barely contains a discursive explosion. In its major voice it speaks a concrete language, a language of facts and things. But it has other, more liquid voices too . . . legends, rumors, whispers, and shouts. Every one of these is as insistent as the first. For all its abstraction, the dam speaks languages specific to time and place. At every point at which its designers tried to seal it against the historical and the particular, the dam sprang discursive and symbolic leaks.

For example, the principal design motif employed at the dam is an abstract pattern from Pima Indian basketweaving. In part, this was conceived as an homage to the great importance of Native Americans in the history of the West. A series of reliefs on the outside of the dam reinforces this theme. But the artist who conceived them had a different aim as well. In his eyes, there was a strong similarity between these basket patterns and the engineering schematics of the dam. His stylized versions of the Native American designs are supposed to represent a kind of universal hieroglyphic, a fusion of the archetypal and the technological.[41]

Bas-reliefs on the outside of the dam juxtapose images of Native Americans with ones of the various technological benefits of "reclamation."[42] According to the sculptor,

> It was my hope that those who step from the roadway of everyday life onto the polished pavement among the stars of the star-map about the base of the monument may feel the exhilaration of a journey far flung in intent and native to the dynamic and adventurous spirit of America. . . . From the appeal of freedom which existed in the breast of the Red Man as he reaches his hands toward his Great Spirit above to the joint effort for the building of a common destiny depicted in the act of peace on the lower panel, these reliefs express in visible symbolism the abiding values of our Nation.[43]

FIG. 5.5. A 1932 tourist pamphlet, *Romance of Concrete and Steel* (Wayside Press, 1933). Courtesy of the Department of Special Collections, Charles E. Young Research Library, University of California, Los Angeles. Artist Frederick A. Eddy.

In this concrete and asphalt incarnation, the image of the "primordial Indian" expresses the values of "our Nation." But it leaves little room for contemporary Native Americans.[44]

The dam too left little room. While there are no Native Americans buried in the Hoover Dam, the dam was responsible for submerging hundreds of miles of Paiute lands and artifacts under the swelling Lake Mead reservoir, artifacts that archaeologists from the Southwest Museum in Los Angeles raced to extract.[45] It is a strange irony that the first publicity pictures of the recreational paradise of Lake Mead feature a small tour boat that boasts the name *Paiute* on the side.

There were a handful of Native Americans employed on the dam project. They were mostly Apaches, who also distinguished themselves as high-scalers on the skyscraper projects of New York and Chicago.[46] As on the skyscrapers, at the dam their daring and skill were legendary. The otherworldly image of the work fit well enough with a white understanding of Native America to overshadow prejudices that still existed.[47] But from the point of view of the companies that built the dam, there was nothing otherworldly about their employment at all. Their hiring was an exception that tended to prove the racist rule. The few Apaches hired as high-scalers were virtually the only people of color directly employed on the project.

As the NAACP found when it came out to investigate hiring practices at the dam, and as it was to emphasize in its protests to W. A. Bechtel and other officials responsible for hiring, there was no official sanction for the exclusion of blacks from the dam project.[48] But the construction site was segregated, de facto. In the rare instances when black men were actually hired to the project, they were almost always consigned to working in the Arizona gravel pits. They were also prevented from living in Boulder City, the government reservation for dam workers. The blacks that worked in Boulder City establishments could not eat together with whites.[49] In one telling instance, a dark-skinned Apache worker was refused service in a Boulder City café on the mistaken assumption that he was African American.[50]

But while an implicit racism against blacks still tainted hiring practices, racism against Asian workers was explicitly written into the rules.[51] According to the Interior Department, there were two principal hiring guidelines that contractors were required to follow: veterans were to have preference above all others, and "Mongolian" workers were to be completely excluded.

Again here, discourse pours through the cracks in the modernist surface. That first summer of the construction project in 1931, one worker died every other day, and almost all of them from heat and dehydration.[52] This clinched the argument for constructing a new city in the desert where workers could live. Built on a federal government plan and run under its auspices, Boulder City was to be a kind of industrial utopia and anti-Vegas. It was segregated and tightly controlled.[53] And, above all, it was air-conditioned.

According to its designers, the Hoover Dam was to be the first American monument to commemorate "the abiding dignity of those who labor."[54] But in the 1930s, "labor" usually meant "white labor." The dam continues to bear witness to this suppressed but crucial modifier. In the words of the companies that built the dam,

> It would be a bit ironical . . . if . . . climatic restrictions proved too severe for American labor to carry through the largest single construction project it had ever attempted. And there were plenty of persons who predicted this would come to pass. Some prophesied that Orientals would finally have to be imported to cope with the melting temperatures that prevail in Black Canyon for four months out of the year.

To make certain that nothing of this kind would happen, Uncle Sam decided to extend a kindly but firm paternal helping hand to the contractors and to set up

FIG. 5.6. "Workman with Water Bag," the human form as architecture. (U.S. Bureau of Reclamation). Courtesy of the Library of Congress. Photographer Ben Glaha (1934).

a construction town under his control to insure for the workers a high standard of living and a maximum of comfort and general well-being.[55]

Boulder City symbolized and attempted to enforce the physical, moral, and racial purity of the worker.[56] It seems particularly fitting that in 1932 it gave a new home to so many of the decommissioned cottages from the Los Angeles Olympic Village, showplace of the perfected American body.[57]

In fact, Boulder City turned out to be a place as full of chatter as the dam itself. If it was not the hotbed of angry rumor that strike-torn "Ragtown" had

NO ONE IS BURIED IN HOOVER DAM

been before it, it was a place where people talked about the cohabitation of the human and the machine in striking ways.[58] Take, for example, Rose Lawson's memory of living in Boulder City:

> Every house was exactly alike. You couldn't tell your own house. It was always a joke in the olden days about somebody coming into the wrong house. Men coming home from work—if they weren't thinking, they'd come into the wrong house. I do know of cases where people got up in the morning and found a man sleeping on their couch. But they'd just wake him and ask him what he was doing. "My gosh, this is not where I belong!"[59]

The story itself is interesting, a kind of Charlie Chaplin perspective on the home in modern times. But more interesting still is the promiscuity of the narrative. It is a story that loves modern towns. Indeed, it is the archetypal story of Levittown, the archetypal postwar American suburb. It speaks not so much about one place in particular as about the particular textures of living modernity in general.[60]

Mercury, Nevada, inherited another discursive artifact of Boulder City: the name of its highway. Again, the echoes are striking. In both Mercury and Boulder City, talk about the "Widowmaker" referred mainly to the dangers of the treacherous (sometimes drunken and often late-night) drive home from Las Vegas. But in the case of both, there was at least some ambivalence about where the danger lay. Boulder City's "widowmaker" led from Vegas to the dam. Mercury's led from Vegas to the Nevada Nuclear Test Site.[61]

Out of the Colorado River the Hoover dam created Lake Mead, the world's largest reservoir. But it also created an enormous reservoir of discourse about body and technology, labor and death, race and nation, the immediate and the timeless. Despite their best efforts at making the Hoover Dam into a vehicle of propaganda of one sort or another, neither government nor industry was able finally to control it. The dam leaks secondary voices. To this day, these powerful currents circulate constantly around it.

In recent years, a controversy developed over a plaque that some veterans of the construction crews of the 1930s had put up on the dam. It bore the image of a black dog and the word "Nig." The plaque commemorated the passing of a companion to workers at the dam, a mascot who was the subject of powerful stories and dreams. According to workers, he wandered the construction site impervious to rules, rode the transports, "inspected" the work the men were doing. He knew how to get everywhere on the project and seemed almost to pass through concrete walls. One worker speculated that he "must have been a reincarnated construction stiff."[62]

To the consternation of many Boulder City residents, in 1979 the Bureau of Reclamation responded to complaints about the racial implications of the name Nig and removed it from the plaque. To the old-timers, this made no sense. The dog was a friend to every man on the project, they said, white or black, regardless of how many white or black workers might have been found there. So, according to a former dam worker, "when the men poured the concrete, they scratched the word Nig in that concrete, and that's still there."[63] But what is still there is difficult to define precisely: particular memories, contested statements, inscriptions, graffiti . . . the dam in miniature.

As both a "reincarnated construction stiff" and a subject of talk, the dog of the dam is the exact counterpart of the buried worker. He is a conduit between worlds. And he really does pass through walls. In passing he leaves traces, a palimpsest of stories not only of labor at the dam but of race and of spirit too. There are no workers buried in the dam, but there are stories buried there, scratching just through the surface.

NOTES

1. U.S. Department of the Interior, Bureau of Reclamation, Web page, "Concrete Dams": http:// www.usbr.gov/cdams/dams/hoover_fatalities.html: "Is Anyone Buried in Hoover Dam?" (July 22, 1997).

   For simplicity, throughout this essay I will use the term "Hoover Dam." In fact, there is much to be said about the controversy over the name of the dam and about the name calling and vitriol that it produced. It is an excellent example of the kind of discursive leakage with which this essay is concerned. In brief, the original act of Congress (June 25, 1929) that authorized construction was called the Boulder Canyon Act. It did not name the dam. Within a year, Herbert Hoover's secretary of the interior, Ray Lyman Wilbur, began calling it Hoover Dam. Wilbur's successor, Harold Ickes, a Roosevelt appointee, did not continue the convention and changed the name to Boulder Dam, which remained its official name until April 30, 1947, when an act of Congress changed it back to Hoover. More than half of Secretary Wilbur's Hoover Dam papers are devoted to the controversy. A note to the editor of his memoirs defaming Ickes reads, "probably unfit to publish but too good not to put in the rough draft." Ray Lyman Wilbur Personal Papers, Stanford University Special Collection, SC64b Box 95:4, 76, 63. See also L. Ward Bannister, "Why It Is Hoover Dam!" *Los Angeles Times Sunday Magazine*, February 18, 1934, 13–19; and "Charge it to Harold Ickes," *Palo Alto Times*, February 3, 1947, editorial.

2. Joseph E. Stevens, *Hoover Dam: An American Adventure* (Norman: University of Oklahoma Press, 1994), 219–21, 294; Andrew J. Dunar and Dennis McBride, *Building Hoover Dam: An Oral History of the Great Depression* (New York: Twayne, 1993), 106, 163–64; Richard Guy Wilson, "Machine-Age Iconography in the American West: The Design of Hoover Dam," *Pacific Historical Review* 54:4 (November 1985): 463–94.

3. Wilson, "Machine-Age Iconography," 471.

4. A full account of construction deaths can be found at http://donews.do.usbr.gov/cdams/dams/hoover_fatalities_table.html (July 7, 1997) as well as in an appendix to Dunar and McBride, *Building Hoover Dam,* 317–20.

5. Stevens, *Hoover Dam,* 221.

6. George Pettitt, *So Boulder Dam Was Built* (Berkeley: Six Companies, 1935), 96–97.

7. Pettitt, *So Boulder Dam Was Built,* 64–65.

8. Stevens, *Hoover Dam,* 204.

9. Stevens, *Hoover Dam,* 164–66.

10. Gordon B. Kaufmann, "The Architecture of Boulder Dam," *Architectural Concrete* 2:3 (1936): 3–5; Wesley R. Nelson, "Ornamental Features of Boulder Dam," *Compressed Air Magazine* 43:6 (June 1938): 5615–20; Wilson, "Machine-Age Iconography," 478; idem, "Massive Deco Monuments," *Architecture,* December 1983, 45–47; and idem, "The Machine in the Landscape," in Richard Guy Wilson, Dianne H. Pilgrim, and Dickran Tashjian, *The Machine Age in America, 1918–1941* (New York: Brooklyn Museum, 1986), 91–124. Kaufmann was the principal architect of Hoover Dam.

11. May Sarton, *The Lion and the Rose: Poems* (New York: Rinehart, 1948), 22.

12. Paul Lincoln Kleinsorge, *Some Historical and Economic Aspects of the Boulder Canyon Project* (Stanford: Stanford University Press, 1939); U.S. Department of the Interior, Bureau of Reclamation, *Boulder Canyon Project, Final Reports* (7 parts, Washington, D.C., 1938–50); idem, *Boulder Canyon Project—Questions and Answers* (Washington, D.C., 1933); idem, *Construction of Boulder Dam* (Washington, D.C., 1936); idem, *The Story of Hoover Dam* (Washington, D.C., 1955); Donald E. Wolf, *Big Dams and Other Dreams: The Six Companies Story* (Norman: University of Oklahoma Press, 1996).

13. David E. Nye, *American Technological Sublime* (Cambridge: MIT Press, 1994), 136–42. There are excellent archival materials on the Hoover Dam tourist industry. The Bancroft Library at the University of California has a number of handsomely illustrated pamphlets principally produced by the Union Pacific Railroad.

14. J. B. Priestley, "Arizona Desert," *Harper's Monthly Magazine* 174 (March 1937): 365; and see Union Pacific Railroad, *Las Vegas Hoover Dam and Lake Mead Recreational Area* (n.p., n.d.), University of California, Berkeley, Bancroft Library.

DANIEL ROSENBERG

15. Marc Reisner, *Cadillac Desert: The American West and Its Disappearing Water* (New York: Viking, 1986), 129–30.

16. See, for example, U.S. Department of the Interior, *The Story of Hoover Dam* and *The Construction of Boulder Dam*. See also the films of the same names. University of California, Los Angeles, Film and Television Archive.

17. *Reclamation Era,* March 1942, back cover.

18. See, for example, Hearst Metrotone News: "Aerial Footage of Boulder Canyon" (1920–26): VA4592; "Boulder Dam" (1933–49): VA4884; "Diversion of Colorado River" (1932): VA4818; "Work Starts on Hoover Dam," vol. 1, no. 303 (September 24, 1930): VA13886; "Across the U.S. with Roosevelt!" vol. 7, no. 204 (October 2, 1935): VA5494; "Giant Boulder Dam Springs to Life," vol. 7, no. 303 (September 14, 1936): VA12710; "Mormon Choir of 450 Voices of Salt Lake City Tabernacle Singing atop the Boulder Dam," vol. 6, no. 289 (July 29, 1935): VA12749. International Newsreel: "Airplane Survey Shows Impressive Magnitude of Boulder Dam Project," vol. 11, iss. 9 (January 29, 1929): VA12741. News of the Day: "Boulder Dam Spillways in Operation," vol. 12, no. 295 (August 11, 1941): VA12743. University of California, Los Angeles, Film and Television Archive.

19. "Beautiful, isn't it?" says the saboteur who plans to blow the dam to bits. "A great monument to man's unceasing industry and his stubborn faith in the future." *Saboteur,* dir. Alfred Hitchcock (Universal Pictures, 1942). In many films, the Hoover Dam figures as the symbolic end of America. In the Albert Brooks comedy *Lost in America* (Warner Brothers, 1985), it is the place where the hyper-reality of California ends and the fantasy of a trip back through time to a true America begins. The dam plays the same symbolic and historical function in Richard Donner's *Superman* (Warner Brothers, 1978). Here, arch-villain Lex Luthor attempts to make the dam the actual end of America by initiating an earthquake that would drop California into the ocean. Superman fails to prevent the disaster and is forced literally to reverse time in order to restore the dam and the American order of things.

20. Priestley, "Arizona Desert," 365.

21. *Desert Bloom,* dir. Eugene Corr (Columbia Pictures, 1985). For comic versions of this reaction, see *Beavis and Butt-Head Do America,* dir. Mike Judge (MTV/Paramount, 1996) and *Vegas Vacation* (Warner Brothers, 1997). The former also provides a spectacular example of glossolalic dam speak.

22. Herbert Corey, *The Biggest Job in the World,* pamphlet published by the Boulder Dam Association, San Diego. Bancroft Library Collection.

23. U.S. Department of the Interior, *The Story of Hoover Dam,* 61–62.

24. *Viva Las Vegas,* dir. George Sidney II (Metro-Goldwyn-Mayer, 1964). In the scene, Lucky (Elvis) is piloting a helicopter with Rusty (Ann-Margret) beside him. As they pass over the dam, Rusty says: "Oh, that's Hoover Dam, one of the seven modern civil engineering wonders of this century. Do you know

that it's over seven hundred feet from the Colorado River below to the top of the dam? Do you know that the dam helps make enough electricity to light up homes three hundred miles away." Lucky: "Well, well. Fly with Rusty Martin and complete your education." Rusty: "I do sound like a guide, don't I?" . . . Lucky: "Continue, Professor." Rusty: "All right, the lake has five hundred fifty miles of shoreline. That's the marina coming up right there ahead of us . . . and there you can go sailing, boating, fishing, swimming, waterskiing." On the language of angels, see Michel de Certeau, "Vocal Utopias: Glossolalias," trans. Daniel Rosenberg, *Representations* 56 (fall 1996). On the relationship between water and fabulous belief in the West, see Carey McWilliams, *Southern California Country: An Island on the Land* (New York: Duell, Sloan, and Pearce, 1946), 196–200. On the mathematical sublime, see Nye, *American Technological Sublime,* 115.

25. Stevens, *Hoover Dam,* 266–67.
26. U.S. Department of the Interior, Bureau of Reclamation, *Sculptures at Hoover Dam* (Washington, D.C., 1978), 11.
27. U.S. Department of the Interior, *Sculptures,* 9.
28. U.S. Department of the Interior, *Sculptures,* 12.
29. U.S. Department of the Interior, *Sculptures,* 14. The visitor services director at the dam suggests that the inscriptions on the dam might "give extraterrestrials who found [them] a way of knowing when the dam and the star chart were built." Brad Peterson, "Hoover Dam Still a Showplace of U.S. Ingenuity," *Las Vegas Review Journal,* June 24, 1984, 15.
30. Joan Didion, "A Piece of Work for Now and Doomsday," *Life* 63 (March 13, 1970): 25.
31. Allan True, "Color and Decoration at the Boulder Power Plant," *Reclamation Era* 26 (January 1936): 24–25. See also idem, "The Planned Use of Color at the Boulder Dam Power Plant," *Reclamation Era* 26 (February 1936): 48.
32. Dunar and McBride, *Building Hoover Dam,* 273.
33. Chester Hanson, "Awed Thousands See Hoover Dam Dedicated," *Los Angeles Times,* October 1, 1935, I: 1,7; Dunar and McBride, *Building Hoover Dam,* 311.
34. Its architect calls it "the greatest mass of concrete on earth and an imperishable barrier in a mountain gorge." Kaufmann, "Architecture of Boulder Dam," 3. For Marc Reisner, the idea of the permanence of concrete dams leads to a Didion-esque dystopian meditation:

> When archaeologists from some other planet sift through the bleached bones of our civilization, they may well conclude that our temples were dams. Imponderably massive, constructed with exquisite care, our dams will outlast anything else we have built—skyscrapers, cathedrals, bridges, even nuclear power plants. When forests push through the rotting streets of New York and the Empire State Building

is a crumbling hulk, Hoover Dam will sit astride the Colorado River much as it does today—intact, formidable, serene.

Reisner, *Cadillac Desert*, 104.

35. See Reisner, *Cadillac Desert*, 97–100; and, for example, A. J. Wiley, Geo. D. Louderback, F. L. Ransome, et al., *Report of the Commission Appointed by Governor C. C. Young to Investigate the Causes Leading to the Failure of the St. Francis Dam near Saugus, California* (Sacramento: State of California, 1928); and Guy L. Jones, *San Francisquito Canyon Dam Disaster (California), Report to His Excellency Gov. George W. P. Hunt* (Phoenix: Arizona Legislature, 1928). According to Reisner, at least nine separate investigations were conducted. The Arizona study is interesting because it is particularly skeptical of the claims of California and Los Angeles officials. Arizona would be a thorn in the side of the Boulder Dam lobby for years to come.

36. See Reisner, *Cadillac Desert*, 84–103. On minor narratives and resource politics, see Anna Tsing, "On the Salvage Frontier," in *Histories of the Future*, ed. Daniel Rosenberg and Susan Harding (forthcoming, 2001).

37. *Chinatown*, dir. Roman Polanski (Paramount, 1974).

38. Barbara Ann Vilander, "The Hoover Dam Photographs Completed under the Auspices of the United States Bureau of Reclamation" (Ph.D. diss., University of California, Santa Barbara, 1995), 138–87.

39. Vilander, "Hoover Dam Photographs," 180–81. And recent public debate about big dam policy has even made it possible to imagine that long before its decay and even perhaps in our lifetimes, the dam could possibly be undone by human hands. Reisner's book *Cadillac Desert* and John Else and Linda Harber's television documentary by the same name (San Jose: KTEH, 1997) are the most prominent representatives of the general change in public attitude that makes such a thought possible. For an even sharper skepticism, see Donald Worster, "The Hoover Dam: A Study in Domination," in *The Social and Environmental Effects of Large Dams*, vol. 2, ed. Edward Goldsmith and Nicholas Hildyard (Camelford, Cornwall: Walebridge Ecological Centre, 1986). For an analysis of changing representations in art, see Vilander, "Hoover Dam Photographs," epilogue. The prevailing rhetoric of the period prior to the 1970s treats the undammed river as a "thief" and a "menace." A pamphlet issued by the Six Companies refers to "the evil that lay dormant in [the] yellow current" of the Colorado, "a treacherous river in a land just two steps removed from Hell." One put out by the Boulder Dam Association calls the Colorado "a dirty river morally as well as physically." Another put out by the Los Angeles Department of Water and Power prefers to employ one of the old Spanish names for the Colorado, "The River of Martyrs." Pettitt, *So Boulder Dam Was Built*, 65, 111; Corey, *Biggest Job in the World*, 2; Donald J. Kinsey, *The River of Destiny: The Story of the Colorado River* (Los Angeles: Department of Water and Power, 1928), 10. There are

countless other works in this genre. See also Boulder Dam Association, *The Story of a Great Government Project for the Conquest of the Colorado River* (Los Angeles: n.d.); William H. Gates, *Hoover Dam, Including the Story of the Turbulent Colorado River* (Los Angeles: Wetzel, 1932).

40. U.S. Department of the Interior, *Sculptures,* 16–17.

41. True, "Color and Decoration," 13.

42. The official use of the term "reclamation" goes back to the Reclamation Act of 1902. It implies directly that lands that are uncultivated are wastelands. See Reisner, *Cadillac Desert,* 111 ff.

43. U.S. Department of the Interior, *Sculptures,* 19–20.

44. It is no accident that these parallel strips also give a résumé of the two terrains of authority of the Department of the Interior (management of natural resources and native peoples). Many of these different themes are concentrated in the opening incident in Barbara Kingsolver's beautiful novel *Pigs in Heaven* (New York: HarperCollins, 1993). The novel concerns a taciturn Native American girl who suddenly begins to speak as she and her mother drive across the Hoover Dam.

45. E. H. Heinemann, "Lake Mead Disturbs the Ancient Indian," *Reclamation Era* 26:8 (August 1936): 181–83.

46. Dunar and McBride, *Building Hoover Dam,* 141; Stevens, *Hoover Dam,* 177.

47. On the languages of the skyscraper, see Rem Koolhaas, *Delirious New York: A Retroactive Manifesto for Manhattan* (New York: Oxford University Press, 1978).

48. Roosevelt Fitzgerald, "Blacks and the Boulder Dam Project," *Nevada Historical Society Quarterly* 24:3 (fall 1981): 255–60.

49. Stevens, *Hoover Dam,* 176–77, 222–23; Dunar and McBride, *Building Hoover Dam,* 225, 306–7.

50. Dunar and McBride, *Building Hoover Dam,* 144.

51. Ray Lyman Wilbur and Elwood Mead, *The Construction of Hoover Dam: Preliminary Investigations, Design of Dam, and Progress of Construction* (Washington, D.C.: U.S. Department of the Interior, 1933), Specifications, 13: "Pursuant to section 4 of the act of June 17, 1902 (32 Stat. 388, 389), no Mongolian labor shall be employed under this contract." It is interesting to note that the editors of Secretary of the Interior Wilbur's memoirs had some trouble deciding what exactly to say about this issue, even going so far as to write a letter to one of his former deputies inquiring as to whether "there may be some specific Japanese [!] incident you know about." Ray Lyman Wilbur Personal Papers, Stanford University Special Collections, SC64b Box 95:4. See also *The Memoirs of Ray Lyman Wilbur,* ed. Edgar Eugene Robinson and Paul Carrol Edwards with a preface by Herbert Hoover (Stanford: Stanford University Press, 1960), chap. 6. See also Ronald T. Takaki, *Strangers from a Different Shore: A History of Asian Americans* (Boston: Little, Brown, 1989).

6

THE EDGE OF MODERNISM

GENOCIDE AND THE POETICS OF TRAUMATIC MEMORY

Walter Kalaidjian

Seldom in the theories of social, cultural, and aesthetic modernisms has the repeated trauma of genocide appeared on the list of what defines the modern condition. Benchmarks in the critical reception of modernism would include Nietzsche's proclamation of the death of God in *The Gay Science;* the epistemological revolution of Darwinism, Marxism, and Freudian psychoanalysis; the Fordist transformation of industrial society with its proliferation of the latest consumer goods, reified services, and attendant information flows; the fragmentation of representation as seen, say, in the formal techniques of the impressionist, cubist, futurist, and constructivist aesthetic movements, along with analogous tendencies in experimental poetics and prose, avant-garde music, dance, and performance art; the new discourses of, on the one hand, an agonized racial double consciousness and, on the other, a celebration of the "renaissance" of race (albeit complicated by the colonial fetish of "primitivism"); progressive figures of class antagonism, experimental gender roles, "queer" sexual identities, and so on. Yet genocide is curiously elided in the critical reception of modernism.

Amidst the wears and tears of postmodernism, the reigning discourses of the state, the media, and the academy have served arguably to repress, deny, and normalize the extreme experiences of total war and industrial mass murder.[1] Not a phenomenon, however, that belongs to the distant past, genocide first happens within the turbulent forces of social modernism with its emerging systems of technology and rapid information exchange. Accompanying these sophisticated advances, genocide persists as the unthought underside to the so-called progress we have witnessed in the twentieth century. Repressed for the most part in the modern public sphere, the legacy of genocide troubles the closure of modernist periodization with the repetition of its event. Witnessed in Cambodia, Rwanda, Bosnia, and Guatemala, the genocidal edge of modernism cuts through the social fabric of postmodernism. But equally important, the unfinished business of genocide's revisionist historicism and political denial bleeds into our own moment. Thus in discerning literary modernism anew, we might begin with asking, What was the uniquely traumatic force of genocide in dissociating the modernist sensibility?

Although the high moderns were not unmindful of "Old civilizations put to the sword," their psychic tendency was to affirm—as Yeats has it in "Lapis Lazuli"—a Nietzschean "gaiety transfiguring all that dread."[2] Similarly, Eliot's definitive work of modernist mourning, *The Waste Land,* also faces the Eastern European apocalypse of "hooded hordes swarming / Over endless plains, stumbling in cracked earth."[3] Yet *The Waste Land* turns toward the consoling metaphysics of "What the Thunder Said" that prefigure Eliot's later investments in the troubling conjuncture of Anglo-Catholicism and anti-Semitism.[4] It is, of course, a critical commonplace that Eliot's modern verse epic *The Waste Land* (1922) reflects the trauma of the First World War. Nowhere, however, has criticism observed that *The Waste Land* was conceived in the wake of the twentieth century's first case of "total" state-administered genocide, undertaken in 1915 by the Young Turk government against the Armenian people.

Canonical modernists such as, say, Ezra Pound, Ernest Hemingway, John Dos Passos, and Virginia Woolf were fully aware of the novum of human extermination as a modern portent of things to come. Pound, for example, foregrounded the ethicopolitical stakes of the Armenian genocide in his political journalism while a contributor to A. R. Orage's weekly *New Age* in the 1910s. Just six months after the outbreak of mass murder in the Ottoman Empire, Pound cited the massacres as an unacceptable, international atrocity in order to press for U.S. entry into the First World War. Beyond the nationalist interests of its own domestic security, America in 1915, Pound argued, was being challenged by the broader "interest of humanity, concerning which Mr. Wilson has occasionally spoken." Such ethicopolitical concern, he maintained, went to the heart of the "humanitarian aspirations" of the American enterprise both in its Enlightenment foundations and its subsequent Civil War over the abolition of slavery. Extending this humanitarian argument beyond America's national borders and into the new global arrangements of international modernism, Pound sought to extend such state resistance to "tyranny" into the transnational public sphere. Drawing an analogy between American resistance to the "tyranny" of slavery in the Civil War and the present "tyranny" of the Ottoman Empire, he criticized what he called America's "superneutrality," observing that "If tyranny is visible in our modern world, it is visible in the militarism of Germany, in the rule of Ferdinand of Bulgaria and in the Armenian massacres."[5]

It was no accident, of course, that Pound should invoke the Armenian case as part of his political journalism in the mid-1910s for, right from the beginning, it was the era's most riveting story. Not just an unprecedented modern horror, the Armenian genocide was also an inaugural media event. The spectacle of concentration-camp internment, death marches, and mass murder—centrally administered throughout the Ottoman Empire under the watchful eye of the German and Austro-Hungarian alliance—was widely reported in the United States and among the other Entente nations of Britain, France, and Russia. In America alone, such newspapers and journals as the *New York Times, New York Herald Tribune, Boston Herald, Chicago Tribune, Atlantic Monthly, Nation, Outlook,* and *Literary Digest* covered the story. In diplomatic circles, Viscount Bryce in 1916 submitted a massive government blue paper to the British secretary of state for foreign affairs; edited by Arnold J. Toynbee, *The Treatment of Armenians* archived eyewitness accounts of torture, rape, and mass murder reported by missionaries, Red Cross volunteers, consular officials, German health workers, and Armenian survivors.[6] The previous year, Toynbee had published *Armenian Atrocities: The Murder of a Nation,* which included Bryce's address to the House of Lords appealing for British intervention in the Turkish massacres. Quoting from a 1915 *New York Tribune* editorial, Toynbee underscored German complicity with the Young Turk genocide: "What Germany has done," according to the *Tribune,* "is to bring us all back in the Twentieth Century to the condition of the dark ages."[7] German witnesses who dissented from Germany's denial of the massacres included Dr. Johannes Lepsius, head of the Deutsche Orient-Mission. His *Der Todesgang des armenischen Volkes* (The Walk into Death March of the Armenian People) had a 1919 print run of twenty thousand copies, distributed, in part, to the Orient Mission and German Reichstag.

Similarly, Dr. Armin T. Wegner of the German-Ottoman Health Mission Conference published an "Open Letter" to President Wilson for the Paris Peace Conference of 1919 based on two unpublished books documenting the Armenian genocide.[8]

What did it mean in the mid-1910s to pick up, for the first time, any major daily paper around the world and read such headlines as "Armenians Are Sent to Perish in Desert: Turks Accused of Plan to Exterminate Whole Population," "Turks Depopulate Towns of Armenia," and "1,500,000 Armenians Starve"?[9] Just how shocking this new edge of modernism appeared for the expatriate generation can be gleaned from the traumatized persona of Ernest Hemingway's short story "On the Quay at Smyrna." As a foreign correspondent for the *Toronto Star,* Ernest Hemingway was familiar with the Armenian genocide and accepted the assignment of covering the burning of Smyrna and the massacre of its Christian community by the Turks in the early 1920s. Hemingway arrived in Smyrna about three weeks after the ancient city was razed by the Turks during mid-September 1922.[10] The story takes the form of a bystander testimonial given by a British naval officer who has just witnessed the refugee Christian community driven to the quays of the harbor in flight from the atrocities of rape, torture, and mass murder perpetrated by the Turks. Foregrounded in the story's opening lines are the arresting traces of genocide's uncanny presence in the modern scene: "The strange thing was," he said,

> how they screamed every night at midnight. I do not know why they screamed at that time. We were in the harbor and they were all on the pier and at midnight they started screaming. . . . The worst, he said, were the women with dead babies. You couldn't get the women to give up their dead babies. They'd have babies dead for six days. Wouldn't give them up. Nothing you could do about it. Had to take them away finally.[11]

Presenting the shock of the bystander witness to "strange," "unimaginable," and "extraordinary" events, Hemingway registers his character's trauma in the patterns of verbal repetition that are symptomatic of his brush with extremity.[12] Similarly, John Dos Passos's autobiographical account of the Armenian genocide's aftermath, portrayed in *Orient Express* (1927), deflects the full emotive impact of mass murder in the numbed monotones and understated ironies of a deadpan narrative voice. Hoping initially to satisfy his "craving for new sights," Dos Passos received commissions to report on the Middle East from the *Tribune* and *Metropolitan Magazine* and he undertook them in the search after the kind of exoticism that would satisfy his "craving for new sights."[13] Through the assistance of Paxton Hibben, who was serving in Paris as secretary of a Near

East relief mission, Dos Passos booked passage on the Orient Express out of Constantinople. Arriving in the Armenian heartland in Erivan near Mount Ararat, he comes upon the evidence of the recent deportations:

> [A] dead wagon goes round every day to pick up the people who die in the streets. People tell horrible stories of new graves plundered and bodies carved up for food in the villages. . . . Opposite the station a crumbling brown wall. In the shade of it lie men, children, a woman, bundles of rags that writhe feverishly. We ask someone what's the matter with them.—Nothing, they are dying. A boy almost naked, his filthy skin livid green, staggers out of the station, a bit of bread in his hand, and lurches dizzily towards the wall. There he sinks down, too weak to raise it to his mouth. An old man with a stick in his hand hobbles slowly towards the boy. He has blood-filled eyes that look out through an indescribable mat of hair and beard. He stands over the boy a minute and then, propping himself up with his stick, grabs the bread, and scuttles off round the corner of the station. The boy makes a curious whining noise, but lies back silently without moving, his head resting on a stone. Above the wall, against the violet sky of afternoon, Ararat stands up white and cool and smooth like the vision of another world.[14]

Not unlike Hemingway's portrait of the British officer at Smyrna, Dos Passos's autobiographical persona is afflicted with the trauma of the bystander witness assailed by the intrusive memory whose strangeness befalls the modern as if from "another world." Some four decades later in his 1966 memoir *The Best Times,* Dos Passos, writing now after Auschwitz, returns to the Armenian landscape whose uncanny scenes look forward to those of the Holocaust and its world of "cinders" where "corpses were stacked like cordwood" (*BT,* 95). Like Hemingway's fictional persona, however, Dos Passos foregrounds a numbed response to horror that defines the modern response to traumatic knowledge.

Beyond such journalistic accounts of the unspeakable, what consequences, we may well ask, did such massive social trauma entail for the traditional paradigm of Western humanism? Such questionings of social modernism are seldom posed in literary criticism, in part because the ethicopolitical issue of genocidal witnessing in the 1920s was struck from cultural memory along with its encrypted event. Three years after *The Waste Land*'s publication, Virginia Woolf's ironic portrait of *Mrs. Dalloway* (1925) marks the psychic limits of imagining this, by then, unconscious horror beneath the banality of everyday life. Clarissa Dalloway, writes Woolf, cared much more for her roses than for Armenians. Hunted out of existence, maimed, frozen, the victims of cruelty and injustice (she had heard Richard say over and over again)—no, she could feel nothing for the Albanians, or was it the Armenians? But she loved her roses (didn't that help the Armenians?)[15]

In discerning the modern subject, Woolf assigns Clarissa's lapse of conscience, her insensitivity to social justice, not so much to a shallow colonial naïveté: for Clarissa has a thoroughgoing, historicizing grasp of how the Armenians were "hunted out of existence." "No," Woolf observes, Mrs. Dalloway's symptom is that "she could feel nothing" about these disturbing facts of the case. Beyond simply recording the state-administered extermination of a people, Woolf witnesses to an event whose force breaches conventional representation. In the blocked psychic experience of her central character, Woolf gives testimony to how the trauma of genocide haunts modernism as a cognitive gap that necessarily eludes conscious registration in the public mind.

Like Yeats and Eliot, Woolf places the advent of modern genocide under erasure: at once acknowledging and denying its dread historicity. In the later writings of his career, Freud in *Civilization and Its Discontents* (1930) would similarly mark the limits of our empathy "to feel our way into such people" as the "Jew awaiting a pogrom" and other victims of traumatic oppression who suffer from what Robert Jay Lifton has theorized as "acute and chronic forms of psychic numbing."[16] Modernism's failure to mount a sustained cultural response to the genocidal emergency of its own moment may itself be symptomatic of what Lifton and others have studied in the survivors of the Holocaust, Hiroshima, and other human and natural disasters as the latency, or structure of temporal delay, that seems inherent in traumatic experience. Part of modernity's numbed silence may be assignable to such a post-traumatic lag—what Freud characterized as the "incubation period"—intervening between the extreme violence of the event and its later return as a felt stressor.[17]

Across the period of latency between the wars, such signs of cultural numbing, as lapsed witnessings, had devastating social consequences. One outcome of repressing—rather than commemorating—this genocidal moment was its repetition some three decades later in the Holocaust. In 1939 Adolph Hitler's diabolical quip—"Who after all, speaks today of the annihilation of the Armenians? . . . The world believes in success alone"—authorized, in his own mind, not just the invasion of Poland but the "final solution" as such.[18] Few spoke of the extermination of the Armenians due, in part, to the temporal latency of its traumatic event. But there were other, geopolitical interests that had a hand in its active censorship throughout the 1920s. Although the Armenian atrocities riveted world attention during the course of the war, America's diplomatic agenda of securing Turkey as a Middle East client state backgrounded the continuing plight of Armenians in the postwar period. But more to the point, the political silencing of the Armenocide, from the 1920s onward, raises crucial ethical questions concerning America's state complicity with genocide denial.

Following the World War I victory of the Allied powers, a resurgence of Turkish nationalism, coupled with the Allies' failure to lend material support to the creation of an Armenian state, resulted in additional Turkish aggressions against the nominal Armenian republic created under the Treaty of Sèvres in 1920. Three years later, the Allies conciliated Mustafa Kemal by ceding Turkish Armenia back to the Republic of Turkey and by dropping the Armenian question from the language of the Lausanne Treaty of 1923. The reconsolidation of Turkish nationalism during the early 1920s was supported, in part, by American foreign policy. The plan called for alliance with Turkey, whose strategic location would serve as both a hedge against the Soviet Union and a platform for Middle East oil interests. During the Harding administration, former Standard Oil official and secretary of state Charles Evans, in league with Allen Dulles, U.S. commissioner in Constantinople, and Near East high commissioner Admiral Mark L. Bristol, undermined congressional resolutions of support for the Armenian cause. Bristol, in particular, belied a disturbing racism that coincided with the ethnic biases exploited by the Young Turk triumvirate. "The Armenians," Bristol wrote in his 1920 correspondence to Admiral W. S. Sims, "are a race like the Jews—they have little or no national spirit and poor moral character."[19] The same prejudicial logic betrayed in Bristol's ethnic notions had earlier shaped the racial essentialism underwriting the nationalist ideology of Pan-Turkism promulgated by Yusuf Akchura of the Young Turk Committee of Union and Progress. In "The Three Political Systems" (1904), Akchura had defined "political nationality" in terms of "a race, a language, a tradition" that was essentially Turkish and thus exclusive of the long-standing ethnic diversity of the Ottoman Empire, divided as it was into Turk, Armenian, Jewish, Coptic, Kurd, and Greek millets, or enclaves of civil and religious administration.[20]

The conjuncture of American ethnocentrism and what Allen Dulles defined as its perceived "commercial interests" created a national climate favorable to Turkish revisionism and genocidal denial that persists to this day. By the end of the 1920s the American press, the Near East relief agency, and Congress succumbed to the State Department silencing of the century's first genocide. Between the world wars, the Republic of Turkey set out to recode popular perceptions of the Armenocide. Its most visible intervention came in 1934, when Metro-Goldwyn-Mayer planned to produce a Hollywood film version of Franz Werfel's widely read novel *The Forty Days of the Musa Dagh*. Werfel's book chronicled Armenian resistance near Antioch, culminating in the dramatic rescue of four thousand Armenian freedom fighters by the Allied navy. Vigorously lobbied by the Turkish embassy, the State Department brought pressure to bear on the studio to stop production of the Werfel movie and, following a year of fruitless negotiations, MGM canceled the project. By the fiftieth anniversary of the atrocities in 1965, with the passing away of many of the original survivors, the story of the Armenian diaspora received little world attention despite second-generation protests, demonstrations, and commemorations held that year in both the United States and Soviet Armenia. In the 1970s a wave of largely third-generation acts of political reprisals and assassinations of Turkish diplomats again focused attention on the troubled legacy of survivor families of the Turkish massacres. Despite the media attention such acts garnered for the Armenocide, Turkey prevailed in dropping reference to it as "the first case of genocide in the twentieth century" from a 1978 United Nations Subcommission Report on Prevention of Discrimination and Protection of Minorities.[21]

During the 1980s, Turkey successfully lobbied against American congressional attempts to commemorate the Armenian genocide in 1985 (the seventieth anniversary of the Armenocide), in 1987, and in 1990.[22] Trading on its continuing strategic value to the United States as a NATO "listening post" and military base against the former Soviet Union, Turkey was represented in congressional testimony and debate by, among others, secretary of state George Shultz and secretary of defense Caspar Weinberger. By the 1990 Senate resolution, the controversy had shifted onto the rhetorical terrain of denial. Against the evidence of some 1,500,000 Armenian victims of Turkish massacres, Senator Robert Byrd laid down the caveat that "I do not know whether what happened to the Armenians constitutes a genocide. . . . there have been injustices perpetrated against Turks. . . . practically every group has had an injustice done to it."[23] Similarly, Senator J. James Exon's performative uncertainty—"I do not know whether a genocide occurred"—countered appeals to the facts of genocide as Senator Paul Simon reviewed them. "At a minimum," Simon argued, "hundreds of thousands of people were slain simply because they were Armenians. That is reality. Many will put the number higher. . . . But the evidence is just overwhelming that genocide occurred."[24] In the end, however, such appeals to historical fact did not carry the day then and they never have since.

The rhetorical strategies producing such state denials of genocide were grounded in a revisionist movement of academic scholarship that Turkey had nurtured from the 1970s onward in an effort to reshape the record of its nationalist past. Such figures as William L. Langer, Stanford and Ezel Kural Shaw, and Bernard Lewis, among others—have denied the semantic appropriateness of the term "genocide" for what they regard as a civil dispute occasioned by the rise of

Armenian revolutionary nationalism.[25] Advancing what Robert Melson has characterized as the "provocation thesis," these historians have sought to recast Armenian self-defense against the rising incidents of fin-de-siècle pogroms and massacres.[26] In their revisionist accounts, Armenian resistance to Turkish oppression has been recoded as militant, domestic terrorism that escalated the threat of Russian adventurism on Turkey's eastern borders and of European imperialism on its western front. Such strategies of denial have followed the same tactics that Deborah Lipstadt has cogently critiqued in postwar efforts to discredit the Holocaust as a documented event. Rhetorical moves that are common to denials of the Holocaust and Armenocide include blaming the victims for bringing genocide on themselves, accusing the Allied powers of imperialism against Germany and the Ottoman Empire, discounting the actual number of deaths from genocide, rejecting perpetrators' postwar trial confessions as coerced testimony, questioning the evidence that concentration camps were in fact death camps, denying personal guilt, and so on.[27]

In the 1990s, controversy over Turkish support of revisionist historicism reached into the most prestigious institutions of higher education in the dispute sparked by Heath Lowry's 1994 appointment to the Ataturk Chair of Ottoman and Near Eastern Studies at Princeton University. To begin with, the Ataturk professorship is a $1.5 million endowed chair that was established at Princeton through a $750,000 matching grant from the Republic of Turkey. Such Turkish funding has supported similar endowments at Georgetown University, Harvard University, and the University of Chicago. Many in the academic community questioned Lowry's appointment based on his previous position as executive director of the Institute of Turkish Studies, a non-profit "educational" organization funded through the Republic of Turkey and grants from major defense contractors. Lowry's publication record has been meager at best and, other than the institute appointment, he has held no academic teaching post since his stint as a lecturer at Bosporus University in Istanbul from 1973 to 1980.[28] What added urgency to the issue of Lowry's appointment, however, was the 1995 disclosure that he had a history of collaboration with the Turkish Embassy in efforts to undermine scholarship on the Armenian genocide.

Specifically, as executive director of the Institute of Turkish Studies, Lowry drafted a memo advising the Turkish ambassador in Washington on tactics for discrediting Robert Jay Lifton's accounts of the Armenian genocide in his 1986 study *The Nazi Doctors: Medical Killing and the Psychology of Genocide.* In addition, Lowry authored an embassy letter reprimanding Lifton. As it happened, the Turkish embassy accidentally forwarded Lowry's memo with the letter to Lifton, who made it the object of sustained critique in "Professional Ethics and the Denial of the Armenian Genocide," a 1995 *Holocaust and Genocide Studies* essay he coauthored with Roger W. Smith and Eric Markusen.[29] "We feel strongly," Lifton later remarked of the affair in a *Chronicle of Higher Education* follow-up interview, "that there's been a violation of academic standards."[30] The following year, this tangible evidence of academic manipulation became the catalyst for a Concerned Scholars and Writers statement—signed by over a hundred distinguished professors, scholars, writers, and clergy—condemning such state-orchestrated denials of the Armenian holocaust. Not surprisingly, U.S. State Department officials defended Turkish gifts totaling $3 million in endowment grants to major American universities. Such state support symptomatically repeated the same arguments of geopolitical expediency that reached back to the Harding administration in the 1920s. "Turkey," a State Department official remarked in 1995, "is very, very much in the forefront of U.S. interests if you look at the vast oil reserves of the Caucasus and Central Asia and everything else going on in that area of the world. We can only smile on the growth of interest in Turkish studies."[31]

The impasse dividing, on the one hand, the moral imperatives and professional ethics of the scholarly community from, on the other, the politics of big oil and defense-industry interests in Turkey has an eighty-year record that is by now irresolvable. Today in our postmodern moment, when the truth of reference cannot be wholly divorced from discourse and its clashing regimes du savoir, contemporary accounts of modern genocide are met by counter-rhetorics of revision and denial that challenge any fixed claims to knowledge.[32] Within that discursive war of position, however, the traumatic force of genocide presences another historicity, one that cuts against the grain of official state memory. Here, the truth of extreme experience lives on, possessing signified reference precisely within, and not prior to, the performative and symptomatic registers of the signifier. In the writing and testimony of genocide's generational survivors, the referential power of its event speaks through textual revenants encountered in the gaps, catachreses, and fissures that trauma opens in our conscious narratives of personal and cultural memory.[33] Not only does the shock of genocide unsettle linguistic representation as such, but it may well leave an impression in our responses as witnessing readers to its extreme event. Noting the subliminal communication of unconscious contents in his 1915 essay "The Unconscious," Freud allowed as how "It is a very remarkable thing that the Unconscious of one human being can react upon that of another, without passing through the Conscious."[34] In forwarding Freud's observation, Nicolas Abraham and Maria Torok have described the figure of the "phantom" as an unconscious content or otherwise secreted experience that belongs not to the analysand but to another at a second- or even third-generational remove.[35] For the inheritors of generational trauma, such revenants transmit what Maria Torok has characterized as "a story of fear" that is wholly subliminal.[36]

In theorizing the phantom's cross-generational return in literature, I would propose considering how the agency of the letter in poetic discourse testifies to the truth of traumatic reference in ways that make special claims on us in excess of our normal roles as authors and readers. Although literature's fictive grounding in the figurative use of language would hardly seem fitted to disclosures of referential truth, I would argue that the poetry of generational witness—precisely as a linguistic event—manifests its force in revolutionary ways. What is properly an unspeakable or "buried" trauma in the ancestor, no matter how distant, appears like a ghost haunting the symptomatic actions, phobias, "puppet emotions," hallucinations, and—most tellingly—the "staged words" or cryptonyms of the descendant.[37] Not unlike the phenomenon of repetition compulsion, the performative, or "staged" symptom within the register of the poetic signifier does not just express the personal fantasy life of the survivor but serves to vent social trauma into a wider public sphere.[38] It's that repetition of the "unknown" that verse uniquely inscribes in the historical archive of genocide.

Blocked over the course of three generations, the unmourned trauma of the 1915 Armenocide makes a special claim to historical reference through the phantom voices possessing contemporary Armenian American survival literature. Troubling the foreclosure of modernist periodization, this particular body of literature revisits and renegotiates the edge of modernism's repressed historicity. The uncanny psychic effects of genocide have been the focus in over ten books of poetry and translations by Diana Der-Hovanessian, a recipient of awards from the Poetry Society of America, the Columbia/P.E.N. Translation Center, and the Massachusetts Arts Council. Der-Hovanessian's verse supplements the modern event with a postgenocidal poetics whose specter haunts her identity as writer through the formal anaphora of direct address: "Children of massacre, / children of destruction, / children of dispersion, / oh, my diaspora . . . / someone was calling / in my dream" (*Selected Poems,* 9).[39] Hailed in this way by the haunting "someone" of dream, the poet finds her place, paradoxically, in a modern genealogy of massacre, destruction, and dispersion. But what does it mean to be named in this ghostly fashion? What does it mean to accept the call of the diaspora?

As a generational survivor of modern genocide, Der-Hovanessian experiences herself as a perpetual exile and tourist. Like a ghost, she is forever displaced from any homeland, always already estranged from any fixed selfhood: forever herself a revenant haunting someone else's celebration. "I am the stranger / in my father's land," she admits in "Diaspora": "I am the tourist / from far away / where I left the tables of plenty / thirsty and unfed" (*SP,* 11). If Der-Hovanessian chooses, or constructs, diasporic identity as a born-again Armenian in language, she is also chosen—in excess of any conscious intent—by the modern event of genocide.[40]

Traditionally in the Ottoman Empire, Armenians—like the Jews—were considered to be a "chosen people of the book."[41] As a postgenocidal subject, however, Der-Hovanessian is chosen somewhat differently.

Across the latency of three generations, she is claimed now and then by the event of trauma whose questioning phantoms spirit her away to violent scenes of psychic dissociation. Chosen in this way, Der-Hovanessian is also given to her poetic vocation as she voices the phantom sisterhood of ancestresses who did not survive the crime of genocide. "But oh, my sisters," she writes, "now that 75 years / have passed and / no one has spoken for you, / I spit out the ink of words / you swallowed unsaid" (*SP,* 40). Repressed trauma that is here "swallowed unsaid" or—in Abraham and Torok's idiom—incorporated waits for the poet's act of verbal introjection: the linguistic work of mourning.[42] Losses, and lost ones, that lack symbolic expression and figural substitution in language frequent the psychic crypts of their survivors as revenants of what has properly become unspeakable. Unlike the failed mourning of the melancholic, however, Der-Hovanessian's revisitings of the Armenocide express phantom representations not of her own unconscious contents, but the unspoken trauma that befell others at a third-generational remove.[43] Haunting the silences and cryptic gaps of poetic discourse, the phantom signs of that earlier, and largely secreted, trauma possess their own agency—coming and going as they please—as in "For the Unsaid":

> Letterless, tongueless, and unpronounced
> the words sleep under their own heaviness.
> Do not disturb them.
>
> Their silence is not golden,
> is not assent, is not guilty.
> Their silence is not the handmaiden
> of death. They will wake
> in their own time.
>
> They are in that silent place,
> the eye of the storm,
> the edge of the heart,
>
> the day before it knows
> it is struck down. Let words
> wake themselves. (*SP,* 68)

Against the "empty" discourse of official state denial, poetry witnesses through its aesthetic medium to the "full" speech of cross-generational truths.[44] Encrypted in the silence that Der-Hovanessian figures here as the "eye of the storm, / the edge of the heart," the "unsaid words" of the phantom are signs of a subtextual agency that eludes even as it possesses our conscious speaking. Neither "golden" nor "guilty"—inhabiting the in-between of the living and the dead—this awakening into another tongue (hitherto "tongueless"), this presencing of a signifier (formerly "letterless")—takes place in its "own time" of linguistic parapraxis: at once outside and within the official discourse of state and academic history.

Marking the similarities between the Armenocide and the Holocaust, Pierre Vidal-Naquet has also theorized the generational pattern that characterizes the chosen people of diasporic survival:

> One could be tempted summarily to categorize the generations. The first, that which survived the great massacre, led a hard struggle toward adaptation. Today it has largely passed away. The second benefited from the efforts and money accumulated by the first and has provided large numbers of the assimilated. The third is a classic generation, in quest of its roots precisely because in fact it has lost them.[45]

If, as Vidal-Naquet observes, the third generation searches for a past that is "lost" to assimilation, there is also a way in which modern history makes a special claim on the descendants across the latency of the second generation. In this third moment, first-generation trauma returns in the haunting disjuncture between two incommensurate worlds. It is this postgenocidal breach that the poet Peter Balakian explores as a third-generation Armenian American writer.

Similar to the psychic splitting that Der-Hovanessian negotiates, Balakian's poetry shuttles between the banality of postwar suburbia and the trauma of the 1915 death march that his grandmother Nafina Hagop Chilinguirian survived from Diarbekir, Turkey, to Aleppo, Syria. Crossing these antithetical moments creates surreal effects in "The History of Armenia." History, in this poem, does not belong solely to the past; rather, the force of its referent lives on, haunting the present in the figure of Nafina's revenant. The grandmother's ghost appears in a dreamscape split between, on the one hand, a "backdrop of steam hammers / and bulldozers" recollected from the poet's childhood memory of construction along the Oraton Parkway and, on the other hand, memory traces that revisit the primal scene of genocide:

I was running
toward her
in a drizzle

THE EDGE OF MODERNISM

with the morning paper.
When I told her
I was hungry, she said,
in the grocery store
a man is standing
to his ankles in blood,
the babies in East Orange
have disappeared
maybe eaten by
the machinery
on this long road.[46]

Bearing the sign of the "starving Armenians," the poet here is also "hungry" for Nafina's untold story that he will never find in the "morning paper." Yet in voicing his symptom, Balakian enters the historical dialogism of another kind of news. However unreported, the event of what "she said" as a revenant speaks beyond a lifetime otherwise consumed by silence. As a discourse of phantoms, poetry nevertheless offers a redemptive supplement to the dead letter of historical narrative.

However denied by Turkey today, the brutality of modernism's first genocide was, of course, amply documented as it occurred. For his part, Commissioner G. Gorrini, the Italian consul-general at Trebizond, testified to the "unheard-of cruelties" and "execrable crimes" against humanity that were the "work of the Central Government and the 'Committee of Union and Progress.'" Recorded in Gorrini's firsthand account is the shock of genocidal reference, whose "black page," as a rhetorical catachresis, marks a mise en abyme in the historical narrative of Western civilization: "It was a real extermination and slaughter of the innocents, an unheard-of thing, a black page stained with the flagrant violation of the most sacred rights of humanity, of Christianity, of nationality."[47] However unreadable, trauma's "black page" leaves its collective impression in the modern repetition of subsequent genocides in the Holocaust, Cambodia, Bosnia, and Rwanda. Only by working through the accounts of these inaugural massacres—the particular forms atrocities took and the suffering their survivors endured—can we avoid their return that, even now, continues to act out similar scenes of so-called ethnic cleansing.

The eyewitness narratives collected by Viscount Bryce and Arnold Toynbee confirm American ambassador to Turkey Henry Morgenthau's judgment that "the whole history of the human race contains no such horrible episode as this. . . . destruction of a race":[48]

WALTER KALAIDJIAN

In Harpout and Mezré the people have had to endure terrible torture. They have had their eye-brows plucked out, their breasts cut off, their nails torn off; their torturers hew off their feet or else hammer nails into them just as they do in shoeing horses. . . . The shortest method for disposing of the women and children concentrated in the various camps was to burn them. Fire was set to large wooden sheds in Alidjan, Megrakom, Khaskegh, and other Armenian villages, and these absolutely helpless women and children were roasted to death. Many went mad and threw their children away; some knelt down and prayed amid the flames in which their bodies were burning; others shrieked and cried for help which came from nowhere. And the executioners, who seem to have been unmoved by this unparalleled savagery, grasped infants by one leg and hurled them into the fire, calling out to the burning mothers: "Here are your lions."[49]

According to eyewitness testimony, the Turkish method of genocide began with the nominal "arrest" of a community's Armenian men anywhere between the ages of fifteen to seventy. Without trial, the Armenians were then marched to a remote site where they were tied in pairs or larger groups and then hacked, strangled, or shot to death. Following such mass executions, the female survivors with children and the elderly were then forcibly paraded—or "deported"—by Turkish gendarmes into the remote deserts, hills, and back country of the Ottoman Empire. Here, over the course of days, weeks, and months, they were continually robbed, assaulted, raped, and harassed by bands of Kurds, Circassians, Bedouins, and Turkish peasants. Amidst such dire straits, hundreds of thousands of Armenians lost their lives through exposure to the elements, starvation, thirst, murder, or the suicide at times of whole families who, joining hands, would drown themselves in the Euphrates River.[50] The sheer scale of the massacres can be gleaned in such apocalyptic accounts as Dr. Martin Niepage's reportage, *The Horrors of Aleppo*. Relating the Mosul German consul's eyewitness narrative, Niepage writes that "in many places on the road from Mosul to Aleppo, he had seen children's hands lying hacked off in such numbers that one could have paved the road with them."[51]

Not just an efficient means of exterminating the Armenian population, such death trains and deportation caravans—as spectacles of dehumanization—served the nationalist agenda of the Young Turk regime by staging a cultural logic of ethnic subordination. Once Armenians were demonized as infidels (*gâvur*), that nominal status could be acted out in rituals of public scapegoating, as seen in the accounts of American evangelists at the time. Gleaned in the accounts of Anna Harlow Birge, a member of the American Board of Commissioners for Foreign Missions, are the harbingers of the Nazi death trains: "They [Armenian women, children and elderly] were brought into Aleppo the last miles in third-class railway carriages, herded together like so many animals. When the doors of the carriages were opened, they were jeered at by the populace for their nakedness."[52]

Such collective scenes of degradation and scapegoating are symptomatic of larger, nationalist crises at the time. Ottoman anxieties about the integrity of its imperial borders in 1915 were projected arguably in the spectacle of genocide, publicly acted out through the ritualized torture of Armenian bodies.[53] Moreover, Turkish nationalism, like the Aryan ideal of the Nazi period, is constituted only in opposition to a demonized other. In this case, the ethnic difference between Turk and Armenian is recoded through a human/nonhuman binarism inscribed in the performative opposition between the jeering "populace" and naked "herd." The public venting of such widespread cruelty had its roots, arguably, in the shifting social foundations that accompanied modernization in the Ottoman Empire at the time. The influx of European capital and Western industry—coupled with the spread of Enlightenment thinking and missionary efforts during the so-called Tanzimat, or reformist, period of the previous century (1838–76)—not only gave new political power to the non-Muslim ethnic constituencies, but undermined the traditional religious and civic authority of the Ottoman sultans. Educated and financed by American missionary societies, the Christian Armenian community was the agent of such modernization. Not surprisingly, the Armenians' access to European markets bred class resentment in provinces where such sayings as "Two Greeks equal an Armenian, and an Armenian equals two devils" or "One Greek cons two Jews, and one Armenian cons two Greeks" demonized Armenians for their entrepreneurial savvy in much the same way that Jews were stereotyped in Germany and throughout Europe generally.[54]

The recoded figure of the Armenian as infidel was needed as a demonized other against which the imagined community of Turkish nationalism could then be constituted. In what Elaine Scarry has described as the "hidden pedagogy" of scapegoating, the fiction of Pan-Turkism received material transubstantiation through an archaic logic of sacrifice, inscribed on the disfigured Armenian body.[55] In this precursor of contemporary "ethnic cleansing," anxieties over a fragmented Ottoman Empire were projected onto the dismembered, castrated, or beheaded bodies of Armenians. Through the semiology of torture, horseshoes, say, were nailed into the soles of Armenian feet as signs of their subhuman status. Similarly, red-hot crowns applied to the heads of the "infidels," crosses branded into their flesh, stigmata pierced into their hands, feet, and vital organs, and literal crucifixion all signified religious difference on the bodies of Armenians who refused Muslim conversion.

For the genocidal survivors, the psychic work of revisiting such extremely traumatic episodes is fraught with difficulty. Building on the early clinical work of Pierre Janet, the neurologists Bessel A. van der Kolk and Onno van der Hart have contrasted the ways the "speechless terror" of trauma may be "engraved" differently from normal memory encoding in the central nervous system.[56] As a nonlinguistic event, the radical violence of traumatic reference exceeds narrative memory to surface in the form of "somatic sensations, behavioral reenactments, nightmares, and flashbacks."[57] In these hypnoid, dissociated, and hysterical registers, patients reenact the moment of earlier trauma but without conscious awareness of its event. Such a moment where "memory becomes action" (175) happens in the symptomatic return of modern trauma depicted in Peter Balakian's poem "First Nervous Breakdown, Newark 1941":

In the street, she said,
you were walking
past a laundry
muttering to the shirts
hanging without heads
in the window

and when you walked
into the store
you kicked the empty
pants and asked for legs.

Outside the butcher's
those were cows' eyes
and moon-fat black balls
you took and gathered
to your chest
as if to say without
a word, they were alive
and beckoning for care.

And hanging ribs
fresh and red
with the bright white
bone like a scythe
running through—

she said you hit it
with your cane
until it screamed. (*SDL,* 17)

As told to Balakian by his maternal aunt Gladys, this incident is based on the experience of his grandmother Nafina Hagop Chilinguirian, who, as mentioned earlier, endured a 1915 death march from Diarbekir, Turkey, to Aleppo, Syria. Across the latency of twenty-six years, the traumatic memory of that survival—triggered by the reported bombing of Pearl Harbor—recalls the burning of the grandmother's house, the violent deaths of several family members, including her husband, and the unspeakable conditions of her own deportation. Memory becomes action in this work both as it is revisited in the hypnoid behavior of an earlier, dissociated self, and as it signifies within the linguistic registers of poetic discourse. Here, the force of traumatic reference surfaces in the catachresis, or verbal "breakdown," that mistakes the figurative expression "pant leg" for a literal limb. The grandmother's demand as she "kicked the empty / pants" acts out what Abraham and Torok have described as a certain "demetaphorization," or disruptive repression of the sign.[58] In this case, kicking a pair of pants performs the repressed signifier of the missing "leg" that, incorporated as a phantom limb, haunts the poem's psychic topography as a loss denied conscious acknowledgment. Similarly, in the butcher shop, the grandmother, "without a word," acts out a symbolic incorporation of other unspeakable signs of dismemberment in the "cows' eyes" and "moon-fat black balls" that are "gathered to [her] chest." But unlike the castration anxieties that belong to the oedipal domain of repressed infantile sexuality, the repetition of castration here reenacts an event that has a historical, not fantasized, referent.

Signs of psychic dissociation mount in the fourth stanza's surrealist image that projects the scream of the torture victim into a bloody carcass. The poem's final presencing of the "fresh and red" fact of a butchered body alludes, perhaps, to the Turkish practice of bastinadoing: beating the human limbs into pulp with sticks (acted out here in the grandmother's cane). Yet "First Nervous Breakdown, Newark 1941" does not conclude with some grave and memorable pronouncement about torture. More radically, the poem stages it in the distortion of an unreadable thing: a raw torso that is further defamiliarized in the grandmother's symptomatic beating. Nevertheless, as a dramatic disfiguring of the bodily imago, the literal hunk of "hanging ribs" performs what Elaine Scarry has theorized as the intended effect of torture, which is to reduce the victim's world, persona, and voice to the body in pain. "World, self, and voice," Scarry writes, "are lost, or nearly lost, through the intense pain of torture. . . . a destruction experienced spatially as either the contraction of the universe down to the immediate vicinity of the body or as the body swelling to fill the entire universe."[59] Beneath the popular cliché of "having a nervous breakdown," Balakian's poem explores the complex psychosocial topography of trauma and its possessing claim to reference that persists beyond the latency of its event.

Ultimately, it is the authenticity of such revisited trauma that empowers Nafina Hagop Chilinguirian's legal suit for damages against Turkey in "The Claim." Within the American tradition of encyclopedic poetics—as you find it, say, in William Carlos Williams's *Paterson*, Charles Olson's *Maximus Poems*, or Muriel Rukeyser's *Book of the Dead*—Balakian's long poem employs his grandmother's 1919 Department of State "Claims Against Foreign Governments" so as to cut and mix historical documentation with lyric utterance. Part of the poem's pathos stems from the anacoluthon of translating human loss into monetary damages, in the some $4,000 claimed for each of ten family members listed on the government form. By cross-cutting italicized sections of traumatic testimony with the language of government reparations, Balakian's poetic strategy subverts the legal fiction of administrative justice. Such crimes against the humanity of one's murdered family members can never be compensated either by money or, for that matter, by poetry. Nevertheless, Balakian's verse, as an act of mourning, would testify to his grandmother's claim to justice. The "full" utterance of her appeal breaches the "empty" discourse of the legal affidavit and its "documentary evidence" in the signifying absences, gaps, and ellipses of traumatic truth.

In Balakian's verse Nafina's trauma crosses the generational divide of eighty years to reemerge as the grandson's revenant. Yet as poet he does not assume to master, and thus foreclose, the genocidal referent through any mimetic or literal representation of the event. According to Nadine Fresco, genocidal experiences, because they are encounters with mortality as such, are by their very nature ontologically "forbidden" to consciousness. Based on her interviews with children of Holocaust survivors, Fresco has described the generational repression of genocide as a gap in the family narrative of what can be remembered: as a metaphoric "black hole of the unmentionable years in which an impossible 'family romance' had been swallowed up. . . . The forbidden memory of death manifested itself only in the form of incomprehensible attacks of pain."[60] As is the case in Der-Hovanessian's verse, knowledge of the "swallowed" or incorporated event is not accessible by any direct cognition but can only be registered through the agency of its affect and its symptom. In early poems such as, say, "Road to Aleppo, 1915," Balakian revisits the modern experience of the grandmother's deportation, himself possessed by the event of desert survival whose trauma is world-dissolving:

There must have
been a flame
like a leaf
eaten in the sun,
that followed you—
a white light
that rose higher
than the mountain
and singed the corner
of your eye
when you turned
to find the screaming
trees dissolving
to the plain. (*SDL*, 8)

Employing the formal resources of an effaced line length, Balakian registers a certain humility in the face of the other's unspeakable suffering. "Dissolving" into the opaque, unreadable space of the page, such truncated utterances suggest traumatic experience that, in its perceptual intensity, exceeds conventional representation. Indeed, a readable report of genocide, no matter how faithful to the facts of history, would simply mask the properly nonlinguistic event of trauma's "speechless terror."

In *Dyer's Thistle,* Balakian wrestles with this difficult paradox of finding a discourse that will represent the unrepresentable. If trauma is marked—as Cathy Caruth has theorized—by an "inherent latency," then it is that "blankness," "its "space of unconsciousness" that Balakian mines as a poetic resource in presencing its referential force.[61] From the opening lines of *Dyer's Thistle,* Balakian reckons with opaque, unreadable signs of phantom events that underwrite the cognitive gaps and numbed absences of consciousness:

That's how I woke
to a window of chalk sky

like indifference, like the sheet wrapped
around two people,
and the radio sounded like fuzz
on a boom mike
the rhetoric needling in about the dead in Croatia
. . .
I looked out to the Fisher-Price toys
blue and yellow in fog,

silver light, gouache on the spruces,
and the words Pol Pot
the geese chromatic, then gone.

Phnom Penh static like snow the day may bring
like a monsoon sweeping over a menorah

like the falling barn seeming to rise in white air.[62]

White air, fog, "silver light, gouache," a sky "like a numb pillow of radar" (*DT,* 12): such images—cut and mixed with references to genocidal regimes in Croatia, Cambodia, Nazi Germany, and Turkey—punctuate the visible landscape with lacunae and cognitive ellipses:

I was thinking like

the cows by the paddock in a peel of sun

when they cut a wide arrow
their feathers oily with tundra,
the gabbling like field-holler. (*DT,* 11)

In this volume, truncated thoughts trail off into the aposiopesis of lines that fall silent and bleed eerily into the white space of the page. Awareness comes through non sequitur and association; thought wanders through the errancy of anacoluthon. For Balakian, the poetry of witness negotiates between, on the one hand, commemorations of histories that must never be forgotten and, on the other hand, a poetics of traumatic transmission whose inherent latency always already eludes conscious memory.

As the definitive precedent of what the United Nations would later define in 1949 as "genocide-in-whole," the history of the Armenocide lodges a somewhat different claim on our social witnessing than that of the Holocaust.[63] Unlike the Nazi extermination of the Jews, the Turkish massacre of the Armenians has no recognized place in the modern archive of commemoration and mourning. Differing from the Holocaust, the genocide of the Armenian people continues arguably in the extremely proactive agenda of the Republic of Turkey and its representatives. In this highly politicized context, writing the history of genocide always already happens as an intervention fraught with risk. For what is at stake here is a special case of genocidal memory that must be continually defended against the state-sponsored distortion and repression that are acted out, even now, at the highest levels of government, the media, and the academy. Denied, contested, and largely forgotten, the Armenocide persists nevertheless *sous rature*—presenced in contemporary Armenian American poetics as an absence, a phantom event haunting today's public sphere. Negotiating these complex psychopolitical registers, this special body of verse also troubles the received closure of modernist periodization, calling for a new ethics of modernist literary and cultural historicism.

NOTES

1. On this point see Jacques Derrida, *Specters of Marx: The State of the Debt, the Work of Mourning, and the New International*, trans. Peggy Kamuf (New York: Routledge, 1994).
2. W. B. Yeats, *The Collected Poems of W. B. Yeats* (New York: Macmillan, 1956), 292.
3. T. S. Eliot, *The Waste Land and Other Poems* (New York: Harcourt Brace, 1962), 43.
4. See Christopher B. Ricks, *T. S. Eliot and Prejudice* (London: Faber, 1988).
5. Ezra Pound, "This Super-Neutrality," *New Age*, 17: 25 (21 October 1915), 595.
6. See Viscount Bryce, *The Treatment of Armenians in the Ottoman Empire, 1915–16: Documents Presented to Viscount Grey of Fallodon*, ed. Arnold J. Toynbee (London: Sir Joseph Causton and Sons, 1916).
7. *New York Tribune*, 8 October 1915, quoted in Arnold J. Toynbee, *Armenian Atrocities: The Murder of a Nation* (London: Hodder and Stoughton, 1915), 117.
8. See Tessa Hofmann, "German Eyewitness Reports of the Genocide of the Armenians, 1915–1916," in *A Crime of Silence: The Armenian Genocide*, ed. Gerard Libaridian (London: Zed Books; Totowa, NJ: Biblio Distribution Center, 1985), 61–93.
9. *New York Times*, 18 August 1915, 5: 7; *New York Times*, 27 August 1915, 3: 3; *New York Times*, 5 September 1915, II 3: 2; cited in Marjorie Housepian Dobkin, "What Genocide? What Holocaust? News from Turkey, 1915–1923: A Case Study," in *The Armenian Genocide in Perspective*, ed. Richard G. Hovannisian (New Brunswick, NJ: Transaction Books, 1986), 98.
10. For an account of the Turkish massacre of the Christian Armenian and Greek community of Smyrna, as well as Hemingway's journalistic accounts, see Marjorie Housepian Dobkin, *The Smyrna Affair* (New York: Harcourt Brace Jovanovich, 1972).
11. Ernest Hemingway, *The Short Stories of Ernest Hemingway* (New York: Macmillan, 1966), 87.
12. As Louis H. Leiter notes, the serial repetition that structures the officer's narrative "dramatizes the gradual numbing of human responses through repeated horrors." "Neural Projections in Hemingway's 'On the Quai at

WALTER KALAIDJIAN

Smyrna,'" in *Critical Essays on Ernest Hemingway's "In Our Time,"* ed. Michael S. Reynolds (Boston: Hall, 1983), 139.

13. John Dos Passos, *The Best Times* (New York: New American Library, 1966), 90 (hereafter cited in the text as *BT*).

14. John Dos Passos, *Orient Express* (New York: Harper and Brothers, 1927), 58–59.

15. Virginia Woolf, *Mrs. Dalloway* (New York: Harcourt Brace, 1997), 130.

16. Sigmund Freud, *Civilization and Its Discontents,* in *Standard Edition,* vol. 21, ed. James Strachey (London: Hogarth Press, 1953), 89; Robert Jay Lifton, *The Broken Connection: On Death and the Continuity of Life* (New York: Simon and Schuster, 1979), 173.

17. See Sigmund Freud, *Moses and Monotheism,* trans. Katherine Jones (New York: Vintage, 1939), 84.

18. *New York Times,* 24 November 1945, 7. Office of the United States Chief of Council for Prosecution of Axis Criminality, *Nazi Conspiracy and Aggression,* vol. 7 (Washington, DC: Government Printing Office, 1946), 753.

19. Admiral Mark L. Bristol to Admiral W. S. Sims, 5 May 1920, Naval Records, U.S. National Archives, Washington, DC, Subject file WT, Record Group 45; quoted in Dobkin, 105.

20. See Stephan H. Astourian, "Genocidal Process: Reflections on the Armeno-Turkish Polarization," in *The Armenian Genocide: History, Politics, Ethics,* ed. Richard G. Hovannisian (New York: St. Martin's, 1992), 53–79.

21. See Leo Kuper, *Genocide* (Middlesex: Penguin Books, 1981), 219.

22. For a detailed analysis of these congressional sessions, see Vigen Guroian, "The Politics and Morality of Genocide," in Hovannisian, *The Armenian Genocide: History, Politics, Ethics,* 311–39.

23. U.S. Congress, Senate, Senator Byrd speaking against a motion to proceed to Sen. J. Res. 212: 1336; 22 February 1990, Senator Simon speaking in favor of a motion to proceed to S. J. Res. 212: 1211. Cited in Guroian, 330, 329.

24. U.S. Congress, Senate, 21 February 1990, Senator Exon speaking against a motion to proceed to S. J. Res. 212: 1336; 22 February 1990, Senator Simon speaking in favor of a motion to proceed to S. J. Res. 212: 1211. Cited in Guroian, 330, 329.

25. See Stanford J. Shaw and Ezel Kural Shaw, *History of the Ottoman Empire and Modern Turkey,* vol. 2, *Reform, Revolution, and Republic: The Rise of Modern Turkey, 1808–1975* (Cambridge: Cambridge University Press, 1977); William L. Langer, *The Diplomacy of Imperialism* (New York: Knopf, 1935); and Bernard Lewis, *The Emergence of Modern Turkey* (Oxford: Oxford University Press, 1961).

26. See Robert Melson, *Revolution and Genocide: On the Origins of the Armenian Genocide and the Holocaust* (Chicago: University of Chicago Press, 1992), 151–59.

27. See Deborah Lipstadt, *Denying the Holocaust: The Growing Assault on Truth and Memory* (New York: Free Press, 1993), 21–23.

28. Noting the obscurity of Lowry's publishers, Peter Balakian observed that Lowry's first book, a ninety-page diatribe entitled *The Story behind Ambassador Morgenthau's Story,* "is in just 53 of the 20,000 academic and research libraries whose holdings are listed by the On-line Computer Library Center Inc. *Studies in Defterology* is held by 14 libraries, and *The Islamization of and Turkification of the City of Trabzon* is in one library." "Armenian Genocide and Turkish Studies," *Chronicle of Higher Education,* 1 December 1995, B5.

29. Roger W. Smith, Eric Markusen, and Robert Jay Lifton, "Professional Ethics and the Denial of the Armenian Genocide," *Holocaust and Genocide Studies* 9 (spring 1995): 1–22.

30. Amy Magaro Rubin, "Critics Accuse Turkish Government of Manipulating Scholarship," *Chronicle of Higher Education,* 27 October 1995, A44.

31. John Yemma, "Turkish Largess Raises Questions," *Boston Globe,* 25 November 1995, 1, 12.

32. For a sophisticated discussion of genocide and its representation, see Dominick LaCapra, *Representing the Holocaust: History, Theory, Trauma* (Ithaca: Cornell University Press, 1994).

33. For a cogent set of discussions on the topic of reference and textual representation, see Cathy Caruth and Deborah Esch, eds., *Critical Encounters: Reference and Responsibility in Deconstructive Writing* (New Brunswick: Rutgers University Press, 1994).

34. Sigmund Freud, "The Unconscious," in *Standard Edition* 14: 194; quoted in Maria Torok, "Story of Fear: The Symptoms of Phobia —the Return of the Repressed or the Return of the Phantom?" in Nicolas Abraham and Maria Torok, *The Shell and the Kernel: Renewals of Psychoanalysis,* vol. 1, ed. and trans. Nicholas T. Rand (Chicago: University of Chicago Press, 1994), 179.

35. "The presence of the phantom indicates the effects, on the descendants, of something that had inflicted narcissistic injury or even catastrophe on the parents." Nicolas Abraham, "Notes on the Phantom: A Complement to Freud's Metapsychology," in Abraham and Torok, *The Shell and the Kernel,* 174.

36. Torok, 181.

37. For an applied theory of reading cryptonyms in psychoanalysis, see Nicolas Abraham and Maria Torok, *The Wolf Man's Magic Word: A Cryptonymy,* trans. Nicholas Rand (Minneapolis: University of Minnesota Press, 1986).

38. Insofar as the phantom presences trauma unconsciously in the staged word, it "constitutes an attempt at exorcism, an attempt, that is, to relieve the unconscious by placing the effects of the phantom in the social realm." Nicolas Abraham, The Shell and the Kernel, 175.

39. Diana Der-Hovanessian, *Selected Poems* (Riverdale-on-Hudson: Sheep Meadow Press, 1994).

WALTER KALAIDJIAN

40. Shoshana Felman has noted the staging of an involuntary choice that authors encounter as witnesses of trauma "whose effects explode any capacity for explanation or rationalization." Shoshana Felman and Dori Laub, *Testimony: Crises of Witnessing in Literature, Psychoanalysis, and History* (New York: Routledge, 1992), 4.

41. See James J. Reid, "Total War, the Annihilation Ethic, and the Armenian Genocide, 1870–1918," in Hovannisian, *The Armenian Genocide: History, Politics, Ethics,* 26.

42. For Abraham and Torok, mourning's oral moment is analogous to, and has its origin in, the infant's first utterances that attempt to fill the empty mouth: introjecting or "swallowing" words to supplement the loss of the (m)other, or primary caregiver. Nicolas Abraham and Maria Torok, "Mourning or Melancholia: Introjection versus Incorporation," in *The Shell and the Kernel,* 127–28.

43. See Abraham, 171–72, on this point.

44. Jacques Lacan defines the difference between "empty" and "full" speech in "The Function and Field of Speech and Language in Psychoanalysis," in *Ecrits, A Selection,* trans. Alan Sheridan (New York: Norton, 1977), 30–113.

45. Pierre Vidal-Naquet, "By Way of a Preface and by the Power of One Word," in Libaridian, *A Crime of Silence: The Armenian Genocide,* 2–3.

46. Peter Balakian, *Sad Days of Light* (Pittsburgh: Carnegie Mellon University Press, 1993), 3 (hereafter cited in the text as *SDL*).

47. "Extracts from an Interview with Comm. G. Gorrini, Late Italian Consul-General at Trebizond, Published in the Journal 'Il Messaggero,' of Rome, 25th August, 1915," quoted in Bryce, 290–91.

48. Henry Morgenthau, *Ambassador Morgenthau's Story* (1919; Plandome, NY: New Age Publishers, 1975), 321–32, 308; cited in Guroian, 312.

49. Bryce, "Statement by a German Eye-Witness of Occurrences at Moush; Communicated by the American Committee for Armenian and Syrian Relief" and "Record of an Interview with Roupen, of Sassoun, by Mr. A. S. Safrastian; Dated Tiflis, 6th November, 1915" in Bryce, *The Treatment of Armenians in the Ottoman Empire 1915–1916,* 86, 90.

50.

> The Method of suicide in most instances was drowning in the Euphrates River. In fact, this practice was common enough that several survivors told us the words of a song which was sung in the orphanages that included the phrase "Virgin girls holding each others' hands, threw themselves into the River Euphrates". . . . Hundreds of girls often drowned themselves in a single day according to survivors' accounts.

> Donald E. Miller and Lorna Touryan Miller, *Survivors: An Oral History of the Armenian Genocide* (Berkeley: University of California Press, 1993), 103, 104.

51. Martin Niepage, *The Horrors of Aleppo* (London: T. Fisher Unwin, 1917), 12.

52. "Camp to Barton," 21 December 1915, p. 5, ABC-FM archives; quoted in Suzanne Elizabeth Moranian, "Bearing Witness: The Missionary Archives as Evidence of the Armenian Genocide," in *The Armenian Genocide: History, Politics, Ethics,* 120–21.

53. For a discussion of how Paul Virilio and Michel Foucault theorize the visible regime of torture and punishment to shore up monarchical power, see Nácunán Sáez, "Torture: A Discourse on Practice," in *Tattoo, Torture, Mutilation, and Adornment: The Denaturalization of the Body in Culture and Text,* ed. Frances E. Mascia-Lees and Patricia Sharpe (Albany: State University of New York Press, 1992), 126–44.

54. See Astourian, 59, 65.

55. "The body," Scarry writes, "tends to be brought forward in its most extreme and absolute form only on behalf of a cultural artifact or symbolic fragment or made thing (a sentence) that is without any other basis in material reality: that is, it is only brought forward when there is a crisis of substantiation." *The Body in Pain* (New York: Oxford University Press, 1985), 127.

56. On trauma's "speechless terror," see Bessel A. van der Kolk, *Psychological Trauma* (Washington, DC: American Psychiatric Press, 1987).

57. Bessel A. van der Kolk and Onno van der Hart, "The Intrusive Past: The Flexibility of Memory and the Engraving of Trauma," in *Trauma: Explorations in Memory,* ed. Cathy Caruth (Baltimore: Johns Hopkins University Press, 1995), 172.

58. See Abraham and Torok, "Mourning or Melancholia," 133.

59. Scarry, 35.

60. Nadine Fresco, "Remembering the Unknown," *International Review of Psychoanalysis* 11 (1984): 418.

61. Cathy Caruth, "Trauma and Experience: Introduction," in Caruth, *Trauma: Explorations in Memory,* 8.

62. Peter Balakian, *Dyer's Thistle* (Pittsburgh: Carnegie Mellon University Press, 1996), 11 (hereafter cited in the text as *DT*).

63. For a discussion of the Armenocide as a "total" genocide, as opposed to instances of "genocide-in-part," see Melson. For other discussions of the relations between the Armenocide and the Holocaust, see Leo Kuper, *Genocide: Its Political Uses in the Twentieth Century* (New Haven: Yale University Press, 1981); Helen Fein, "A Formula for Genocide: A Comparison of the Turkish Genocide (1915) and the German Holocaust (1939–1945)," *Comparative Studies in Sociology* 1 (1978): 271–93; Vahakn N. Dadrian, "The Convergent Aspects of the Armenian and Jewish Cases of Genocide: A Reinterpretation of the Concept of Holocaust," *Holocaust and Genocide Studies* 3: 2 (1988): 151–70; Hrair R. Dekmejian, "Determinants of Genocide: Armenians and Jews as Case Studies," in Hovannisian, *The Armenian Genocide in Perspective,* 85–96.

7

WRITING, SOCIAL SCIENCE, AND ETHNICITY IN GERTRUDE STEIN AND CERTAIN OTHERS

Maria Damon

In October 1995, "L-A-N-G-U-A-G-E" poet Charles Bernstein and I participated by telephone in a Gertrude Stein hour on WBAI Radio's *Beyond the Pale,* organized by Jews for Racial and Economic Justice. (The gay and lesbian activist wing of the group had requested Stein as the subject of their designated special show, a choice that in itself was interesting to me, since, while there is no consensus on Stein's positions on racial and economic justice, it indicated the degree to which she has herself become a figure of political resonance in queer circles.) We were the "Jews" on the panel; the other two panelists, who were present in the studio along with the JFREJ moderator, were the poet Eileen Myles, who had recently coedited *The New Fuck You Anthology of Lesbian Writing,* and Buffy Johnson, a New York painter who had known Gertrude and Alice in Paris. Charles and I came in on the second half of the hour-long show, and discussed first how we did or didn't see questions of identity arising in Stein's work, and how Stein's interrogation of identity through language play (as well as thematically) could itself be seen as a strong current in the Jewish intellectual tradition. Then came the question of her politics, her survival of World War II under the auspices of Bernard Faÿ in the Vichy government. The moderator challenged any designation of Stein and Toklas as "radical" since they owed their survival to friendship with an anti-Semite whom they refused to repudiate even after Faÿ's disgrace in the wake of Allied victory. Charles and I bristled. Would it have been better that she not survive? She didn't betray anybody. People did what they had to. The whole village knew they were Jewish and protected them. I'd seen their wartime I.D. photos at the Beinecke, and they were terrified little old Jewish ladies (I refer to them in my notes as "suffering, aging, patient, angry and very intelligent"), not callous race-traitors living it up à la Nero, fiddling and diddling while their people perished. And so forth. Our vehement defense was cut off by the hour's expiration. Thank you for being with us but that's all the time we have. Our disembodied, miscreant Jewish voices snipped, our absence doubled. The non-Jewish artists and the political Jew wrapped it up in person.

In an earlier essay I explored Gertrude Stein's writing as "minority discourse" in the sense expressed by Deleuze and Guattari in their *Kafka: Toward a Minor Literature*.[1] I had thought, before I began writing that piece, that I'd be most compelled in this direction by Stein's status as a sexual minority and as a woman. However, her Jewishness emerged as an at least equal site of creative contestation, not in opposition to those other elements of social difference, but implicated, of a piece, with them. In the present essay I want to continue that inquiry by situating work produced during Stein's middle period (roughly, from World War I to just before the emergence of the Final Solution—primarily the works collected as *Painted Lace, and Other Pieces, 1914–1937*) in the discourse of Jewish social science. I will refer primarily to Otto Weininger's work, but also, more cursorily, to that of Freud, Maurice Fishberg, and Melville Herskovits (whom I always misname Herman Melvillowitz), all secularized Jews.

Let me say at the outset that, though I find Stein's and Toklas's gratitude and loyalty vis-à-vis Bernard Faÿ completely defensible and understandable, there is no point in exonerating Stein's occasional displays of colossal political naïveté, most spectacularly her enthusiastic support for Marshal Pétain as the savior of France. That was not my aim in the JFREJ radio show, nor is it in the current essay. Rather, I want to argue for the ways Stein, in spite of her sometimes dubious enthusiasms (such as her early excitement about the sociologist Otto Weininger), actively participated in the debates surrounding the scientization of ethnocultural characteristics and did so in a way not wholly reducible to either a simple repudiation of her Jewishness or an affirmation thereof in conventionally recognizable terms. In fact, the complex relationship of Stein, as a proto-postmodernist, to Jewishness and Jewish history anticipates current debates about the emancipationist and/or dangerously apolitical potentials of postmodern writing practice and poststructuralist, language-oriented philosophies.

The Jewish social scientist's inquiry into systems of character, physical type, and mental processes may reflect an attempt to understand the origins of his or her socially perceived "difference," and to affirm that difference. However, the inquiry may also indicate an attempt to control by intellectual mastery a system of exclusion; the anxiety of "passing" generates a search for systemic order in which one can find one's own safety zone. This essay has its autobiographical imperative: I am the daughter of an ambivalently Jewish medical anthropologist. I read my father's professional life as an attempt to both assert his (ethnically affirmed) intelligence and efface his (socially despised) ethnicity within a larger culture that deemed his bookishness, his verbal acumen and sensitivity, his passion for Western culture unmanly even as it rewarded his achievements. Gertrude Stein's early novelistic experiments with African American language, for example, and the novel *QED,* in which each person of the lesbian love triangle in the plot typifies a different "national" temperament, constitute a similarly problematic move to study (the otherness of) oneself by attending to the otherness of an/other Other. Her move to Europe, in which she plunged herself into a culture alien yet somehow evocative of an older, familiar world ("we [singulars, queer people] fly to the kindly comfort of an older world accustomed to take all manner of strange forms to its bosom"), could constitute a kind of sociolinguistic fieldwork in which the real subject of study (as in most ethnographies, after all) is herself.[2] The writing Stein produced in France, though less thematically concerned with "types" and character, became a practice in which language itself, in a process of experiment, undertakes and undergoes a dissolution of category.

Since until recently it has been assumed that an inquiry into someone's ethnicity involves establishing how they themselves "felt about" being *x* or *y,* Steinians have maintained that Stein's radical anti-identitarianism foreclosed such inquiry, except to assert that "it simply wasn't important to her"; this foreclosure is exacerbated by the ongoing debates about whether Judaism/Jewishness is a religion, an ethnicity, a culture, and so on. It seems indecorous to "out" Stein as a Jew, especially since it is not at all clear what that really means for someone who was not religiously observant, did not observe dietary laws (Toklas's cookbook is full of pork and shellfish recipes), and had no interest in Zionism. On the other side, staunchly culturally identified, nonreligious Jews like the WBAI moderator from JFREJ take issue with Stein's lack of public solidarity with other Jews, seeing her as an assimilationist of a worse type than the secular Jews Freud, Marx, and Emma Goldman, the latter of whom qualify as (JFREJ-type) Jews by their political engagements. Claims such as mine—that Stein's Jewishness is, arguably, a language practice—can sound vaguely essentialistic, in the vein of Otto Weininger's thought, which I will discuss in more detail below (preview: he's one of the "villains" in what follows, though I find a certain pathos in the configurations of his particular dementia Judaica). Thus Stein's Jewishness is a topic that is best approached obliquely, as she herself does; with narrative tentativeness; with an openness toward the inclusion of fragment-clues and minutiae free-floating through her work like sidereal flotsam, as well as toward broad disciplinary inquiries into "the status of the social sciences at the turn of the century" and other such currents of humanistic cliché that, when delved into, relinquish their apparent predictability and turn into discoveries maybe intuited but nonetheless finally surprising. For many, it is not a topic whose viability is immediately self-evident; I was told by another scholar whose specialty is Jewish women poets, "If you can find Jewishness in Stein you can find it anywhere." I have learned, moreover, that the editors of a forthcoming encyclopedia of Jewish American playwrights and poets almost decided to exclude Stein, changing their minds only at the insistence of a prominent avant-gardist who was one of their advisors on the project. Likewise, although the very useful *Jews and Gender: Responses to Otto Weininger,* edited by Nancy Harrowitz and Barbara Hyams, refers correctly to Stein as having been influenced by Weininger's writings, there is no essay on this subject in the book, which deals copiously with Weininger and Joyce (fully three essays dedicated to this topic), as well as Apollinaire, Heine, and German novels in general.[3] Split into strict halves, the book addresses first the "scientific," social-context aspect of its thorny subject—Weininger as a Viennese, as a liberal, Weininger and Freud, Lombroso, and Wittgenstein respectively; the second half comprises the literary essays enumerated above. And where, indeed, given the scope of Stein's inquiry, would one "place" such an essay? Anyone wanting to investigate Stein's relationship to the forms and styles of "Jewishness" that prevailed during her long life needs to be, as she believed herself to be, both social "scientist" and "artist." These comprise a specious binarism, of course; they also express the becoming-oxymoron of the "social scientist" as that disciplinary identity took shape during Stein's era.

It is precisely this binarism to which Otto Weininger appeals in the introduction to his notorious *Sex and Character* (1903), a volume inaugurating (according to the German publisher's preface to the posthumous—post-suicide—authorized edition) the psycho-philosophical science of "characterology."[4]

Briefly, Weininger, working out of a European tradition of first religious and then scientific anti-Semitism and misogyny, proposes that "genius"—that is, the capacity to develop to the fullest extent the rational, humanistic spirituality necessary to become a fully actualized (as contemporary New Agers might say) individual—is the sole province of the Aryan male, and is inaccessible to (Aryan) women and (male) Jews. This is because characterologically (character being a combination of biological, moral, and intellectual temperament), Jews and women are incapable of self-sufficiency—that is, they have no "center," no soul, no being-in-themselves; they are reactive and parasitic, concerned only with physical survival. Weininger stresses that he is not concerned, in his scheme, with literal Jews and Aryans, with literal men and women; these are "platonic" conceptions, which in some measure are manifested in real individuals but function more nearly as tendencies; all Jews and Christians are combinations of Jew and Christian, all men and women are properly bisexual, with a tendency toward one pole or the other.[5] Thus, for example, the crowning achievement of Jesus, the act that represented his genius, was that, though he was Jewish, he killed the Jew in him to found Christianity.[6] For Weininger, this example provides the only possible solution to the Jewish question. The individual Jew must, through "steady resolution, united to the highest self-respect," overcome, like Jesus, his own Judaism. Zionism is out of the question, for it does not save the Jew; it merely isolates him.[7]

Weininger's insistence on a wholistic, rational/moral individualism and on the perfectibility of society in a clear-cut and narrow teleology of values, through the self-initiated perfectibility of the individual, constitutes his liberalism. The belief in human progress along individual lines, but conforming nonetheless to a universally applicable ideal, comprises the heart of liberalism. Steven Beller has drawn a useful distinction between "intolerant" and "tolerant" liberalism; pluralism is intrinsic to the latter, but has no place in the former (we can see this distinction played out in contemporary debates about multiculturalism: will "difference" strengthen or weaken national unity? The question liberalism cannot ask is, Why should national unity be the bottom line?).[8] Weininger clearly falls in the former camp; human rationality is defined as a single style of thinking—that of the Aryan/Christian male; human morality has one universal code—that of the Aryan/Christian male. One can also see the nature of Weininger's assimilationism, which was a strange twist on the progressive thought of his time. While many liberal Jews, the sociologist Maurice Fishberg among them, advocated assimilation under the aegis of a pluralistic tolerance (i.e., Jews should not be forced to be other than Jews, but they should enjoy full and egalitarian contact with the Gentile mainstream—short of intermarriage in which the offspring become non-Jewish—and have full access to rights and opportunities enjoyed by Gentiles), Weininger's solution resonates with an older model of assimilation—that is, conversion.[9] But it is not so much a religious conversion as a characterological one, and it must, of course, be voluntary, individually undertaken, and profound, not cosmetic—the result of rigorous soul-searching and ruthless introspective asceticism. Weininger brings the Protestant work ethic to bear on the self-help project of Jewish assimilation.

However, this linear logic, meant to save Western civilization, doomed him to suicide. Trapped in a system of thinking in which he believed himself to have found the answer, but unable to actualize it in the world (in his own being), he was condemned to a certain teleological track that was self-canceling.

The overdeterminism of Weininger's binarisms—Jew/Aryan, woman/man, Hebraism/Christianity, body/soul—articulates an almost decadently extreme dialectic—the end point of modernism, perhaps, a line of reasoning atrophied from inbreeding. Weininger does in fact advocate letting the human race perish rather than perpetrate the immorality of coitus—immorality because it requires that man partake of woman's lack of identity by objectifying her; though she is in fact nothing but an object of man's projections, his moral integrity rests on him treating her as if she were capable of humanity.[10] It is not hard to see how Stein may have found Weininger's ethically argued distaste for heterosexual coitus reassuring (Charlotte Perkins Gilman, an American feminist and economist, was also taken with his work); likewise, his theory of universal bisexuality, which Freud later adopted, gave philosophical permission for sexual minorities to place themselves within a continuum of social normativity. What is fascinating is how Stein's early enthusiasm for this straightforwardly misogynistic, anti-Semitic tract is later reworked; she revises its uncompromisingly unilinear premise of progress (Weininger argues that at least in theory all people can and must kill the woman and the Jew in them to become the supreme individual, the Aryan male) into an emergent dialogic, one that finds emancipationist possibilities in precisely the putatively unwholesome elements of character, speech, and thought in woman and Jew that Weininger contemned.

Like Stein, other Jewish contemporaries of Weininger, such as Freud (*Jokes and Their Relation to the Unconscious,* essentially an affectionate ethnic manifesto whose closest contemporary analogue is Henry Louis Gates Jr.'s *Signifying Monkey*), Theodore Reik, and Maurice Fishberg (*The Jews: A Study in Race and Environment,* 1911), also studied the "problem" of "Jewishness" as social scientists (Freud, unlike Fishberg, tending also toward an essayistic, humanistic model of exposition) in ways that affirmed, rather than denounced, the Jews' perceived specialness as an ethnic group.[11] Stein, too, in her very challenge to the concept or desirability of identity, in her very claim that identity is relational rather than innate and autonomous, enacted and affirmed a kind of Jew-ishness that eschewed fixed categories and unilinear ways of thinking, thus in-stantiating Weininger's charges of Jews' faulty reasoning-cum-being-in-the-world while championing that psychic style as valid, liberating, and intellectu-ally and aesthetically rewarding.

Sander Gilman has thoroughly documented how Weininger's ideas grow out of a history of first religious, then scientific anti-Semitism in Europe, in which stock indices of Jewish difference were codified into a normative discourse that influenced Jewish social scientists such as Cesare Lombroso, Arthur Schnitzler, Joseph Jacobs, Maurice Fishberg, and Freud, as well as their Gentile colleagues. Jewish creativity, insofar as it existed at all (which Weininger ruled out), was in-tertwined with Jewish "madness" and melancholia, Jewish sexuality was linked with Jewish pathology, Jewish "inauthenticity" was seen to be either innate (Weininger) or a result of millennia of oppression, and so on. And Gilman bluntly asserts biographical detail as crucial in understanding these men's intel-lectual formations, and conversely reads intellectual treatises as barely veiled au-tobiographical position papers: "The self-hating Jew Otto Weininger . . . was both a baptized Jew and a repressed homosexual";[12] "Like the Jew in Viennese society [i.e., Freud, whose theory of creativity and sublimation Gilman is reca-pitulating], the creative figure must deny his essence to become what he can be-come."[13] Gilman's own projections give permission to see Stein's oeuvre as, if not representationally autobiographical (though that too, in some pieces), at least firmly situated within the context of debates about Jewishness that were part of the psycho-philosophical backdrop of modernist (theories and practice of) creativity.

As Gilman, again, has argued, the emergence of the twentieth century marked not only the emergence of European and American Jews and women as political actors on their own behalf, but also the rise of a host of sciences de-signed in part to contain these insurgencies through the establishment of racial, ethnic, and gender characteristics that determined immutable differences be-tween demographic groups.[14] For Jews placing themselves in the mainstream in-tellectual life of the twentieth century, the challenge was to position themselves in relation to these sociobiological, psychological, sexological, and anthropolog-ical systems in a way that did not subordinate them to these discourses of classi-fication and control but rather enabled them to participate affirmatively in the process of social definition. Unlike Weininger, many did not repudiate their own Jewishness but rather used the concept of ethnic classification to affirm what they felt to be special about their culture. Gilman has shown that Freud goes further than simple affirmation; his theory of creativity disentangles what had been articulated (by Cesare Lombroso and others) as the nexus of creativity and madness characterizing the Jewish psyche. In Freud's view, creativity is part of everyday life and everyone's working consciousness and unconscious, rather than the special and pathological purview of one "race"; "madness" is recast as "psychopathology," a current running through everyday life—part of, one might say, "everybody's autobiography." Freud, in other words, takes what is Other and universalizes it, not as a way of robbing Jews/we Others of their specialness but instead, as the Jewish orchestrator of theory, to give the Jewish gift (noblesse oblige, a bit) to the world, alerting it to its own unplumbed resources of wit, imagination, and magical logic.

On the other end of the century's first half, on the other side of the cultural loss comprising the Holocaust, Euro-Jewish anthropologists like Franz Boas and Melville Herskovits could no longer be naive or even fearfully premonitory about the potentially genocidal implications of their chosen science. After World War II their task became, rather than building the social sciences, a rescue mission for the reputation of their now-tarnished-beyond-mere-speculation discipline: its assumptions, methodologies, and responsibilities.

An egregious typographical error concludes the anthropologist Melville Herskovits's tribute to his mentor Franz Boas, an error that reveals the anxiety that plagued Jewish social scientists of the early twentieth century. The passage is meant to be the climax of an appeal to the ethical responsibility of the ethnographic or anthropometric researcher, but gets twisted up in a double negative that directly countermands that appeal. Herskovits oulines the two clear duties of the ethical social scientist:

> as a scientist, the anthropologist studies his problem and publishes his results. With other scientists, he seeks the answer to this basic ethical problem, as yet unsolved, of how to ensure that his findings *are used* by those who would direct them toward ends *inimical* to the canons of morality of the scientific tradition within which he works. (my emphasis)[15]

Herskovits writes in the 1950s, after the world had witnessed the ways the Nazis had used the discourse of anthropometry and racial difference in the service of genocidal imperialism. However, he points to the care with which progressive social scientists like Boas had to position themselves even before the Nazi decimation. Placing his ultimate faith in scientific objectivity, Herskovits describes the perversion of the "science" of anthropometry to enable rationales for fascism: the "cephalic index," the famous head-shape index, was "transmuted (from a 'simple device to further the quantitative analysis of differences in physical type') into a qualitative expression to designate a presumably superior 'race,' first called Teutonic, then Nordic, and still later Aryan." He then cites another problem, namely, that the destruction of indigenous cultures, a phenomenon now called "ethnocide," can be brought about by (Western) people with advanced technology, even those with good intentions vis-à-vis indigenous well-being—a group in which the ethnographer would certainly claim membership. But for all his insight about anthropologists' complicity with systems of world domination they putatively abhor (prescient of the debates surrounding the "new ethnography" of today), his belief that careful and disinterested research can save the day is dramatically negated by the text itself. The typographical error perfectly, though unintentionally, reveals the contradiction embedded in progressive Jewish social scientists' agenda, and the poignancy of their predicament: they were trying to do emancipatory work in a discourse inimical to such work—and to them as subjects marginal to the predominant Western humanist project.

Both Herskovits and Boas were towering figures in the development of American anthropology; both considered themselves firmly in the tradition of anthropometrics and "physical anthropology," though they are now known more for their work in African American and Native American culture, respectively. Boas's influence reached across disciplines: in literary studies, he is perhaps best known for having encouraged his student Zora Neale Hurston to collect folk materials from her own ethnic group. Herskovits, whose students included Katherine Dunham, the revolutionary choreographer who drew heavily on traditional Afro-Caribbean dance, is pivotal in arguing for recognition of an African diaspora culture that included pre-slavery, West African ethnic elements. Though it has come under critique and revision in contemporary diaspora studies, this project is acknowledged to be a quite consciously antiracist attempt to establish a preexisting culture for a people cast in popular discourse as atavistic and cultureless. (And, we might add to our discussion of the displaced fascination with displacement that befalls some Jewish anthropologists whose subject is non-Jews, Herskovits's project establishes a cultural "home" or point of origin—West Africa—for a people exiled into slavery. While the fetishizing of origins is precisely one of the tenets now challenged by contemporary anthropological, African diaspora, and Jewish cultural studies, it is important to remember that the Jewish Herskovits was writing about American blacks at the same time that Stalin was describing Jews pejoratively with the epithet "homeless cosmopolitans").

Chronologically, Gertrude Stein wrote the works collected posthumously as *Painted Lace, and Other Pieces, 1914–1937,* the text I examine most closely in this essay, between the eras of Weininger's wild popularity and the postwar reckoning of the humanistic sciences and the Jews who participated in them, which I have epitomized in Herskovits's garbled tribute to his mentor.[16] Though written well beyond the period of her early enthusiasm for Weininger's book (which was published when she was still living in Baltimore), and after she had definitively left the field of psychology, *Painted Lace* evinces a preoccupation with nationalism, race/religion/ethnicity, gender and sexuality, and most important, the way writing and language inform and/or "unmean" these social categories. The volume's governing metaphor, painted lace, moreover, serves as a slightly defamiliarized image of alphabetic writing on a page, calling to mind Derrida's well-known essay "The Violence of the Letter," which centrally features the juxtaposed images of a tribal chief "writing" incomprehensibly in imitation of his Western visitors and the traditional linear cross-hatchings and other designs on the ceramic pots produced by the indigenes.[17] Why not recognize the latter as a form of writing that predates the arrival of Western culture with its "corrupting" (read literate) influence? Why not recognize "painted lace," esoteric, "precious," or eccentric—"corrupt"—"Jewish"—"womanish"— modes of inscription as worthy emblems of expressive culture alongside and permeating those of the Aryan Male Speaking/Writing?

I have learned that one dear colleague, whose anthropological work treats American Jews, characterizes my work as addressing "Jews who are hated by other Jews." "Bad" Jews? Like Stein, Lenny Bruce, myself, and my dear elusive father the head-measurer? Like Weininger? I have no love for the latter, so rest assured, though the pathos of his tragic vision and life has a chrysalis-like cachet that seals him from the utter contempt he'd have merited had he "successfully" "transcended" his "Jewishness." But the pathos that constitutes his one saving grace (in addition, perhaps, to his theory of universal bisexuality, which Freud made famous) meets its match in Gertrude Stein's assertive appropriation of his damning characteristics of Jewish men and all women; though Stein's Jewishness has many times been dismissed as a minor aspect of her life and work, and her qualifications as a "good Jew" many times challenged, it simply cannot be argued that she was ashamed or conflicted about her status as a Jew, though often her work questions what exactly being a "Jew" means. That she, like Freud and Weininger, was a secular Jew is quite obvious; that she, like Freud and Weininger, held a (then considered liberal) assimilationist position could be argued for or against; that she, like Freud and unlike Weininger, enjoyed being Jewish is, I believe, palpably demonstrable.

I have written elsewhere of Stein's affirmative though only symbolic use of Yiddish (as I read her title "Yet Dish") as a metaphor for modernist language use and sensibility. I use the qualifying phrase "only symbolic" because Stein, as a German Jew, probably never spoke Yiddish (though Alice, as a Hungarian Jew, may have; Stein called her "my little Hebrew," indicating that she may have felt

Alice to be "more Jewish" than herself), and she certainly doesn't use Yiddish phrases in her work; she uses, rather, the idea of Yiddish as a flexible, makeshift emergency-condition collage-n that stretches across homelands and host lands, history and geography—to conflate Czeslaw Milosz's phrase that "language is the only homeland" and Jonathan Boyarin's image of the book as portable homeland, Stein creates makeshift homelands in books composed of language that itself is not stable, but portable, mobile, motile. In other words, language for Stein is not the safe haven it may be for Milosz, but enacts the instability that necessarily informs a Jewish notion of home.[18]

Through this type of practice, I would claim, Stein valorizes verbal styles— repetition, circularity, "imprecision," unconventional syntactic and semantic constructions—that were despised as primitive, and that were literally thought to mark the speaker or writer as less than fully human. As Daniel Boyarin has written, it is considered a religious obligation in Jewish intellectual tradition to push language—both production and interpretation thereof—to its limits.[19] While Stein is obviously not religious, her practice demonstrates the secularization of this tenet with regard to production; Freud's and Walter Benjamin's oeuvres amply instantiate its interpretive aspect. (In *QED*, the Stein character asserts, "I have the failing of my tribe. I believe in the sacred right of conversation even when it is a monologue."[20]) Also, I feel compelled to draw attention to her championing of the "Old Testament" as a model for "new" (experimental) American writing because of its stylistic tendency toward parataxis in "Lecture II: Narration." Erich Auerbach makes much the same point in *Mimesis,* which is generally acknowledged to have been written in response to the Holocaust he was surviving in Turkey—and, interestingly, complicity is not a charge commonly leveled at him as it is at Stein, who made her plea for the Old Testament's centrality to Western culture in 1935.

At the same time, however, Stein's apprehension of the instability of language (and her concerted experiments in language use) and of domicile does not have the catastrophizing angst of a Weininger, who understood psycholinguistic flux, polyvocality, multiple identity, and diffuse proliferation as atavistic and profoundly detrimental to the progress of a rational humanity. "The psychological contents of the Jewish mind are always double or multiple," writes Weininger.

> There are always before him two or many possibilities, where the Aryan, although he sees as widely, feels himself limited in his choice. I think that the idea of Judaism consists in this want of reality, this absence of any fundamental relation to the thing-in-and-for-itself. . . . He

can never make himself one with anything—never enter into any real relationships.[21]

For him this was tragic; Jews (and women) were the ultimate negation of all that Man could and should be, and this nadir of human potential was bodied forth in language use, which is the medium of exchange in human relations. For Stein, the instability of identity, or its illusory nature, permitted community, social being-in-flux, and relationality to flourish and create new ways of apprehending reality as non-possessive:

> I am I because my little dog knows me. The figure wanders on alone.
> . . . The person and the dog are there and the dog is there and the person is there and where oh where is their identity, is the identity there anywhere.[22]

Knowing that for Stein "there"-ness is a suspect category, one can understand this as a challenge rather than a plaint; the poem, the first sentence of which functions as a kind of talisman sentence for Stein, becomes a treatise on the difference between "entity" (the unfixability of an apprehended "other"/object/ being) and "identity," a need to be fixed, recognized, and given meaning by an other. For Stein, making oneself One with anything, recognizing something in and for itself (whatever that may be), would be the kiss of death—as it was for Weininger.

It would bespeak a naive need for absolutes, however, to impute a callousness to Stein's ludic writing; one has only to look at work produced during the Reich to see that she and other secularized Jews were acutely tuned to the underside of displacement and instability. The tinge of melancholy in, say, *Paris France* or Walter Benjamin's "Berlin Chronicle" (a piece that makes clear Benjamin's felt relationship between urban *flânerie* and global uprootedness) is not due to a thwarted faith in origins but rather to the thwarted desire (to be encouraged) to explore—through memory and language—the processes of memory, language, and human being itself.[23] This exploration had been these writers' most compelling raison d'être. The wistful meanderings of these works in style and content—tentative here, sure there; sketchy and aphoristic here, humorously detailed and obsessively developed there—enact a non-identitarian, historically contingent "Jewish" writing practice that is most beautiful and exemplary where (when) it is most—literally—under the gun. The fear I saw in Stein's and Toklas's I.D. photos for wartime travel—and the excessive absurdity of Benjamin's (as it turns out) unnecessary suicide—indicate both the fragility and resilience of this living-in-style—this lived style, this writing life.

DIS PLAYST READINGS

The phrase "Painted Lace" serves as title for volume 5 of Stein's unpublished writings written during and after, and much affected by, World War I. It is also the name of a piece within that volume. The phrase offers a marvelous metaphor for the sense of redundancy-that-is-not-redundant, gilding the lily, "independent embroidery" (the title of another poem in the volume), a sense of performative excess that is, nonethless, not expendable. Yet another title in that volume, "Emp Lace," combines the two phrases and simultaneously fractures the word "emplace(ment/ meant)," whose militaristic positionality is untenable in a nomadic, free-range exilic language style implied by lace, by "independent embroidery." What can "emp lace" mean? Caveat emptor: language as commodity, as excuse for world-warfare, is being "unmeant," emp-tied and untied, loosened like lace that lets the light through, like a writing we can't read straight and shouldn't, if we want in on the shaggy dog joke, the endless yarns spun by an a-mused, Fate/fé/friend-of-Faÿ/lady-fairy who never cuts that thread after all. In the art of "lace," threads derive their aesthetic power from interplay with "negative" space, emptiness (which Weininger claims to be the essence, insofar as there is one, of both Jews—"the absolute Jew is devoid of a soul"—and women),[24] just as Steinian non-sense derives its power to "unmean" from the rigidly semantical context of most discursive forms, including that of social science, our special concern here, and its relation to the "Jewish question." In lacing language, Stein ties the "not" that Melvillowitz forgot and that Weininger fought.

Likewise "Painted Lace" splits, opens, enlaces, and aerates Place by interjecting a space and the extra lace of "ainted" letters. "Ainted" elaborates and negates ungrammatically in a stage aside (P-lace is still there, though displaced); Stein is "Arthur/ author(ing) a Grammar" (How to Write). Decentered? You bet. Weininger's worst fears flaunted: himself, the Jewish homosexual, in drag, camping it up, reveling in his/her defects. "I'm a Jew, how 'bout u?" Stein teases Wein's ghost, by performing her tainted JEWOMANISH writing in calm, experimental tones. "What happens," the Jewoman scientist asks, "when we separate these two letters?" Oy, such cold experimentation, treating language as if it were dead matter: Jews excel in the field of chemistry, says Weininger, because "they cling naturally to matter, and expect to find the solution of everything in its properties."[25] Unlike Goethe's, the greatest genius of Weininger's imagining, Stein's work is not about Feelings, not about individual self-consciousness developing ethically. Vey iz mir! It doesn't track like the transparent thoughts of the male Aryan, O mighty hunter

He, following the lettered spoor of The Great Idea to its Godly punctum, a humble manger that is the origin of all meaning. Instead, the Fat Lady's text winds around and around, has no beginning and no end, not even any middle or edge. It's all marginalia to itself, Talmudic bordering on borders, embroidery that has taken off from an always-already infinite regress of no regrets and plenty of rsvps.

As its name suggests, the section of *Painted Lace* entitled "Voice Lessons and Calligraphy" addresses, among other subjects, writing style, composition, the relationship between orality and graphology, domesticity and the "feminine" arts. By presenting both media (speaking and writing) in terms of refined, mannered mastery of a relatively old-fashioned (and thus cosmetic/frivolous) "finishing school" type of art, Stein foregrounds the artificiality, the made-ness (constructedness, as we might say now), of both speech and writing, anticipating the Derridean controversy and placing herself in the stream of the latter's argument, that is, in accord with his challenge to the supremacy and presumed anteriority of "the Voice." The section opens with "Independent Embroidery," which phrase operates, as I have suggested above, as a kind of governing trope for "Jewomanish" language use: diffuse, elaborative, inauthentic, and defective, according to Weiningerian Austro-liberal values. Within this section, a short poem called "The Reverie of the Zionist" concludes,

> I saw [*sic*] all this to prove that Judaism should be a question of religion.
> Don't talk about race. Race is disgusting if you don't love your country.
> I don't want to go to Zion.
> This is an expression of Shem.[26]

Insofar as Judaism is a race, race should be uncoupled from nationalism; the notion that countries should be the provenance or teleological punctum of particular ethnicities is abhorrent to Stein, who loves living in France and also, from a distance, at least claims to love America, and has no similar feelings about Zion. Some have read this piece as Stein's repudiation of her Jewishness; however, the argument that Jews did not constitute a "race" was a popular one among progressive Jews in the interbellum period, Boas and Herskovits among them. Concerned about the anti-Semitic repercussions of how National Socialism had scientized (racialized) the Jewish question, they took the position that Jews should not be persecuted on the basis of race; and in order to argue this attempted to demonstrate that Jews were not a racial group. Moreover, in line with these secular Jews who on the one hand were not particularly observant but on the other hand did not want to be perceived/persecuted as a race, the last line suggests that the foregoing ought to be a legitimate opinion to hold as a

Jew. The piece appears to be shot through with contradictions; the "reverie" of the Zionist is anti-Zionist, Stein deliberately distances herself from some Jews ("Can we believe that all Jews are these") while claiming the right to speak as a Jew, and so forth. It must be remembered that the word "reverie" may have had negative overtones for Stein, who stubbornly resisted any charges of mysticism in her work, and who saw herself as a phenomenological empiricist, tracking the minutiae of the changes of human mind for the pleasure of it—a disinterested scientist. Thus the Zionist is indulging in pipe dreams; Zionism is the opiate of the Jewish masses. The piece also has in it some of the anxiety betrayed by the error in Herskovits's book (which may not have been his error at all, but that of a typesetter, copyeditor, etc.; one Jewish colleague even suggested to me that an anti-Semitic publisher may have purposefully allowed the error to stand—this seems far-fetched to me, but the fact that someone had that idea indicates the depth of even ostensibly assimilated Jews' fears)—how to "rationalize" a situation whose irrationality threatens to (and did) overwhelm and exterminate an entire people? The apparent contradictions also enact the internal heterogeneity, the contentious pluralism that comprises the Jewish interpretive community. These concerns about the nature of race and its relation to geography run throughout the rest of the volume, particularly in "Landscapes and Geography: 1925–1934," in which the words "natural" and "national" are juxtaposed,[27] and in which the ideological manipulation of social categories such as matrilineality, difference, and race/religion are subject to inquiry:

Can a Christian father have a Christian mother.
Yes.
Can a Christian mother have a Christian father.
Yes.[28]

It is very necessary that natural phenomena are usual. It is very much it is very much used it is used very much in that way.
    There are three Negroes they do not at all resemble one another.
    Moreover there are three Negroes Negroes and women five of them and they do not at all resemble one another. It is not at all astonishing that one seeing them and seeing them knows very well then that it is another thing.[29]

When Stein writes, "Authorize natural phenomena" (215), natural phenomena are understood to be that which can be written—that is constructed creatively, as in "arthur a grammar." Nationalism and claims of naturalism are both systems of meaning created by and not anterior to "human mind," "never having been meant to be Natural Phenomena" (207) as commonly understood—that is, as bio-essential hardwiring. However, "Natural Phenomena" is also queer girl sex: "Aroused and dedicated to natural phenomena . . . pearly and seized" (207). What has been declared deviant by racial nationalist logic is as natural a phenomenon as landscapes, geography and writing. That is, it is all authored, all emptied, all painted lace, a vocal exercise.

One could say that Herskovitz espouses Weiningerian teleology when he appeals to the twin virtues of hard science and humane citizenship, those golden sons of the Western metaphysics of unity, that Enlightenment legacy that ended, as he knew but did not want to know, in Auschwitz. Someone's typographical error that put him in the "wrong" camp may not have been as much of a wandering as one might have wished for. While there is, obviously, a vast difference between racist and antiracist anthropology (and its cousins philosophy, "characterology," psychology, sociology, etc.), between Weininger and Herskovits, they have a common ideology that anxiety-induced lapses can throw into relief. Stein's language experiments eviscerate the truth claims of the modern(ist) achievements—rationalism and liberal morality—that the philosopher Weininger and the scientist Herskovitz continue to cling to. This evisceration carries with it a different set of risks, which are becoming apparent in a world where, for example, Jean Baudrillard can claim that there was no Gulf War. Stein's work, however, neither collapses in despairing self-immolation nor issues prescriptives in a tinny, would-be heroic resistance to history. Relatively early in her career, it seems, Stein abandoned the idea of progress to which her two coreligionists were tightly bound—but she did not do so in a gesture of nihilism. And while thematically her writing continues to participate in their concerns— concerns about her own survival—her writing process and practice have already created an escape route, a "line of flight." Her work doesn't strive to get "there"—no landscape, nation, or race except in words, and even those words are not a place but a naughty, knotty emp lace, but, but . . .

In revisiting this essay, an earlier version of which appeared in *Modern Fiction Studies* a few years ago, I realize that what might appear as an implicit apologetics for Stein's politics (or lack thereof), most notably the stylistic excursions into flights of—of fun but slightly triumphalist lyricism, shouldn't necessarily be allowed the "last word," though formally it would be very satisfying to do so. So let me add to that extremely final-sounding finale above the monition to hold our "three faces of modernism"—Weininger, Herskovits, and Stein—in an unresolved tension that highlights the tangled conflicts and confluences of liberalisms, radicalisms, and politics of style that marked assimilated and/or secularized Jews' participation in the mainstream modernist project.

NOTES

1. See Maria Damon, "Gertrude Stein's Doggerel 'Yiddish': Women, Dogs, and Jews," in *The Dark End of the Street: Margins in American Vanguard Poetry* (Minneapolis: University of Minnesota Press, 1993), 202–35.

2. Gertrude Stein, *The Making of Americans* (New York: Harcourt, Brace, 1934), 21.

3. See Nancy A. Harrowitz and Barbara Hyams, *Jews and Gender: Responses to Otto Weininger* (Philadelphia: Temple University Press, 1995), esp. p. 5.

4. Otto Weininger, *Sex and Character,* authorized and anonymous translation from the 6th German edition (London: Heinemann, 1906).

5. Weininger, 311.

6. Weininger, 327–28.

7. Weininger, 312.

8. Steven Beller, "Otto Weininger as Liberal?" in Harrowitz and Hyams, *Jews and Gender: Responses to Otto Weininger,* 91–101, 91–92.

9. See Maurice Fishberg, *The Jews: A Study in Race and Environment* (London: Walter Scott, 1911).

10. Weininger, 343ff.

11. See Freud, *Jokes and Their Relation to the Unconscious,* trans. James Strachey (New York: Norton, 1960).

12. Sander Gilman, *The Jew's Body* (New York: Routledge, 1991), 133.

13. Gilman, 138.

14. See Sander Gilman, *Jewish Self-Hatred: Anti-Semitism and the Hidden Language of the Jews* (Baltimore: Johns Hopkins University Press, 1986).

15. Melville Herskovits, *Franz Boas: The Science of Man in the Making* (New York: Charles Scribner's Sons, 1953), 104.

16. Gertrude Stein, *Painted Lace, and Other Pieces, 1914–1937* (New Haven: Yale University Press, 1955).

17. Jacques Derrida, "The Violence of the Letter: From Levi-Strauss to Rousseau," in *Of Grammatology,* trans. Gayatri Chakravorty Spivak (Baltimore: Johns Hopkins University Press, 1974), 101–40.

18. Jonathan Boyarin, "Jewish Ethnography and the Question of the Book," in *Storm from Paradise: The Politics of Jewish Memory* (Minneapolis: University of Minnesota Press, 1992).

19. Daniel Boyarin is cited in Jonathan Boyarin, *Palestine and Jewish History: Criticism at the Borders of Ethnography* (Minneapolis: University of Minnesota Press, 1996).

20. Gertrude Stein, *QED,* in *Fernhurst, QED and Other Early Writings* (New York: Liveright, 1971), 57.

21. Weininger, 321–22.

22. Gertrude Stein, "Identity a Poem," in *A Stein Reader,* ed. Ulla E. Dydo (Evanston: Northwestern University Press, 1993), 588–94, 588.

23. See Walter Benjamin, "A Berlin Chronicle," in *Reflections,* ed. Peter Demetz,

trans. Edmund Jephcott (New York: Harcourt Brace Jovanovich, 1978), 3–60; Gertrude Stein, *Paris France* (1940, New York: Liveright, 1970).

24. Weininger, 313.
25. Weininger, 315.
26. Stein, *Painted Lace,* 94.
27. Stein, *Painted Lace,* 209.
28. Stein, *Painted Lace,* 202.
29. Stein, *Painted Lace,* 203.

8

JEAN TOOMER'S *CANE,* MODERNIZATION, AND THE SPECTRAL FOLK

David G. Nicholls

Cane's engagement with both modernity and modernization has been at once the book's most attractive and elusive feature. Because Toomer's 1923 text addresses daily life in the rural South at the beginning of its transformation, it has about it the air of portent, of bearing witness to the passage of history. The book offers both the speculative pleasures of nostalgia and the certainty of historical testimony after the fact of modernization. Toomer's use of modernist formal gestures, such as imagism and pastiche, has underscored his interaction with the metropolitan literary culture of the 1920s and has contributed to *Cane*'s reception as that paradoxical entity, the modernist classic. *Cane* can be seen as both an interpretation of the modernization of African America and a product of that very transformation, for *Cane* would seem to enact the process by which metropolitan cultural forms came to predominate: Toomer published a modernist book that included lyric poems about folk songs. In short, *Cane* is a particularly attractive work for readers attentive to the economic and cultural changes affecting African America in the 1920s.

When *Cane* addresses the status of life in the rural South, it does so less to inquire whether agrarian culture could be maintained than to pay tribute to its passing. Toomer referred to the book as a "swan-song"[1] for the African American "folk," indicating that he took "folk" life to be vanishing and worthy of a final artistic expression: "the Negro of the folk-song has all but passed away," he would tell Waldo Frank.[2] In *Cane*'s first section, set in rural Georgia, we encounter a poem in which the speaker is an auditor to the singing of both the soil and a "song-lit race of slaves."[3] In "Song of the Son," the son is a migrant, now returned to the place of his birth in the South. The second stanza presents the son speaking in apostrophe to the land, his parent:

> O land and soil, red soil and sweet-gum tree,
> So scant of grass, so profligate of pines,
> Now just before an epoch's sun declines
> Thy son, in time, I have returned to thee,
> Thy son, I have in time returned to thee. (14)

The son returns to a denuded pastoral scene "in time," but by this he does not mean he is in time to stop the milling of its forests. Rather, he is in time to catch the "plaintive soul" (14, l. 14) of the soil transmuted into a song that rides through the valley on pine smoke. The son's relief is that he has not missed the brilliance of a sunset, the setting of the "song-lit race of slaves," and his motivation for seeing this spectacle is primarily aesthetic. This motivation is underscored in his second apostrophe, which he makes to "Negro slaves" whom he likens to "dark purple ripened plums" (14, l. 16). Since they are ripened and the tree has grown bare, he is happy to find that one plum and its seed have been saved for him. This seed will turn into "a singing tree" (14, l. 20) in the final stanza of the poem, "Caroling softly souls of slavery" (14, l. 21). The "folk" in this poem has a spectral presence, for the souls of former slaves are transformed into the voice of a singing tree caroling an "everlasting song" (14, l. 20).[4] The landscape at the end of "Song of the Son" holds only an ornamental plum tree that sings instead of bearing fruit.

The son's return to the southern countryside resembles the sojourn Toomer took to Sparta, Georgia, in 1921. Toomer spent two months as a substitute principal for a Negro agricultural and industrial training school there, and his encounter with students and sharecroppers led him to begin writing *Cane* while taking the train home to Washington, D.C.[5] While he may well have expected to have encountered a timeless rural South, Toomer discovered a Georgia in the midst of great economic change. In his recent historical account, *Rural Worlds Lost,* Jack Temple Kirby describes the state of affairs in Georgia's Black Belt:

> By the 1920s its lands were badly worn and eroded and infested with the dreaded boll weevil. Planters cut and sold their second-growth pine, leaving nothing of value on the land. They then began to withdraw, abandoning their property to the poor, or more commonly, to banks and insurance companies. . . . [W]here slaves first planted cotton, the plantation had broken down. This South was no longer modern in any sense.[6]

But if soil exhaustion and the boll weevil had rendered the South "no longer modern," Kirby shows us that "roughly between 1920 and 1960 the American South was modernized; it was not developed."[7] While paved roads, farm machinery, supermarkets, and the cash nexus reorganized agricultural labor and markets, there was no concomitant effort to assure economic autonomy and political modernity for the agricultural workers who were displaced in this period. Accordingly, most displaced workers either migrated or lived in poverty. But when Toomer came to Hancock County in 1921, what we see now as a massive historical change was only beginning. Hancock County's population had been relatively stable from the turn of the century through 1920, but diminished by 29 percent between 1920 and 1930;[8] neighboring Greene County recorded its largest population to date in 1920, before losing nearly half of its black population by 1930.[9] Consequently, while a poem such as "Song of the Son" aims to lament the end of an era, it would seem to do so prematurely. Toomer's intervention on the scene of the changing Georgia countryside is curious, for he imagines the people who attend his school and work the nearby fields as spirits who will live on through their songs. This curious attitude arises out of an ambivalence toward the prospects for cultural and agricultural sustenance in this landscape. In some of the other works in *Cane,* the "ripened plums" (14, l. 16) Toomer sees would be read as an agricultural metaphor for the fertile cultural circumstances here: a bountiful harvest would give rise to joyous singing in the community. Here, however, the plum's seed produces disembodied songs from the antebellum era; the land sustains neither agricultural nor live cultural production. The book, then, seems both to honor rural life and to hasten its passing.

THE "IDENTITY THROUGH FORM" ARGUMENT AND MODERNIST PASTICHE

Cane's position on modern culture has been a frustratingly elusive feature of the book. *Cane*'s modernism—its lack of a coherent formal affiliation or overarching point of view—has made it difficult for readers to name the book's position on modernity. Most scholars have turned to Toomer's own writing on the book and to biographical information to claim that *Cane* is an allegory of the author's achievement of "identity through form."[10] Here, *Cane* is a transitional space in which the author achieves "wholeness" through redemptive contact with the past. Nellie McKay, for example, describes Toomer's trip to Georgia and its generative effects: "He was moved by the folk spirit and the folk as by nothing else before, and he felt that he had found the missing element that he needed to harness his creative talents: a self-confirming sense of wholeness."[11] McKay's analysis, like that of many other critics, is both intentionalist and New Critical: it accepts the author's statements about his intentions for the book and uses these statements to demonstrate how the book fulfills his aspirations for a unified form, an organic whole. By accepting these assumptions, these scholars tend to subsume the book's engagement with modernity to their preoccupation with the artist's consciousness, as in Bernard Bell's description of the book as a poetic *Künstlerroman*.[12] McKay, for instance, locates modernization in Toomer's consciousness:

> [T]he external pressures that created the black folk culture also prevented it from comprehending its own historical and cultural significance. That was the responsibility of those who came later, those sufficiently removed from its influence to temper vision with objectivity and who were yet close enough to feel racial and/or emotional kinship with it.[13]

McKay's assumptions lead her to the questionable conclusion that members of the African American "folk" were incapable of self-consciousness. Further, her analysis would suggest that the value of a work like *Cane* lies in its contribution to a progressive teleology of racial development. The "identity through form" argument understands the book's engagement with modernity and modernization only as an enabling aspect of the artist's cognitive development.

When the "identity through form" argument addresses the formal qualities of *Cane*, it usually attempts to derive the transition narrative of modernization from the book's division into three sections, assigning each a position in various theories of development. Thus Bernard Bell argues,

> Part 1, with its focus on the Southern past and the libido, presents the rural thesis, while Part 2, with its emphasis on the centers of commerce and the superego, offers the urban antithesis. Part 3 then functions as a synthesis of the earlier sections with Kabnis representing the black writer whose difficulty in resolving the tension of his double-consciousness prevents him from tapping the creative reservoir of his soul.[14]

This schematization of the book is compatible with the New Critical under-pinnings of the "identity through form" argument in that it sees the movement of the book as progressing toward wholeness.[15] While the incorporation of the "rural thesis" and "urban antithesis" into the "identity through form" argument complicates our understanding of the book's relation to its historical moment, this gesture fails to capture the full resonance of *Cane*'s engagement with history because the argument is fundamentally committed to proving that the book is a unified and fully formed masterpiece. Indeed, this argument collapses the multiple histories of rural and urban lives presented in *Cane* into one history, the history of the artist and his search for a satisfyingly complete expressive form.

One way to read history back into *Cane* is to address its status as pastiche.[16] The pages of *Cane* present multiple forms, including poetry, fiction, and drama. Rather than seeing Toomer's incorporation of rural and urban settings into *Cane* as productive of a synthetic dialectic striving toward wholeness, we might instead see the book as presenting multiple settings through which to interpret the changes affecting 1920s America. *Cane* understands that the widespread effects of this historic change occurred in different sites, and that they could be interpreted through different forms of representation. My introductory reading of "Song of the Son" has suggested one way aesthetic form mediates historical change in the book: Toomer presents a lyric poem in which the speaker returns to a denuded southern landscape in time to catch the plaintive songs of a spectral "folk." *Cane*, as pastiche, presents many other settings through which to understand economic and cultural change, and yet these multiple settings do not simply provide a benign plurality of points of view. Rather, Toomer's book settles on a pattern of interests. As we will see, this pattern emerges as a preoccupation with male subjectivity, with female reproductive crisis, and with the tension between the crowd and individuality.

ABUNDANCE AND SCARCITY IN THE GEORGIA LANDSCAPE

In *Cane*'s first section, we witness a southern landscape perpetually at dusk, hazy with the smoke from the many timber mills converting the forest into a saleable commodity. "Georgia Dusk," a poem that immediately follows "Song of the Son," situates dusk at the end of the workday at a sawmill and shows how both dusk and the mill have transformed the countryside:

> The sawmill blows its whistle, buzz-saws stop,
> And silence breaks the bud of knoll and hill,
> Soft settling pollen where plowed lands fulfill
> Their early promise of a bumper crop.

Smoke from the pyramidal sawdust pile
Curls up, blue ghosts of trees, tarrying low
Where only chips and stumps are left to show
The solid proof of former domicile. (15)

The ghostly trace of the forest, blue smoke, wends its way through the detritus of its own destruction. The "dusky cane-lipped throngs" (15, l. 28) are accompanied by "the chorus of the cane" (15, l. 23) and the strumming of pine needles. In "Georgia Dusk," a collective voice arises out of the terrain and its populace that bears witness to its passing. The speaker in "Georgia Dusk" is an appreciative but relatively detached auditor to the chorus of its "throngs."

"Georgia Dusk" relates a conflicted message about the countryside's productivity. While the spectral "folk" we heard singing through a tree in "Song of the Son" is now pantheistically heard through pine needles and cane, the landscape here is not so barren as in the other poem.[17] Instead, we read that the "plowed lands fulfill / Their early promise of a bumper crop" (15, l. 11–12), and night is portrayed as a "barbecue" (15, l. 4) and "A feast of moon and men" (15, l. 5). The land would seem to provide an excess of food even as the mills were stripping it of its trees. The fecundity of the land here contributes to the sense in the poem that dusk is a time of leisure. The whistle has blown and work has stopped; it's time to sing and eat. This time is then "an orgy for some genius of the South" (15, l. 6), while it is also the opportunity for spiritual recreation, as the speaker suggests when he calls on the singers to "Give virgin lips to cornfield concubines" (15, l. 27). But if the land was so abundant, why bother to do the work of cutting down the trees to sell them on the lumber market?

Arthur Raper's classic 1936 sociological account, *Preface to Peasantry: A Tale of Two Black Belt Counties,* gives us another view of the Georgia Toomer encountered in 1921. One of the counties Raper studies, Greene County, is only ten miles to the north of Sparta, and they share the same climate, agricultural resources, and cultural dynamics. Raper demonstrates that the collapse of the Black Belt plantation system "leaves in its wake depleted soil, shoddy livestock, inadequate farm equipment, crude agricultural practices, crippled institutions, a defeated and impoverished people."[18] He argues that the collapse provides a preface to peasantry rather than to independent farming, since the workers who inherit the remains of the plantation do not have enough personal or natural resources to sustain themselves. They are consequently open to exploitation as sharecroppers. Raper's sociological analysis concludes that in Greene County in the 1920s and 1930s,

> while a few rural families . . . live well enough, the vast majority have
> but little money; that they buy much of their food, and many of them

are dependent upon landlords for subsistence while growing a crop; that they produce only a small proportion of the meat, milk, eggs, and cereals which they need for their own tables; that they live in unattractive and uncomfortable dwellings; that they have scant household furnishings and but little reading matter; and that they own and work with the crudest kind of agricultural tools—in short, that they maintain a very low plane of living.[19]

This plane of living was precarious and susceptible to collapse. Greene and Hancock Counties had been largely unaffected when the boll weevil invaded its cotton crops in 1916, and speculators thought that the area was "weevil-proof" and invested most of the area's wealth in cotton crops over the following years. When the weevil returned in 1921, the year of Toomer's trip to Sparta, it was not so gracious; a "severe plunge of agricultural prices in 1920" did not help matters.[20] "The year 1921, with very low prices added to the weevil devastation, was a particularly bad one in all parts of the cotton region," concluded one economist.[21] Land value diminished and credit evaporated, and the economy collapsed. Hungry and out of work, 43 percent of Greene County's black population left. In response to the economic crisis, landowners turned to the forest as the last saleable commodity: "By 1923 sawmills were puffing away all over the county. They had become Greene County's major source of income. From the car windows of the Atlanta-Augusta train, as it ran across the county, one could see a score of sawdust piles in 1925."[22] One can imagine Toomer enjoying a similar view on his travels to Sparta and back: as *The History of Hancock County* reports, "the lumber industry has always been profitable in the county, but it was most prosperous from 1920–27. During this period there were 50 to 75 sawmills in operation in various parts of the county. . . . In late years, since most of the original timber had been cut, pulpwood has been the main item in this industry."[23] Even this sector of the economy was under stress in 1921, however; Barbara Foley's recent research indicates that a depression in the lumber industry closed several mills and provoked layoffs.[24]

If Raper's account of the Black Belt during the 1920s explains the place of the sawmill in "Georgia Dusk," it also raises questions about the feast available to the throngs in the evening. Certainly, Toomer was misreading the scene before him. And yet the inconsistency Toomer presents between a fecund Georgia landscape and the stubble of a countryside literally going up in smoke is also endorsed, in part, by Raper. At the end of his study, Raper holds out the possibility that "peasantry in America" could also offer autonomy for former Black Belt sharecroppers.[25] He explains that a constructive land policy for the area will not try to rejuvenate the plantation system, but will succeed "if it enables the

157

poorest farmers to build up the soil, to own livestock, to raise vegetables and fruits for their own tables, to coöperate with their fellows making their purchases and in producing and marketing crops—in short, if it enables the landless farmers to attain ownership on an adequate plane."[26] This never happened, as Kirby has shown us. But as Toomer wrote, the possibility existed, and this may contribute to an explanation of the inconsistency in Toomer's attitude toward agricultural production in the South, for he would seem to celebrate the fecundity of the farm and its promise of economic autonomy and political modernity, while he also proclaims its doom under modernization.

This inconsistency may be mapped across the remainder of the poems in *Cane*'s first section. Some poems, like "Reapers" and "Cotton Song," present scenes of agricultural work without adding the dimension of temporal change. Indeed, in "Reapers" (5), Toomer presents the repetitive motion of "Black reapers" (5, l. 1) swinging their scythes "one by one" (5, l. 4), and when the scene is interrupted by the blade of a mower cutting a field rat, the poem stresses the continuity of the work: "I see the blade, / Blood-stained, continue cutting weeds and shade" (5, l. 7–8). Likewise, "Cotton Song" (11) is a work song in which the speaker invokes his fellow workers to "roll, roll!" (11, l. 8 and 20) as they work: "Come, brother, come. Lets [*sic*] lift it; / Come now, hewit! roll away!" (11, l. 1–2). But while "Cotton Song" represents agricultural labor as a repetitive and continuing activity, "November Cotton Flower" notes the presence of the boll weevil and the effects it has on the crops: "Boll-weevil's coming, and the winter's cold, / Made cotton-stalks look rusty, seasons old, / And cotton, scarce as any southern snow, / Was vanishing" (6, l. 1–4). The poem continues to describe how drought dried up the streams and sent birds into wells in search of water. When the cotton suddenly blooms out of season, "Old folks were startled" (6, l. 10) and the sudden beauty of the event urges fearlessness on those who had lived with the doom of the failed crops. In contrast, then, to "Reapers" and "Cotton Song," this poem presents the field as a site of crisis, and it shows that site transformed by sudden beauty. "November Cotton Flower" shows both agricultural crisis and the potential of renewal.

MALE MIGRATION AND FEMALE REPRODUCTIVE CRISIS

Where the poems in the first section vacillate between celebrating the fecundity of the land and pronouncing it barren, the poems and vignettes in this section are far more consistent when it comes to the topic of women's reproductive prospects. The poems I have discussed so far have generally been enunciated through a man's lyric voice: "Song of the Son" presents the subjectivity of a migrant man, while "Cotton Song" addresses fellow laborers as "brother" (11, l. 1). Two poems present flat descriptions of women as a catalog of traits, and these poems emphasize grotesque and corpselike features. In "Face," a woman's brows are "recurved canoes / quivered by the ripples blown by pain" (10, l. 5–6), while the flesh of her face resembles rotting fruit: "And her channeled muscles / are cluster grapes of sorrow / purple in the evening sun / nearly ripe for worms" (10, 1. 10–13). While the poem's understatement conveys pathos for the woman, it also imparts the message that she is nearly done for. "Portrait in Georgia" also uses the method of cataloging traits—both poems begin with "Hair—" (10; 29)—and continues the practice of portraying woman as corpse. Here, each trait of a white woman's body is revealed as an element of a black man's lynching: "her slim body, white as the ash / of black flesh after flame" (29, l. 6–7). This is a coupling that will result not in reproduction, but death. Women's flesh in these two poems is either rotting or burnt up, and both scarred and "blown by pain" (10, l. 6). These poems help set the context for the vignettes, in which six women are portrayed in various situations of social and reproductive crisis. Given the prevalence in "folk" aesthetics of linking the figure of the mother with agrarian labor so as to secure the perpetuity of peasant life, we might expect the women here to be strong maternal figures working the land.[27] As we will see, none of these women is featured in such a vision, for in *Cane*, the "folk" world is not expected to survive the onset of modernization.

The opening story of the book, "Karintha," begins with an invocation that serves as a call to witness: "Her skin is like dusk on the eastern horizon, / O cant [*sic*] you see it, O cant you see it, / Her skin is like dusk on the eastern horizon / . . . When the sun goes down" (3). The story repeats this invocation midway through its narrative, and again at the end, and we can see the intervening fictional prose as filling in the context for Karintha's association with the dusk. Karintha has been beautiful since birth, and men are anxiously waiting to mate with her, an ominous sign: "This interest of the male, who wishes to ripen a growing thing too soon, could mean no good to her" (3). The scene in "Karintha" could be played against the backdrop of "Georgia Dusk," and it would seem that Karintha will become one of the "cornfield concubines" referred to in the last stanza of that poem. Indeed, we encounter a sawmill in this poem, and the smoke provides a contrast to the "wild flash" (3) of Karintha at twelve: "At sunset, when there was no wind, and the pine-smoke from over by the sawmill hugged the earth, and you couldnt [*sic*] see more than a few feet in front, her sudden darting past you was a bit of vivid color, like a black bird that flashes in light" (3). But her wildness is portentous: Karintha lives in a two-room home, and she "had seen or heard, perhaps she had felt her parents loving" (4), and we discover that "the soul of her was a growing thing ripened too soon" (4). In other words, she starts gratifying men's desires, and in so doing she brings in a lot of capital: "Young men run stills to make her money. Young men go to the big cities and run on the road. Young men go away to college. They all want to bring her money. These are the young men who thought that all they had to do was to count time" (4). Karintha gets pregnant. After she has a child on a bed of pine needles in the forest, the smoke from the smoldering sawdust pile at the nearby mill thickens, suggesting that the child has been burned there as well. The scene in "Karintha" recalls the smoky landscape that animates the spectral "folk" to sing in "Georgia Dusk." The smoke "curls up and hangs in odd wraiths" and was "so heavy you tasted it in water," and a song urges spiritual redemption: "Smoke is on the hills, O rise / And take my soul to Jesus" (4). This tale presents a rural woman who has ripened on the vine, and it blames this spoilage on both the woman's desire for capital and the broad network of exchange by which young men can go off to get capital for her. Karintha's crisis represents—in gendered terms—the crisis of modernization: instead of playing the role of the premodern "earth mother" who reproduces the labor force for the fields, she desires capital, and men abandon the small farm to get money for her through the cash nexus. The story also intermingles the child's soul with the smoke from the burning sawdust, linking the fate of the forest with the child's; it would seem that the dusky beauty of Karintha warns of the setting of an era.

As the sun sets on Karintha, the young men continue to circulate in the world. The women in *Cane*'s first section are stuck in the past, reserved for the admiration of returning migrant men, and they generally do not survive the move from country to city.[28] The narrator of "Fern," an African American man from the North, considers bringing Fern back north with him, but quickly notes "the futility of mere change of place": "Besides, picture if you can, this cream-colored solitary girl sitting at a tenement window looking down on the indifferent throngs of Harlem. Better that she listen to folk-songs at dusk in Georgia, you would say, and so would I" (17). "Fern" tells of the migrant's fascination with a woman whom no man can satisfy. She is presented as a transparent eyeball, for "the whole countryside seemed to flow into her eyes" (17), and one night when he takes her into the canebrake she falls into a religious trance. She speaks in tongues, and sings as a Jewish cantor, then faints. This episode serves to further mystify the woman, while it also provokes gossip: although the narrator is not forced to leave town, he decides to do so after experiencing some insinuating stares. As he leaves, he positions Fern as a permanent fixture of the countryside: "From the train window I saw her as I crossed her road. Saw her on her porch, head tilted a little forward . . . eyes vaguely focused on the sunset. Saw her face flow into them, the countryside and something that I call God, flowing into them" (19). He concludes the story by noting that she is still living there, further emphasizing her immobility.

As I noted earlier, the women in the first section are in various states of social and sexual crisis. The heroine of "Becky," for example, is a white woman with two Negro sons; she is "islandized" (7) by her community in a shack between a road and a railroad track, where she is ostracized and yet supported by the anonymous charity of passersby who leave food and prayers in her yard. One day a train rumbles by and the chimney of her house collapses, killing her; her sons had wandered off long before, "drift[ing] around from job to job" (8). While this story continues the pattern of stressing women's immobility in comparison to men, at least one story ends with a man's entrapment and lynching. The final story of the section, "Blood-Burning Moon," has a black man kill a white man in rivalry for a black woman; predictably, the killer is lynched by a white mob. More than the other elements of the first section, these stories emphasize the agony incumbent on sexual relations across race in Jim Crow society. Where "Karintha" links the heroine's fall to her desire for capital, and where "Fern" fixes its heroine as a spiritual medium, these stories blame social ostracism and its extreme, the mob, for women's reproductive crises; all the stories situate women's crises within the problematic of modernization and migration.

The first section of *Cane* presents a Georgia with an unpromising future. The persistence of smoke denotes the depletion of the last saleable commodity in this area, while the infestation of the boll weevil as noted in "November Cotton Flower" threatens the area's agricultural economy. Toomer's occasional praise of the fecundity of the land and the cultural wealth of the folk songs produced by its workers suggests that he sometimes yearns to endorse the ideal of independent farmers Raper put forth at the conclusion of *Preface to Peasantry.* But Toomer also insists on the depopulation of the landscape, in part by making the singers of "folk" songs a spectral presence, which reveals itself pantheistically through a singing tree, pine needles, the wind in the cane, and blue smoke, and in part by demonstrating in various ways that women cannot provide children in this landscape. The presence of male migrants returning for a visit suggests what Raper confirms empirically: 43 percent of black Americans left Greene County between 1920 and 1930.[29] While many migrants were economic refugees who moved to the closest town that could provide work and food, many others set their hopes on urban life and moved to big cities like Chicago and New York.

THE URBAN CROWD AND THE DRONE'S FANTASY

Washington, D.C., also attracted its share of immigrants from the South, and when Toomer returned home from his sojourn to Sparta, he had a deeper appreciation of the origins of the "wedge of nigger life" (41) on the city's Seventh Street.[30] "Seventh Street" is the opening sketch of *Cane*'s second section, which is set primarily in Washington, and the wedge cuts through the wood we saw being milled in the South: "black reddish blood into the white and white-washed wood of Washington. Stale soggy wood of Washington. Wedges rust in soggy wood. . . . Split it! In two! Again! Shred it!" (41). Urban blacks, the sketch argues, have money to burn, and this allows them to add vitality to a blanched Washington culture: "Money burns the pocket, pocket hurts, / Bootleggers in silken shirts" (41). Washington offers black migrants the pleasures of *flânerie*: members of the crowd breathe the "loafer air" (41) of Seventh Street as they stroll aimlessly in the city's leisure district. Much like the *flâneur* of Baudelaire's Paris, whom Walter Benjamin describes as an idler who "seeks refuge in the crowd," the stroller on Seventh Street spends leisure hours seeking experiences and things to consume.[31] The second section of *Cane* will not endorse cheap amusements as the route to happiness, however. Instead, the section repeats a scene in which the speaker yearns for the pastoral landscape from which the "stale soggy wood" comes, and it imagines this departure as an escape from the urban crowd. In this way, Toomer imitates Baudelaire's ambivalent attitude toward the crowd: "He becomes deeply involved with them, only to relegate them to oblivion with a single glance of contempt," Benjamin writes.[32] But where in Paris the "city dilates to become landscape"[33] in the perception of the *flâneur* and in the lyric practice of the poet, Toomer and his idler project themselves away from Washington toward pastoral solitude in the southern landscape.

Midway through the second section of *Cane*, we encounter a lyric poem whose speaker enjoys a reverie in which he takes flight from an urban crowd and wings himself into the embrace of a farmyard flower. In "Beehive," the speaker is a drone who distinguishes himself from the black masses swarming through an urban nightclub district. The drone, perhaps the insect world's most notorious *flâneur*, drinks with his fellow bees, while he also abstracts himself from the scene and into an agrarian landscape. The poem reads as follows:

> Within this black hive to-night
> There swarm a million bees;
> Bees passing in and out the moon,
> Bees escaping out the moon,
> Bees returning through the moon,
> Silver bees intently buzzing,
> Silver honey dripping from the swarm of bees
> Earth is a waxen cell of the world comb,
> And I, a drone,
> Lying on my back,
> Lipping honey,
> Getting drunk with silver honey,

Wish that I might fly out past the moon
And curl forever in some far-off farmyard flower. (50)

The drone's abstraction from the scene takes him to a pastoral utopia in which he can "curl forever" in the petals of a flower. Never mind that it is the female worker bee, not the drone, who gleans pollen and nectar for the hive; Toomer's error here simply underscores the drone's intention for leisure and his inattention to the collective needs of the hive. Significantly, the poem stops when the bee comes to rest in the flower; solitude, rather than connection with a rural collectivity, is the aim of the fantasy.

For the migrant man in the North, the "mass-heart of black people" (52), as the narrator of "Theater" describes an audience, presents the threat of constraint and isolation. In "Box Seat," Dan Moore is a migrant who feels equally isolated from the middle class and the urban crowd. "Bona and Paul," a story in which Paul is a migrant from the South living in Chicago, dwells on the problems of courtship in an urban setting. Paul, who is dark-skinned, goes on a date with white-skinned Bona at the Crimson Gardens, a white nightclub. Toward the beginning of the story, Paul prepares for his date in his bedroom. His room has two windows, and "Bona is one window. One window, Paul" (73). Paul looks west from his window and sees the South:

> Gray slanting roofs of houses are tinted lavender in the setting sun. Paul follows the sun, over the stock-yards where a fresh stench is just arising, across wheat lands that are still waving above their stubble, into the sun. Paul follows the sun to a pine-matted hillock in Georgia. He sees the slanting roofs of gray unpainted cabins tinted lavender. A Negress chants a lullaby beneath the mate-eyes of a southern planter. Her breasts are ample for the suckling of a song. She weans it, and sends it, curiously weaving, among lush melodies of cane and corn. Paul follows the sun into himself in Chicago. (73)

This passage is remarkable in part because Paul's fantasy turns the earth on its axis, so that the sun sets in the South. In this way, the passage continues the practice of the first section in seeing the South at dusk. The Georgian landscape in Paul's window is fertile, filled with wheat, pines, cane, and corn. The woman, too, is fecund, breaking with the first section's preoccupation with women's reproductive crises. And yet this woman is not nursing a child, but a song, and she weans the song from her breast to send it weaving, like the smoke smoldering in the hills of "Georgia Dusk" and "Song of the Son," through the fields. Similarly, Paul is weaned from his nostalgic projection and "follows the sun into himself in Chicago." He faces the other window, Bona's window, and "with his own glow he looks through a dark pane" (73). This look is ominous, for it foreshadows the scrutiny white customers in the nightclub will pay to his dusky complexion. In contrast to "Box Seat," in which a black crowd proves suffocating, this story displays a white crowd as the source of alienation. But like the drone in "Beehive," Paul experiences a nostalgic projection of a rural utopia, and this experience in "Bona and Paul" provides a contrast to the alienation of an urban scene in which racial difference is a source of scrutiny and shame.

Where the first section of the book conveys a conflicted understanding of the fertility of the southern landscape, such that it is both barren and depopulated and yet holds the possibility of renewal and sustainable peasant autonomy, the second section of *Cane* does not hold out hope for sustenance in the countryside. Here, the South supports the prospect of pastoral solitude, as in the drone's fantasy, but this abundance is also something from which one must be weaned, as Paul understands. This section advocates a speculative return back to agrarian life rather than actual migration. As an argument that this world will not sustain its workers, Toomer provides the poem "Harvest Song," for example, as a bleak counterpoint to the earlier "Cotton Song." This poem is told through the voice of a reaper who cannot eat the harvest he has exhausted himself to reap. Where "Cotton Song" stressed the repetitive nature of field work, the importance of collective camaraderie, and the eventual redemption of the workers by God, "Harvest Song" presents a lone worker who is not likely to survive under current conditions: "I am a reaper. (Eoho!) All my oats are cradled. But I am too / fatigued to bind them. And I hunger. I crack a grain. It / has no taste to it. My throat is dry" (71, l. 26–28). This poem reminds us that if the rural South is utopia, as "Beehive" and "Bona and Paul" have encouraged us to see it, it is a lost utopia even for those who work there. In the second section, the pastoral South offers a point of contrast through which to develop an argument against the crowdedness of urban life; while the section does not praise modern life in the city, it does not offer the prospect of return to rural life, either.

NEW DAWN, EVERLASTING SONG

If the second section of *Cane* would seem to draw the shades decisively, though wistfully, on the vision of rural life Paul saw in the sunset from his Chicago apartment, the third section of the book will return us once again to the Georgia countryside. The third section consists of a closet drama, "Kabnis," in which Ralph Kabnis is a mixed-race northerner returned to a small Georgia town to teach in a Negro school. Toomer, we will recall, had traveled to Sparta to work in such a school in 1921, and we can safely assume that the situation inspired the premise for this story. Like the first section of *Cane*, "Kabnis" expresses an ambivalence about the fertility of the southern landscape. In the first segment of the drama, Kabnis has insomnia, and his restlessness brings him out of his cabin, haunted by his surroundings and the spectral presence of "folk" songs, to beg for salvation: "Dear Jesus, do not chain me to myself and set these hills and valleys, heaving with folk-songs, so close to me that I cannot reach them. There is a radiant beauty in the night that touches and . . . tortures me" (85). Kabnis feels out of touch with his environment, in part because he is a northerner, and this leads him to pine nostalgically for the North, while he also contrasts his situation to the supposed immediacy rural blacks feel for their surroundings: "Christ, how cut off from everything he is. And hours, hours north, why not say a lifetime north? Washington sleeps. Its still, peaceful streets, how desirable they are. Its people whom he had always halfway despised. New York? Impossible. It was a fiction. He had dreamed it. An impotent nostalgia grips him" (86). If Kabnis had "halfway despised" the urban blacks from the North, he now projects the first nostalgic vision in the book of that setting. But in order to relieve himself from a nostalgia that cannot be satisfied, he chooses to construct a pastoralizing interpretive frame around the cabin in the landscape before him: "It becomes intolerable. He forces himself to narrow to a cabin silhouetted on a knoll about a mile away. Peace. Negroes within it are content. They farm. They sing. They love. They sleep. Kabnis wonders if perhaps they can feel him. If perhaps he gives them bad dreams. Things are so immediate in Georgia" (86). As an antidote to his "intolerable" nostalgia for urban life, he appreciates the putative immediacy and peace of the contented Negroes in the cabin. To fully appreciate the "radiant beauty" (85) of the landscape, he must be unchained from himself.

In the drama, Kabnis becomes rather more unhinged than unchained. He becomes terrified of lynching, a terror made palpable when, during a Sunday-morning chat with other middle-class men, a rock hurtles through the window with the message "*You northern nigger, its [sic] time fer y t leave. Git along now*" (92).[34] Kabnis's fear drives him to seek spiritual comfort in alcohol, and he is consequently fired by the principal of the school because, according to the school's principal, "the progress of the Negro race is jeopardized whenever the personal habits and examples set by its guides and mentors fall below the acknowledged and hard-won standard of its average member" (95). Where Kabnis had tried to console himself earlier that his status as a middle-class northerner would protect him from lynching, he now loses that status as well as any assurance that the status would have protected him. Fired, he becomes an apprentice blacksmith, and he discovers the condescension whites convey toward laborers as he struggles to learn on the job. He continues his descent, literally, in a drunken party in the basement of the shop. Here, he denies his black lineage and berates an old man, Father John, a mystic. Kabnis is contemptuous when Father John declares, after years of silence, that the sin the white folks committed during the era of slavery was to make the Bible lie. Kabnis wants "somethin new and up t date" (116). After Kabnis trudges up the stairs to return to work in the shop, we are asked to see Father John and Carrie, a devout woman who cares for him, in a circle of light streaking through the "iron-barred cellar window" (117): Father John and Carrie share out-of-date beliefs that imprison them in the shop's cellar. The slow pace of work in the blacksmith's shop indicates that this trade is out of date too; Kabnis will find nothing new there. But Toomer does not close this hopeless scene by dimming the lights; rather, the narrator presents the image of a southern landscape at dawn, a departure from the prevalent image of the South at dusk: "Outside, the sun arises from its cradle in the tree-tops of the forest. Shadows of pines are dreams the sun shakes from its eyes. The sun arises. Gold-glowing child, it steps into the sky and sends a birth-song slanting down gray dust streets and sleepy windows of the southern town" (117). While Kabnis himself does not become "unchained" from his ambivalence about his racial heritage and his place in the South, the story endorses the possibility of a new dawn for the South through pastoral renewal.

"Kabnis" returns us once again to a conflicted vision of southern prosperity. Where the second section of *Cane* had been fairly decisive about the fate of southern agrarian life, the concluding scene of "Kabnis"—and of the book as a whole—asks us to contemplate the prospect of a new day for the South. For Arthur Raper, this new day would emerge from a constructive land policy and the development of peasant-owned, self-sufficient farms. But Toomer urges spiritual rather than material renewal in *Cane*, and the final scene characteristically features a "birth-song" rather than an actual efflorescence of life. Just as the woman whose "breasts are ample for the suckling of a song" (73) in Paul's vision of the rural South, the sun too sends out a song, and here we can remember the singing of the caroling tree in "Song of the Son" as lyrics that haunted the modernized landscape.

It is telling that when Toomer settles on an image of a productive southern landscape, the landscape's chief product is a new song. While Toomer's project was to articulate a swan song for the "folk," the book also served as an invocation in the most literal sense: as so many critics have noted, *Cane* served as a touchstone for many writers of the New Negro movement and after who chose to produce more "folk"-based aesthetic works. This was not the project Toomer would choose for himself, however; like *Cane* itself, Toomer was preoccupied with spiritual matters after quitting his work in the South. *Cane*'s engagement with the prospects for political modernity in the context of modernization gives us an intricate, if sometimes inconsistent, picture of the transformation of the southern landscape as well as an understanding of the psychological experience of migration and dislocation.[35] His text helps us to understand the rich cultural products of a once-rich agricultural region. As an intervention into the economic consequences of modernization, however, *Cane* presents a dubious legacy: *Cane* conjures up a spectral "folk" singing an "everlasting song" (14, l. 20) when the daily needs of rural southerners were both dire and immediate.

NOTES

This essay is a condensed version of a chapter from my book, *Conjuring the Folk: Forms of Modernity in African America* (Ann Arbor: University of Michigan Press, 1999).

I thank George Hutchinson, Loren Kruger, Jani Scandura, Michael Thurston, and Kenneth Warren for their attention to earlier drafts of this essay, Elizabeth Alexander and Thomas Holt and other members of the African American Studies Workshop at the University of Chicago for their comments, Barbara Foley for sharing her work-in-progress with me, the Mellon and Rockefeller Foundations for funding time to complete the research on the project of which this essay is one part, and the Center for Afroamerican and African Studies at the University of Michigan and the Center for the Study of Race, Politics, and Culture at the University of Chicago for providing comfortable places in which to work.

1. See *The Wayward and the Seeking: A Collection of Writings by Jean Toomer*, ed. Darwin T. Turner (Washington, D.C.: Howard University Press, 1980), 123.

2. *A Jean Toomer Reader: Selected Unpublished Writings,* ed. Frederik L. Rusch (New York: Oxford University Press, 1993), 24.

   As in my larger project exploring the discursive deployment of the "folk" in various narrative contexts during the Harlem Renaissance era, I have put the term "folk" in quotation marks to signal that it is the signification of the term, rather than a particular empirical group, that forms the object of my inquiry here.

3. Jean Toomer, *Cane*, ed. Darwin T. Turner (1923; reprint, New York: Norton, 1988), 14. All further references are to this edition and are cited parenthetically in the text.

4. In describing the "folk" in *Cane* as spectral, I take inspiration from Vera Kutzinski, who has written, "The text's purportedly sensual lyricism, much like the 'radiant beauty' of the southern landscape, has to it an eerie, nightmarish quality that unsettles its readers (or at least this reader) more than it communicates an abiding sense of 'spiritual fusion' and 'harmony.'" See Vera M. Kutzinski, "Unseasonal Flowers: Nature and History in Plácido and Jean Toomer," *Yale Journal of Criticism* 3.2 (1990): 166.

5. The details of this trip have been frequently recounted in the critical literature on Toomer. See in particular Cynthia Earl Kerman and Richard Eldridge, *The*

Lives of Jean Toomer: A Hunger for Wholeness (Baton Rouge: Louisiana State University Press, 1987), 79–116. However, it is possible that some parts of the second section of *Cane* were written prior to his trip to Sparta: see George B. Hutchinson, "Jean Toomer and the 'New Negroes' of Washington," *American Literature* 63.4 (December 1991): 683–92.

6. Jack Temple Kirby, *Rural Worlds Lost: The American South, 1920–1960* (Baton Rouge: Louisiana State University Press, 1987), 31.

7. Kirby, *Rural Worlds Lost,* 119.

8. Forrest Shivers, *The Land Between: A History of Hancock County, Georgia, to 1940* (Spartanburg, S.C.: Reprint Company, 1990), 288.

9. See Arthur F. Raper, *Preface to Peasantry: A Tale of Two Black Belt Counties* (Chapel Hill: University of North Carolina Press, 1936), 184, table 41.

10. See Alan Golding, "Jean Toomer's *Cane*: The Search for Identity through Form," *Arizona Quarterly* 39.3 (autumn 1983): 197–214. Major attempts to articulate the "identity through form" argument include John M. Reilly, "The Search for Black Redemption: Jean Toomer's *Cane*," *Studies in the Novel* 2 (1970): 312–24; Patricia Watkins, "Is There a Unifying Theme in *Cane*?" *College Language Association Journal* 15 (1971–72): 303–5; Bernard W. Bell, "Portrait of the Artist as High Priest of Soul: Jean Toomer's *Cane*," *Black World* 23.11 (September 1974): 4–19, 92–97; Odette C. Martin, "*Cane*: Method and Myth," *Obsidian* 2.1 (1976): 5–20; Howard Faulkner, "The Buried Life: Jean Toomer's *Cane*," *Studies in Black Literature* 7.1 (winter 1976): 1–5. See also the various positions elaborated in Therman O'Daniel, ed., *Jean Toomer: A Critical Evaluation* (Washington, D.C.: Howard University Press, 1988).

11. Nellie Y. McKay, *Jean Toomer, Artist: A Study of His Literary Life and Work, 1894–1936* (Chapel Hill: University of North Carolina Press, 1984), 46.

12. Bernard W. Bell, *The Afro-American Novel and Its Tradition* (Amherst: University of Massachusetts Press, 1987), 97.

   A *Künstlerroman* is a novel of development in which the hero is an artist, and it is the defining subgenre of the *Bildungsroman* (e.g., Goethe's *Wilhelm Meister* or Joyce's *Portrait of the Artist as a Young Man*). While *Cane* engages the figure of the male artist enjoying a *Wanderjahr* in the rural South, it does not insist on totality and closure in the same way as its generic antecedents have—or, indeed, as critics like Bell and McKay have insisted.

13. McKay, *Jean Toomer, Artist,* 108.

14. Bell, *The Afro-American Novel and Its Tradition,* 97–98.

15. Bernard Bell is not the only critic to schematize the book in this way. See, among many others, William K. Spofford, "The Unity of Part One of Jean Toomer's *Cane*," *Markham Review* 3 (1972): 58–60; Clyde Taylor, "The Second Coming of Jean Toomer," *Obsidian* 1 (winter 1975): 37–57; Robert Jones, "Jean Toomer as Poet: A Phenomenology of the Spirit," *Black American Literature Forum* 21.3 (fall 1987): 253–73; and the more elaborate

schematic provided in Robert Jones, *Jean Toomer and the Prison-House of Thought* (Amherst: University of Massachusetts Press, 1993); Jeanne Kerblat-Houghton, "Mythes ruraux et urbains dans *Cane* de Jean Toomer (1894–1967)," in Groupe Recherche et d'Études Nord-Américaines, *Mythes ruraux et urbains dans la culture Américaine* (Provence: Université de Provence Service des Publications, 1990), 67–77.

16. Michael North's recent description of the book would seem to endorse my view: in contrast to the understanding of the book as a circle, "it would be more accurate to say that there is a constant shuttling back and forth between literary forms such as lyric in a simple state and complex variations on them or mixtures of them." See Michael North, *The Dialect of Modernism: Race, Language, and Twentieth-Century Literature* (New York: Oxford University Press, 1994), 167.

Another way to read history back into *Cane* is through extensive research of the text's historical references: Barbara Foley's recent work demonstrates that "once one recognizes Toomer's veiled historical allusions, it becomes difficult, if not impossible, to read *Cane* as an abstractly lyrical representation of Southern life" (754); see Barbara Foley, "Jean Toomer's Sparta," *American Literature* 67.4 (December 1995): 747–75.

17. Toomer's text contrasts with Lawrence Levine's expectation that "although it happened neither suddenly nor completely, the sacred worldview so central to black slaves was to be shattered in the twentieth century"; rather than show the shattering of a stable worldview, Toomer's text entertains the possibility of an alternative modernity. See Lawrence W. Levine, *Black Culture and Black Consciousness: Afro-American Folk Thought from Slavery to Freedom* (New York: Oxford University Press, 1977), 158.

18. Raper, *Preface to Peasantry*, 3.

19. Raper, *Preface to Peasantry*, 87.

20. Shivers, *The Land Between*, 291.

21. Edward E. Lewis, *The Mobility of the Negro: A Study in the American Labor Supply* (New York: Columbia University Press, 1931), 112.

22. Shivers, *The Land Between*, 211.

23. Elizabeth Wiley Smith, *The History of Hancock County, Georgia*, vol. 1 (Washington, GA: Wilkes, 1974), 123–24.

24. Barbara Foley, "'In the Land of Cotton': Economics and Violence in Jean Toomer's *Cane*," *African American Review* 32.2 (1998): 183. Foley provides an account of Toomer's "somewhat shallow" (187) economic analysis in *Cane* that is both compatible with the one I've provided here and more extensive.

25. Raper, *Preface to Peasantry*, 406.

26. Raper, *Preface to Peasantry*, 406.

27. This practice is discussed in Nicholls, *Conjuring the Folk*, chaps. 4 and 5, in relation to Claude McKay's *Banana Bottom* and George Wylie Henderson's *Ollie Miss*, respectively.

28. Most migration narratives feature male protagonists, while "folk" narratives tend to center on women: see my discussion of this pattern in *Conjuring the Folk*, chap. 5.

29. Migration patterns by gender tend to suggest that more males than females migrated, although most measures of the trend focus on immigrants in urban centers rather than on out-migration sex ratios. See the long version of this essay in Nicholls, *Conjuring the Folk*, for an extensive discussion of this topic.

30. For a general discussion of "the ways in which migrants creatively use the commercial media to build communities around shared aesthetics of place and to mediate place as well" in Washington, D.C., and elsewhere, see Brett Williams, "The South in the City," *Journal of Popular Culture* 16.3 (winter 1982): 30–41.

31. Walter Benjamin, "Paris, Capital of the Nineteenth Century," in *Reflections*, ed. Peter Demetz (New York: Schocken, 1986), 156.

32. Walter Benjamin, "On Some Motifs in Baudelaire," in *Illuminations*, ed. Hannah Arendt (New York: Schocken, 1969), 172.

33. Benjamin, "Paris, Capital of the Nineteenth Century," 150.

34. As Barbara Foley has recently argued, Kabnis's fear had a concrete referent: lynching was on the rise in 1921. See Foley, 'In the Land of Cotton,'" 192. Foley's contention is that Toomer's strongest historical engagement with the scene in Sparta arose through his representation of racial violence, which many historians have correlated to the depressed economy, although she notes that Toomer does not make this connection himself.

    Farah Griffin's recent discussions of *Cane* also stress the immediacy of racial violence (instead of emphasizing the notion of mythic pastoralism) in Toomer's Georgia. See Farah Jasmine Griffin, *"Who Set You Flowin'?": The African-American Migration Narrative* (New York: Oxford University Press, 1995), passim.

35. In this sense, I concur with Barbara Foley's assertion that "Toomer's class politics were as contradictory as his racial politics." See Foley, "Jean Toomer's Washington and the Politics of Class: From 'Blue Veins' to Seventh-Street Rebels," *Modern Fiction Studies* 42.2 (summer 1996): 313.

9

GRAFTS, TRANSPLANTS, TRANSLATION
THE AMERICANIZING OF YOUNGHILL KANG

Walter K. Lew

> This graft, this hybridization, this composition that puts heterogeneous
> bodies together may be called a monster. This in fact happens in certain
> kinds of writing.
> —Jacques Derrida, "Passages—from Traumatism to Promise"

The birth date of Younghill Kang, the first prominent Korean American
author, remains unclear. According to some sources, "Kang Yong-hŭl"
(Kang's Korean name) was born in or around 1898 in Hongwŏn County, in the
northeastern Korean province of Hamgyŏng Nam-do.[1] In 1920 Kang himself
wrote that he was born on May 10, 1899, when registering at Dalhousie University in Nova Scotia after leaving Korea the year before, but regularly stated
during his subsequent career in the United States that he was born four years
later, on May 10, 1903—sometimes specifying that this is a lunar calendar date
and sometimes not.[2] Where Kang was born is also an unsolved puzzle. Although he normally gave Hongwŏn as his natal town, Kang has Chung-Pa
Han,[3] the reminiscing narrator of Kang's first, often autobiographical novel *The
Grass Roof* (1931), confuse the issue by saying,

I was told by one of my aunts that I was born somewhere in Northern Korea, while my mother was on a trip to China with my father. Since I cannot verify my birthplace accurately, it is safe to say that I was born in that village where I was brought up, not far from Asiatic Russia and Manchuria. (*GR* 4)

Hongwŏn is actually quite far from either Manchuria or "Asiatic Russia," especially for someone who did his childhood traveling on foot,[4] and the statement that Han was born in Korea while his "mother was on a trip to China" can be read as an oxymoron. Kang's calendrical and geographical "imprecision" declines allegiance to nation-state boundaries and unilinear chronology. Over and against the various nationalisms of his time, Kang's equivocations suggest that, as an immigrant Korean novelist writing for an Anglophone audience about a "backward" country colonized by "modern" Japan, he considered his sensibility to have been formed from the "beginning" at the confluence of many shifting cultural and historical currents.[5]

In the metaphysical preamble to Kang's third book, *East Goes West: The Making of an Oriental Yankee* (1937), time is both uniform ("the same time that occupied the Roman lovers is the same that Hamlet was insane in, and in the same I write and think of time" [*EGW* 3]) and shaped by the intensity and "trajectory" of one's historically specific actions and culture:

> I seem to have traversed much time, more than most men, although I am still in my early thirties. My own life in actual books still extant in my Korean village was traced far back to ancestors with the bodies of men and heads of cows. This lifetime, threaded to theirs over the mellow-gold distances of time, can it be the same which now sees New York City? And I ask, did I fall from a different star? (*EGW* 4)

The tension between vitalistically seizing one's time "as long as there is life to use it" (*EGW* 3) and drifting like innumerable predecessors across its great indifferent manifold was one to which Kang himself had grown accustomed by the 1930s. It characterizes his ability to cross (in some cases, infiltrate) widely different arenas of culture, aesthetics, society, and ethnicity. Such a life required Kang to continually recalibrate his descents from dynamically heterogeneous origins, mapping and remapping an autobio-grafting as perpetual roamer, fallen from an always already "different star."[6] In the present essay, I analyze certain struggles *East Goes West* has undergone, as well as ingenious intertextual grafts it performed, to achieve the type of ambitious yet wandering flight across times and geographies figured in its opening meditation—challenged as it became by a series of powerfully reductive and institutionalized readings.

In drawing these conclusions, I am not proposing that *East Goes West* be read simply as autobiography—a reduction that has plagued both the novel's publication history and most Kang scholarship. Although it is clear that much of the novel draws on events in Kang's life, connections between those events and the narrative are not all of one type, they sometimes vanish, and are inevitably couched in various stylistic registers that should affect how we interpret them.[7] As I will discuss, Kang resisted readings that either framed his novel as a recounting of his own supposedly happy assimilation into American society or lambasted it as the narrow product of an elite betrayer of Korea.

The opposition between assimilation into (or exclusion from) mainstream American society and nativist loyalty to (or betrayal of) Asian cultural, political, and socioeconomic values appears in some form in most of the writing on Asian American culture and society produced in both the United States and various Asian nations.[8] In its most extreme form (advocated at one time by many Asian American intellectuals themselves), assimilationism encouraged erasure, through acculturation and interracial marriage, of any difference between Asian American and mainstream Anglo-American culture and physiognomy.[9] As Sucheng Chan notes, assimilationism adheres to the "facile assumption that all immigrants can and should transform themselves" and "overlooks the fact that people of color have encountered enormous hurdles—legal, political, social, and economic—whenever they have tried to enter mainstream society."[10] Beginning in the 1970s, it was the assimilationist paradigm that, to a large extent, Asian American activists rejected. Since part of what they rebelled against was "negative portrayals of their forebears and themselves," nativist declarations of reverent continuity with Asian ancestral or homelands and cultures became one of several alternative ideological stances.[11]

As we shall see, the dichotomy between assimilationism and nativism overlooks other more complex positions and gives little consideration to issues of agency.[12] These paradigms are nonetheless helpful for discussing the ideological underpinnings of *East Goes West*'s reception among a variety of readers, ranging from midcentury newspaper reviewers to more recent academic critics. The two most influential interpretations, on which I focus in this essay, have been what I consider to be the assimilationist manuscript revisions of Maxwell Perkins, Kang's renowned editor at Charles Scribner's Sons, and the disparaging nativist assessments published by Elaine H. Kim, author of the most widely used textbook on Asian American literature.[13] Both interpretations eradicate important levels of literary play between *East Goes West*'s story of Chungpa Han's life in

North America and Kang's own pre–World War II career, forcing the novel into one tightly constrained "lifetime."

MAXWELL PERKINS ON "THE MORE FRIVOLOUS KOREANS"

It is safe to say that Kang cut at least 150 manuscript pages from a late draft of *East Goes West*, following recommendations by Perkins, the vice president of Charles Scribner's Sons, who played a crucial role in the careers of such authors as Ernest Hemingway, F. Scott Fitzgerald, and Kang's close friend Thomas Wolfe.[14] Although Perkins deemed the cuts necessary in "order to sell [the novel] at a suitable price," they were not solely market-driven. Perkins's editorial suggestions are consistently geared toward transforming the narrative into a text more palatable for Euro-American audiences than the one Kang had planned.[15] Taken as a whole, they propose a vision of the successful assimilation of an individual immigrant gradually "freed" from ethnic community and identity as he strives to enter mainstream White society. It is significant, for example, that Perkins felt that the writing was more consistently marked by "real deep reflection and episodes of more serious significance" once Han moves to Canada, since it is then that he becomes severed for the first time from the company of other "more frivolous Easterners."[16] Indeed, Perkins remarked that the novel was "in the first place the story of a man, and in the second, of an Easterner in the West."[17]

Perkins unambiguously used Kang's own life as the standard against which to judge the manuscript's narrative, viewing the book not as a novel, but as autobiography, even suggesting that it be titled "The Americanizing of Younghill Kang."[18] Indeed, the one major element that Perkins asked Kang to *add* was explicit depiction of marriage between Han and Trip, the young Caucasian poet with whom Han is desperately enamored, justifying his request with an appeal to Kang's own life experience:

> [I]t seems to me that the main change should be at the end, to make much more of Trip, and to show definitely that you [i.e., Kang] married her, because the fact that you did, makes one of the principal points of the book, in that the Easterner became a Westerner through this experience.[19]

By invoking the fact of Kang's marriage to Frances Keely (supposedly the real-life model for Trip) and suggesting matrimony as the means through which "the Easterner [becomes] a Westerner," Perkins may have wanted to dissipate the indictment of America implied in the tragic parallel story of the novel's other interracial couple, the disaffected Korean intellectual To Wan Kim and his beloved Helen Hancock, scion of an elite, racist Boston family.[20] To prevent her from seeing Kim, Helen's family sends her to Europe and then a sanitarium, where she eventually dies, her illness precipitated by the cruel separation. Crushed by these events and destitution in New York, Kim commits suicide.

In terms of the manuscript's word count per se, Kang allowed himself to be guided by Perkins's proven expertise. Nonetheless, Kang often subverted his editor by working like a Korean American trickster "wreak[ing] havoc upon the signified" through rhetorical indirection.[21] Indeed, he ironicized or problematized the surface meaning of the novel with embedded allusions and symbolic codes, many of which are legible only to Korean or Korea-knowledgeable readers, as I show in the final section of this essay. Kang also outright opposed particular recommendations as to what to write or revise. In the case of the "main change" advised by Perkins, Kang contrived no epithalamium to dispel the self-mockery and ambivalence of *East Goes West*'s portrayal of the relationship between Han and the young woman of his dreams. The novel insists to the very end that Han's trip to the West—for all its opportunities and peculiar delights—was humiliatingly "tripped up" by relentless materialism and racism. Though an echo of tripping the light fantastic on the sidewalks of New York, Trip remains a frivolous Westerner who offers no real escape from such sufferings.[22] Moreover, in another point I return to later, by devoting much of the novel's closing passages—its final depiction of America—to a nightmare in which the narrator is herded together with African Americans about to be immolated in a race riot, Kang ensured that his simultaneously market-calculating and humanistically intentioned editor's hope of success for him (and Han) could only be a hollow one.

THE PROBLEM OF PROPER REPRESENTATION

Interpretations of *East Goes West* in the field of Asian American studies tend to be guided by nativist assumptions, ironically without heeding the codes of Korean signification Kang employed. The main points of Elaine Kim's literalist yet unchallenged readings of *East Goes West*, first presented in such pieces as her 1977 article "Searching for a Door to America: Younghill Kang, Korean American Writer" (hereafter *SD*), are reproduced and extended in her influential textbook, *Asian American Literature* (hereafter *AA*).[23] It is important, therefore, to reevaluate an analysis that has helped to marginalize Kang's writing in accounts of Asian American cultural history. Assuming that Koreans are a politically and culturally uniform community and that the ultimate value of a writer or character in a novel is how well he or she typifies a particular ethnic group, Kim's interpretation repeatedly accuses Kang of being both inauthentically Korean and politically suspect, even as she fails to explore not only the novel's intricate intertextualities but also the abundant, published record of Kang's contributions to Korean political and cultural causes. She argues that as an "aristocrat" by birth, "one of the last immigrants to reach America before Oriental immigration was prohibited," and "the only Korean immigrant to have written book-length fiction in English until recent years," Kang could not legitimately represent Korean and Korean American society and aspirations, nor his protagonist Chungpa Han (*SD* 38, 46; *AA* 33, 43).[24]

Kim makes no effort to qualify her statement that "the majority of Koreans in America were concentrating their thoughts on their homeland" and anti-Japanese movements (*SD* 38), a dictum she uses to ostracize both Kang and Han (dissolved together in a transmogrification that I shall call "Khan") for what she sees as their unpatriotic pursuit of humanistic "Western learning" and their qualms about terrorism. Kim thus fails to acknowledge that such educational goals and pacifism were common among nationalist Korean intellectuals of the time.[25] Ignoring the ironic tone in Kang's writing, she surmises that Khan is "hopelessly in thrall of Western culture," and thus "unable to fully analyze the significance of his experience beyond metaphysical hopes and dreams" (*SD* 46).[26] In her estimation, Khan "would have left behind, if he could have, his Korean past, his Korean identity, and perhaps his Korean compatriots in America" (*SD* 41),[27] squandering "his energies trying to establish a place for himself in his adopted land" (*SD* 40).

Serious problems emerge, of course, when one recklessly neglects differences between a novelist and his protagonist or narrator. As already mentioned, merging Kang and Han prevents Kim from developing a sufficient sense of, among other things, *East Goes West*'s trenchant ironies and satire. Even taken as assertions about Khan's "biography," however, Kim's accusations are demonstrably false.

It is, for instance, misleading to use the term "aristocrat" to describe Khan's *yangban* (i.e., literati or scholar-official class) background when the case at hand is that of non-officeholding families in remote villages of northeastern Korea, a politically estranged region throughout the Chosŏn dynasty (1392–1910); by the nineteenth century especially such households often survived on the fruits of their own farming.[28] This is confirmed in *The Grass Roof* and *East Goes West*, both of which depict Chungpa Han's means as being severely limited during his childhood and student years. Besides earning a few meals in Korean villages and New York Chinatown on the strength of either his skills as a poet and calligrapher or the literary reputation of his uncles, Han survives not through *yangban* emoluments and privilege, but through the pragmatic devising of temporary employments for himself. He has, after all, gone deeply against his father's wishes by pursuing a Western education, rejecting a traditionally arranged marriage, and almost completely cutting himself off from communication with his home region and whatever local esteem *yangban* status could provide. More-over, far from being blithely unconcerned with the consequences of Korea's "an-nexation," several of Han's relatives are brutally treated by Japanese police and are consumed with anguish over Korea's loss of sovereignty.

Most calumnious is Kim's condemnation of Kang for his "peripheral" in-volvement in both domestic and overseas movements for Korean independence (*SD* 39). In the case of the watershed 1919 March First Movement, in which Kang marched and was consequently wounded and imprisoned, one wonders at the criteria Kim sets for being legitimately at the center of pacifist demonstra-tions celebrated for their extremely diverse, nationwide participation. It is quite clear that Kang did, in fact, participate intensely in nationalist activities as a bold author, editor, translator, demonstrator, and critic. One of the reasons *The Grass Roof* received international acclaim and was translated into numerous lan-guages was its harsh critique of Japanese nationalism and jingoism.[29] "Mansei (O Live Ten Thousand Years!)," the chapter that is devoted to a firsthand ac-count of the March First Movement and its aftermath, is among the most im-passioned writing in English on the events of that time (*GR* 335–53). *The Grass Roof* also includes a harrowing description of Chung-Pa Han's failed attempts to escape Japanese police at the Chinese border and in Russia—the first time in collaboration with Koreans trying to aid the government-in-exile in Shanghai. Han's exhausting and terrified efforts result in three months of imprisonment and torture (*GR* 354–66).

Influential American reviews praised Kang for countering previous apolo-gists for Japanese rule that had portrayed Korea as degenerate.[30] Throughout most of his writing and speaking career, Kang readily spoke out against tyranny, corruption, and militarism in Asia, whether Japanese colonialism, Korean dicta-torship, or American involvement in the Vietnam War, even when his views made him the object of both U.S. and South Korean surveillance.[31] An un-daunted, erudite reviewer of Asia-related books in such periodicals as the *New York Times Book Review* and the *New Republic*, Kang did not hesitate to casti-gate ill-informed, Orientalist, imperialist, or racist writing.[32] In a 1931 *New Republic* review that sparked several rounds of debate, Kang criticized Pearl Buck's *The Good Earth* for what he considered typical missionary prejudice against Chinese culture and ignorance of the background of events it portrayed; it was the only negative review of the immensely successful novel in a major American periodical.[33]

In the Korean American community Kang was often lauded in the pages of such publications as the *Korean Student Bulletin*, where he was described as a "one-man protagonist of the new Korean Literary Renaissance."[34] He was an editor of the *Bulletin*'s stirring issue on the Kwangju Student Uprising of

November 1929, the largest mass protest against Japanese rule after the March First Movement.[35] Later he extended his criticism to the post-liberation policies of the U.S. Army Military Government in Korea (1945–48), which, on the eve of McCarthyism, had already branded Kang an author possessing "leftist tendencies."[36] In the article "How It Feels to Be a Korean in Korea," Kang was harshly critical of both American betrayal of Koreans' hopes for independence and Syngman Rhee's political operatives, which he likened to "the Black Shirts of Italy and Hitler's Brown Shirts."[37]

Finally, with the collaboration of Frances Keely, Kang made pioneering, persistent efforts to translate and introduce both classical and modern Korean literature to American audiences, much of which was profoundly patriotic, such as Kang's most cherished work: the poetry of the Buddhist reformer and freedom fighter Manhae Han Yong-un.[38]

TRANSPLANTING RESISTANCE

In light of the combination of romantic poetry, Confucian learning and rusticity, high modernist poetics, acerbic social critique, Buddhist equanimity, picaresque individualism, and Taoist principles of continual change and spontaneity that characterize much of *East Goes West*, neither assimilationist nor nativist paradigms can do justice to Chungpa Han's complexly coordinated, mobile relations to the cultures he transits and performs. As Alice Scharper has argued, a fundamental metaphor that Han himself uses to describe his ambitions in America is a botanical one: "the *engrafting* of one set of cultural experiences onto another." Citing the work of William Boelhower, she adds that the "botanical metaphor [of engrafting] is common to many ethnic immigrant narratives."[38]

Such metaphors were also commonly used in late-nineteenth-century Chinese debates on how to incorporate new Western knowledge and soon afterwards in Korea and Japan as well, especially once the renowned Chinese scholar and political leader Liang Qichao (1873–1929) began to publish his *Xinmin shuo* (Treatise on a people made new) in various forms from 1902 onward while taking political refuge in Japan.[40] According to Liang, previous pseudo-Westernizers had wanted merely to graft (or "attach") the flowers, fruit, or branches of Western technology onto the eternal trunk or roots of fundamental Chinese values, statecraft, and philosophy.[41] Liang himself, in this early stage of his thought, argued from a Social Darwinist perspective that superficial, intermittent grafting could not help China survive in the brutal international arena: "If [intellectuals] neglect the roots [of Western culture] but tend the branches, it will be no different from seeing the luxuriant growth of another tree and wishing to graft its branches onto our withered trunk."[42] Instead, he urged a more drastic *transplantation* of the fundamental values, ideas, and spirit of the West, to the point of even replacing the diseased trees of Chinese traditions now seen, through an act of self-Orientalization, as incapable of progress and Enlightenment.[43]

In Korean literary discussions this trope became especially important under the coerced modernization of Japanese colonial rule (1910–45). The most influential example is an assertion by the leftist actor, poet, and scholar Im Hwa (1908–53), who claimed that since Korea's new or modern literature had absorbed a tremendous variety of translated Western influences within an extremely concentrated period of time, it was a fundamentally "transplanted literature" (*ishik munhak*).[44] Im Hwa had studied in Japan, where tropes of cultural transplantation (*ishoku*) or grafting (*tsugiki*) were used to support widely different views vis-à-vis the West and modernity.[45]

In his 1938 article "The Fate of Thought," the Japanese philosopher Hayashi Tatsuo advanced a cosmopolitan view about ideological transplantation:

> The notion of being native is sometimes used as if it were a synonym for vital energy and for implacably seated depth, yet it is a fact that plants that have been replanted in new ground turn out to be superior plants far more often than do native ones. Isn't it the case, too, that superior thought does not weaken or wither when uprooted, but instead—through being transplanted into new ground and a new environment—gains vigor, sees flourishing growth, and takes root all the more deeply in the soil?"[46]

Unlike the Chinese or Korean situations, however, metaphors of *ishoku* were here being used in a nation that was itself a colonizer of Asia (the Chinese-based logographs of "colonization" and "colonialist" [*shokumin*] literally mean "planting people"). Although not all discussants of cultural transplantation and grafting were imperialist ideologues, some were, such as Naitō Konan (1866–1934), one of the founders of Japanese Orientalist studies.[47] When Naitō claimed in 1924 that "the new culture in the orient is not that which has completely cut away the trunk of oriental culture and grafted on (*tsugi kisuru*) western culture," he was not merely echoing the late-nineteenth-century Chinese debates that Liang Qichao, who was an early influence on Naitó, had engaged in; he was also promoting the idea that it was not the West but imperialist Japan, guided in part by the type of research Naitó helped develop, that knew how to properly guide Asia toward modernity.[48]

Kang, a frequent commentator in American venues on both contemporary and traditional Chinese, Korean, and Japanese literature and philosophy, was certainly familiar with the intercultural complexities of East Asian metaphors of transplantation. He reversed, however, their geopolitical direction by vowing to engraft/transplant Eastern culture onto (rather than from) the West within the cosmopolitan center of American literary activity (Scribner's, the *New Republic*, the *New York Times*, etc.). His primary techniques were, as we shall see, translation and various forms of trickster disguise and intertextuality. Thus, what had been a figure of (at least partially) appropriating the West by the East thereby became one of aggressively suturing the East *onto* the West, in Derrida's sense of "monstrous" grafting, a controlled yet violent process whereby a text "while continuing to work through tradition emerges at a given moment as a *monster*, a monstrous mutation without tradition or normative precedent."[49] Kang's diasporic translation of metaphors of cultural grafting and transplantation is not a displacement that misrecognizes in America the "original" source of oppression, Japan. Instead, it relies on an astute tactic of intertextuality that draws on a triangular paradigm of colony (Korea), semiperipheral colonizer (Japan), and diasporically discovered "core" metropole (United States) that interpretations such as Elaine Kim's or even postcolonial theories of hybridity and nationalist redeployment of essentialism do not easily accommodate.[50] Such approaches remain bipolar even when positing a "Third Space."[51]

In a key passage, Han contrasts his own mission of cultural engrafting to the futility of *yangban* scholars and patriots mourning the demise of traditional Korean society:

> I could take away my slip cut from the roots, and try to engraft my scholar-inherited kingdom upon the world's thought. But what I could not bear was the thought of futility, the futility of the martyr, or the death-stifled scholar back home. It was so that the individualist was born, the individualist, demanding life and more life—some anchor in thin air to bring him to earth though he seems cut off from the very roots of being.
>
> And this it was—this naked individual slip—I had brought to New York. (*EGW* 9)

Bearing this precious "slip," Han aims to engender a hybrid flowering not possible before in either East or West. Indeed, Han reflects, the suicide of his fellow expatriate, To Wan Kim, was due not only to the agony inflicted by racism, but also to Kim's inability to clearly realize and resolutely perform such a mission. The result is that Kim's life became one that had "never accepted its real worldliness [and] did not know if it came once to be *transplanted* or was hopelessly in exile" (*EGW* 390; emphasis added). That the material form and practice of transplantation referred to here are literary can be seen in Han's mournful meditation on Kim's destruction of his own writings and calligraphy:

> All [of Kim's] work had been burned in that Bleecker Street fireplace, nothing was left. But the greatest loss to me, Kim's friend, was himself, his brain which bore in its fine involutions our ancient characters deeply and simply incised, familiar to me. And over their classic economy, their primitive chaste elegance, was scrawled the West's handwriting, in incoherent labyrinth. . . . [A] priceless and awful parchment was in him destroyed. Could it not have been deciphered, conveyed to the world? (*EGW* 395)

This image of double inscription can also be thought of as a metaphor of failed transplantation: weed-like English writing strewn chaotically over Chinese characters in the wasted soil of Kim's brain.[52] Han, however, defies both the idea of the inescapable rootedness of culture in only one local soil (that of its origin and earlier development) and the notion that all environments are equivalent. What is needed to make the "naked, individual slip" develop in a different habitat is a unique grafting, which—if we return to the deciphering called for in Han's elegiac thoughts on Kim's death—is a process of imaginative *translation*.

That transplantation requires translation[53] is implied by another image of the cerebral inscription of cultures that emerges during a scene of humiliation in which Han tries to impress Trip and her friends with his rote knowledge of nationally delineated literatures—of, on the one hand, "a Chinese poem in the old-fashioned singing" and, on the other, "Keats, Shelley, Browning, Tennyson, Ruskin, Carlyle, and Shakespeare roll[ing] out in pages and sheets, all that had imprinted itself word for word on the retentive Oriental memory of one classically trained" (*EGW* 348). The unfortunate result is that Han is mocked for his presumably superficial mimicry of canonical English literature and quaint show of Oriental aestheticism, although Han (but not Kang) insists on idealizing the juvenile party to the point of pathetic denial as a timeless soiree filled with race-transcending literary companionship. He has, after all, not translated or transplanted either body of poetry into some new cultural form, such as the intricately imbricated *East Goes West* itself.

In short, a trope that had signified both the movement of Western epistemology across Asia and Japanese colonization was redirected by Kang against a racist America that, since 1924, had excluded his countrymen and whose literary market, according to Perkins, ascribed no value to his depiction of "frivolous Easterners," those unassimilated members of Asian American communities in Boston and New York. Without denying Han's desire for Western knowledge and modernity, such an analysis emphasizes the menace contained in such images as the "projectile" arching toward America that he describes himself as becoming near the outset of the novel (*EGW* 5).

Delicately worded images of trees, flowers, and leaves occur throughout both *The Grass Roof* and *East Goes West*, as do metaphors of fragile, tendril-like connections to the past. In a chapter of *The Grass Roof* titled "The Invisible Ribbon," Han, departing for America, speaks of streamers of farewell "unwinding longer and longer as the ship slowly moves out to sea." Rather than a ribbon that one gazes at playing out over the water, however, Han celebrates the "ribbon that you hold only with your imagination" (*GR* 362). Yet by the end of *East Goes West*, published six years later, even this deeply held connection threatens to snap in midair. The closing episode of the novel, in which Han tells of a nostalgic dream-turned-nightmare, becomes a scene of grief over the loss of Han's ties to village life in Korea and his imprisonment in American mercantilism and racism.

To gain a richer sense of this final episode, we need to pay attention to relations between *East Goes West* and several intertexts, only two of which I have space to address here: first, the previously mentioned letter in which Perkins requests a scene of marriage between Han and Trip as a symbol of Han's successful Westernization, and second, a well-known Korean folktale in which a tiger falls to its death from a tree after being tricked into climbing up a rotten rope by two escaping children. Grafting together such culturally disparate narratives, Kang achieved a translating polysemy complex enough to resist both complete assimilation into a deeply hostile America and futile attachment to a lost past.

The description of Han's nightmare is one of the few passages in *East Goes West* where it might be construed that Chungpa Han marries Trip. Their time together, however, is associated not with contentment, but entry into a life of obsessive materialism and the loss of Han's psychic relationship with Korea. Han dreams that he is high up in a "lofty tree" to which a "tightrope"-like bridge has been attached that can lead him back to his childhood village (*EGW* 400). Two village friends, Yunkoo and Chak-doo-shay, excitedly beckon him to cross over to them, but before he can reach the bridge,

> all in a moment, things began tumbling out of my pockets, money and keys, contracts and business letters. Especially the key to my car, my American car. I clutched, but I saw it falling.
>
> Now, always before in my dreams when I entered that village, it was with Trip, in a car. . . . I must not lose the car key. "The car key, the car key!" I cried to myself in my dream, forgetting Yunkoo and Chak-doo-shay. "It fell in the bushes at the foot of the tree. I must find it."

> I half climbed, half slid down the tree and began grubbing in the
> leaves and sticks, and ever present in my mind was the urgency of find-
> ing the car key, of recovering all of the money. (*EGW* 400–401)

When compared to the sort of connubial vision that Perkins urged on Kang, the
appearance of this farcical scene near the harrowing conclusion of the novel
must be seen as a defiant one. The "contracts and business letters" (perhaps including correspondence from Scribner's?) falling out of Han's pockets might
even be read as ambivalence about the intrusions of the marketplace on Kang's
writing.

The image of Han "half climb[ing], half slid[ing] down the tree" is also reminiscent of the tiger in the Korean folktale mentioned above, who clumsily
slides down a tree because the two children perched in it have tricked him into
coating it with sesame oil. After the children ascend from the tree into the safety
of Heaven, they confound the tiger again by leading him to believe that he can
pursue them by climbing up a rope. It snaps and he falls to his death, pierced by
the stalks of a corn field.[54]

Read against this intertext, Han's dream may be seen as an ominous parable
aimed at Korean and Korean American readers, most of whom would be familiar with the tale: successful as the narrator may have become in the United
States—with a car, a winsome, highly-educated Caucasian wife, and pockets
filled with cash and business letters—his return to the Korea of his youth could
only be a monstrous one. He has become a tiger whose American voraciousness
would devour the ways of its inhabitants, and whose long-lost friends, in turn,
might find it necessary to deceive him into crossing a rope bridge that will send
him plunging to his death. Return from diaspora, as Trinh T. Minh-Ha has elo-
quently written, requires yet another redeparture from one's homeland, or a less
direct arrival.[55] Thus, across an intertextual network—invisible, yet more extensive than rope—Kang attempted to convey an intimate, conflicted message to
his folk, "frivolous Easterners" or not.

In the nightmare's final scene, analogous to Ralph Ellison's *Invisible Man*,
published fifteen years later, Han descends "into a dark and cryptlike cellar, still
looking for [his] money and keys—under the pavements of a vast city" and becomes desperately trapped in a race riot:

> Other men were in that cellar with me—some frightened-looking Ne-
> groes, I remember. Then looking back, I saw, through an iron grating
> into the upper air, men with clubs and knives. The cellar was being at-
> tacked. The Negroes were about to be mobbed. I shut the door and
> bolted it, and called to my frightened fellows to help me hold the door.

"Fire, bring fire," called the red-faced men outside.

And through the grating I saw the flaring torches being brought. And applied. Being shoved, crackling, through the gratings. (*EGW* 401)

The narrator has tumbled into the nether regions of the type of city in which he once aspired to literary fame, engulfed in a race riot that, to Kang's American readers in 1937, would have eerily recalled the Harlem insurrection of two years before.[56]

The torches thrust at the trapped African Americans and Han are like the cornstalks piercing the fallen tiger bleeding to death in a distant field. According to one version of the folktale, that brutal end is how leopards came to have spots and, in another, why broom-corn leaves are marked with blood-red dots. Here the image signals a different transformation: Han recognizes his allegiance with the "Negroes [who] were about to be mobbed" and ineluctably joins them in collective opposition to America's murderous racism. For readers troubled by the novel's previous, often patronizing portrayal of African American individuals and communities, this may serve as a redemptive turn in the narrative.

Yet it is within this seemingly inescapable inferno raging between Black and White that Han resorts one final time to an image of monstrous fusion along the axis of East and West. He awakens "like the phenix [*sic*] out of a burst of flames," embracing the Buddhistic hope of "growth and rebirth and a happier reincarnation" (*EGW* 401).[57] Sustaining the ambition of both East Asian modernists and American immigrant authors who searched for forms of cultural transplantation, Kang concludes his novel with a hopeful "cross-fertilization" of Eastern and Western motifs.[58] Given the context of the immediately preceding scene, however, this resolution is unconvincing or simply mystifying, possibly because its drive to make East go West so blindly and forcibly extricates itself from yet another deadly racialized chasm (Black vs. White) into which Han, misrecognized, had tumbled almost accidentally—a chasm so threatening that Younghill Kang never returned to its precipice in any of his subsequent writing.

NOTES

This essay is dedicated to Lucy Lynn Kang Sammis (1930–1995): "We all need a country. And I, in desperation, needed two."

Versions of parts of this essay were delivered at a series of conferences between 1995 and 1997. I thank Juliana C. Chang, Heinz Insu Fenkl, Ted Hughes, Hyungji Park, Michael E. Robinson, Sam E. Solberg, Dorothy Wang, and especially Jani Scandura and Michael Thurston for their comments. Charles Armour, Hasig Bahng, Michael

Bourdaghs, Maria Damon, Steven G. Doi, John B. Duncan, Theodore Huters, Christopher Kang, K. W. Lee, Seiji M. Lippit, Michael E. MacMillan, Hiromi Mizuno, Alice M. Scharper, Shu-mei Shih, Michael D. Shin, Miriam Silverberg, Min Suh Son, Brian Kim Stefans, Tim Tangherlini, K. Scott Wong, and Wu Shengqing generously provided information, source materials, and suggestions of related scholarship.

1. See, among others, Chang Mun-p'yŏng, "Tongyang chôngshin ûi chôngsu <Ch'odang>" (Purity of the Eastern spirit: *The Grass Roof*), in Kang Yong-hûl, *Ch'odang* (The grass roof), *Segye munhak sok ûi Han'guk* (Korea in world literature), vol. 2 (Seoul: Chônghan Ch'ulp'an Sa, 1975), 465–70; Kim Jong-gil, "Kang Showed Korean Culture to World," *Korea Times* (Seoul), 17 December 1972, 3.

2. University Archive, Dalhousie University (Halifax, Nova Scotia, Canada). Although Kang states in his first two books (*GR* 5, *HG* 1) that he was "born on the tenth day of May, by the Korean calendar (which is about a month later than by the American)," from 1920 onward, he simply gives May 10, 1899 or May 10, 1903, without conversion to a Gregorian calendar date in his correspondence and official forms. All citations from *The Grass Roof* (Follett, 1966) (hereafter *GR*) and *East Goes West* (Follett, 1965) (hereafter *EGW*) refer to the Follett Publishing Company editions, since these are the most recent authorized and relatively error-free texts. *GR* (1931), *EGW* (1937), and *The Happy Grove* (1933) (hereafter *HG*) were all originally published by Charles Scribner's Sons (New York). The Kaya edition of *EGW*, printed in 1997 over the strenuous objections of the Kang estate and its agent, is error-ridden in both its main text and supplementary material.

3. Han's given name is spelled "Chung-Pa" in *GR* and *HG*, but "Chungpa" in *EGW*.

4. I thank Gari Ledyard for this observation.

5. The frequently posited definition of Japan as the one nation that could accommodate all Asian difference was itself fundamentally ambivalent. For the "insoluble paradoxes" of national identity in Japanese imperialist ideology, see, among others, Tessa Morris-Suzuki, *Re-Inventing Japan: Time, Space, Nation* (Armonk, NY: M. E. Sharpe, 1998).

6. Jacques Derrida, *Dissemination*, trans., intro., and notes by Barbara Johnson (Chicago: University of Chicago Press, 1981), 355–58; and Jacques Derrida, "Passages—from Traumatism to Promise," interview, 1990, in *Points . . . : Interviews, 1974–1994*, ed. Elisabeth Weber, trans. Peggy Kamuf et al. (Stanford: Stanford University Press, 1995).

7. Walter K. Lew, "Before *The Grass Roof*: Younghill Kang's University Days," *Korean Culture* 19/1 (spring 1998): 22–29.

8. Ling-chi Wang, "The Structure of Dual Domination: Toward a Paradigm for the Study of the Chinese Diaspora in the United States," *Amerasia Journal*

21/1–2 (1995): 149–69; Aihwa Ong and Donald Nonini introduction to *Ungrounded Empires: The Cultural Politics of Modern Chinese Transnationalism,* ed. Aihwa Ong and Donald Nonini (New York: Routledge, 1997), 5–9.

9. See, for instance, the discussion of Rose Hum Lee's sociological writings in Henry Yu, "The 'Oriental Problem' in America, 1920–1960: Linking the Identities of Chinese American and Japanese American Intellectuals," in *Claiming America, Constructing Chinese American Identities during the Exclusion Era,* ed. K. Scott Wong and Sucheng Chan (Philadelphia: Temple University Press, 1998), 191–214.

10. Sucheng Chan, "Asian American Historiography," *Pacific Historical Review* 65/3 (1996): 363–99; the quotation is on p. 371.

11. Ibid., 370.

12. See ibid.; and the preface to Wong and Chan, *Claiming America.* For a discussion of the dilemmas of assimilation as portrayed in Asian American literature, see Sau-ling Cynthia Wong's landmark study, *Reading Asian American Literature: From Necessity to Extravagance* (Princeton: Princeton University Press, 1993).

13. Elaine H. Kim, *Asian American Literature: An Introduction to the Writings and Their Social Context* (hereafter *AA*) (Philadelphia: Temple University Press, 1982); the section on Kang comprises pp. 32–43.

14. Maxwell Perkins to Younghill Kang, 8 February 1937. Perkins's correspondence to and about Kang, which I uncovered in 1993, is housed in the Charles Scribner's and Sons Archive, Rare Books and Special Collections Department, Princeton University Library, Princeton, New Jersey. For more on the relationship between Kang and Wolfe, see, among others, K. W. Lee, "Kang and Wolfe: East-West Friendship," *Koreatown Weekly* (Los Angeles), 7 January 1980, 1.

15. For an early conception of the project that resulted in *East Goes West,* see Kang's 1931 Guggenheim fellowship application. Archive, John Simon Guggenheim Memorial Foundation, New York.

16. Perkins to Kang, 8 December 1936, 8 February 1937.

17. Perkins to Kang, 8 February 1937.

18. Perkins to Kang, 5 April 1937.

19. Perkins to Kang, 8 February 1937.

20. It has even been surmised that Kang's early plan for the novel was to make this story its main focus; its original working title was "Death of an Exile." Guggenheim fellowship application, 1931.

21. I draw here on Henry Louis Gates, Jr.'s analysis of the "signifying monkey"; see especially Gates's *Figures in Black: Words, Signs, and the "Racial" Self* (New York: Oxford University Press, 1989), 236–40.

22. Trip's apartment mate remarks, "The only thing light about her was her nickname" (*EGW* 327).

23. See Elaine H. Kim, "Searching for a Door to America: Younghill Kang, Ko-

rean American Writer" (hereafter *SD*), *Korea Journal* 17/4 (April 1977): 38–47, and *AA* 32–43. While Kim seems to retract some of her earlier criticism of Kang in a more recent essay (Elaine H. Kim, "Korean American Literature," in *An Interethnic Companion to Asian American Literature*, ed. King-kok Cheung [New York: Cambridge University Press, 1997], 156–91), she still maintains that Kang is severely limited for "speak[ing] primarily from the perspectives of members of an elite class of educated, nonlaboring [*sic*] immigrants" (158). She also inaccurately characterizes early Korean American writers—which would, of course, include Kang as the most prominent and prolific instance—as often considering "dealing with subtleties, hybridities, paradoxes, and layers . . . impossibly luxurious" (157–58). As I argue, these complexities are what helped produce Kang's writing and are reinscribed in its eclectic structures.

24. During the early twentieth century, Congress passed a series of laws that either barred Asians from entering the United States or severely restricted their number. Kim is referring to the Immigration Act of 1924, which also limited immigration from southern and eastern Europe.

25. Michael E. Robinson, *Cultural Nationalism in Colonial Korea, 1920–1925* (Seattle: University of Washington Press, 1988).

26. Also see *AA* 43.

27. Also see *AA* 36.

28. The exclusion of northern province *yangban* from political power and the quickly expanding class of fallen or impoverished *yangban* (*ch'anban*) are only mentioned briefly in English-language sources, such as Ki-baik Lee, *A New History of Korea*, trans. Edward W. Wagner (Cambridge: Harvard University Press, 1984), 174, 250; and Carter J. Eckert et al., *Korea Old and New: A History* (Seoul: Ilchogak, 1990), 109, 181. Kim Sŏn-ju is currently writing a dissertation at the University of Washington that gives a much more extensive treatment. Kang himself resorted to farming on Long Island in the 1950s after losing his teaching position at New York University.

29. See, for instance, the publisher's preface to the French edition, which garnered the 1937 Prix Halperine Kaminsky for best book in French translation: Younghill Kang, *Au pays du matin calme*, trans. Claudine De Courcelle (1935; Paris: PLON, 1967), 5–6.

30. See, among others, Isador Schneider, "Youth in Korea," review of *The Grass Roof*, by Younghill Kang, *New Republic* 1 April 1931, 187. Kang also published anti-Japanese propaganda during World War II, such as "When the Japs March In," *American Magazine*, August 1942, 42–43.

31. Interviews I have conducted and documents I have obtained through the Freedom of Information Act from various federal agencies, such as the U.S. army and the State Department, make it clear that Kang was frequently spied on, especially after the end of World War II.

32. See, for instance, Younghill Kang, "China and Korea in Revolt," review of

Korea of the Japanese, by H. B. Drake, *The Inner History of the Chinese Revolution*, by T'ang Leang-li, and *The Spirit of the Chinese Revolution*, by A. N. Holcombe, *New Republic*, 7 January 1931, 224–25.

33. Younghill Kang, "China Is Different," review of *The Good Earth*, by Pearl S. Buck, and *The Tragedy of Ah Qui, and Other Modern Chinese Stories*, translated from the Chinese by Kyn Yn Yu and from the French by E. H. F. Mills, *New Republic*, 1 July 1931, 185–86.

34. "Our Own Hall of Fame, Five New Stars in the Firmament of Korean Scholarship," *Korean Student Bulletin* 12/1 (April–May 1934): 7; Joanne Haewon Kim, "Asian American Consciousness before and during the Second World War: A Comparative Study of Younghill Kang and Carlos Bulosan" (senior thesis, University of California, Berkeley, 1997), 32.

35. "Koreans Rise Again for Independence," *Korean Student Bulletin* 8/1 (February 1930).

36. National Archives, RG 338, USAFIK, unit 11070, box 103, file 350/09.

37. Younghill Kang, "How It Feels to Be a Korean in Korea," *U.N. World* 2/4 (May 1948): 18–21: the quotation is from p. 20. Also see Younghill Kang, foreword to Bong-youn Choy, *Korea: A History* (Rutland, VT: Charles E. Tuttle, 1971), 13–15. At a Long Island University colloquium in the late 1960s, Kang was the one speaker who criticized U.S. military involvement in the Vietnam War (Gari Ledyard, e-mail, 8 April 1997).

38. See, for instance, Kang's contributions to Hiram Haydn and Edmund Fuller, comps., *Thesaurus of Book Digests: Digests of the World's Permanent Writings from the Ancient Classics to Current Literature* (New York: Crown, 1949); and Kang's co-translation with Keely of Manhae's *Nim ŭi ch'immuk*: Han Yong-Woon [*sic*], *Meditations of the Lover* (Seoul: Yonsei University Press, 1970).

39. Alice M. Scharper, "The Golden Thread: Younghill Kang and the Origins of Korean American Literature" (Ph.D. diss., University of California, Davis, 1997), 49; emphasis added.

40. For examples of Liang's extensive, nearly instantaneous impact on both Japanese intellectuals like the Sinologist Naitō Konan and Korean nationalists like Shin Ch'ae-ho and An Ch'ang-ho, see Joshua Fogel, *Politics and Sinology: The Case of Naitō Konan (1866–1934)* (Cambridge: Harvard University Press, 1984), 84–91; Lee Kwang-rin [Yi Kwang-nin], "Korea's Responses to Social Darwinism," parts 1 and 2, *Korea Journal* 18/4 (April 1978): 36–47; 18/5 (May 1978): 42–49.

41. Liang Ch'i-ch'ao [Liang Qichao], *Intellectual Trends in the Ch'ing Period*, trans., intro., notes by Immanuel C. Y. Hsu (Cambridge: Harvard University Press, 1959), 104.

42. Translation modified from the one that appears in William Theodore de Bary, Wing-tsit Chan, and Chester Tan, comps., *Sources of Chinese Tradition*, vol. 2 (New York: Columbia University Press, 1964), 95.

43. Liang, *Intellectual Trends in the Ch'ing Period*, 104. In 1930 Younghill Kang

reviewed an English translation of Liang's 1922 *Xianqin Zhengzhi Sixiang Shi*. "China's Thinkers," review of *History of Chinese Political Thought*, by Liang Chi-Chao, *New York Herald Tribune Books*, 2 November 1930, XI, 10. Not surprisingly, Liang's preface to the book includes an extended example of the transplantation conceit, though by then, disillusioned with Western political and economic systems in the aftermath of World War I, Liang had grown skeptical about the "wholesale transplantation of the thoughts of another society." Liang Chi-Chao [Liang Qichao], *History of Chinese Political Thought during the Early Tsin Period*, trans. L. T. Chen (New York: Harcourt, Brace, 1930), 13.

44. Im Hwa, *Sinmunhak sa* (History of the new literature), ed. Im Kyu-ch'an and Han Chin-il (Seoul: Han'gil Sa, 1993), 18. This major history of Korean literature was originally published in 1940, but Im Hwa also discussed literary transplantation in earlier articles. Kang mentions Im Hwa (spelled "Yim Wha") as one of the "best-known writers" included in a 1938 Korean literary anthology. Haydn and Fuller, *Thesaurus of Book Digests*, 360.

45. Sometimes *ishoku* denotes "grafting" as well; it is the Japanese pronunciation of the same Chinese logographs that are used by Liang Qichao and Im Hwa to mean only "transplant."

46. An unpublished translation by Michael Bourdaghs of "Shisó no unmei" (1938), reprinted in *Hayashi Tatsuo chosakushú* (Collected writings of Hayashi Tatsuo), vol. 5 (Tokyo: Heibonsha, 1971), 97–109. Hayashi (1896–1984) was a liberal social critic and philosopher.

47. Fogel, *Politics and Sinology*. Fogel argues rather unpersuasively that Naitó has been wrongly accused of being an apologist for Japanese imperialism. For a summary of organic models and metaphors of Japanese imperialist thought, see Morris-Suzuki, *Re-Inventing Japan*.

48. Quoted in Stefan Tanaka, *Japan's Orient: Rendering Pasts into History* (Berkeley: University of California Press, 1993), 207.

49. Derrida, "Passages—from Traumatism to Promise," 123; emphasis in the original.

50. I refer here to Wallersteinian World System theory, which posits a semiperipheral, sub-imperial Japan. See also Bruce Cumings, "Archaeology, Descent, Emergence: Japan in British/American Hegemony, 1900–1950," in *Japan in the World*, ed. Masao Miyoshi and H. D. Harootunian (Durham: Duke University Press, 1993).

51. Homi K. Bhabha, *The Location of Culture* (New York: Routledge, 1994); Partha Chatterjee, *Nationalist Thought and the Colonial World* (Minneapolis: University of Minnesota Press, 1986).

52. In the first decades of the twentieth century, it was still common for well-educated Koreans such as Han and Kim to be skilled in Chinese calligraphy.

53. Lack of space prevents me from discussing Kang's thoughts on principles of literary translation and their relation to the critiques of translation's work in

the "cofiguration" of national languages and identity given in such works as Naoki Sakai, *Translation and Subjectivity* (Minneapolis: University of Minnesota Press, 1997) and Lydia Liu, *Translingual Practice: Literature, National Culture, and Translated Modernity—China, 1900–1937* (Stanford: Stanford University Press, 1995).

54. I originally heard this tale from my parents as a child in Baltimore. There are, of course, many variations, such as the more extended version in In-sob Zong, ed., trans., *Folk Tales from Korea* (1952; New York: Grove, 1979), 7–10.

55. Trinh T. Minh-Ha, *When the Moon Waxes Red: Representation, Gender, and Cultural Politics* (New York: Routledge, 1991), 14–15. For alternative routes of postcoloniality and "return" for the diasporic subject, see R. Radhakrishnan, *Diasporic Mediations: Between Home and Location* (Minneapolis: University of Minnesota Press, 1996), 164–67.

56. For more on the 1935 riot, see Cheryl Lynn Greenberg, *Or Does It Explode? Black Harlem in the Great Depression* (New York: Oxford University Press, 1991).

57. This maneuver, away from African American collectivity to the "calm center" of individual transcendence, is considered a typical modernist trope in Edward Pavlić, 'Come On in My Kitchen': Asymmetry, Angularity, and Incremental Repetition in Zora Neale Hurston's Diasporic Modernism," *Xcp: cross cultural poetics* 6 (2000): 10–19. Although here I treat the combination of the Western phoenix and Buddhist reincarnation as *East Goes West*'s concluding instance of hybridity, both the phoenix and soteriological vision themselves are results of a complex East-West grafting. Kang's "phenix" fuses the firebird of Roman myth and the Chinese *feng huang* (commonly termed a phoenix in translations of Chinese poetry), while his description of reincarnation has puzzling non-Buddhist elements in it. I shall address elsewhere the additional meanings generated by this complexity and its literary precedents in both Chinese and Western modernist poems that Kang studied.

58. In his unsuccessful Guggenheim fellowship application of 1954, Kang used the term "cross-fertilizations" in relation to his earlier advocacy of F. S. C. Northrop's 1946 treatise *The Meeting of East and West: An Inquiry concerning World Understanding*. Archive, John Simon Guggenheim Memorial Foundation.

CAPITAL

If in a literal sense incorporation refers to a specific form of industrial and business organization, in a figurative sense it encompasses a more comprehensive pattern of change.
                    —Alan Trachtenberg, *The Incorporation of America*

The essays in part 3 consider the cultural and political legacies of economic Americanization and corporatization, and the production of a laboring and consuming subject. Paula Rabinowitz argues that feminism may be read as a vernacular modernism. "In both celebrating female artists and commodifying their art as a means of consolidating a mass movement," Rabinowitz writes, "contemporary feminism has fulfilled both the optimistic and pessimistic aspects of mechanical reproduction as mass production." Pushing the limits of modernism, nationalism, and feminism in the proliferation of "too many words, too many images," art, gender, and citizenship become kitsch. Yet in collectively considering the reception and production of the "Great Lady Painters" of the United States, Canada, and Mexico, Georgia O'Keeffe, Emily Carr, and Frida Kahlo, Rabinowitz also destabilizes the spatial and temporal incorporation of all "America" into the United States. Rather than "forgetting the threats to cohesion" of the nation, she remembers the "forgetting of the cohesion of that which was formerly combined."

In "Kitchen Mechanics and Parlor Nationalists," William Maxwell challenges prevailing histories of the Harlem Renaissance that focus on the cultural nationalism of African America to the exclusion of the multiple concurrent internationalist movements, including black bolshevism, a movement largely comprised of Caribbean immigrants who had been impressed by the Soviet Union's overtures to the colonized world. Focusing particularly on the work and politics of the largely forgotten poet and lyricist Andy Razaf, who composed the words to more than eight hundred jazz and "blues-flavored" popular songs during the middle part of the twentieth century, Maxwell argues that Razaf's leftist politics and radical poetry both anticipated and influenced much of the better-known writing of the renaissance. Sharing a belief in the promise of diaspora that Marcus Garvey advocated, while simultaneously rejecting the romanticist erudition of the Lockean New Negroes as well as Garvey's ventures into capitalism and his quasi-imperialist ambitions for a repatriated Africa, Razaf's songwriting and poetry drew on two distinct countercultures of modernity—Soviet Marxism and the vernacular arts of the African diaspora—to celebrate black service workers and suggest that "underpaid black labor is the breeding ground of black art."

In "Reno-vating Gender: Place, Production, and the Reno Divorce Factory," Jani Scandura argues that 1930s Reno, Nevada, was constructed as a place in which femininity, female sexuality, and gendered divisions of labor and migration were questioned, produced, and revised. Projecting a twisted Fordist industrialism onto a regendered American Frontier, the "Reno Divorce Factory" proposed to Reno-vate independent divorcées into New Industrial Wives: heterosexual mothers who shopped. Yet, as Scandura points out, the discursive struggles underpinning the production of "Reno" also reveal the gendered performative that is modern place.

Finally in a move to recuperate and preserve the writings and collections of turn-of-the-century worker-poets whose forgotten publications circulated on meeting cards and in newspapers and pamphlets, Cary Nelson establishes a "tradition in the American labor movement in which poems and songs help workers interpret and articulate their lives and draw them toward solidarity with their peers." The labor movement used poetry not only to build and unify membership, he argues, but also to educate workers and restate core beliefs and values.

10

GREAT LADY PAINTERS, INC.

ICONS OF FEMINISM, MODERNISM, AND THE NATION

Paula Rabinowitz

As always art is the pulse of a nation.
—Gertrude Stein, *Paris France*

Half of the things they had me send are in the basement too.
—Emily Carr, *Hundreds and Thousands*

The art of Frida Kahlo is a ribbon around a bomb.
—Andre Breton, *Surrealism and Painting*

America, she [O'Keeffe] says, can give her all she wants.
—Peyton Boswell, Jr., *Modern American Painting*

In 1996, to honor the hundredth anniversary of the birth of "the most renowned of . . . American women painters," the United States Postal Service issued a commemorative stamp featuring one of Georgia O'Keeffe's *Red Poppy* paintings.[1] That same year, the Canadian government began a massive project designed to produce a new national school curriculum about "Canada's most famous woman painter," Emily Carr.[2] A few years earlier, in 1991, Mexican journalists coined a neologism, "Fridamania," to describe the quasi-hysteria erupting over Frida Kahlo's life and work after Madonna announced that she had purchased a number of the artists' paintings and had plans to acquire the rights to her life story.[3] It would seem that the 1990s ushered in an astonishing interest in these North American women's work, an interest that coincides with new understandings of hemispheric interdependency and exploitation resulting from NAFTA, the Internet, and changing immigration policies. That these women painters, who forged their careers during the heyday of American modernism (1920s–1930s), have become accessible (even marketable) icons of womanhood, creativity, national identity, and modernism in the 1990s is both perfectly logical and truly bizarre.

Lately, it seems, modernism—that which we thought we had successfully posted—has returned, like the repressed it was supposed to have unleashed, postmarked for a second, post-post time. Modernism is being revisited, pluralized, resuscitated, resurrected, rethought, reinscribed, reincorporated. No longer can we be sure of what modernism, once a stable/staple movement, is or was. Where once there was a certain consensus about the tenets of modernism—formal innovation, surface over depth, self-referentiality—now there are one, two, many modernisms, spanning various continents, unevenly developed among multiple populations. Modernism has acquired gender, sexuality, race, even class identities that complicate and alter its "structure."[4] Yet these complications remain dependent on certain modernist notions of identity and difference (such as gender), of representation and form (such as landscape), of space and time (such as nationalism) that tend to collapse into its structure itself.[5]

Feminism, which in its (so-called) second wave organized under the banner of international solidarity among women against capitalist exploitation and male chauvinism, has, paradoxically, been central to this modernist structure and has as such aided the recent rise of O'Keeffe, Kahlo, and Carr beyond celebrity status to iconicity.[6] So has the emergence of various forms of commercialized art trophies—posters, postcards, refrigerator magnets, coffee mugs, and so forth. The intersection of feminism and the marketplace has been both an effect of modern culture and one of its primary supports. That women's lives, voices, paintings are part of a modern national discourse should be obvious, but is not easily recognized because the heuristic of the public/private split laces the personal to women, placing them apart from the political, keeping them separate from the larger realm of power—the modern nation.

Women's lives do not conform to traditional autobiographical narratives of great men: they are about daily life of those closeted off in the domestic routines of home and family, so the story goes—and women's paintings lack the tradition, even more so than women's writings, to fit into a national canon of landscape or heroic portraiture.[7] "For most women," writes Germaine Greer, "portraiture was not one of the multifarious media of well-developed painterly genius but the outer limit of their capacity, a calling followed by constraint."[8] In a sense, never having been premodern, women's art can hardly embrace modernism. Moreover, modernism itself has a curious history in the Americas, where the most modern movements were found in industrial design—the Chrysler Building, grain elevators, the River Rouge Ford Plant (i.e., in the service of capital)—rather than as oppositional antibourgeois aesthetic movements in art and literature. The very aspects that symbolized American modernity—its rapid industrialization and urbanization—are monuments to accumulation and mobility, which would seem to offer little to modern women. Nevertheless, I want to argue that feminism itself is part of a modern nationalist identity. Its politics of subjectivity paradoxically place it in the service of collectivity by emphasizing a counter-modernist stance of the local, the personal, the vernacular, which have become, in effect, the culture of the modern national-feminine. The nation and modernism depend on the figure of private woman as much as feminism depends on the modern liberal nation-state to express identity, and if "art is the pulse of the nation," as that consummate modernist woman Gertrude Stein asserts, then one might look to it for some clues to the marketing of these three modern icons.

Why does modern feminism produce heroic female icons? These often come in the form of what the critic Susan Kollin calls, speaking of colonialist discourse, "the first (white) woman trope" of a nationalist project of expansion.[9] This powerful need to name an originary yet thoroughly modern mother is connected to another equally powerful one: the rediscovery of the unrecognized genius, the woman artist unappreciated in her own time, her own place, shrunken by the men surrounding her, waiting for her true audience—we women from another era, perhaps another country, who can pierce the veil of invisibility gender produces in history and bring these works up from the basement. I don't want to dissociate myself from this project of feminist archaeology and genealogy—I've made a career of it, like many feminists working as revisionist historians in one field or another. Rather, I want to understand it. To do so, I read some poems (and I might have chosen any number of other works) alongside the images of the three artists these poems memorialize to begin to unpack four interlinking concerns: how these artists used the nation and modernism to create an identity for themselves; how feminists use these artists to embody a modern female identity; how the nation uses this feminist identity and these women's modern art to celebrate itself; and finally, how mechanical reproduction makes it all possible—a circulation, among painting, poetry, feminism, nation, and reproduction, within the Americas then (the modern times of the 1920s and 1930s) and now (roughly since the postmodern late 1970s).

A 1978 poem by Patti Smith to "georgia o'keefe"—sweetly misspelling her name—begins, "great lady painter."[10] Adrienne Rich's volume *Your Native Land, Your Life* takes its title from her 1985 poem to "Emily Carr."[11] Both speak back to the past, as one woman artist retrieves another because "you were alone in this / Nobody knew or cared," until Rich spoke to and for Carr. Smith screams O'Keeffe's defiance: "she's no fool / started out pretty / pretty pretty girl / georgia o'keefe / until she had her fill." A generation later, Nicole Cooley, in a recent poem to Frida Kahlo, "want[s] to feel her pain / . . . want[s] to save her as Diego could not . . . / want[s] to slip / into her clothes . . . to save her."[12] In this urge to give voice, they repeat a gesture performed by the Canadian protofeminist and proletarian poet Dorothy Livesay in her 1953 poem, "The Three Emilys." "These women crying in my head / Walk alone, uncomforted: / The Emilys, these three / Cry to be set free—."[13] Contemporary women artists, now armed with an American modernist feminism (concerned with a "return to the sources of tradition"[14]), will know these women, will save these women, whose lives and landscapes fuse them into their nation's female heritage and their own feminine creativity.

Ironically, in this way, these heroines are reappropriated, stripped of their (national) identities, and carried away to do other work elsewhere. In the Americas, where the national project entails land conquest and colonial expansion, these women's struggles to embody, to incorporate, to vivify the trees, sky, mountains, ground, plants, and first peoples within their spaces and themselves mirror their nations' histories. Mechanical reproduction, the culture industry, has spread their images, making them ubiquitous symbols of unrecognized female pain and power now ripe to be reinhabited by our newer, more insightful postmodern American feminist selves. This subsequent effort at reclamation seems to place feminism itself at the service of the national culture and its industry also.

The belief that these lives and the lands they represent are open for feminist identification derives in part from the modernist Virginia Woolf's famous remark in *A Room of One's Own* (1928) that "we think back through our mothers if we are women." Woolf had traced a genealogy of British women's literary history in her search as Mary Beton, Mary Seton, or Mary Carmichael find something to say about "Women and Fiction." Appropriating a kitchen maid's ballad about court intrigue, Woolf positioned herself just outside the doors of literary history among minor ladies-in-waiting, wondering whether this time a mother would appear; after all, sons create mothers as much as mothers bear sons. But who are "our mothers"? For Woolf, our mothers are clearly not biological—they are not any woman, nor any woman writing, not even any woman writing in English, they are, finds Woolf's many Marys, British women—of a certain class—writing modern British fiction. Woolf's female antecedents connect a female heritage to a nation, a class, and a genre, and also provide a map for charting her own self, that historical oxymoron—the female genius. Woolf may have revised her nationalist sentiments in *Three Guineas*—"As a woman I have no country"—but the unconscious connection between mothers and modern national narratives continued in her work and in much subsequent feminist critical histories of literature.

Yet, like Woolf herself, the mothers she thinks back through were not themselves mothers. Dorothy Livesay's poem laments her own limitations as a poet—unable to "possess another kindom" and be "an Emily on mountain snows"—because she "move[s] as mother in a frame." The modern woman artist—novelist or painter—cannot be burdened by children. Maternity itself is somehow antimodern, a throwback. Ecstatic merger with landscape requires mobility—social, economic, sexual. The female self can embody the nation only when it has not already bodied forth its own offspring. The modern woman's sexuality is virginal, almost girlish, or tomboyish as the flat-chested, narrow-hipped, bobbed flapper. She must be free to "move triumphant," like the Emilys, like O'Keeffe, who Stieglitz insisted remain childless, like Kahlo, left unable to bear children after her accident, like Carr, a Victorian spinster aunt. Her only labor must be her "work"; "I think work is best," wrote Kahlo of her painting and childlessness.

The last public appearance Frida Kahlo made before her death was at a demonstration protesting CIA involvement in the overthrow of Guatemalan president Jacobo Arbenz. In a famous wire service photo of July 2, 1954, she raises one fist in the air in international solidarity and in the other holds a placard reading "Por la Paz." Behind her, pushing her wheelchair, marches Diego Rivera. Two weeks before her death, Kahlo was an amputee wracked by disease and drugs; her wheelchair was still her means of mobility as it had been on and off since her freak streetcar accident at the age of eighteen. Kahlo's paintings—primarily self-portraits and still lifes—were in some part a result of her limited mobility; yet her signature self-image, almost always set in an imagined Mexican landscape—for example, her 1943 painting *Roots*—like the photograph of her, linked her face and body to her nation and land.[15]

Being out on the streets, "nightwalking in stranger cities," as Muriel Rukeyser called it, has been an essential activity for modern radical political activism and for urban aesthetic epiphanies.[16] Walter Benjamin's image of the *flâneur* walking his turtle through the Paris arcades fixes the quintessential vision of modernity as bourgeois, dandyish. However, feminist scholars have questioned its relevance for women.[17] Streetwalking means something different when the one taking a stroll is female. Still, Louise Michel striding along the Paris Commune barricades codes modern revolution within the working-class woman's body. Benjamin's fascination with prostitutes (in "A Berlin Chronicle" and elsewhere) suggests that the modern city streets, where women offer themselves as both commodities and their purveyors, give rise to a new form of subjectivity. This is a subjectivity of loneliness, desire, and transgression, Benjamin notes, founded in the empty Paris streets of Atget's photographs—the scene of a crime, Benjamin calls them—a woman alone on the street, night-walking, serves as the emblem of modernity.

By the 1930s, many middle-class women hit the road in search of their nations' stark natural beauty and squalid social ills besieging their poorer contemporaries; in a curious marriage of capital and its critics, both the automobile and the Left made this possible. Movement rearranged, for a time, traditional American mythos of sedate feminine bourgeois culture, as artists, political activists, and social workers sought to document and ameliorate the ravages of the Dust Bowl and the Depression. For middle-class women, paradoxically, the economic constrictions of the 1930s offered a widened world of travel, work, and responsibility. Georgia O'Keeffe left her husband and mentor, Alfred Stieglitz, and New York for New Mexico in the Ford V8 she fitted as a mobile studio, replacing the back seat with an easel, to keep cool in the burning desert sun as she reinvented landscape painting into a feminine erotic abstraction. Among the photographic "Portrait" Stieglitz and O'Keeffe choreographed together are a striking series of O'Keeffe and her car. Ranging from abstract studies of fingers on the shiny hubcaps to severe portraits of O'Keeffe in the driver's seat, these studies suggest not only her freedom from her mentor/husband, but her ability to discover her landscape herself through mastery of Detroit's modern machine.

In her diary, *Hundreds and Thousands,* Emily Carr related that in 1933 she bought an old caravan, which she dubbed "The Elephant," to lumber through the backwoods of British Columbia with her menagerie, an entourage of monkeys, cats, birds, dogs, rats, to spend long weeks painting the towering red cedars that became her subject matter as she sought a visual vernacular for Canada's West. "Oh, these mountains, great bundles of contradiction, hard, cold, austere, disdainful, remote yet gentle, spiritual, appealing! Oh, you mountains, I am at your feet—humble pleading! Speak to me in your wordless words! I claim my brotherhood to you. We are the same substance," ecstatically proclaimed Carr (36).

Kahlo, by inhabiting her self-portraits with a mythical Mexican landscape of desert, volcanoes, cactus, and palm, at once arid and fecund, fused her face, body, and land. Sporting her "Mexican petticoats" against the cold, during the early 1930s she traveled "Gringolandia" while Diego Rivera worked on murals in San Francisco, Detroit, and New York, collecting images; then in 1938 she set off for Paris to exhibit her "message of pain" with Andre Breton and other surrealists.[18] Contemporary feminism didn't invent these women's identification with a modernist national-feminine landscape. Each painter first presented, even promoted, herself as a modern woman and national heroine, almost hysterically placing herself in the landscape of her nation.

Coming into artistic power during the late 1920s and early 1930s, each woman was as acutely aware of her national identity as a modern identity. The 1910–17 revolution forged Mexican independence and the imperial conferences (resulting in the 1931 Statutes of Westminster) strengthened Canada's dominion status; national pride inspired movements that sought a distinctly Mexican *mestizo* and Canadian mosaic vernacular. Meanwhile during the 1920s, "the States were asserting: The U.S.A. is now grown up artistically."[19] "Today," enthused the author of *Modern American Painting* in 1939, "America need no longer dwell in Europe's house and live with Europe's art. America, in art, as in national progress, has native spirit."[20] "No advertising / No institution / No isms / No theories. . . . The doors of An American Place are ever open to all." Thus did Stieglitz's "An American Place" declare itself a new kind of gallery more democratic and more open to all Americans than the brand new Museum of Modern Art. An American Place held "No cocktail parties."[21] Modern American arts, stemming from a rejection of European influences and embracing a kind of industrial primitivism, had varying national sources in the teens and twenties. For both personal and professional reasons, Stieglitz's galleries promoted American art and photography. Mexico's revolution drew the Muralistas to peasant and *mestizo* themes to connect their art with an illiterate population.[22] The Group of Seven came home from Europe to catalogue Canada's vast landscapes.

These nationalist impulses were of course reinforced by the politics and economics of the 1930s as worldwide depression and Hitler's Germany closed off the social milieux of Europe's avant-garde. In the United States, the New Deal's Federal Arts Projects encouraged an expanded audience for the arts as it helped support unemployed artists. Art became part of popular culture as well. *Life* magazine's "Pageant of America" series commissioning "Modern American Paintings," inaugurated in 1936 by Henry Luce, was "a further step in the program of art education, which has made *Life* the most significant single force of art appreciation in America," according to the Corcoran Gallery's director, C. Powell Minnegerode. By 1939, *Life's* circulation of more than 2.3 million produced a "mass-impact of art upon the dormant sensitivies of an entire nation," claimed Peyton Boswell, editor of *Art Digest*.[23]

The language of national destiny, even when encoded in the singular visions of artists setting out to invent a new iconography of landscape, however, took on ominous and sinister connotations during the 1920s and 1930s, tinged as it was with fascist overtones everywhere. Still, the 1920s represent for Canada and

Mexico the emergence of modern nationhood from colonial domination by Europe and the United States and the beginning of reckoning with the cultural imperialism of a xenophobic and increasingly powerful United States, which has only increased over the years, culminating with NAFTA. Moreover, because these artists were women, they never held the stature of the men with whom they were linked as lovers, spouses, protégés, and models in the traditional gender patterns of Western art history. Thus claiming national identity provided a means for them to enter history and reshape the vision of the land as eternally feminized. If they were hardly feminists, these women were daughters of the first wave of feminism, which opened careers for creative middle-class women and offered an education and freedom to travel.

O'Keeffe painted *Red Hills White Sky* and *Skull—Red, White and Blue* (1930), a still life composed in Lake George of bones brought back from her trip to New Mexico, in response to "the men of New York City and their 'Great American Everything.'"[24] Natural forms of dead animals, dried white in the hot southwestern sun, undermine the patriotic vision, even as the red, white, and blue so common to O'Keeffe's palette enhance the simple objects she painted. *Blunden Harbor* and *Forest British Columbia* by Carr and *On the Borderline between Mexico and United States,* and *My Grandparents, My Parents and Me* by Kahlo are also responses by these women artists to a modernist fusion of female self-identity with national terrain. Each painting traces a history of the nation: working from photographs, Carr's recover a lost tribal presence by replacing the totems that no longer stood in their original locations; Kahlo's locate herself, on the one hand, between U.S. commodity capitalism and Mexican indigenous socialism, and within her family tree—linking Europe and Mexico—on the other. They make explicit a reading of nation, native, and nature as feminized; at the same time, they mock male fantasies of maternal nature by exaggerating the legacy of the feminist and antifeminist rhetoric about womanhood, nature, and nation circulating since the mid-nineteenth century. (Think of the map of Scotland superimposed on Lucy Mannheim's face as she describes to Robert Donat the grave danger to Britain posed by the foreign gentleman with the missing little finger in Hitchcock's 1937 thriller *The 39 Steps*). Typical of the backhanded trivializing celebration of a woman artist as modernist emblem was this remark by Holger Cahill, curator at MOMA during the 1930s: "Georgia O'Keeffe articulates her design with great clarity, and shows in her work a combination of delicacy and austerity which is essentially feminine."[25]

Nevertheless, the paintings subvert regional iconography by obsessively and idiosyncratically reinscribing it and in so doing alienating it from the nation. O'Keeffe remarked that her New York paintings were never really accepted by the "men" because the modern city was a masculine space. She could paint flowers, but not skyscapers.[26] They told her to "Leave New York to the men."[27] Kahlo noted that the 'big shits' of surrealism," who with Diego Rivera and Trotsky were arguing "Pour an art revolutionaire independant" had just published a manifesto denouncing "nationalism in art." They liked her work; but in Mexico, at "the University gallery, which is a small and rotten place, but the only one which admits any kind of stuff . . . four or five people told me they were swel [sic], the rest think they are too crazy."[28] Carr wrote a friend, "The History of Art and the things that are written about the men have never interested me greatly. . . . Only the work."[29] Elsewhere—symbolically located, because it might be next door—was where these women were headed.

The road became a space for female fantasies of movement and merger, forging a new aesthetics out of intense looking: O'Keeffe magnifying a cow skull; Carr absorbed by the swirls of Red Cedar and the huge tongues looming from the lost totems of native peoples; Kahlo tracing Mexico in the lines of her brow.[30] Kahlo intimately coiled together her genealogy with the great land despoiled by imperialism, its people debased and dislocated as a result, "A hidden materialism," wrote Rivera, "Frida's art is collectively individual."[31] (Just look at her 1930s paintings *My Dress Hangs There* or *Henry Ford Hospital.*) Despite being thrilled and appalled by what they found in their travels, the women on the road felt that they had connected with their nation and its places and people. However, unlike Kahlo, who was actively involved with the Fourth International and Communist Party, neither Carr nor O'Keeffe had any truck with left-wing class-based politics. (Of course, O'Keeffe was involved in the National Women's Party and advocated for passage of the Equal Rights Amendment.) Theirs was a more traditional modernist sentiment of the artist achieving her vision apart from current events; O'Keeffe even argued with *New Masses* editor Michael Gold about the importance for women artists of remaining independent and unaligned.

Part of the labor of modernist thinking back through our mothers entails discovering their latent feminism (and, even better, lesbianism).[32] Even if the evidence is missing, it becomes a willed desire of the feminist critic. Carr had a deep connection to her sisters and a few women artists, yet she did not identify with women's issues. While she identified herself with Canada's mountains and trees and sky and sea, turning them into deeply erotic sites of interiority, the nation served to free her from the bounds of conventional middle-class womanhood. It allowed her to forge a "brotherhood" through its landscape with the other male artists of the Group of Seven. In a watercolor from 1912 she paints her sister, a schoolteacher, at her desk, a map of Canada hanging on the wall behind her. These feminine interiors were soon replaced by an envaginated nature, eerie and dark, yet clearly home to Carr in ways traditional domesticity

201

was not. As early as 1927, Carr's paintings were hanging in Canadian art museums along with her revered and, at that time, still popularly reviled Group of Seven. However, her work, like theirs, was "down in the basement, turned face to the wall, four beautiful canvases . . . rejected, hidden away, scorned—beautiful thoughts of fine men picturing beautiful Canada" (12). If there was little critical sympathy for fine men picturing beautiful Canada, Carr's chances of attaining national recognition appeared hopeless.

Carr's commitment to finding a pictorial expression of the nature and history of coastal British Columbia developed incrementally. It took her time to discover her landscape and its visual language, one that would let her escape from the clutches of Victorian femininity and from the phallic influences of her mentor. By 1933, as she was struggling to paint heroic, spiritual mountains in the manner of her friend Lawren Harris, Carr groused in her diary that "the women's clubs are sending 'Vanquished' to Amsterdam for the Convention of the Confederation of Women Something-or-Other" (46). Her only consolation at what she saw as a double failure—inability to paint the mountains and impatience with Women Something-or-Others—came from her deep identification with her nation, or more specifically, her region. "Only one point I give to mine. I loved the country and the people more than the others who have painted her. It was my own country, part of the West and me" (12).

From the beginning, O'Keeffe positioned herself as the exceptional woman; while she encouraged other women artists, as Carr put it in her memoir, *Growing Pains,* "O'keefe [*sic*] wants to be the greatest painter."[33] As C. S. Merrill notes in her verse tribute to O'Keeffe (one of the many examples of how proximity to an icon bestows limited fame), "If she was not on top, then she wanted out."[34] The photographic portrait on which O'Keeffe and Stieglitz collaborated during the 1920s and 1930s, first exhibited in 1921, "put her at once on the map. Everybody knew the name. She became what is known as a newspaper personality."[35] The exceptional woman, the personality, are two sides of the same modernist coin: a romantic holdover notion of genius as a condition of the modernist aesthete; and the emergence of a popular culture of celebrity against which modernist aesthetics rebels. Moreover, the pictures, featuring her gorgeous body, face, and hands posed before her paintings, often described as "gorgeous," reaffirmed a connection between her youthful sexuality and her painting.[36] Two years later, the one-person show Stieglitz mounted of her new work at Anderson Gallery was jammed as five hundred people (mostly women) a day came to see her work, interested in this woman artist and lover of her impresario. Her gigantic flowers and other curvilinear objects suggested to the critic Paul Rosenfeld that "Women, one would judge, always feel, when they feel strongly, through the womb."[37]

Despite her dismissals of these pop-Freudian interpretations, critics persisted in viewing her work as "quite outblaz[ing] masculine masterpieces," its "dissonances . . . analogous to modern music and poetry."[38] This love goddess and exceptional woman artist embodied a curious amalgam of modern American culture; tabloids called her the "Lindbergh of art," after her 1928 sale of her calla lily painting to a French collector for $25,000. Under Stieglitz's guidance, she had successfully packaged herself as typically American; "a prim ex-country schoolmistress," the *New York Evening Graphic* called her.[39] This echoed the *Nation*'s "series of personality portraits, Americans We Like," which begins with the observation, "A tall slender woman dressed in black with an apron thrown over her lap . . . carefully scraped . . . the palette, which thus retains always its air of virginity."[40] By 1938, after *Life* had featured her in its Pageant of America series, O'Keeffe began receiving commissions from Steuben Glass and other corporations to design glassware, dishes, and so forth for mass reproduction and sale. Her move west and discovery of her ultimate subject in its bleak spaces solidified her position as heroic woman unveiling her unconscious desires. Through her painting of the landscape as "colors and shapes," her eroticized desert places hiding secret spaces had invented a "language," which, according to her contemporary, the critic Lewis Mumford, "conveyed directly and chastely in paint experiences for which language conveys only obscenities."[41] She was making the desert speak of female power and independence, as she had spoken a few years before to an assembly of the National Woman's Party (of which she had been a member since 1913).[42]

Kahlo, while connected deeply to a number of women—Ella Wolfe, Lucienne Bloch, her sisters—found her political identity through her connections to international socialism and communism; moreover, much of her artistic identity developed from her difficult relationship with Rivera, who in addition to being Mexico's revered artist, had had affairs with many of her female intimates. "I wear again my crazy mexican [*sic*] dress, my hair grew longer again. . . . I have painted about twelve paintings, all small and unimportant, with the same personal subjects that only appeal to myself and nobody else," she wrote Bloch in 1938 after Julien Levy offered to mount the first show of her work. This self-appraisal contrasted with her assessment of Rivera's "serie [*sic*] of landscapes. Two of them, if you trust my own taste, are the best things he ever painted . . . simply gorgeous . . . they are magnificent . . . so perfect and strong."[43] Kahlo's insistence on the diminutive quality of her work, especially compared to Rivera's monumental landscapes, suggests her focus on the self, rather than the land and nation. As Susan Stewart notes, "We find the miniature at the origin of private, individual history, . . . the gigantic at the origin of public and natural history." Yet Gaston Bachelard insists that the miniature incorporates a universe: "large is contained in small."[44] Kahlo's miniature canvases—which appeal only to herself—allow her to embrace, even embody, the Mexican nation, its land and people completely. Kahlo's 1953 autobiography—small, just three paragraphs long—concludes,

> My paintings are well-painted, not nimbly but patiently. My painting contains in it the message of pain. I think that at least a few people are interested in it. It's not revolutionary. Why keep wishing for it to be belligerent? I can't.
>
> Painting completed my life. I lost three children and a series of other things that would have fulfilled my horrible life. My painting took the place of all this, I think work is best.[45]

Again, emphasizing the miniature, paintings replace children; a reminder, like the references to O'Keeffe's virginal palette, to Carr's collection of stories about her alter ego, *The Book of Small,* that the modern female painter is not maternal. Their legacies are as "women" painters, partly because of the overwhelming sexism of art history, but also because of the deeply erotic vaginal iconography each developed to claim her landscape. As such, they can never be truly modern, if modernism presumes a certain international style, for their subject matter—no matter how physically inaccessible it was—remains resolutely personal, local, idiosyncratic, particular. Because of this vernacular quality, these women are also coded as profoundly national (or regional) figures.[46] Carr is "Canada's most famous woman painter." Frida Kahlo "conjures mystery and magic and Mexico"—"Her house must belong to the penitent Mother, the stone/virgin in Juarez." O'Keeffe is redundantly America's "great lady painter." In claiming to be icons of Canadianness or Mexicanness or Americanness, the artists themselves, their contemporary mentors, and their current promoters—feminist or not—are reproducing another aspect of the woman/artist/nation identity: isolation and uniqueness. Diego Rivera crowed that "[i]n the panorama of Mexican painting of the last 20 years the work of Frida Kahlo shines like a diamond in the midst of many inferior jewels; clear and hard with precisely defined facets."[47] Ironically, in 1932 O'Keeffe won a contest sponsored by the newly created Museum of Modern Art for a mural to grace Radio City Music Hall after enraged New Yorkers demanded that Rivera, who was completing the ill-fated Rockefeller Center mural, be replaced as the commissioned artist by an "American."[48] Her commission to paint the women's powder room with a gigantic triptych (Stuart Davis won the men's room) infuriated Stieglitz, who had spent almost two decades cultivating a reputation (and decent price) for her canvases. (As cruel fate would have it, O'Keeffe's first commission expressly aimed at a female audience ended in disaster. As she was putting the fin-ishing touches on the canvas-lined walls, they began to lift from the surface, peeling off and disintegrating, and sending O'Keeffe into convalescence for a nervous breakdown, that most unmodern female malady.) The burden of repre-senting modern/woman/nation appears at once as liberating and confining. Consider the image of loneliness and sexual alienation projected in the poems by Rich, Smith, and Cooley: Carr has "no personal leanings" and so is cut off from the vital culture of lesbian modernism; O'Keeffe, "what she do now / go and beat the desert / stir dust bowl" as a solitary shaman; and Kahlo "wish[es] that lightning could erase my body." Either in "pain" as Kahlo is or "joy" as is Carr, she has "been around forever," like O'Keeffe, as the condition of nature and of woman, and in this argument, of modernism and nation, which be-comes an eternal state, outside history, alone, isolated. Yet Carr had traveled ex-tensively—to San Francisco, London, Paris to study art, and across Canada and the United States to visit artists, museums, and galleries; Andrea Mariani writes persuasively of Emily Carr's internationalism. The same is true for O'Keeffe, despite her constant assertion that "she has never been to Europe and . . . never had a desire to go [because] America can give her all she wants."[49] Stieglitz served as an important link to Europe while O'Keeffe was in New York. Later, after her move to New Mexico, O'Keeffe was approached by artists from around the world seeking advice about how to exhibit in New York and other international art centers.[50] Kahlo regularly traveled abroad and hosted foreign guests and was part of international movements, both artistic and political. None of these painters was cut off from vital connections to other painters—even women painters—worldwide. Clearly historical accuracy is beside the point; rather, it is the status of these women as national icons that determines their legends as isolated visionaries.

Their visions circulate through mechanically reproduced images, which, at least since the advent of photography, become a means to incorporate an imagi-native space/place into one's identity, to project a self outward onto a nation.[51] Gertrude Stein speaks of her passionately intense relationship with France begin-ning when she first saw Millet's *Man with a Hoe*, which made her understand "the french [*sic*] country" as "different, it was ground not country." That "France is made of ground, of earth" she knew from the photograph of this painting she ac-quired as a girl. Landscape painting fuses identity, nation, and nature in powerful ways, in each of these painters' works as sensuous, sometimes violent, displays of female genitalia. The uses to which feminists have put these women's landscapes, ironically because of the culture industry's commodification of art, reinforce the acutely nationalist aspects of women's artistic identities. Just as Stein's picture of the Millet painting "was all the Paris France I really knew then," O'Keeffe posters

GREAT LADY PAINTERS, INC.

and Carr calendars and Kahlo shopping bags provide access to women's imaginary landscapes of desire, enabling them to claim the nation as an erotic and, finally, maternal female space, reinstating the modernist collapse of woman and consumption (this time in the form of shopping).[52]

In their differing and contradictory theories of modern popular culture both Walter Benjamin and Theodor Adorno and Max Horkheimer describe mechanical reproduction as a process of mass production. What they mean is not only the industrial procedures of Fordism and Taylorism enabling the rapid production of huge amounts of identical objects, but the ancillary, yet ultimately more significant, production of the masses who become at once their objects' producers and consumers. Benjamin's more optimistic view sees the sense of mass—of a population simultaneously experiencing its self as a mass—as a potentially revolutionary formation. This symbiosis of modern mass production is akin to his description of the streetwalker—simultaneously worker, commodity, and capitalist—as a figure of modernity. "Mechanical reproduction of art changes the reaction of the masses toward art. The reactionary attitude toward a Picasso painting changes into the progressive reaction towards a Chaplin movie." For Benjamin, "Painting simply is in no position to represent an object for simultaneous collective experience" and so it is to film he turns for the mass "intimate fusion of visual and emotional enjoyment."[53]

Benjamin hadn't fully grasped what the invention of cheap photo-textual printing would mean for painting (not to mention what digitizing entire museum collections for the World Wide Web might do to art); it, too, might become a mechanically reproduced form through the circulation of postcards, calendars, T-shirts, refrigerator magnets, posters, and so forth, turning what seems to be a unique contemplative encounter with the "aura—a unique phenomenon of distance however close it may be" of art into an easily reproducible, commonly held instantaneous reaction to a series of images.[54] Of course, the difference between postcards of paintings and films is that film's mechanical reproduction is essential to its medium; however, in the case of the overcirculation of reproductions, images are reproduced from copies of images, which amounts to the same thing.

Madonna as Kahlo and the cartoon of it on the Internet (on the Madonna home page) are aspects of the ease with which "trademarks" can be replicated. Madonna's endless self-styling as first one then another female icon mimics Kahlo's self-fashioning as an emblem of Mexico. Lupe Rivera concludes her cookbook/memoir of her stepmother with the comment, "Because of the demands of her egocentric personality she played both icon and devotee. Her clothes created the Frida Kahlo style . . . only Frida and the women of Oaxaca wore their hair in that style. . . . With her own image in a mirror Frida painted

FIG. 10.1. Emily Carr meets Andy Warhol. T-shirt from the Vancouver Art Museum Shop. Photograph by Paula Rabinowitz. Printed by Mark Jensen.

ritualized icons surrounded by magic."[55] The museum shop of the Vancouver Museum of Art sells an Emily Carr T-shirt placing her face in a faux-Warhol series print.

The O'Keeffe industry of postcards, greeting cards, and calendars has produced staples found in virtually every museum and bookstore. They are designed, like film, to foreground, even require their replication and mass dispersal as "trademarks" for modern art, feminism, and nation.

Far less sanguine about Chaplin, the movies, and replicable mass culture were Adorno and Horkheimer, writing after the war and in the brightly noirish Hollywood of America, overcrowded with the "cult" of the "trademark" and its reinvention of language and thus identity.[56] "Perfect similarity is the absolute difference. . . . Ironically, man as a member of a species has been made a reality by the culture industry. Now any person signifies only those attributes by which he can replace everybody else; he is interchangeable, a copy." Mechanical reproduction continued the alienation of production apparent in mass culture—the industry of culture/the culture of industry—the same:

> The assembly-line character of the culture industry, the synthetic, planned method of turning out its products (factory-like not only in

the studio but more or less, in the compilation of cheap biographies, pseudo documentary novels, and hit songs) is very suited to advertising; the important individual points, by becoming detachable, interchangeable, and even technically alienated from any connected meaning, lend themselves to ends external to the work.

As if to prove their point, there are literally dozens of plays, operas, films, tapes, Web sites, poems, postcards, coffee table books, and tchotchkes circulating the visages, names, and images of these three painters. Kahlo, Carr, and O'Keeffe actively contributed to the construction of their images—dressing and posing in starkly recognizable outfits, Kahlo in her huuipils and flowers posing as a Tehuana for her self-portraits or Tina Modotti's photographs; Carr with her pet monkey, bobbed hair, and skullcap; O'Keeffe's stark visage and graceful long fingers photographed endlessly by Stieglitz. This culture, "a paradoxical commodity . . . it amalgamates with advertising," was both an object and so a representation of and an actual expression and so experience of the latent fascism they called late capitalism; and becomes, as such, the final stage of Enlightenment modernity.[57]

In both celebrating female artists and commodifying their art as a means of consolidating a mass movement, it would seem that contemporary feminism has fulfilled both the optimistic and pessimistic aspects of mechanical reproduction as mass production. In and through the circulation of these images of and by "great lady painters," feminism constructs a female genealogy and charts a feminized landscape—"painted desert / flower cactus"—and in so doing etches a space for female solidarity. In Rich's poem, the speaker's access to Carr's painting *Skidegate Pole* is highly mediated: "All I know is, it is here / even postcard-size can't diminish / the great eye, nostril, tongue." Rich's speaker, like millions of tourists to Canada's museums, has picked up a postcard of "Canada's most famous woman painter" and is reliving the visual experience of Skidegate Pole as Carr herself revived its eerie magnificence in her painting.

Actually, Carr's trips into the densely forested islands of British Columbia seldom yielded "the great eye." Instead, she found ruins as in *Koskemo Village*:

It is D'Sonoqua on the housepost up in the burnt part, strangled round by undergrowth. I want the pole vague and the tangle of growth strenuous. I want the ferocious, strangled lonesomeness of that place, creepy, nervy, forsaken, dank, dirty, dilapidated, the rank smell of nettles and rotting wood, the lush greens of the rank sea grass and the overgrown bushes, and the great dense forest behind full of unseen things and great silence, and on the sea the sun beating down, and on

FIG. 10.2. Poster advertising O'Keeffe prints available for sale at a Santa Fe gallery. Photograph by Paula Rabinowitz. Printed by Mark Jensen.

the sand everywhere, circling me, that army of cats, purring and rubbing, following my every footstep.[58]

If Rich uses the postcard to invent an identity for Carr—as a woman who "found / yourself facing the one great art / of your native land, your life" and dreams into this life the expression of desire: "Wait for me. I have waited so long for you,"[59] Carr merely "sensed" the Indian presence, finding rather that "among the nutbushes are picnickers with shrieking children bashing and destroying, and flappers in pyjamas. And there are wood waggons and gravel waggons [*sic*] blatantly snorting in and out, cutting up the rude natural roads, smelling and snorting like evil monsters among the cedars."[60]

Carr's expressionistic cedars and totems were already disappearing when, as Rich declares to Carr, she was "facing the one great art / of your native land." Most of her efforts did not land her face to face with totems. These had been defaced, burnt, rotted, stolen, or retrieved to the Museum of Anthropology at the University of British Columbia, where in a more tame setting Carr could study them at her leisure. Her 1931 (or 1932) painting *Blunden Harbor* was done from a 1901 photograph. Carr noted that her work was "history"; whether she felt she was recording a dying history or making it up whole, I am not sure from her cryptic remark. There is no doubt, however, that Rich rewrites history: "But you never said that I / am ashamed to have thought it / You had no personal leanings."[61] She turns Canada and Carr's work into a pristine prepatriarchal space where native land and a woman's life come together in nature, lesbianism, and art. In this, she follows Carr, who sees the red cedars as the "primeval," and Canada's scenery as "Mountains towering—snow mountains, blue mountains, green mountains, brown mountains, tree-covered, barren rock, cruel mountains with awful waterfalls and chasms and avalanches, tender mountains all shining. Spiritual peaks way up among the clouds."[62]

In the American imagination, Canada's vast northlands signify a pure, strenuous nature so tremendous it leads inevitably to annihilation—I need only mention Jack London or the movie *The Blob*. Carr's struggle to paint became a struggle for identity: "I had got the spirit of the country and the people more than others who had been there. . . . I long to return to it and wrestle something out for myself, to look for things I did not know of before, and to feel and strive and earnestly try to be true and sincere to the country and to myself."[63] Carr's ecstatic merger with her nation and its landscape reenacts part of an American mythos of purity and salvation—"plumbing and saving the world," in Lawrence's words. Rich's investment repeats the desire to inhabit a place; after *Your Native Land, Your Life,* her next book, *An Atlas of the Difficult World,* continued to map a space for herself as woman/poet/lesbian/mother/Jew/leftist/feminist.

The incorporation of all "America" into the United States continues in the recent identification with these previous heroines. John Sanford's *Book of American Women,* addressed to a female "you," presumably his wife, suggests that this solidarity comes from a history of shared suffering, the price women pay for the "gang-hooked dig" they receive (as he surmises O'Keeffe did on hearing Nathanael West's comment, "It's all right, if you like barns")[64] from their male contemporaries. That Kahlo and Carr (to a less extent), as much as O'Keeffe, are objects of U.S. feminist identification should hardly surprise us. Miriam Shapiro appropriates Kahlo's classic head-on self-portrait for her *Frida and Me,* Mary Beth Edelson turns O'Keeffe into a feminist Christ, sacrificed on the altar of male art history.[65] United States citizens speak of ourselves as Americans, inhabiting the entire continent—even hemisphere—as our nation, ourselves. Furthermore, each of these women was drawn to an imagined conception of their nations as haunted by the presences of submerged, marginal first peoples. Their own discoveries of the increasingly hidden traces of native peoples in their native (adopted) lands (and for Kahlo in and through her body) foreshadow contemporary feminist attention to female differences, even as they reveal a modernist fascination with the primitive and syncretic, and with borderlands.

As feminists in the Americas struggling with the racialist overtones of much liberal feminism, we search through our mothers, tracing the "indistinctly mapped and terribly difficult space of the self" represented through their imaginative connections with native peoples.[66] Carr forged that link through her canvas, shaping beautiful things, and separating her from most of Canada's citizens who understood neither its history, its nature, nor its art: "The Indian used the cedars, shaped beautiful things from them: canoes, ropes, baskets, mats, totem poles. It was his tree of trees. The picnickers mutilate them with their hideous initials, light fires against them, throw tin cans and rubbish into their hollow boles, size up how many cords, etc." If Carr could never master the mountains celebrated by her theosophist mentor Harris, she was able, like the Indians, to transform the tree from its phallic enormity into an emanation of her connection to place: "The individual mighty trees stagger me. I become engaged with the figures . . . the total. Nothing stands alone; each is only a part. A picture must be a portrayal of relationships."[67]

At this moment, the concepts of nation, woman, and modern art are up for grabs in the face of globalization and ethnic conflict, feminism and right-wing backlash; in 1999, the Museum of Modern Art transferred to the Metropolitan Museum two Van Gogh prints bequeathed by Abby Rockefeller, who insisted fifty years later they could no longer be called "modern." Yet the mania for objects and images naming these "female icons," as the *New York Times* dubbed Kahlo a few years ago, expands. An insatiable market circulates their work, domesticating whatever subversive qualities each artist had as a woman or modernist. "Frida. Her name conjures mystery and magic and Mexico."[68] O'Keeffe and Kahlo are two of the only nine women (out of the hundred listed artists in a recent book) to be featured as "icons of modern art."[69] The mass marketing of feminist icons of national identity is part of Modernism, Inc. Each of these women's houses has become a national museum—pilgrimages to their houses (for a twenty-dollar "donation" one can spend an hour at Abiquiu, O'Keeffe's last residence and the most recent domestic museum, though not yet accredited as such) provide the opportunity to purchase replicas of their work or children's coloring books, or their recipes. The domestication of the modern woman artist onto coffee mugs and refrigerator magnets is repeated in the public sphere in the gesture to turn their houses (which served also as studios) into museums.

In 1996 Madonna appeared on the Dave Letterman show dressed as Kahlo after news reports revealed her interest in collecting Kahlo's work. She had purchased the rights to Kahlo's life story with plans of starring as the artist now that her Latina credits were secured after playing Evita and becoming the mother of Lourdes. Madonna's desire to embody Frida—coming months after her resurrection of Marilyn Monroe—confirmed the message that Kahlo was, like Madonna and Marilyn, an iconic international woman artist already circulating when her work capped the huge show of Mexican art mounted by the Metropolitan Museum. For a time, Frida's face haunted every other shopping bag in New York. Paola Pierini, assistant to the USIS (United States Information Service) cultural attaché, hangs two of Georgia O'Keeffe's *Red Poppy* paintings on the walls of her office in the American embassy in Rome, and I was able to receive high-level clearance to take a picture of it in the agency devoted to promoting American culture abroad. The promotional poster for the *Red Poppy* stamp had hung on post office walls across the nation after it was issued. When I inquired at my local post office about getting a copy, I was told that the workers had already claimed them all; so I asked if I might photograph the walls as part of my research. Permission refused; high-level clearance must be given to film within the walls of a government office and by the time I could get it a whole new stamp collection was in the offing. Every word Carr wrote, every image she painted and drew, every word written about her, the floor plan of her home in Victoria, BC, including its contents, are being digitized and put online so that students across the vast regions of Canada can have instant access to a virtual Carrnocopia—walking through her Victorian house, searching every library and archive, strolling through every gallery for all available information and imagery. The great lady painters, whose works and names, faces and homes establish feminist national modernism in venues as public as Blockbuster museum exhibits and the World Wide Web and as intimate as one's earlobes, have been overexposed. Too many words, too many images circulate. This ubiquity pushes the limits of modernism, of nationalism, and of feminism as art, citizenship, and gender become kitsch. The incorporation of feminine modernism in the bodies of these women's art—and in their actual bodies—helps market national identity; feminism itself becomes a form of vernacular modernism—contaminating the landscapes of nations, media, and histories. If art is the pulse of the nation, and feminism offers a modern national identity, then we are united; and Modernism, Inc. declares itself one nation under Georgia, Frida, and Emily! Patti Smith is on the road again.

NOTES

1. Peyton Boswell Jr., *Modern American Painting* (New York: Dodd, Mead, 1939), 176. This same kind of commentary gets repeated in books on women's art published after the 1970s. For instance, Charlotte Streifer Rubenstein writes, "O'Keeffe is considered by many art historians and critics to be America's greatest living painter." *American Women Artists* (New York: Avon, 1982), 181. The hagiography has only grown since then, causing Hilton Kramer, bad-boy critic for the *New York Observer*, to lambaste O'Keeffe as "a provincial talent" and decry the P.C. forces that have put her work at the forefront of twentieth-century American art: "How much did O'Keeffe's initial reputation as an American modernist owe to her romance with Stieglitz in the earlier decades of this century, and how much does her current status as an American classic owe to the tidal wave of feminist politics and so-called gender studies that had lately engulfed the study of art history in the academy, the museums and the art press?" "Georgia O'Keeffe, Artist with Inflated Reputation," *New York Observer*, May 31, 1999, 1, 25.

2. Emily Carr, *Hundreds and Thousands: The Journals of an Artist* (Toronto: Irwin, 1966), book jacket, back panel.

3. Thanks to unpublished research papers by Thea Petchler and Anne Basting, University of Minnesota, 1991.

4. Holger Cahill describes the "modern search for structure" as the crucial element of "American modernist pioneers" in "American Art, 1862–1932," in Catalogue of Museum of Modern Art exhibition *American Painting and Sculpture, 1862–1932* (1932; reprint, New York: Arno Press, 1969), 18–19.

5. See, for instance, Bonnie Kime Scott, ed., *The Gender of Modernism* (Bloomington: Indiana University Press, 1990); or Mary Loeffleholz, *Experimental Lives: Women and Literature, 1900–1945* (New York: Twayne, 1992), both of which acknowledge differences among women, even as they return to a high modernist concept of woman (and lesbians) and of women writers that ultimately precludes anyone who wasn't hanging out on the Left Bank with Natalie Barney as satirized by Djuna Barnes, *Ladies Alamanack* (1928; reprint, Normal, IL: Dalkey Archive Press, 1997). For critiques of Benedict Anderson's *Imagined Communities* (London: Verso, 1983), see the work of subaltern studies.

6. See Maureen Dowd, "Icon and I Will Survive," *New York Times,* December 9, 1998, A31 on the rise of Hillary Rodham Clinton from celebrity to icon. In fact, the first book-length study of these three modernist North American

female art icons has appeared as a catalog for an exhibition opening Spring 2001 at the McMichael Canadian Art Collection Gallery: Sharyn Rohlfsen Udall, *Carr, O'Keeffe, Kahlo: Places of Their Own* (New Haven: Yale University Press, 2000).

7. The locus classicus for this argument remains Linda Nochlin, "Why Have There Been No Great Women Artists?" *Art News* 1 (February–March 1973).

8. Germaine Greer, *The Obstacle Race: The Fortunes of Women Painters and Their Work* (New York : Farrar, Straus and Giroux, 1979), 251.

9. Susan Kollin, "Frontier Nostalgia and the Invention of Alaska" (Ph.D. diss., University of Minnesota, 1995).

10. Patti Smith, *Babel* (New York: Putnam, 1978), 84.

11. Adrienne Rich, "Emily Carr," *Parnassus* 12.2 (1985): 244, reprinted in *Your Native Land, Your Life* (New York: Norton, 1986). Rich is not the first woman poet to pronounce Carr a national-feminine heroine; see Dorothy Livesay's 1953 poem "The Three Emilys," in *Collected Poems: The Two Seasons* (Toronto: McGraw-Hill, 1982), 202.

12. Nicole Cooley, "Self-Portrait: Frida Kahlo," *Nation,* December 25, 1995, 834, reprinted in *Resurrections* (Baton Rouge: Louisiana State University Press, 1996).

13. Livesay, "The Three Emilys," 202. The three Emilys are, of course, Emily Bronte, Emily Dickinson, and Emily Carr. (This poem also appears in *The Norton Anthology of Women's Literature,* 2d ed.)

14. Cahill, 18.

15. In *Foundational Fictions: The National Romances of Latin America,* Doris Sommer argues that the nation-building work of Latin American fiction required a narrative indebted to romance in which the Indian or *mestiza* woman marries the Creole man, thus instating bourgeois national stability. Crucial to this narrative is the image of native woman as embodiment of nature and nation. See also Jean Franco, *Plotting Women: Gender and Representation in Mexico* (New York: Columbia University Press, 1989) on the mythic embodiment of woman in Mexican literary history.

16. Muriel Rukeyser, "Fifth Elegy—A Turning Wind," in *A Turning Wind* (New York: Viking, 1939).

17. Giuliana Bruno, *Streetwalking on a Ruined Map: Cultural Theory and the City in the Films of Elvira Notari* (Princeton: Princeton University Press, 1992).

18. Frida Kahlo, *The Letters of Frida Kahlo: Cartas Apasionadas,* ed. Martha Zamora (San Francisco: Chronical Books, 1995), 50–51, 157.

19. D. H. Lawrence, *Studies in Classic American Literature* (1923; New York: Viking, 1961), 7.

20. Boswell, 11.

21. Quoted in Sue Davidson Lowe, *Stieglitz: A Memoir/Biography* (New York: Farrar, Straus and Giroux, 1983), 307.

22. The Muralistas also worked extensively in the United States, painting murals

in California, Detroit, and New York. Paradoxically, at the other end of this border economy, this was the era of the Bracero program, which imported migrant farm laborers from Mexico to the San Fernando Valley.

23. Quoted in Boswell, foreword to *Modern American Painting,* n.p.

24. Quoted in Marsha Bellavance-Johnson, *Georgia O'Keeffe in New Mexico* (Ketchum, ID: Computer Lab, 1988), 9.

25. Cahill, 19. This important exhibit featured two of O'Keeffe's works contributed by Stieglitz's An American Place collection, *Cow's Skull and White Roses* (1931) and *Pink Dish and Green Leaves* (pastel, 1928). Mary Cassatt was the only other woman painter included.

26. Ann Douglas, *Terrible Honesty: Mongrel Manhattan in the 1920s* (New York: Farrar, Straus and Giroux, 1995) describes the masculine space of skyscrapers.

27. Ralph Looney, *O'Keeffe and Me: A Treasured Friendship* (Niwot, CO: University Press of Colorado, 1995), 30.

28. Kahlo, 88 (big shits and university gallery); Maurice Nadeau, *The History of Surrealism,* trans. Richard Howard (New York: Collier, 1965), 209.

29. Edythe Hembroff-Schleicher, *M.E.: A Portrayal of Emily Carr* (Toronto: Calerke, Irwin, 1969), 95–96.

30. As I have noted in previous work, women photographers and poets also hit the road in search of a hidden, ruined America; also finding beauty in the microscopic inspection of objects. Or as Edmund Wilson put it in a review of O'Keeffe's paintings, "women seem to charge the objects they represent with some immediate and personal emotion that they absorb the subject into themselves instead of incorporating the subject into themselves." "The Stieglitz Exhibition," *New Republic* 46 (March 18, 1925): 97.

31. Quoted in Keto von Waberer, *Frida Kahlo: Masterpieces* (New York: Norton, 1994), n.p., opposite plate 15.

32. Virginia Woolf, *A Room of One's Own* (New York: Harcourt, Brace and World, 1929). Alice Walker, *In Search of Our Mothers' Gardens: Womanist Prose* (San Diego: Harcourt Brace Jovanovich, 1983). Alice Echols, in *Scars of Sweet Paradise: The Life and Times of Janis Joplin* (New York: Metropolitan Books, 1999) discusses the desire to rewrite pre-Stonewall sexual history to make someone like Joplin into a lesbian. See also a Frida Kahlo Web site that includes a "page" picturing a "few of the women she is rumored to have romanced—Dolores Del Rio, Paulette Goddard, Georgia O'Keeffe": http://members.aol.com/fridanet/affairs.htm.

33. Emily Carr, *Growing Pains* (Toronto: Irwin, 1966), 338. Laurie Lisle, *Portrait of an Artist: A Biography of Georgia O'Keeffe* (New York: Seaview Books, 1980) suggests that O'Keeffe was uncomfortable with female competition, especially after her sister Catherine's close-up paintings of morning glories and other flowers were exhibited in New York and acclaimed in a *New York Times* article entitled "Another O'Keeffe Emerges" (202–3).

34. C. S. Merrill, *O'Keeffe: Days in a Life* (New Mexico: La Alameda Press,

1995), n.p., entry 14. This is one of a number of books about Georgia O'-Keeffe that feed off a limited intimacy with the artist. Merrill visited O'Keeffe for a few weeks in the 1970s, when she composed the "poems"—really brief journal entries—in this volume. Why she waited until 1995 to apparently self-publish them is anyone's guess (but the fact that many such books have emerged since O'Keeffe's death is perhaps significant).

35. Henry McBride, quoted in Lisle, 100.
36. On "this decorative gorgeousness," see Wilson, 97; and Frances O'Brien, "Georgia O'Keeffe," *Nation* 125 (October 12, 1927): 361.
37. Paul Rosenfeld, "American Painting," *Dial,* December 1921, 666.
38. Wilson, 98.
39. Quoted in Lisle, 154–55.
40. O'Brien, 361.
41. Quoted in Andrea Mariani, "Emily Carr: Il contesto internazionale," *Merope,* no. 16 (September 1995): 43–73, 64. See 63–69 on Carr's and O'-Keeffe's connections.
42. See Lowe, 280. O'Keeffe became associated with the National Women's Party through her friend Anita Pollitzer (the woman responsible for showing O'Keeffe's work to Stieglitz, eliciting his exclamation, "Finally a woman on paper!"). See Clive Giboire, ed., *Lovingly, Georgia: The Complete Correspondence of Georgia O'Keeffe and Anita Pollitzer* (New York: Simon and Schuster, 1990), 269, 275.
43. Kahlo, 87–88.
44. Susan Stewart, *On Longing: Narratives of the Miniature, the Gigantic, the Souvenir, the Collection* (Durham: Duke University Press, 1993), 71. Gaston Bachelard, *The Poetics of Space,* trans. Maria Jolas (Boston: Beacon Press, 1964), 157.
45. Kahlo, 157.
46. Houston A. Baker Jr., *Modernism and the Harlem Renaissance* (Chicago: University of Chicago Press, 1987) argues for distinctive vernacular and local modernisms as resistances and counter-histories.
47. Diego Rivera, "Frida Kahlo and Mexican Art," *Bulletin of the Mexican Cultural Seminary,* no. 2 (Ministry of Public Education, Mexico City) (October 1943): 89–101, 89.
48. Rivera had gotten the mural commission for Radio City Music Hall while working on the Rockefeller Center mural, which was destroyed by John D. Rockefeller when Rivera refused to remove Lenin's portrait from it. See Lisle, 207–12 and Lowe, 318–23 for accounts of this incident.
49. Boswell, 176. This point is repeated again and again in 1920s and 1930s descriptions of O'Keeffe.
50. The Japanese artist Yayoi Kusama, for instance, wrote a letter and "sought out the advice of Georgia O'Keeffe whose work she had discovered in an art magazine." While the report about this incident on *All Things Considered* in

1998 indicated that O'Keeffe's reply to Kusama was that, to become famous, you had to walk around everywhere with your work, Alexandra Munroe quotes a more discouraging letter from O'Keeffe: "It seems to me very odd that you are so ambitious to show your paintings here, but I wish the best for you. "Yayoi Kusama: The 1950s and 1960s Paintings, Sculptures and Works on Paper," Catalogue introduction, Paula Cooper Gallery, 1996, n.p.

51. See John Berger, "Understanding a Photograph," in *The Look of Things* (New York: Viking, 1974) on the lack of "property value" associated with photographs as reproducible objects, which is even more exaggerated with postcards. As Malek Alloula writes, "The postcard . . . becomes the poor man's phantasm: for a few pennies, display racks full of dreams. . . . The postcard is ubiquitous. It can be found not only at the scene of the crime but at a far venue as well." *The Colonial Harem,* trans. Myrna Godzich and Wlad Godzich (Minneapolis: University of Minnesota Press, 1986), 4.

52. Gertrude Stein, *Paris France* (New York: Liveright, 1940), 6, 7. The Walker Art Center in Minneapolis used its O'Keeffe barn painting to advertise its 1999 Mother's Day events.

53. Walter Benjamin, "The Work of Art in the Age of Mechanical Reproduction," in *Illuminations,* ed. Hannah Arendt, trans. Harry Zohn (New York: Harcourt Brace and World, 1968), 234.

54. Benjamin, 243.

55. Guadalupe Rivera and Marie-Pierre Colle, *Frida's Fiesta: Recipes and Reminiscences of Life with Frida Kahlo* (New York: Clarkson N. Potter, 1994), 219.

56. "Cult" is Benjamin's term (223). "Trade-mark" is Adorno's and Horkheimer's, *Dialectic of Enlightenment,* trans. John Cumming (New York: Continuum, 1989), 166.

57. Adorno and Horkheimer, 145, 163, 161.

58. Carr, *Hundreds and Thousands,* 26.

59. Rich, "Emily Carr," 244.

60. Carr, *Hundreds and Thousands,* 56.

61. I'd like to thank Marilyn Young for pointing this out to me.

62. Carr, *Hundreds and Thousands,* 35, 54.

63. Carr, *Hundreds and Thousands,* 17–18.

64. John Sanford, *A Book of American Women* (1980; reprint, Urbana: University of Illinois Press, 1995), 190. Just as Sanford's book offers a male feminist revisionism about American women, other men have stepped in to authorize O'Keeffe's work. See Bram Dijkstra, *Georgia O'Keeffe and the Eros of Place* (Princeton: Princeton University Press, 1998). Kahlo, too, has been reclaimed as a serious modernist by Terry Smith, *Making the Modern: Industry, Art, and Design in America* (Chicago: University of Chicago Press, 1993).

65. See Norma Broude and Mary D. Garrard, eds., *The Power of Feminist Art: The American Movement of the 1970s, History and Impact* (New York: Harry Abrams, 1994), front cover and 17. Kahlo has also served as icon for

Latino artists. See the works of Las Mujeres Muralistas, especially the mural "Pan America," in Broude and Garrard, 240; Nahum Zenil's self-portrait *Frida in My Heart, Boston Magazine,* April 1998; and the notecards by Hector J. Guerra, including "Frida and Her World," from Designs for Better Living, Inc.

66. Judith Fryer, "Women and Space," *Prospects* 9 (1984): 221.
67. Carr, *Hundreds and Thousands,* 56, 54.
68. Rivera and Colle, Jacket blurb.
69. Jurgen Tesch and Eckhard Hollmann, eds., *Icons of Art: The Twentieth Century* (Munich: Prestel, 1997).

11

KITCHEN MECHANICS AND PARLOR NATIONALISTS

ANDY RAZAF, BLACK BOLSHEVISM, AND HARLEM'S RENAISSANCE

William J. Maxwell

The first extended musical allusion in Ralph Ellison's *Invisible Man* (1952), African American modernism's most insistently allusive and musical novel, involves a bluesy torch song with an axe to grind. Near the climax of the monologue that fills the novel's prologue, Ellison's unnamed, invisible narrator admits to a desire that would provoke his New York neighbors to violence if he lived anywhere but in an abandoned coal cellar. "I'd like to hear five recordings of Louis Armstrong playing and singing 'What Did I Do to Be so Black and Blue,'" he divulges, "all at the same time."[1] One recording won't do, he explains, because "when I have music I want to *feel* its vibration, not only with my ear but with my whole body" (emphasis in original).[2] Yet the narrator is excited by more than the sensual pleasures of pumped-up volume. The alchemy to be heard as "Louis bends that military instrument into a beam of lyrical sound" offers Ellison's unseen hero rare insights into African American time and history.[3] "But what did *I* do to be so black and blue?" he asks in the prologue's concluding lines, annexing Armstrong's musical question as the key to his own Bildung and casting the novel that reveals it as "Black and Blue's" libretto (emphasis in original).[4]

Apart from its status as an overture and narrative inducement, the version of "Black and Blue" heard by the invisible man earns its honored place among the novel's intertexts for its distillation of some of Ellison's abiding concerns: concerns with the masquerading of black tricksters who, like Satchmo, counter whites wearing their own visible and invisible blackface; with the attitudes toward history of those seemingly "outside the groove" of classical Marxism's teleological plottings;[5] with jazz generally and the rehabilitation of Armstrong's post-bebop profile as a gifted Uncle Tom specifically. Given the novel's focal theme of black invisibility and its encyclopedic ransacking of black cultural archives, however, its failure to unveil the African American who first posed the overwhelming question of "Black and Blue" is at least ironic. Before Armstrong mock-innocently asked, "(What Did I Do to Be So) Black and Blue," the inquiry had been raised by Andy Razaf, who wrote the lyrics to the tune in 1929. Before the song appeared on any Armstrong disc, it had been the showstopper in a New York black-cast musical called *Hot Chocolates*. Razaf's words were the fruit of the kind of improvisational bravado that Ellison counted among the black gifts to American democracy. During rehearsals, the Jewish mobster and impresario Dutch Schultz confronted the lyricist with a nonrefusable offer to add "a little 'colored girl' singing how tough it is to be 'colored.'"[6] Razaf and his dazzling pianist, Fats Waller, responded with what has often been called America's first popular song of racial protest. In its original form, "Black and Blue" led with wickedly punning lyrics lamenting an interracial gentlemen's agreement from the point of view of a lonely, dark-skinned black woman. "Browns and yellers / All have fellers," went an introductory verse Armstrong would excise, "Gentlemen prefer them light. / Wish I could fade, / Can't make the grade, / Nothin' but dark days in sight."[7]

Why are readers of *Invisible Man* still unlikely to know that the novel unwittingly perpetuates Razaf's invisibility along with Armstrong's edit of "Black and Blue's" antiracist satire?[8] Barry Singer, Razaf's biographer, attributes his subject's absence from a variety of historical repertoires to an anomalous career as a black song lyricist on Tin Pan Alley, a walking contradiction of the myth of the effortlessness of black musicianship.[9] But Razaf's U.S. semi-obscurity may also be due to his typicality. Some of the forgetting of Razaf, I believe, is an aspect of the forgetting of the black anticapitalists among whom he wrote and argued, New Yorkers who bid to direct a racial renaissance powered by the black working class years before Harlem's canonical vogue was declared in the mid-1920s. While Razaf's personal history seems bent on disproving that the self only signifies as a symptom, my main concern in what follows is thus not to drag a singular popular artist up from the basement of cultural history and the enormous condescension of the canon. Without regarding Razaf as a plaything of discursive or historical forces, I will retrieve him as a partial product and gauge of the place of black bolshevism within the cultural field of the Harlem Renaissance, the formative location of a self-conscious African American modernism.

In contrast to Andy Razaf, anticapitalist radicalism is a topic that many histories of the Harlem Renaissance have felt bound to raise. If, as George Hutchinson remarks, virtually all criticism of the Harlem movement has pivoted on evaluation of "its interracial dynamics,"[10] much has also set the historical parameters of these dynamics with reference to the "Old," pro-Soviet Left. Proudly identified with total revolution and the forced entrance of the future, readily envisioned as a perpetrator of radical historical breaks, this Left has regularly been sighted at scenes of the renaissance's birth and death. From Harold Cruse, to Nathan Huggins, to David Levering Lewis, to Henry Louis Gates, the Old Left is painted as both a leading cause of the rebirth's demise and part of an insurgent Red Summer prehistory it must squash to be born.[11] Communism here becomes something like a repressed precondition and a determinate negation of the renaissance pursuit of politics through cultural means. If, like a suspicious absentee parent, the Old Left thus fled the movement after its birth and reappeared only at its death, several questions are begged: Where was this Left during the movement's maturity? Were it and the Harlem Renaissance not just distinct but antipathetic modern projects?

The best recent intellectual history of the renaissance, George Hutchinson's heavyweight *Harlem Renaissance in Black and White* (1995), answers by precluding most discoveries of the Old Left inside renaissance walls. To orient his voluminous research, Hutchinson borrows from Pierre Bourdieu's theory of the "cultural field," a three-dimensional model of the terrain of forces and struggles in which writers, publishers, and other cultural agents battle to impose a ruling definition of literary capital.[12] Hutchinson proves the utility of Bourdieu's un-unified field theory in rescripting the renaissance as an outwardly focused yet internally divided ensemble, and the ability to define the movement as an honor fought for by a variety of cultural catalysts. His account falters, however, in its imposition of American national identity as "the dominant problematic," or unavoidable language and stake of competition, "structuring the literary field relevant to the Harlem Renaissance."[13] Concurrent with the cultural nationalism of African

America in the early twentieth century grew a transnational imagining of blackness, institutionalized by the Pan-Africanism of W. E. B. Du Bois and by Marcus Garvey's immensely popular Universal Negro Improvement Association (accent on the "Universal"). At best, then, Hutchinson's choice of American national identity as the master problematic of the renaissance discounts one operative sense of the territory which fighting over the movement meant fighting for. At its least productive, it decrees that some of the most influential modern black internationalists be severed from the rebirth. For example, "Garvey's [seeming] insistence on separation from American culture and society" places him beyond the pale, nowhere to be seen within Hutchinson's meticulous topography of the movement's contending forces.[14]

Hutchinson's extraction of black internationalists from the Harlem Renaissance ironically also results in the banishment of those who became Garvey's most vocal Harlem enemies: namely, Razaf and the rest of uptown's black bolsheviks. This loose collective shared Garvey's diasporan prospect while rejecting what they considered his ill-fated ventures in black capitalism and his quasi-imperial ambitions for a repatriated Africa. Caribbean immigrants or their close associates, they were impressed by the Soviet Union's overtures to the colonized world and convinced by Lenin's declaration that imperialism was the highest (and last) stage of capitalism, the true cause of world war, but the bearer of the preconditions for worldwide socialist revolution. The view through the eyes of these overlooked black bolsheviks, I believe, in fact pleads that the Old Left never fully deserted or opposed the renaissance cultural field. With Razaf's typifying help, I'll thus be challenging prevailing renaissance histories that either banish anticapitalism from the Harlem movement or confine it to a negative presence at its creation and disintegration. I'll instead suggest that the Old Left was an invited guest at the birth of Harlem's rebirth; that its Harlem proponents sponsored expressive culture with a configuring impact on high and low renaissance art; and that its responsibility for the death of the movement is greatly exaggerated.

Casting Andy Razaf as a window onto Harlem Renaissance bolshevism is counterintuitive: he was of royal birth, and he could swing. Born in 1895 with the Malagasy name of Andreamentania Razafkeriefo, Razaf was a living, breathing New World scion of African royalty. Razaf's father, Henri, was a nephew of Madagascar's queen, Ranavalona III. Razaf's mother, Jennie Maria Waller (no relation to Fats), sprang from the African American aristocracy attached to the party of Lincoln. Her father, the Republican lawyer John Louis Waller, was appointed U.S. consul to Madagascar in 1891. Had French colonial policy not interfered, Andy might have attained the elevated position projected for Jennie's children when she married into one of Africa's last intact monarchies. As it happened, however, 1895 saw Razaf's grandfather dragged aboard a steamship and imprisoned in Marseilles, a victim of French resistance to his campaign to strengthen official U.S. ties to the island and, failing that, to transform the French protectorate into "Wallerland," an African American settler colony on the model of Liberia. Razaf's mother was thus forced to return to the United States, where she settled in Washington, D.C., and delivered her first child as a fifteen-year-old with a workaday future.[15]

The teenaged Razaf's response to his prenatal dispossession was to conceive an ambition to become a self-supporting poet-lyricist. From the time he was seventeen until his death in 1973 at seventy-seven, Razaf would compose the words to more than eight hundred jazz- and blues-flavored popular songs. Nat "King" Cole, Duke Ellington, Ella Fitzgerald, Paul Robeson, Frank Sinatra, and Bessie Smith followed Fats Waller in recording from his songbook, the highlights of which include "Ain't Misbehavin'," "Honeysuckle Rose," "Memories of You," "This Joint Is Jumpin'," "Stompin' at the Savoy," and "In the Mood." Despite this enormous volume of lyrical production, Razaf never stopped writing in support of the left wing of progressive black politics, perhaps because his mature career as a professional lyricist never stopped colliding with the voluble racism and fraud of Tin Pan Alley music publishers. In the late teens and during the twenties, Razaf frequently published poetry in Marcus Garvey's *Negro World*, A. Philip Randolph's *Messenger*, and Cyril Briggs's *Crusader*, the radical Harlem magazines that led the postwar celebration of a self-assertive, comfortably modern "New Negro." For much of his adult life, Razaf contributed playful but trenchant essays to the *New York Amsterdam News* and other black papers, more than once calling for a black songwriters' union, praising the employment of dark-skinned black actresses, and protesting the inadequate material footing for an independent black theater.[16]

This remarkable profile makes Razaf's absence from most Harlem Renaissance commentary more mystifying than his absence from Ellison's *Invisible Man*. It would be hard to invent someone who could better serve as a confluence of disparate renaissance energies: Razaf, who once worked as a Harlem telephone operator, fashioned himself as a switchboard through which many of the movement's contraries were patched. Renaissance oppositions meet in the exiled African nobleman turned poetic and musical purveyor of Harlem: the typically divided modernist enthusiasm for ostensibly premodern, primitive zones (Africa) and for modern, metropolitan ones (Harlem); the simultaneous achievements in formal literature (especially poetry) and popular music (especially jazz); the often dissimilar uses and significances of this music in Harlem and on Broadway and Tin Pan Alley; and the usually inimical conceptions of the Harlem movement as the birth of black cultural autonomy and a rebirth of white appreciation for black culture's entertainment value. In the early 1920s it appeared that this talent for mediation had won Razaf a place on the renaissance literary roster. Robert T. Kerlin's *Negro Poets and Their Poems,* a pathbreaking 1923 anthology of the "renaissance of the Negro," praised Razaf's verse for its "great variety of forms[,] . . . moods and traits."[17] By the second half of the 1920s, however, Razaf's disappearance from the movement's literary anthologies would barely be noticed, a pre-echo of his unremarked absence from scholarly histories of the movement. A volume of selected poems, perhaps enough to challenge this vanishing, was contracted in the 1950s but never saw print; Langston Hughes's introduction, complimenting Razaf as a democratic "philosopher-poet" with "a talent for the concise line," languished along with it.[18]

Razaf's literary disappearance, best understood in conjunction with a larger realignment of renaissance forces, can begin to suggest why the singular Razaf also furnishes a stage from which to view Harlem Renaissance bolshevism. In the mid-1920s, the declining fortunes of Razaf's poetry matched the worsening position of anticapitalism in the renaissance field. And for good reason: though Razaf never seems to have carried a Communist Party card, most of his poetry had its objective social origin in Harlem's postwar subculture of anti-imperialist agitation; some of it had been composed in Razaf's capacity as a staff member of the Harlem journal that pictured the straightest of roads from Soviet Moscow to New Negro New York. In the fall of 1918, Razaf became the house poet at the *Crusader,* a monthly launched by the West Indian–born journalist Cyril V. Briggs. Briggs's enterprise should be required reading for those periodizing Harlem's renaissance. In November 1918, seven years before Alain Locke's signal New Negro anthology, the journal was already promoting what it called "a renaissance of Negro power and culture throughout the world."[19]

From Razaf's perspective, the *Crusader*'s vision of Harlem's renaissance was most valuable for its class consciousness, not its precociousness. Like most of the journal's staff, and a greater percentage of the renaissance's talented tenth than is usually acknowledged,[20] Razaf earned his rent money through the service jobs that then occupied a majority of Harlem men.[21] Between 1913 and 1920 alone he put in time as a telephone operator, a butler, a "coater" in a Chinese laundry, a custodian in a government building, and an elevator operator shuttling audiences to the roof garden home of Ziegfeld's Follies.[22] To adapt E. P. Thompson's adage, class as much as race was "something which in fact happen[ed] . . . in [the] human relationships" these jobs thrust on Razaf.[23] Catering to the Follies stars and audiences who later sang his words, he shouldered both the historical burden of African American servitude and the high cost of having nothing to sell but a smile and unsolicited song lyrics. The *Crusader*'s renaissance promised to remove some of the weight. For one thing, it recognized that most Harlemites were not dusty, still rural-minded folks but metropolitan wage workers; even those whom the Great Migration had lured from the South were more than likely to have been city-dwelling, nonagricultural employees before the move.[24] For another thing, the *Crusader's* renaissance celebrated this New York state of mind, projecting urban proletarianization as the renaissance's motor rather than as a sidelight or hazard to the main business of upgrading the vernacular culture of black folk. From Cyril Briggs's editorials, Razaf could learn that it was forward-looking metropolitan workers such as he who would snatch the baton of the New Negro from returning troops and guide a rebirth that might level American capitalism, not win favorable cultural recognition within it. Unlike many nineteenth-century white American workers, devoted to the language of civic republicanism, the *Crusader* writers talked labor ideology in unembarrassed socialist-internationalist accents. It would be tough, they bet, to red-bait a population too familiar with race-baiting: "Don't mind being called 'Bolsheviki,'" they cracked, "by the same people who called you 'nigger.'"[25] Without prompting from the fractious American Communist Party that emerged in 1919, the journal for which Razaf volunteered thus imagined pro-Soviet, working-class radicalism as an irreplaceable element within Harlem's racial revival. For the *Crusader* staff, the anticapitalist Left did not menace a fully formed New Negro from without but inhered within the modern mix that compelled this ideal's creation and ensured its combustible novelty.

The poetry that Razaf composed for Briggs's publication pleads that cultural history is doubly mistaken when it proposes a clean breach between a superstructure-averse, anticapitalist prerenaissance and a Harlem Renaissance proper of cultural sublimation and aesthetic heroism. First, Razaf's verse indicates that the supposed prerenaissance was nearly as convinced of the political use-value of black literature as Alain Locke and other framers of the "civil rights by copyright" position.[26] Second, it affirms that the literary position-takings of the *Crusader* writers played a role in jump-starting renaissance writing by helping to detach it from an unusable portion of the black literary past. I'd like now to consider one of Razaf's poems in some detail, a ballad entitled "Don't Tread on Me." First published in the April 1919 *Crusader,* the poem draws on the insignia of the Fifteenth Infantry, the all-black New York regiment whose heroism in France won them the Croix de Guerre and the nickname the Harlem Hell-Fighters:

There is a wondrous symbol
Which has come from 'cross the sea
It's worn by every member
Of the Fifteenth Infantry:

A snake, curled up, prepared to strike—
And one can plainly see
That by its threat'ning attitude
It says, "DON'T TREAD ON ME!"

O! race! make this your battle-cry—
Engrave it on your heart
It's time for us to "do or die,"
To play a bolder part.
For by the blood you've spilled in France
You must—and will—be free
So, from now on, let us advance
With this, "DON'T TREAD ON ME!"[27]

Even after repeated arguments for the contingency of aesthetic value and the politically interested repressions of the modernist poetic canon, it's initially difficult to read this poem without nostalgia for the old-time religion of complexity, ambiguity, and non-metronomic rhythm. With a singsong ballad measure and insistent iambs that predict Razaf's success as a pop lyricist, "Don't Tread on Me" seems to ask readers simply to internalize its identical title and refrain. To put the brakes on interpretation here, however, would be to ignore the intersection between Razaf's verse and that believed to have opened the floodgates of Harlem Renaissance literature. At the very least, "Don't Tread on Me" stands out for its insistence that the military-issue image of "[a] snake, curled up, prepared to strike" is fit for engraving on all black hearts. As David Roediger remarks of another text in another context, "a greater appreciation of African American patterns of resistance might have argued for using" one of the non-venomous trickster creatures who get the last laugh in New World black oral literature.[28] Yet Razaf's contention that it is time for all of black America to imitate its most honored returning soldiers and "play a bolder part" in securing liberation required a symbol of active, even predatory defiance, not one associated with the caginess the hunted are compelled to master. A less subtle, ultimately less symbolic mode of black struggle called for an immediately readable icon of the intent to secure emancipation by any means necessary, and the uniforms of the Fifteenth Infantry had come preequipped. In "Don't Tread on Me," the transition from Old Negro to New Negro accordingly hinges on a transfer of black identification from Brer Rabbit to Brer Snake.

Just as important, Razaf's poem suggests that the rearticulated significance of the "Don't Tread on Me" snake should be expressible and interpretable both inside and outside the race. The slogan to be used as a "battle cry" in the public

WILLIAM J. MAXWELL

campaign for freedom is no different from that to be inscribed on the private "heart" of black combatants; this script of black resistance is neither hermetic nor double-voiced. Houston Baker maintains that renaissance verse in conventional (read Western or white) form stealthily adopts a black modernist discursive strategy he calls the "mastery of form." The faithful English sonnets and ballads of poets such as Countee Cullen and Claude McKay, claims Baker, "are just as much mastered masks as the minstrel manipulations of Booker T. Washington and Charles Chesnutt."[29] Driven to display the outward signs of Anglo-American formal competence, these poems in whiteface effect a "denigration of form—a necessary . . . adoption of the standard that results in an effective *blackening*" (emphasis in original).[30] Readers in the know can detect the dark tones beneath the ivory surfaces, just as they would have eyes to see the trickster-hero's rebellious face beneath the pious mask. Perhaps Razaf's employment of the ballad is a sign of such poetic "denigration." His seizing of the "Don't Tread on Me" legend from Revolutionary War patriots, Confederate secessionists, and a segregated World War I American expeditionary force is an inspired act of black appropriation. Yet the overriding project of Razaf's poem declines the mastery of form along with the motif of the grinning, lying mask woven throughout turn-of-the-century African American poetry. "Don't Tread on Me" is a brief for black literary and political *un*masking, an impatient dictate that black belligerence must reveal itself in an interracial public sphere most impressed by displays of strength. The poem embodies not so much a fugitive mastery of white literary form as an overt request to begin contesting white mastery in its chosen language of force.

What's most noteworthy about "Don't Tread on Me," however, is what now seems least remarkable about it: its synthesis of standard English and the expression of black militancy without tears. Several months before the Red Summer prompted Claude McKay to write "If We Must Die," African American literature's canonical statement on black regeneration through violent resistance, "Don't Tread on Me" had enacted the tectonic shift in black poetry's diction and thematic range that would soon be seen as McKay's achievement. Much like McKay's furious yet decorous sonnet, Razaf's ballad smashes what Melvin Tolson called the "mold of the Dialect School and the Booker T. Washington Compromise."[31] The subject of "Don't Tread on Me," replacing black accommodation with either liberty or death, anticipates the farewell in "If We Must Die" to the Bookerite gospel of racial progress through forbearance. Razaf's diction banishes the "hyeah"s and "chillen"s representing black linguistic difference in Dunbar and the turn-of-the-century Dialect School, installing a standard English that indeed was less soaked in the idiom of English romanticism than McKay's. With the same enthusiasm as "If We Must Die," "Don't Tread on Me" thus takes on the job assigned to renaissance verse in James Weldon Johnson's famous preface to 1922's *Book of American Negro Poetry:* replacing an overtaxed approximation of rural black speech seemingly chained to plantation apologetics with "a form freer and larger than dialect."[32] Several early (and warring) audiences thought the similarities between the McKay and Razaf texts were obvious. The *Crusader* reprinted both poems to point up the moral of its September 1919 riot issue, while a Department of Justice report on black radicalism introduced the pair as parallel documentations of New Negro subversion.[33]

For present-day audiences, the similarities between the poems ought to make it harder to believe that the literary sea change traditionally associated with McKay flows from his typewriter alone. Beginning with Johnson's anthology, the McKay of "If We Must Die" has been viewed as "one of the principal forces in bringing about the Negro literary awakening."[34] Accounts of renaissance literature often identify the sonnet and its likenesses, collected in *Harlem Shadows* (1922), as final divorces from the age of Dunbar and invitations to New Negro letters. Placing "If We Must Die" next to "Don't Tread on Me" suggests, however, that in shrinking the earliest campaign of renaissance literature to a duel between New Negro McKay and Old Negro Dunbar, we reproduce an artificially foreshortened relationship between the two poets and ratify their major white publishers' nearsighted views of the black poetic landscape. McKay and Razaf, each *Crusader* readers and contributors, built their poetic projects in conference with each other and with the journal's best wishes. The "mold of the Dialect School and the Booker T. Washington Compromise" that McKay is said to have shattered was exactly the mold the journal's New Negro defied. In a sonnet that declared this New Negro a necessary archetype, McKay stood on Razaf's shoulders to present the Harlem Renaissance with a literary calling card. "If We Must Die" of course did not set a single direction for renaissance poetry, let alone renaissance literature: Langston Hughes and Sterling Brown would save dialect poetry from the Dialect School, just as Zora Neale Hurston rescued dialect narrative. To the extent that the sonnet's cry for self-defense helped clear the ground for the plurality of renaissance literary forms that followed, however, it did so by adapting the frank and proper language of New Negro militancy employed by the *Crusader* and similarly carved into verse by Razaf. McKay may have provided African American writing with the recognized break from a literary "dark ages" the logic of cultural renaissance demanded, but not without the aid of black bolshevism and another of its preferred poets.

It is tempting to conclude that Harlem Renaissance bolshevism ends with this chronic modernist irony: an avant-garde aspires to depose capitalist relations and succeeds in overthrowing a cultural style. By the mid-1920s Razaf was writing fewer poems and spending more time with midtown music publishers than with Harlem Marxists. The timing of Razaf's increased devotion to music correlates with two developments that paved the way for Langston Hughes's quip that "ordinary Negroes hadn't heard of the Negro Renaissance. And if they had, it hadn't raised their wages any."[35] The first was a political double whammy obvious to the U.S. Left by 1925. The wartime wave of U.S. labor insurgency had been sent to a historic defeat between 1919 and 1924, just as the prospects for revolution in European capitals had collapsed. The second development—made easier by the first—was the spectacular transvaluation of Harlem's rebirth instigated by Alain Locke's 1925 New Negro anthology, a volume commonly read as the renaissance's birth certificate and blueprint. With aid from the NAACP, the National Urban League, and the well-connected white liberals Zora Neale Hurston appointed "Negrotarians," *The New Negro* redefined the type invoked in its title as someone more likely to turn to Fauvists than Bolsheviks when consulting the muses of Europe. In the process, Locke's anthology assembled a model that has commanded the description, marketing, and consumption of Harlem's renaissance for over seventy years.

The takeoff of Razaf's music career in the middle of the 1920s thus appears to be a sign of the concurrent rout of renaissance bolshevism, done in by forces inside and outside black New York. But such a conclusion is not wary enough of the shortcut of constructing a contested, nonstatic movement that still unfolds in an orderly progression of discrete, uniform stages. By 1925 the black bolsheviks were short of one species of capital they actively sought—the kind collected by those able to define the stakes and meaning of modern black renovation. Their distinctive stance on the renaissance had not simply vanished, however, exiled once and for all by a Lockean renaissance of artistic suasion. Their proposals for urban, working-class leadership would inflect renaissance culture produced following the ground-clearing gestures of McKay's poetry, itself reposited in *The New Negro;* and their position in the renaissance field, though weakened, would make itself felt into the 1930s. Deep-seated changes in the Harlem audience and population, if not red victories, continued to license their ventures.

The song lyrics Razaf composed after 1925, for example, would continue to bear the imprint of "Don't Tread on Me" and the subculture-cum-political tendency in which it took shape. One of Razaf's major efforts in 1930 can tell the tale. In that year, he was commissioned to compose the book and lyrics for a floor show at Ed Smalls's Paradise, an integrated, "black and tan" nightclub just below the Cotton Club on the Harlem pecking order. James P. Johnson, the dean of Harlem's bounding stride-piano style, was hired to furnish the show's music. What emerged from Razaf and Johnson's collaboration was *A Kitchen Mechanic's Revue,* a plotless but tightly themed musical celebrating service workers as Harlem's fountains of wealth, sanity, pleasure, and art. From one angle, the revue's tribute to maids, porters, and cooks ("kitchen mechanics," in Harlem slang) seems to be a repetition of Razaf's *Crusader* history as farce. Consider the resolutely offensive lyrics of a number called "Sambo's Syncopated Russian Dance":

> Both Lenin and Trotsky
> They do the Kazotsky
> To Sambo's syncopated Russian dance.
> This hamsky from Bamsky [Alabama]
> Is now the man what-amsky,
> All through his syncopated Russian dance.
> Once they were about to shoot him
> Where the Volga flows,
> Now the Soviets salute him,
> Ev'rywhere he goes;
> They say this tarsky,
> Will soon be the Czarsky,
> All through his syncopated Russian dance.[36]

At what, exactly, does Razaf take aim with his absurd and ingenious "-sky" rhymes, inventing a synthetic Afro-Soviet dialect from dizzy cross-cultural juxtapositions? Perhaps he focuses on radical Harlem's beeline for the Soviets and thus on an aspect of his *Crusader* self. The 1929 stock market crash and Comintern resolutions on the so-called Negro Question in 1928 and 1930 had done little to dull the enthusiasm of Harlem Marxists for things Soviet. Lovett Fort-Whiteman, for one, a Caribbean-born radical who journeyed to the Soviet Union in the mid-1920s and returned a decade later to die in Stalin's gulag, continued wearing Russian costume when back in Harlem.[37] The satiric target behind Sambo's Soviet tour might thus be escalating Russophilia and the related impression that communism required disconnection from black cultural wealth. But the performance through which Razaf's hoofer gains fame seems as indebted to the Black Bottom as the Kazotsky. It's the syncopation of his Russian dance, and thus his capacity for cultural syncretism, that's stressed. Razaf's Sambo invents moves that fit somewhere between Lenin and Trotsky's habitual steps and his own; he's a compulsory but wildly successful cultural arbitrator, another fact suggesting that the song is self-ironizing. Like the protagonist of his lyrics, Razaf was practiced in negotiating between bolsheviks and jazzbos, comfortable in both radical Harlem and a Tin Pan Alley untouched by multicultural sensitivity training. The song's satire also homes in, however, on the

WILLIAM J. MAXWELL

communist state "[w]here the Volga flows." Razaf gives us a bolshevik pantheon that succumbs to fascinatin' rhythm despite itself, in the process hinting at the hypocritical squareness of those Soviet officials who refused to welcome black music while embracing African American comrades. The novelist Maxim Gorky had denounced jazz as the "music of the gross" in 1928, while other protectors of Soviet proletarian culture tried to ban the saxophone and succeeded in frightening prospective importers of American jazz records with six months in jail.[38] "Sambo's Dance" jokingly protests such censorship with a narrative germ close to the rock-and-roll films of the 1950s, in which authorities ban but then helplessly dance to the kids' music.

What is to be done with such fuzzy, multidirectional satire? The remainder of *A Kitchen Mechanic's Revue* answers that the irresolution of "Sambo's Dance" was one price Razaf paid to lend a left accent to genuinely popular Harlem theater. Theophilus Lewis of the *Messenger* was isolated among renaissance-era critics in arguing that any African American drama worth its salt would build from black stage performance as working-class Harlem knew and liked it. He instructed proponents of an indigenously black theater to study the comic revue, an entertainment George Hutchinson nicely describes as "modern, urban, erotic, both morally and culturally 'impure.'"[39] Lewis seems to have sparked at least one black artist to put his proposals to the test. As an author of comic musical theater, Razaf was equally unawed by Lockean folk authenticity or the kind of proletcult solemnity in which Lenin never dances and never sins. Yet he still hoped to produce purposeful dramatic amusement, discreetly slipping doses of the *Crusader's* working-class renaissance into Harlem club life where they were least expected. The revue accordingly took up an impure, if not illegitimate, task: breeding the casual, risqué, and urbane theatrical mode that ruled Harlem evenings with the service work that filled most Harlemites' days.

Consider the revue's biggest hit, "A Porter's Love Song (to a Chambermaid)," which reveals the black labor hidden within saleable Harlem melodies:

> Tho' my position is of low degree
> And all the others may look down on me,
> I'll go smiling thru,
> That's if I have you;
> I am the happiest of troubadours,
> Thinking of you, while I'm massaging floors,
> At my leisure time, I made up this rhyme:
>
> I will be the oil mop,
> If you'll be the oil,

Then we both could mingle
Ev'ry time we toil.
I will be the washboard,
If you will be the tub,
Think of all the Mondays
We can rub-a-dub.[40]

Through their bluesy double entendres, one of Razaf's specialties, these lyrics sound a Marxian overtone: underpaid black labor is the breeding ground of the African American art that "Jes Grew" from Harlem to the land where the Volga flows. Razaf's porter needs little prodding to rival Cole Porter and composes a clever rhyme at the drop of a mop. The bawdy results are an extended play on the multiaccentuality of the word "work" in African American speech, where it can signify "dancing, labor, sexual activity or any nuanced combination of all three."[41] The porter's introductory lines emphasize work as mere drudgery, but then his love song diverges from Prufrock's and becomes a catalog of the domestic chores and erotic acts a maid and porter could share. We might think that this drift from preface to catalog, from work alone to work as sex, coincides with a flight from sexually repressive labor to erotically fulfilling artistic production. The introduction indeed presents a lonely porter reckoning with his paying "position . . . of low degree," whereas the verses that follow represent his autonomous, pleasurable creation. But Razaf's worker-writer can't quite bring himself to segregate eros and labor, unalienated song composition and alienated service work. In his 1924 book *The Gift of Black Folk,* W. E. B. Du Bois had argued that African Americans gave all U.S. workers a precious donation in "the idea of toil as a necessary evil ministering to the pleasures of life."[42] Razaf's porter might agree with Du Bois but add that another gift worth giving was the idea that the pleasures of life could minister to—and mingle with—toil. The sliver of utopia within the slightly dirty joke of "A Porter's Love Song" is thus not the promise that sexuality and art might escape cleanly from the discipline of the wage but the prospect that the common labor in making love, "massaging floors," and fabricating rhymes could be freely acknowledged and enjoyed.

It would be too cute to propose that *A Kitchen Mechanic's Revue* consciously works to synthesize Marx's secret of surplus value with popular, uncodified forms of African American labor resistance. Razaf's Moscow-on-the-Harlem musical nevertheless suggests that his contact with the renaissance of Harlem bolshevism allowed his songwriting to draw on two distinct countercultures of modernity: Marxism, with its materialist accent on labor's primacy and exploitation under capitalism; and the vernacular arts of the descendants of

African slaves, whose utopian "politics of transfiguration" Paul Gilroy distills as a "desire . . . to conjure up and enact the new modes of friendship, happiness, and solidarity that are consequent on the overcoming of [modernity's] racial oppression."[43] The revue draws from black music's "posing [of] the world as it is against the world as the racially subordinated would like it to be,"[44] evoking the deliverance of maids and porters through songs of liberation from dormant bosses. It draws from Marxism as it discloses the oddly personal yet still hidden and naturalized labor of service work. It braids the two borrowings together in its suggestion that black emancipation might emerge through a generous enrichment of productive labor, a proposition as distinct from most black radical thought, forged in the memory of slavery, as from the severe work ethic of Booker T.-ism. "Sambo's Dance" affirms that the Razaf of 1930 was less infatuated with the Soviet Union than his *Crusader* comrades, many now party officials. All the same, the whole of the revue bespeaks his continued infatuation with the *Crusader* group's understanding of Harlem's rebirth. Renaissance principals from onetime chauffeur Zora Neale Hurston to onetime busboy Langston Hughes sometimes suspected that the Harlem movement was as much in service to white New York as was Harlem's workforce. Their anxiety has been passed down to renaissance criticism, where it lurks behind numberless discussions of the deforming effects of white artistic patronage.[45] Razaf, though troubled by the estrangements inherent in running both the *Crusader* and an elevator, learned that service jobs could finance contributions to institutions servicing black liberation. In 1930, he thus filled the floor of Smalls's with a performance proud to suggest that Harlem service workers were authoring renaissance culture even as they earned their wages.

Crucial Harlem Renaissance texts from *Fine Clothes to the Jew* (1927) to *Home to Harlem* (1928) might be added to the case I have pursued through *A Kitchen Mechanic's Revue*. Neither Hughes's cooks and elevator boys nor McKay's uninhibited, pro-union longshoreman Jake seem to believe that the renaissance of Harlem's proletariat had failed entirely by 1925. The sweep of Razaf's renaissance radicalism alone, however, should serve to suggest that black bolshevism is best seen as a fluctuating but consistently fertile position within the full lifespan of the renaissance cultural field. The primary aim of this conclusion does not need belaboring at a moment when the history of the renaissance's black modernism is back in vogue and back in flux. Under the combined pressure of black feminism, black vernacular theory, new and newer historicisms, and what I've elsewhere called the new integrationism in modernist studies,[46] the self-defeating and melodramatic problem of the movement's "failure" has finally been tabled. Clearly, I intend my work to join the reopened questions of the renaissance's parameters and balance of power. Why, however, should we believe that recalling Razaf is valuable to projects other than mapping the renaissance field with greater precision?

For at least four reasons, I submit. First, retrieving Razaf argues that we have just begun exploring the continuities between putatively hostile periods of black cultural life: the renaissance of the 1920s and the black proletarianism of the 1930s sustained by the Great Depression, the Federal Writers' Project, and an aggressively antiracist Communist Party. Might the crash and the resulting reorientation of political, economic, and cultural capital in fact have forced a weakened renaissance position—black bolshevism—into dominance and equipped it to install a compelling problematic for black literary culture? Second, retrieving Razaf argues that the engagement between the New Negro and the Old Left was commenced much earlier than usually thought, and by parties usually deemed passive in its grip. The pages of the *Crusader* testify that this engagement was first proposed at the dawning of a Harlem modernism, and at the instigation of black intellectuals who never suspected that communism and black renaissances were bad neighbors. Third, retrieving Razaf argues that we go awry in assuming that the meeting of the New Negro and the Old Left is purely an installment in the history of modern interracial organization or black-Jewish relations. As the sparring renaissances of Alain Locke and the black bolsheviks suggest, this meeting was also played out from its inception within African American ranks. Fourth, and finally, retrieving Razaf argues that we have little reason to fear that black intellectual freedom was necessarily compromised when black intellectuals eyed communism as a fraternal relation. From the *Crusader*'s renaissance, we learn that Harlem's modern unveiling of such freedom tapped and accommodated bolshevism with liberty. For all these reasons—the details and consequences of which require other essays to explore—Razaf should not remain an invisible man.

NOTES

1. Ralph Ellison, *Invisible Man* (1952; New York: Vintage, 1989), 8.
2. Ellison 8.
3. Ellison 8.
4. Ellison 14.
5. Ellison 443.
6. Barry Singer, *Black and Blue: The Life and Lyrics of Andy Razaf* (New York: Schirmer, 1992), 216.
7. Andy Razaf, "(What Did I Do to Be So) Black and Blue." Music by Thomas "Fats" Waller and Harry Brooks. Copyright © 1929 by EMI Mills Music; ©

renewed, assigned to Razaf Music, Co., EMI Mills Music, Inc., and Chapell and Co.

8. There is a chance that forgetting the writer of "Black and Blue's" lyric—the least mediated trace of Armstrong's performance Ellison can reproduce—will be less common in the future. Eric J. Sundquist's helpful guidebook *Cultural Contexts for Ralph Ellison's* Invisible Man (Boston: St. Martin's, 1995) acknowledges Razaf's authorship and reproduces the song's words in full, as does the section on "The Vernacular Tradition" in Henry Louis Gates and Nellie Y. McKay, eds., *The Norton Anthology of African American Literature* (New York: Norton, 1997).

9. Singer 338.

10. George Hutchinson, *The Harlem Renaissance in Black and White* (Cambridge: Belknap-Harvard University Press, 1995), 15.

11. See the accounts of the Old Left's involvement in the genesis and passing of the renaissance in Harold Cruse, *The Crisis of the Negro Intellectual* (New York: William Morrow, 1967); Nathan Huggins's introduction to the anthology *Voices from the Harlem Renaissance* (New York; Oxford University Press, 1976); David Levering Lewis, *When Harlem Was in Vogue* (1981; New York: Vintage, 1982) and his introduction to *The Portable Harlem Renaissance Reader* (New York: Viking, 1994); and Henry Louis Gates, "The Trope of a New Negro and the Reconstruction of the Image of the Black," *Representations* 24 (1988): 129–55.

12. For a more adequate introduction to Pierre Bourdieu's theory of the cultural field, see the English-language translation of his associated essays in *The Field of Cultural Production,* ed. and intro. Randal Johnson (New York: Columbia University Press, 1993).

13. Hutchinson 13.

14. Hutchinson 146.

15. Singer 6–23.

16. Singer 29–347.

17. Robert T. Kerlin, ed., *Negro Poets and Their Poems* (Washington, D.C.: Associated Publishers, 1923), 51, 199.

18. Andy Razaf, *Poems for a Mixed-Up World,* intro. Langston Hughes, manuscript 35, Andy Razaf Papers, Manuscripts, Archives, and Rare Books Division, Schomburg Center for Research in Black Culture, New York Public Library, 2.

19. "Aims of *The Crusader,*" *Crusader* 1.3 (November 1918): 1.

20. In one of the few admissions that a significant portion of the staff of the literary renaissance was not safely ensconced in nationalist parlors "far beyond the menial labor and poverty of Harlem's vast working class," Sidney H. Bremer, *Urban Intersections: Meetings of Life and Literature in United States Cities* (Urbana: University of Illinois Press, 1992) notes that "Claude McKay worked as a railroad steward while he wrote the clarion poem for the New

Negro, 'If We Must Die' (1919); Hughes was waiting on tables—having just returned from one of his several stints as a messboy at sea—when *The Weary Blues* (1925) was going to press" (138). Less likely proletarian Countee Cullen, who joined the Communist Party in the 1930s, had early work experience as a busboy, whereas Zora Neale Hurston labored as a maid and manicurist as well as "a popular novelist's secretary and chauffeur" (138).

21. Herbert G. Gutman, *The Black Family in Slavery and Freedom, 1750–1925* (New York: Vintage, 1976), 453.
22. Singer 44–57.
23. E. P. Thompson, *The Making of the English Working Class* (New York: Vintage, 1966), 9.
24. Carole Marks, *Farewell—We're Good and Gone: The Great Black Migration* (Bloomington: Indiana University Press, 1989), 32–41.
25. "The African Blood Brotherhood," *Crusader* 2.10 (June 1920): 22.
26. David Levering Lewis, "Parallels and Divergences: Assimilationist Strategies of Afro-American and Jewish Elites from 1910 to the Early 1930s," in *Bridges and Boundaries: African Americans and American Jews,* ed. Jack Salzman (New York: George Braziller, 1992), 29.
27. Andy Razaf, "Don't Tread on Me," *Crusader* 1.8 (April 1919): 7.
28. David R. Roediger, *Towards the Abolition of Whiteness: Essays on Race, Politics, and Working Class History* (New York: Verso, 1994), 168.
29. Houston A. Baker Jr., *Modernism and the Harlem Renaissance* (Chicago: University of Chicago Press, 1987), 85.
30. Baker 85.
31. Melvin B. Tolson, "Claude McKay's Art," *Poetry* 83.4 (1954): 288.
32. James Weldon Johnson, ed., *The Book of American Negro Poetry* (1922; rev. ed. 1931; New York: Harcourt Brace, 1959), 41.
33. "We 'Rile' the Crackerized Department of Justice," *Crusader* 2.9 (May 1920): 5–6.
34. Johnson 168.
35. Langston Hughes, *The Big Sea* (New York: Knopf, 1940), 228.
36. Andy Razaf, "Sambo's Syncopated Russian Dance." Music by Jimmy Johnson. Copyright © 1930 (renewed) Edwin H. Morris and Co., a Division of MPL Communications, Inc., and Razaf Music. Copyright renewed by Morley Music Co. All rights reserved.
37. Harvey Klehr, John Earl Haynes, and Kyrill M. Anderson, *The Soviet World of American Communism* (New Haven: Yale University Press, 1998), 218–27; Mark Naison, *Communists in Harlem During the Depression* (New York: Grove, 1984), 13–14.
38. Paul R. Gorman, *Left Intellectuals and Popular Culture in Twentieth-Century America* (Chapel Hill: University of North Carolina Press, 1996), 133.
39. Hutchinson 311.
40. Andy Razaf, "A Porter's Love Song (to a Chambermaid)." Music by Jimmy

Johnson. Copyright © 1930 Edwin H. Morris and Co., a Division of MPL Communications, Inc., and Razaf Music. Copyright renewed by Morley Music Co. All rights reserved.

41. Paul Gilroy, *"There Ain't No Black in the Union Jack": The Cultural Politics of Race and Nation* (1987; Chicago: University of Chicago Press, 1991), 203.

42. W. E. B. Du Bois, *The Gift of Black Folk* (1924; Millwood, NY: Kraus-Thomson, 1975), 79.

43. Paul Gilroy, *The Black Atlantic: Modernity and Double Consciousness* (Cambridge: Harvard University Press, 1993), 38. Recently adapted by Gilroy, the term "counter-culture of modernity" was introduced by Zygmunt Bauman to describe the Western Left's immanent, surprisingly respectful critique of modern capitalist democracy and rationality; see his "The Left as the Counter-Culture of Modernity," *Telos* 70 (winter 1986–87): 81–93.

44. Gilroy, *The Black Atlantic*, 36.

45. I am partly indebted to Sidney H. Bremer's insightful chapter "The Urban Home of the Harlem Renaissance" (132–64) in *Urban Intersections* for these thoughts on the relationship between Harlem service labor and the anxiety of renaissance patronage.

46. William J. Maxwell, "Black and White, Unite and Write: New Integrationist Criticism of U.S. Literary Modernism," review of *The Dialect of Modernism: Race, Language, and Twentieth-Century Literature,* by Michael North; *The Harlem Renaissance in Black and White,* by George Hutchinson; and *Radical Representations: Politics and Form in U.S. Proletarian Fiction, 1929–1941,* by Barbara Foley, *minnesota review* 47 (1996): 205–15.

RENO-VATING GENDER

PLACE, PRODUCTION, AND THE RENO DIVORCE FACTORY

Jani Scandura

PART I: THE WASTE OF PROGRESS

Divorcées always arrived in Reno by train. They hopped on the Twentieth Century at Grand Central, switched in Chicago to the Overland Limited, and three days later stepped out of their Pullman cars at the Reno Union Pacific Station, where fatherly divorce attorneys gathered them up "like great sheep dogs, shepherding their lambs."[1] Reno was the 1930s Mecca of the controversial "quickie" divorce, easy to be had on almost any grounds as long as one stayed in the state for six weeks.[2]

That is how the story goes.[3] And this is another story, a story not simply of how to read that complex place, but of what it means to perform critical historiography in a postmodern era. Reno is a wasteland, as we shall see, but it is a wasteland that subverts any pretensions to the universalized space that T. S. Eliot proposed.[4] Reno is a peculiarly American wasteland, a wasteland of the feminine, of divorcées and prostitutes. It is a non-elegiac wasteland that reveals the grotesque machinery of modernity in crisis and relies on the economically and ideologically beneficial mass production of trash. This is a story, then, about Reno and gender, but also a critique of the current methodologies of reading modernisms and modernity. This is a story about modern place.

Places, as the geographer Doreen Massey points out, are "constructed out of the juxtaposition, the intersection, the articulation, of multiple social relations."[5] Far from being fixed, cohesive, or bounded—materially, ideologically, or otherwise—"the identity of place is always and controversially being produced."[6] At stake in the productions of modern places are not simply social relations in the neo-Marxist sense of much contemporary cultural geography,[7] but the struggle for cultural belonging, collective memory, and representational forms.[8] Because places simultaneously conserve even as they undermine the foundations of cultural hegemony, it is crucial to consider those ideas that stabilize or "fix" place-identity in addition to those that unmake them.[9] Reconstructing places of the past becomes an act of "visual consumption" as well as imagination,[10] a kind of historicist *flânerie* that seeks out the "new intermingled with the old," the ruins of the past in the seams of the present and the dreams for the present in what has gone before.[11] For "every place is many places," the textual composite of myriad representations and simultaneous temporalities.[12] As Edward Casey astutely remarks, "place is more an event than an entity."[13] Projecting a model of regulated assembly-line production onto communities of women who were discarded from socially sanctioned American society, then transforming these transported eastern women in the post-frontier West, the place-text that is "Reno" relies on a refuse economy that negotiates between two of the fictional monuments of American progressive modernity: Fordist industrial "Americanism" and imperialist frontier "Americanization."[14]

That a railroad quest set Reno "production" in motion underscores the ideological import of the destination—and of this means of getting there. "Railroads were the referent, and progress the sign, as spatial movement became so wedded to the concept of historical movement that these could no longer be distinguished," writes Susan Buck-Morss in *The Dialectics of Seeing: Walter Benjamin and the Arcades Project*.[15] If Marx, perhaps optimistically, used the locomotive as a metaphor for revolutionary progress, Walter Benjamin suggested instead that "perhaps revolutions are the reaching of humanity traveling in this train for the emergency brake."[16] Social revolution, Benjamin implies, necessitates a slowing down or stopping of modernist progress. At the very least, a price must be paid to race through time en route to Somewhere.

The departure for Reno

• For now, alas, not secretly nor under cover, but openly, with al sense of shame put aside, now by word, again by writing, by theat cal productions of every kind, by romantic fiction, by amorous an frivolous novels, by cinematographs portraying in vivid scene, al dresses broadcast by radio-telephony, in short, by all the inventio of modern science, the sanctity of marriage is being trampled upo and derided . . . Pope Pius XI. From the ENCYCLICAL ON MARRIAG

FIG. 12.1. New York women took the "Divorcée Special" to Reno from Grand Central Station. The metaphor was apt. As the above remarks from this August 1931 *Vanity Fair* cartoon suggest, divorce was seen as a by-product of modern technology. © 1931 Galbraith/*Vanity Fair*, Condé Nast Publications, Inc.

In contrast to megalomaniac, monumentalist narratives of competitive capitalism and imperialism, those allegorized by the train, Benjamin insisted on focusing on the "small, discarded, objects," the waste products of progressive narratives of history. The dialectical relationship he posits between allegories of trains and those of trash seems abundantly clear. Not only do trains produce trash, the waste and refuse of fuel, machinery, and bodies in transit, but trash itself implies movement, history, and labor. Trash is the exhausted material of "no worth or value," the abject defilement that "is jettisoned from the symbolic system[s]" of modernity.[17] It is the mess that spews forth from the historical gaps that narratives of progress have thrown out, ridden over, stitched between, glossed. And it defines its own mode of production. To trash, according to the 1911 *Century Dictionary*, is to "walk or run with exertion, to fatigue, to labor a point"; while "to be trashed" is to be worn out, "bungled, spoiled; ill-treated or injured; run down" and, implicitly, to have had a past when one was new, healthy, cherished, and whole.[18]

Certainly, the train station at Reno made material the metaphoric intersection between progressive narratives of modernity and the mess left in their wake. Reno flaunted its trash at the tracks. "Reno throws its worst face directly at the station," wrote Max Miller in his 1941 cultural history of the city, "and [it] appears to take pleasure in doing so, appears to take pleasure in indicating a turmoil of shack-stores, cheap saloons, a burleycue of gambling houses, even a tattoo shop, tough alleys—and a blur of constant excitement."[19]

Moreover, it is telling that the "Divorcée Special" to Reno was itself a train filled

FIG. 12.2. Reno is a multivalenced text that continually, cyclically builds and unbuilds itself. Its name stays the same, but the surface changes. The famed Virginia Street arch, at the gateway to the casino district in downtown Reno, has been rebuilt several times. The one standing today was built during the 1970s, replacing an earlier neon version built in 1964, which replaced an electrically torched gateway constructed in 1938, which replaced the first arch; pictured above circa 1931, a bulb-lit wrought iron structure that was designed for the Nevada Transcontinental Exposition in 1927. Courtesy of the Nevada Historical Society.

with trash, the rejected partners and families that refused—or were refused by—the impositions of American progressive modernity. Nor is it surprising that 1930s Reno was largely narrated by trash—pulp novels, sensation magazines, cartoons, and B-films. In undergoing a materialist quest to reread Reno's monumentalist fictions, we must wade through this waste, must gather signs, symbols, and clues, piece these together, and build a textual construction that reveals the ongoing dialectic between Reno as metaphor and Reno as material place.

An American Tale

A joke in the *Nevada Review*, May 1928:

> A San Francisco couple had decided that they were no longer compatable [*sic*] and were making plans for their little girl and the lady of the family to spend 3 months in Reno. One evening before the departure of the wife and daughter the better half said to the husband: "What have you been telling our little girl about Reno, I just heard her saying her prayers and she said, 'Good-bye God, we are going to Reno.'"
>
> "That's queer," answered the husband, "I will listen to her tomorrow night and see what she says then, as I have not been telling her any tales about Reno."
>
> The next evening after listening to the daughter say her prayers, the husband said to the wife: "You must have been wrong, for she only said, 'Good! By God we are going to Reno.'"[20]

"Mass Culture as Woman"

For Reno, divorce—and its by-products—proved a lucrative industry.[21] The Nevada residency period was carefully designed to guarantee that divorcées would pay several months' rent and purchase a multitude of other necessary and luxury services during their stay.[22] A 1933 *Fortune* magazine article estimated that divorce brought in approximately $3 to $4 million in income to Reno and that individual divorce seekers spent an average of $1,500 during a six-week stay (although the writers admit that exceptionally frugal women could get by on as little as $225).[23]

Famous for attracting movie stars and socialites, Reno also became the temporary home of the divorcing literati. Over the years, Sherwood Anderson, Katherine Anne Porter, Mary McCarthy, Arthur Miller, Clare Boothe, Kay Boyle, and the wives of Eugene O'Neill, Sinclair Lewis, and Waldo Frank all came to Reno to get their decrees. By the 1930s, questing to Reno seemed almost inevitable in the lives of modern middle-class women—at least according to the plethora of Reno narratives that flooded popular culture. In the year fol-

lowing the 1931 change in the Nevada residency requirement, no fewer than eight novels about Reno divorces were published.[24]

Hollywood followed suit, not simply with a smattering of "Reno" references and a plenitude of divorce films (what Stanley Cavell calls the 1930s "films of remarriage"),[25] but with films in which the Reno divorce quest occupied center screen. MGM's star-studded 1939 film adaption of Clare Boothe's satirical play *The Women* is simply the most expensive and best-known of a fairly rich genre of motion pictures.[26] Yet it is this film that sums up the prevailing popular sentiment about middle-class marriage when thrice-married Countess DeLave (Mary Boland) laments, "No matter what you pick [your husbands] for where does it get you?" "On the train to Reno," the soon-to-be-divorced Mary (Norma Shearer) and Miriam (Paulette Goddard) answer in refrain.

Despite all the brouhaha, Reno divorces never amounted to much. During the seven years following Mary Pickford's much-publicized 1920 Reno breakup from Owen Moore, Nevada courts granted about a thousand divorces a year.[27] In 1927 Nevada reduced its nineteenth-century residency requirement from six months to three months, and increased its annual divorce quotient to 2,500. Three years later, in 1931, the same year that gambling was legalized, Nevada lowered its residency requirement to six weeks, again doubling its rate of divorce "production." Yet in 1931—when an unprecedented 5,260 divorces were performed in Reno—Reno divorces still constituted less than 3 percent of those nationwide.[28] Nonetheless, to most Americans, Reno meant divorce—as well as a number of other illicit vices. A 1936 article in the pulp magazine *True Detective* gushed, "Whatever you want—wine, women, or song—gambling, prostitution, marriage or divorce—Reno has it. And it's legal. Reno's motto is: 'You can't do wrong—we'll legalize it!'"[29]

Much of the anxiety about divorce derived from and deflected cultural anxieties about the psychosocial effects of advanced industrial capitalism. Indeed, rising divorce rates after the Great War were attributed to all the supposed pollutants of modern life, including the "entry of women into industry" and "the movement for women's rights," as well as a myriad of causes such as "low mentality," "nerves," "yellow journalism," "jazz," "the Ford car," and "irreligion."[30] Alfred Cahen's influential 1932 study statistically derived "four important factors" that he believed were the cause of increasing divorce rates: the rise in economic production; the growth of cities; the increase in women wage earners; and the declining birthrate.[31] Following Cahen's logic, the rupture of the patriarchal family system became a toxic by-product of modern industrialism and urbanization. Divorce was construed as a problem of laboring women who had been seduced by the products and processes of modernity and had thereby become less dependent on men.

Certainly, modern marketing and mass production threatened to erase the visible markers of social distinction that distinguished the good girls from the bad. "Since the jazz age gave cosmetology and 'sex appeal' to all women, prostitutes have lost their monopoly on traditional means of allure," comments Richard Lillard in his 1942 history of Nevada.[32] After all, like prostitution, modern marriage relied on an economy of sex. The unofficial, but supposedly authentic, cause of all Reno marital breakups was sexual incompatibility.[33] "Consciously or unconsciously, my dear young ladies, sex dissatisfaction is at the bottom of every divorce," Nairn's Reno lawyer tells her and Elisabeth in Dorothy Walworth Carmen's 1932 novel *Reno Fever*.[34]

In this context, a Reno divorce can be considered a product—indeed *the* product—of a modernity that had been built to "redo" and "renew" the institution of marriage. "But you will divorce, *nicht wahr?*" Susan Hale's German friend asks her in *Half a Loaf,* Grace Hegger Lewis's *roman à clef* about her breakup with Sinclair Lewis. "It is so easy I am told in America in this place so funnily named Renoo. You have also the word 'renew'? Renoo, renew—the same thing?"[35] What's more, divorce seemed to "modernize" Reno. In John Hamlin's 1931 novel *Whirlpool of Reno,* stodgy Minnie Brooks exclaims, "Why Reno is a real up-to-date town now, thanks to our divorcées." A fellow permanent resident, Jane, snaps back the plaint of many critics of modernity in its Depression-era guise: "A shame we're not as we used to be. . . . Far better to be provincial and pure than up-to-date and corrupted."[36]

PART II: THE GENDER FACTORY

Partial transcript from case no. 38,192 in the Second Judicial Court of the state of Nevada, county of Washoe, November 27, 1931, 4:07 P.M.:

> *Q:* Please state why the defendant deserted you at that time.
> *A:* My husband told me at that time that he no longer cared for me and absolutely refused to support me.
> *Q:* Did you give him any cause to leave you?
> *A:* No, sir.
> *Q:* Now, you have also alleged that for more than one year last past before the filing of this complaint, as a second cause of action, that since November, 1926, he neglected and refused to provide you with the common necessities of life. Is that true?
> *A:* Yes, sir.
> *Q:* And could he have provided you with clothing, food, and shelter if he had wanted to?
> *A:* Yes, sir.
> *Q:* Was he an able-bodied man?
> *A:* Yes.
> *Q:* And was he at that time?
> *A:* Yes, sir.
> *The Court:* I think that is sufficient, Mr. Rafetto.

Women at Work

The possibility that domestic life could be modeled to function on modern paradigms was an ominous as well as utopian prospect for social theorists—and a premise already put into practice by Henry Ford, who made no secret of attempting to intervene in the private life of his workers.[37] If Fordism seemed to be gender-neutral because it distinguished between concrete tasks rather than individual workers, then the logical outgrowth of its practice would be to "take to pieces" the machinery of the patriarchal family and the stay-at-home wife. In practice, however, Fordism relied on a logic where gender superseded task differentiation, where workers first were distinguished through gender-appropriate jobs. As Peter Wollen remarks in his analysis of Antonio Gramsci's writings on Fordism, "the workforce of a factory . . . is itself 'like a machine which cannot, without considerable loss, be taken to pieces too often and renewed with single parts.' The wife waiting at home becomes another such permanent machine part."[38]

The gender-appropriateness of jobs for women was a point of contention during the Depression, when the economic hardship of the 1930s forced an increasing percentage of married women into wage labor. By 1940, 35 percent of all wage-earning women were married, as opposed to 28.5 percent a decade earlier.[39] Moreover, the proportion of unemployed women, while significant, was generally lower than that of men, especially in states that largely relied on heavy industries such as mining, metal work, and building.[40] This disproportion caused a backlash against women workers, according to Alice Kessler-Harris, who quotes Norman Cousin's 1939 solution to unemployment: "There are approximately 10,000,000 people out of work in the United States today . . . there are also 10,000,000 or more women, married and single, who are job holders. Simply fire the women, who shouldn't be working anyway, and hire the men. Presto! No unemployment. No Relief rolls. No depression."[41] Some industries had done just that. Section 213 of the 1932 Federal Economy Act legislated that married employees (usually women) should be fired first in the event of a personnel reduction if their spouses (usually men) also held federal government jobs. Public school systems both refused to hire and often fired women teachers. Railroads and other transportation industries were barred to married women. Unions refused women admission. Until 1939, legislatures in twenty-six states were reviewing bills to ban married women from state employment.[42]

Representations of Depression-era Reno addressed these controversies head-on. For the Reno economy quite literally projected a Fordist ideology onto the public regulation of private life and in doing so revealed its ruptures. The legal assembly line of the Reno "divorce mill," as it was popularly called, relied on the specialized labor of interchangeable lawyers, defendants, and prosecutors to mass produce trials that were grounded on identical evidence (a vague assertion of cruelty and desertion); from prosecutors with identical residency status (exactly six weeks continuous residency and the supposed intention to make Nevada a permanent home); affirmed by identical witness testimonies (landlords who swore, "I saw her every day for six weeks"); which resulted in identical judgments (a divorce decree). Reno divorcées were metaphorized as factory workers. In *Half a Loaf*, Susan Hale comments that in moving to Reno she "had bound herself to a definite six months' job."[43] And like assembly-line work, the routine of getting "Reno-vated" is so monotonous a labor for divorcées that an "asterisk" or "a line of stars" would be quite adequate to cover the narratives of

FIG. 12.4. A *New York World Telegram* cartoon depicting the Reno divorce factory—an updated version of the early-twentieth-century divorce mill. Reprinted in 1931 in the short-lived scandal sheet, *The Reno Divorce Racket*. Courtesy of the Nevada Historical Society.

the "empty five months and twenty-nine days in the lives of many of the women Susan met."[44]

If divorcées were workers, however, they also were processed like so much raw material in an industrial mill. The tenets of Nevada's residency laws made all of Reno's temporary citizens not just "created equal," but interchangeable like industrial parts. In *Half a Loaf*, Susan's lawyer reminds her of the generic testimony she is to give in court: "Don't forget to say 'yes' when you are asked if you intend to make Reno your permanent residence."[45] Just before her divorce trial, Sheila Randolph's Reno attorney, in Charles Parmer's 1932 novel *After Divorce?* reminds her, "Just remember—answer as I coached you."[46]

Fordism always unbuilds while building, renovating means of construction to build ever more identical products faster, more cheaply than ever before, to make, as Terry Smith argues in *Making the Modern: Industry, Art and Design in America*, "nothing original, but everything new."[47] Reno divorce legislation, as organizing structure, transformed itself simply by shortening the residency requirement allowed in the state, thereby offsetting threatened competition for divorce from Arkansas, Florida, the Virgin Islands, and Mexico. But though standardized divorce production became increasingly time-efficient in Reno, the product, like the Model T, didn't change. Nor did the power dynamics of the Reno factory's patriarchal management structure—the lawyers, judges, politicians, and police—ever substantially alter. Individual men bucked for money and power within the system itself. Each change in legislation seemed to promise the arrival of more prospective divorcées and a bundle in easy income for the residents of Reno.

By 1932 Reno employed 127 lawyers, compared to the 44 in Ogden, Utah, a town that had over twice Reno's population at the time.[48] Litigation revenue averaged $250 in lawyers' fees plus $40 in court costs per client for an uncontested divorce and could run well into the thousands of dollars for contested cases or where large settlements were being negotiated.[49] In *Reno Fever*, Elisabeth Wane reflects, "The law had been carefully administered to bring money to the town. Every broken life means so many dollars."[50] "We are all caught in the legal machinery of marriage and divorce," comments Nairn in Carmen's novel before she does herself in.[51]

Factory Life

An inquiry from William D. Shew, Attorney at Law, Hartford, Connecticut, to George A. Bartlett, Esq., Reno, Nevada, April 3, 1943:

> I have been consulted in the last few days by three girls, all of whom are factory workers in Hartford, relative to the possibilities of securing Reno divorces. I believe they are live prospects and are held back solely by the question of finances and what I would like to find out are two things. First, if two or three of these girls came out, just what could you see your way clear to secure their divorces for? Let me know, including costs. Secondly, they desire to know whether there is a reasonable possibility of their securing work of any kind while they are in Reno. It could either be factory work or even restaurant work, just so long as some of their living expenses were paid.

Reply from George A. Bartlett to William D. Shew, April 8, 1943:

it is difficult, of course, without discussing with clients so as to know the amount of labor that might be involved with their particular case, to fix fees in advance but with people who have to work for a living, as the girls you refer to must, I usually, after discussing conditions with them, fix a very moderate fee, depending, of course, upon their capacity to pay, either at the close of the case or later on; rarely, however, charging above $150 and sometimes cutting that to $100 or less. The costs of Court approximate $53. inclusive of both sides; defendants' appearance fee, I think I can arrange to have done for $25. each.

There is a reasonable possibility of securing work, but of course I cannot guarantee it. It would be more apt to be a restaurant or housework, as we have no factory enterprises here; however, please be assured I will do my best to secure work for them and fix fees according to capacity to pay.[52]

Sex and Standardization

The new methods of work required by the "planned economy" of Fordist Americanism were "inseparable from a specific mode of living and of thinking and feeling life," according to Antonio Gramsci. Therefore, they necessitated the production of a new type of worker and a new type of man—a man whose sexual instinct had been "suitably regulated" and rationalized.[53] Gramsci points out, however, that American attempts at rationalizing the sexual instinct had backfired, producing "unhealthy 'feministic' deviations," sexually liberated upper-class divorcées who had achieved economic independence through favorable divorce settlements.[54] Although this group never constituted more than a tiny percentage of American women who divorced, it came to represent the norm.

Gramsci harps at length on the divorcée as an emergent American class and the modern counterpart to the European "parasitic" noble classes. Even the male industrialist does not seem to warrant such wrath. While the male industrialist labors, Gramsci writes,

> [his wife and daughters] . . . travel; they are continually crossing the ocean to Europe. . . . (It is worth recalling that ship's captains in the United States have been deprived of their right to celebrate marriage on board ship, since so many couples get married on leaving Europe and divorced again before disembarking in America.) Prostitution in a real sense is spreading, in a form barely disguised by fragile legal formulae.[55]

For women, temporal, spatial, economic, or marital displacement, divorce, becomes prostitution, the *real* thing, according to Gramsci, which regulated

FIG. 12.5. The entrance to the Stockade, circa 1943. The Stockade was the most famous Reno house of prostitution in the 1920s and 1930s. Legal prostitution in Reno functioned as a kind of factory labor in itself. Prostitutes paid a management company about $2.50 to rent a "crib" for an eight-hour shift. They reaped whatever profits could be had in that time. Charging an average $2.00 per trick, they garnered between $20 and $40 in eight hours. Prostitutes registered their off-hour addresses with the police and submitted to a weekly medical examination. Courtesy of the Nevada Historical Society.

prostitution presumably is not. He claims that "the new industrialism wants monogamy," while simultaneously warning against the "abolition of organized, legal prostitution," which in 1930s Reno was a legally sanctioned gendered division of labor.[56] During the 1920s and 1930s, Reno housed the last legal red-light district in the United States.[57]

Federal law already scripted mobile women as transgressive and sexually promiscuous. The Mann Act of 1910 prohibited women from crossing state lines with any man other than a spouse or relative.[58] In supposedly preventing the hypothesis of "white slavery," the act presupposed all unmarried women to be potential prostitutes and all unregulated movement illicit.

Still, a narrative collapse between prostitutes and divorcées obscures the specificity of Reno's divorce machinery, a machinery that was particularly modern both in what threatened it (single, financially independent and productive women) and what sustained it (refused or refusing married and marrying women, geographic and social displacement, economic viability). To be transgressive in this system was not to be a prostitute, but to be "unprofessional," in other words, to be unregistered or unexamined or to perform sexual services outside legally sanctioned spatial or temporal boundaries.

The so-called floating population of Reno divorce seekers, Reno's "foster children," as one writer names them, lived in a liminal state.[59] They were transient but fully viable citizens of Nevada. They belonged both to Reno and, presumably, to the homes they had left. Moreover, their status as divorcées-in-waiting, or even divorcées, was temporary at best. Most Reno narratives end with the divorcée remarrying and returning back east in the same social position she left.

Reno Notes

A letter from playwright Clare Brokaw (later Clare Boothe Luce) to Judge George A. Bartlett, July 15, 1929:

> Judgie it is two months since I left Nevada with a divorce decree in my hand, and in my heart a conviction that events have not born out (you could have told me this!) that the major decree would settle all my problems, all the major ones, at least. Alas! I find that a decree is very much like a peace-treaty which ends a state of war, but leaves the countries in an infinitely more precarious and delicate psoition [*sic*] of reconstructions and readjustment. At first you are wildly glad that it is over, and you are inflated with a feeling of victory and power, but then, as you survey the little ruins and desolation around you, you are

overwhelmed with remorse that it ever had to be. Then you resolutely turn your face to the future, resolving all sorts of intelligent things, and start in painfully, a little wearily to reconstruct your life anew.[60]

New Industrial Wives

It is crucial to remember that for the bulk of their stay in Nevada, the heroines of Reno narratives, although referred to as divorcées, are not yet divorced. It is the potentiality of these divorcées-to-be that makes their position so ideologically resonant. They are unfinished, uncompleted. They stand in the midst of a process of building an institution (divorce) that relies on a simultaneous unbuilding and rebuilding of institutions that already stand (marriage, citizenship, gendered roles of production, renovation, reproduction, and consumption). In *The Company She Keeps,* Mary McCarthy points out that *potential* Reno divorcées are accorded a state that is "deeply pleasurable in somewhat the same way that being an engaged girl had been."[61] The divorcée is empowered in her unfinishedness, in her potential to play the game either way, in not yet being easily narrated, finalized, closed.

The processes of the Reno divorce mill inevitably prevailed, however, taking transgressive women who had been overly "modernized" and Reno-vating them to fit the old frame. Reno-vated divorcées adopted a new "feminine personality" that was assembled ever more efficiently from the same, unchanging societal parts. They were built, retroactively, as "raw material," as the crude, unfinished, *transient* mass of divorce seekers who must be labored upon. The past integrity of these raw materials (as married women) was incidental to the process that dismantled and refashioned them into what Gramsci called a "new feminine personality," a woman who was "independent of men," *individual men,* but not from the patriarchal structures already in place. Women's sexuality and sexual pleasure must be subordinated to the tasks of running a home. A contemporary evangelist, U. E. Harding, advised young wives, for example, that "cooking cleaning and keeping yourself up" would prevent the need for Reno-vation.[62] As Ford himself hoped, mass production had become morally upright.

Renovation of women as raw materials, or Reno-vation, actually put modern women back in their (traditional) place. Both "the cogs and the products," women were "mechanized according to the general norms" of an advanced industrial society.[63] Like the assembly-line laborers at Ford's factory, women, as workers, were automated in this model, stripped of the authority or ability to alter the end product, themselves, or even to alter the speed with which it (this newly remade woman) was self-produced. Remade and refeminized, Reno-

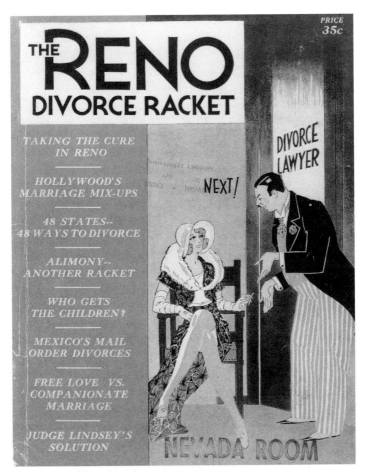

THE **RENO**
DIVORCE RACKET

TAKING THE CURE
IN RENO

HOLLYWOOD'S
MARRIAGE MIX-UPS

48 STATES--
48 WAYS TO DIVORCE

ALIMONY--
ANOTHER RACKET

WHO GETS
THE CHILDREN?

MEXICO'S MAIL
ORDER DIVORCES

FREE LOVE VS.
COMPANIONATE
MARRIAGE

JUDGE LINDSEY'S
SOLUTION

DIVORCE
LAWYER

NEXT!

NEVADA ROOM

FIG. 12.6. Cover from a 1931 publication designed to give an insider's guide to the divorce colony. Courtesy of the Nevada Historical Society.

vated into (re)marriage and traditional roles, divorcées became ironic New Women, a far cry from their feminist predecessors, though perhaps not from Victorian wives. A contemporary *Good Housekeeping* article goes so far as to conclude that "marriage can profit from divorce."[64]

The opening of MGM's film *The Women* is telling in this regard. A tracking shot follows a young woman through the different rooms of Sydney's, the Taylorized beauty salon in which beauticians perform specialized functions, undoing society women—through manicures, permanents, massages, and exercise instruction. The clients pass from room to room becoming increasingly monstrous and contorted until they exit the salon, finally remade, but looking the same as when they entered. In this context, divorce becomes another "normalizing" gender process—along with grooming and fashion. To be Reno-vated is not simply to get divorced, but to be quickly married again, to be renewed, in other words, but not made original. As Reno local Minnie Borne points out in *Whirlpool of Reno*, "Free and easy as all get out in their talk; smokin' cigarettes, drinkin' cocktails, wearin' as few clothes as law 'n order'll let 'em; but under their pretty skins [young divorcées are] prezactly the same as we used to be, now ain't they?"[65]

The Reno-vated wife, however, was the same with a difference. She was also "new and improved," making Reno-vation less akin to traditional Fordism than to the 1930s marketing philosophy of "progressive obsolescence," in which products were actively and consciously outmoded in order to initiate their faster, more regular replacement. The New Deal drive to boost the economy focused on increasing consumption by perpetuating a waste economy that mass produced trash. Progressive obsolescence made Ford's eschewal of style, what Stuart Ewen calls "Ford's puritanical commitment to 'homeliness,'" outmoded and a thing of the past.[66]

The production of Reno-vated wives ensured reproduction as a means through which to increase the populace of consumers. Therefore, semen might be seen as the ultimate Reno-vator, and children the preferred products of the New Industrial domestic machine. In *Reno Fever*, Elisabeth wonders whether a divorced woman with children were in a better way. For "at least she had something to show for the years. And yet, a child was always a link with the past. She could never make a fresh beginning."[67] Certainly, *The Women* relies on a progressive narrative that directs women to a life of dependent motherhood. Peggy Day (Joan Fontaine) is reunited with her husband only when she phones him from Reno to tell him there is a baby on the way. And Edith Potter (Phyllis Povah), the only married New Yorker who does not get divorced in the film, is a regular (re)production machine. While her companions wait out their six weeks at a Reno dude ranch, she gives birth to her eighth child.

In contrast to Edith Potter's healthy brood, the child of the overdressed and "over-sexed" Delia in *Reno Fever* is disastrously "pale and meager"; he has the

> undersized, second-rate look of an unwanted child. He kissed his mother timidly on the cheek. Delia treated him with that condescension which women, who make a career of sex, use for their children— by-products of the main industry. No Delia was not a perfect animal because she could not reproduce healthy young. A stock breeder would have shot her.[68]

In Reno, independent, sexual, career women become prostitutes or livestock, transforming their own children into trash. They are, in fact, worthy of little more than social and bodily erasure.

Reno becomes not a divorce mill, but "a regular matrimonial exchange. The air reeks of it."[69] And divorce is, in fact, only an odorous by-product, pollution, blown off during a production process that transforms modern women into New Industrial Wives. If women leave Reno without the prospect of remarriage and (re)commodification, the noxious stench of divorce tends to cling. Like their transgressive Victorian mothers, Reno women who refuse to remarry, refuse Reno-vation, refuse to become New (Industrial) Wives, become disruptive by-products and must be discarded as pollution, rubbish, societal trash.

Being "refused," according to Adele Leyton in *Whirlpool of Reno,* transforms one into refuse. She surmises, "It was to get away from this depressing, horrid sensation of being cast off, alone in the world, that threw these women into the reckless whirlpool of Reno's divorce colony."[70] Adele, née Addie Brooks, avoids this fate by paying for plastic surgery with her stock market winnings to lose and forget "her hideously twisted nose."[71] She returns remade to Reno, posing as a seductive divorcée, Adele Leyton, and claims that without such reconstruction she had only two choices: "Suicide or a nunnery—I couldn't decide which."[72] Refashioning her body and identity even before she puts herself on the Reno assembly line, Adele profits from Reno-vation, ultimately marrying a rich rancher without having to go through a divorce. Yet un-Reno-vated women who refuse remarriage, domesticity, and reproductive bliss go crazy (like Sheila in Latifa Johnson's novel *Sheila Goes to Reno*), are abandoned after having abortions (like Dee in *Whirlpool of Reno*), take lethal doses of pills (like Nairn in *Reno Fever*), or, like Delia, are preferably shot.

On Consumption
From Reno lawyer Clel Georgetta's diary, September 11, 1933:

> This A.M. I ran off Frank L——'s (New York) divorce case. The courtroom was full. He testified his wife drank and gave wild parties. I asked him if she ever did anything that embarrassed him. He said yes. So I asked him to relate to the Court a specific incident. He said that one night, while living in an apt. house the wife was staging a party. The landlord put his head in the dumbwaiter shaft and called upstairs to be quiet. The wife walked over and dumped a pail of garbage down on the landlord's head. He came up and put them out of the apt. that night. Frank said, Well, yes I was embarrassed. The whole court room broke out in a roar, even the Judge laughed and continued to laugh for some time.

PART III: THE CURE FACTORY

The popular press, which published accounts of prospective divorcées who went to Nevada to be Reno-vated at the divorce mill, also joked that divorcées quested west to "take the cure." Reno was variously described as a "hospital for hopeless marriages"[73] or for the "victims of apartment house quarrels, for the victims of city nerves, for the victims of what Bill said to Jane and what Jane hurried and told Julia and what Julia told to Johnny,"[74] a "Clinic like the Mayo Clinic,"[75] and a hybrid "Cure factory."[76]

Certainly divorce, that symptom of modernity, seemed an illness in many Reno narratives. Millicent describes the process of self-surveillance to Elisabeth Wane in *Reno Fever*, a novel whose title makes the connection explicit: "We were all brought up to believe that divorce is horrible. So we watch ourselves to see how we're living through it, just as we watch ourselves when we're sick."[77] Elisabeth earlier notes that she told others of her divorce "warily as news of cancer."[78] The hypothetical "Patsy," who narrates her Reno quest for the *Richmond Times,* sums up Reno of 1931 as a "symptom" of the American modernist problem of transitioning from a pioneer mentality to a modern, urban one.[79] And Julia Johnsen makes the point more succinctly in her 1925 introduction to *Selected Articles on Marriage and Divorce* when she argues that since "divorce is a symptom and not a cause of ills in the social body, efforts should be made to improve conditions at the source."[80]

The Reno "cure" ironically regendered Theodore Roosevelt's prescription for "the strenuous life," popular in the early part of the century, which provided the means through which men could counter the feminizing effects of living in the "sick society" of urban America. Roosevelt sought a sanitized national body composed of individuals who "lead clean, vigorous, healthy lives."[81] A "West cure"—which consisted of a few weeks camping and hiking in the western wilderness—often was prescribed as a cleansing mechanism, a kind of masculinization holiday that simulated pioneer trials without the tribulation. Droves of middle-class male "brain-workers" suffering from the ills of neurasthenia, "over-civilization"—and potential femininity—took temporary trips to remasculinize and re-Americanize themselves in unsettled conservation parks in the West.[82]

If the "frontier" immersion of Roosevelt's "strenuous life" cured individuals from the effects of contemporary urbanization, then the Reno "cure" might "heal" American women from the infection of modern life. But Reno as cure ironically repositioned marriage, not divorce, in the disease-bearing position. Moreover, if the West cured by masculinizing overly modernized subjects, the Reno cure became yet more problematic. For rather than gaining behavioral freedom, cured Reno women simply lost control of their shapes. "Without

FIG. 12.7. The Cure Factory specialized in the production of divorce. Postcard. Courtesy of Special Collections, University of Nevada-Reno Library.

shame," Susan Hale notes in *Half a Loaf,* Reno divorcées "would pull out a persistently offending black hair from a white chin, and discuss the methods of a chiropractor who had special thumps for reducing the hips."[83]

In time, these bearded, big-hipped women became veritable androgynes. Their supposed attempts to walk like a man and look like a woman are subverted: as they "slim down" and masculinize their hips, they sprout unwanted facial hair. Reno divorcées don't risk losing their gender identity, but their embodied, sexual one. If not, they are made ridiculous for attempting to try. A 1930s cartoon in *Pic* shows a young, voluptuous, and hyperfeminine divorcée leaving the Reno courthouse accompanied by her lawyer. "Boy," she exclaims, "I feel like a new man!"[84] Clearly, the cartoon satirizes the economy of marriage produced in Reno, in which men rather than women become progressively obsolescent, and where modern women periodically need to exchange a new man for the old. In doing so, it mocks the authority of modern women who seem to participate in a "traffic in men," for to initiate a transaction in which men become the sign of exchange is to overturn the authority of patriarchal kinship networks.[85] The potential political import of this kind of resignification is immediately squashed when the cartoon is taken literally. A woman so well endowed could no more "feel" like a man than she could look like one. Certainly, she is kidding herself. And this is the point. Underlying all this gender blurring is not the fear that women will turn into men, but that the masculinity inherent in all women might be exposed. Those black facial hairs are horrific not because women possess them but because they flaunt them without shame. In the end, if women temporary residents are cured in Reno, then the disease from which they seem to be freed is not marriage, but masculinity (or at least the attempt to adopt—and expose—some of its traits).

If Reno threatens to make women men, for divorcing men it has the opposite effect. "Normal men don't usually come out here [to Reno]. They send their wives. They're too much tied up in business," explains a world-weary Gretchen to two new Reno arrivals in *Reno Fever*.[86] Millicent replies, "I'd rather go around with a native rather than a male colonist. They are all so queer."[87] Men who divorce in Reno are often portrayed at the least as effeminate (especially in contrast to cowboys or even dude "wranglers") and perhaps homosexual. At the very least, men in this feminine community threaten to become "queer," losing their wives to predatory lesbians. In *Reno Fever*, "the hero of [Gretchen's] crowd was Edgar Ray, who had come out [there] for a divorce because his wife was seduced by a woman."[88]

In fact, the threat of queer desire underwrites most Reno narratives.[89] In *Reno Fever*, "somehow the thought that she would love Nairn forever [comforts] Elisabeth's heart."[90] And Nairn responds likewise, asking Elisabeth, "Promise me one thing, Elisabeth. No matter what man is in your life—no matter what happens—we'll spend our last Reno night together." To which Elisabeth replies, "There won't be any man. Nairn, I love you."[91] Nairn and Elisabeth's romance is cut short by Nairn's suicide. Potential lesbian desire (like all female sexual desire outside marriage) is not simply subdued, but made deadly.

Modern marriage that produces lesbians and androgynes becomes the noxious culprit for which divorce is the cure. And ultimately, Reno divorcées are "cured" by becoming (re)diseased. To catch "Reno-itis" is to participate in a constant circulation of Reno gossip, that "drivel about love and marriage."[92]

FIG. 12.8. In *The Women,* marriage ruining seems the particular occupation of working-class women, who cause divorce not by "stealing" men's jobs, but by "stealing" rich husbands from their socialite wives. Mary Haines (Norma Shearer) loses her husband, Stephen, to the ambitious and deceptive perfume clerk, Crystal Allen (Joan Crawford). That Shearer, Crawford, Russell, and the other actors in the film were themselves working women, a point underscored by the fact that the film served as an advertising vehicle for MGM's bevy of female stars, is all the more ironic. After all, Hollywood's working women were often blamed for glamorizing divorce. Here, socialites Sylvia Fowler (Rosalind Russell) and Edith Potter (Phyllis Povah) shop for gossip more than goods. Courtesy of the Academy of Motion Picture Arts and Sciences. *The Women* © 1939 Turner Entertainment Co. A Time Warner Company. All rights reserved.

The virulent "Reno fever," to which all are exposed as they are being Renovated, transforms women into enthusiastic consumers of material goods. A Reno clerk tells Elisabeth, "[Divorcées] all buy clothes just before they go home. It's a fever that gets hold of them. We store clerks all notice it."[93] Renovation and rehabilitation, *Sanierung,* are etymologically linked to curing, the Latin *sanare.*[94] So, finally, to be Reno-vated means not just to remarry, but to be cured by becoming what Ellen Wiley Todd calls a 1930s "revised New Woman," a woman who shops.[95]

Remember, however, that for Gramsci, although the American frontier (or pioneer) spirit enabled Americans to embrace Fordist industrialization more wholly than Europeans, it was also responsible for the modern "moral gap" found among American (divorced and divorcing) women, those "luxury mammals" who threatened to idly consume. Yet female consumerism is precisely the point. Fordism is predicated not simply on a division of labor, but on the creation of a laborer who consumes what (s)he builds. The connection between consumption and femininity has a long and well-charted history in modernity in which consumption becomes simultaneously a gender disease and gender cure.[96] Reno-vation as process seems to mollify this bind, producing a self-surveying and self-regulating consumer.

It now makes sense why MGM's film *The Women* is really about shopping—in salons and restaurants, at perfume counters and fashion shows. Though the women traipse out to a dude ranch in Reno, the train that they take actually sends them *back* to New York and the patriarchy and products they have left. "Mary, listen to the wheels, don't they seem to be saying something," asks saccharine-sweet Peggy Day (Joan Fontaine), who shares a Pullman sleeping berth with Mary Haines. "Don't they seem to be saying, 'Go back. Go back. Go back . . .' The camera closes in and fixes on a close-up of the two women, who cuddle cheek-to-cheek. A moment passes. Mary breaks away and declares to Peggy, "Go back to him."

The train Peggy hears directs her away from the possibility of a supportive (and potentially self-contained) female community in a Reno ranch that the film depicts as far from department stores. Indeed, Peggy's train doesn't reach for the "emergency brake," as Walter Benjamin suggests, but actually moves in reverse. Peggy's train "goes back" to a world where narratives of progress are devoid of independent modern women, where middle-class women join forces only to preserve the middle-class family from women who labor,[97] where women need only reproduce. Inevitably, all the Women do "go back" finally Reno-vated to the east, where they remarry the same or new—but interchangeable—husbands and become mothers and Reno-vated shoppers of mass-produced goods.

What they finally purchase is Reno itself—and their remade selves as its advertisements. If the West is a masculinizing space, then the Reno divorce factory is not simply a feminine place—or even a feminizing place—but a woman, a so-called "gay blond little haven of freedom."[98] Reno comes to allegorize both the feminization of place generally and the degraded and eroticized production of the modern tourist site which sells its notoriety as a commodity.[99] For if the story of 1930s Reno is a story about how gender is produced, remade, and practiced, it is also, not coincidentally, a story about the performative compulsion of making modern place. Place, both gendered and as gender, is made through "imitation," to paraphrase Judith Butler, an imitation for which there is no original and which "may be said to exceed any definitive narrativization."[100] Thus, Reno, amnesiac, though ever in flux, exposes the irreducibility of the performative itself. We know it when we see it. But when we see it, it's not there. Reno, as place, is produced both retroactively and in advance through the instable repetition, approximation, and improvisation of the detritus of generic tropes, in the iteration of recognizable aesthetic, discursive, and material forms, and in the exploitative commodification and codification of those iterations. As a divorce colony, "Reno was losing its old identity, but it was making money. Reno was a prostitute," surmises Elisabeth in *Reno Fever.* "Well, weren't most places?"[101]

NOTES

1. See Charles B. Parmer, *After Divorce?* (New York: A. L. Burt, 1932), 31.
2. Nevada's residency requirement for citizenship, voting, and divorce was the shortest in the nation. Designed in the nineteenth century to benefit a mobile mining population, the lenient legislation took on a new meaning in the first decades of the twentieth century, when an increasing number of easterners—mostly from New York, where the divorce laws were especially stringent—began to quest west to Reno for a "quickie" divorce. The residency requirement was reduced twice, from six months to three months in 1927 and from three months to six weeks in 1931. For more information on Nevada divorce laws, see Glenda Riley, *Divorce: An American Tradition* (New York: Oxford University Press, 1991), 135–38. See also Nelson Manfred Blake, *The Road to Reno: A History of Divorce in the United States* (New York: Macmillan, 1962).
3. The train quest and arrival at the Reno train station are standard tropes in the divorce novel and film genres.
4. Eliot appropriates vernacular tropes, but employs them in order to make a universalizing and transhistorical statement about modernity and its spaces. Indeed, *The Waste Land* seeks to erase the cultural, spatial, and historical particularity of individual place-texts. When *The Waste Land* is read for its vernacular peculiarities, the poem reveals Eliot's collapse of vernacular spaces, such as the English pub, into both Western classical history and Eastern philosophy. The poem sublimates both Eliot's own national identity and those with a history outside imperial Britain who not only contribute to, but have been the victim of Anglo-American industrial modernity's waste. More potently, the poem's appropriation of "all history" as English modernist history and its suggestion that English modernist history is "all history" become a form of imperialism that mimics Britain's cultural imperialism, an imperialism that albeit self-destructively, is nonetheless nostalgically in decline.
5. Doreen Massey, *Space, Place, and Gender* (Minneapolis: University of Minnesota Press, 1994), 137.

6. Massey 171.

7. I refer here specifically to work following David Harvey's influential book, *The Condition of Postmodernity* (Cambridge, MA: Blackwell, 1990). But I also am responding to a larger matrix of British, Canadian, and American geography theory that has dominated the discipline over the past two decades.

8. In *The Architecture of the City,* Aldo Rossi argues that "the city is the locus of the collective memory," and one might say the same of place, which always embodies traces of the past in its present. See *The Architecture of the City* (Cambridge: MIT Press, 1982), 130.

9. Massey points out, for instance, that stable or fixed ideas of place-identity are also "always constructed by reference to [an autochthonous historical] past" (8).

10. Sharon Zukin, "Postmodern Urban Landscapes: Mapping Culture and Power," in *Modernity and Identity,* ed. Scott Lash and Jonathan Friedman (Oxford: Blackwell, 1992), 241.

11. Walter Benjamin, "Paris, Capital of the Nineteenth Century," in *Reflections: Essays, Aphorisms, Autobiographical Writings,* ed. Peter Demetz, trans. Edmund Jephcott (New York: Schocken, 1986), 148.

12. Edward S. Casey, *The Fate of Place: A Philosophical History* (Berkeley: University of California Press, 1997).

13. Casey 339.

14. This essay is a fragment of a longer essay on Reno that will be published in my forthcoming book, *Down in the Dumps: Place, Modernity, and the American Depression.* The longer version contains, among other things, a much more extensive analysis of the reconstruction of frontier mythology that is played out in Reno than is included here.

15. Susan Buck-Morss, *The Dialectics of Seeing: Walter Benjamin and the Arcades Project* (Cambridge: MIT Press, 1991), 92.

16. Under the conditions of "competitive capitalism," speed was only one of the "advertisements" of progress, according to Buck-Morss, who argues that abundance or excess, monumental size, and expansion (industrial and imperial) were also crucial metaphors (91).

17. See Julia Kristeva, *Powers of Horror: An Essay on Abjection,* trans. Leon S. Roudiez (New York: Columbia University Press, 1982), 65.

18. *The Century Dictionary and Cyclopedia,* vol. 9 (New York: Century, 1911). The *Century Dictionary* refers largely to American usage.

19. Max Miller, *Reno* (New York: Dodd, Mead, 1941), 25.

20. Courtesy of the Nevada Historical Society.

21. I take the title for this section from Andreas Huyssen, *After the Great Divide: Modernism, Mass Culture, Postmodernism* (Bloomington: Indiana University Press, 1986). In the late nineteenth and early twentieth centuries, however, Huyssen writes, "the fear of the masses in this age of declining liberalism is

also a fear of women, a fear of nature out of control, a fear of the unconscious, of sexuality, of the loss of identity and stable ego boundaries in the mass" (52). The conflation between woman and mass gets played out in Reno, which is narrated as feminine, hypersexual, and unstable.

22. Gambling did not make as large a contribution to Nevada income until Las Vegas took precedence over the state in the 1950s. In the years just after World War II, gambling was estimated to bring in just $330,000 to the city annually. See Oscar Lewis, *Sagebrush Casinos: The Story of Legal Gambling in Nevada* (Garden City: Doubleday, 1953), 115.

23. "Passion in the Desert," *Fortune,* 9 no. 4 (April 1934): 101. Private rooms could be had for as little as $15 a month. But apartment houses that catered to divorcées usually ranged in 1930 from $50 a month for a tiny efficiency to $200 and up for a suite at the Riverside Hotel. See "Letters from a Richmond Wife in Reno," *Richmond Times Dispatch,* April 6, 1930: 44–45, reprinted in *Washoe Rambler* (Reno: Washoe County Historical Society; n.d.). In later years, chic stays at dude ranches could cost between $30 and $75 a week for meals, lodging, and the use of a saddle horse. Nevada Dude Ranch Association brochure, Chamber of Commerce, Reno. Courtesy of the Nevada Historical Society.

24. Divorce narratives were plentiful in the United States during the late nineteenth and early twentieth centuries, and divorces took place in a variety of locales (particularly Paris) during the nineteenth century. For a summary of some of these works, see James Harwood Barnett, "Divorce and the American Divorce Novel 1858–1937: A Study in Literary Reflections of Social Influences" (Ph.D. diss., University of Pennsylvania, 1939). See also Donald Nelson Koster, "The Theme of Divorce in American Drama, 1871–1939" (Ph.D. diss., University of Pennsylvania, 1942). For an account of some Reno novels, see Ann Ronald, "Reno: Myth, Mystique, or Madness?" in *East of Eden, West of Zion: Essays on Nevada,* ed. Wilbur Shepperson (Reno: University of Nevada Press, 1989), 134–48.

25. Stanley Cavell, *Pursuits of Happiness: The Hollywood Comedy of Remarriage* (Cambridge: Harvard University Press, 1981).

26. Most of these were B-pictures, starring lesser-known actors and filmed on cheap sets. Often they were titled simply, aptly, *Reno.* (Warner Brothers produced several B-films devoted to Reno during the 1930s.) "Reno" films include, among others, *Reno* (Son Art World Pictures, 1930), an adaption of his novel by the same name by Cornelius Vanderbilt Jr., which is notable for location shots of the city; Warner Brothers' *Merry Wives of Reno* (1933), which is a more middle-class version of the classic Reno narrative; *The Women* (1939), MGM's adaption of Clare Boothe's 1937 play by the same name; *The Opposite Sex* (1956), an MGM musical remake of *The Women; Maisie Goes to Reno* (MGM, 1944), a film version of the 1931 Kathleen Norris novel *Second Hand Wife;* John Huston's dystopic western, *The Misfits*

(1961); and *Desert Hearts* (1985), Donna Dietch's adaption of Jane Rule's novel *Desert of the Heart*. Reno is mentioned in many 1930s screwball comedies, including *Libeled Lady*, *Mr. and Mrs. Smith*, and others.

27. For more information on the Pickford divorce and on divorce sensationalism, see John D. Stevens, "Social Utility of Sensational News: Murder and Divorce in the 1920s," *Journalism Quarterly* 62.1 (spring 1985): 53–58. See also Richard Lillard, *Desert Challenge: An Interpretation of Nevada* (New York: Knopf, 1942), 346–47.

28. That year, a total of 183,695 divorces were granted in the United States (17 percent of the married population).

29. Con Ryan, "The City That Sex Built," *True Detective* 39:1 (November 1936): 12–17, 79–82.

30. In Julia E. Johnsen, ed., *Selected Articles on Marriage and Divorce* (New York: H. W. Wilson, 1925), 19–20, 28–39.

31. Alfred Cahen, *Statistical Analysis of American Divorce* (New York: Columbia University Press, 1932), 129.

32. Lillard 330.

33. Sally Springmeyer Zanjani, *The Unspiked Rail: Memoir of a Nevada Rebel* (Reno: University of Nevada Press, 1981), 343.

34. Dorothy Walworth Carmen, *Reno Fever* (New York: Ray Long and Richard R. Smith, 1932), 219.

35. Grace Hegger Lewis, *Half a Loaf* (New York: Horace Liveright, 1931), 337. Although *Half a Loaf* was published in 1931, after the residency requirement was shortened to six weeks, it is a *roman à clef* that describes Grace Hegger Lewis's experience divorcing Sinclair Lewis in the 1920s, before legislation changed.

36. John Hamlin, *Whirlpool of Reno* (New York: Dial Press, 1931), 132.

37. Antonio Gramsci points this out, as I address in this essay, but also see James R. Barrett, "Americanization from the Bottom Up: Immigration and the Remaking of the Working Class in the United States, 1880–1930," in *Discovering America: Essays on the Search for an Identity*, ed. David Thelen and Frederick E. Hoxie (Urbana: University of Illinois Press, 1994), 162–86. For more on the narrative implications of the Taylorization of domesticity, see Martha Banta, *Taylored Lives: Narrative Productions in the Age of Taylor, Veblen, and Ford* (Chicago: University of Chicago Press, 1993).

38. Peter Wollen, "Cinema/Americanism/the Robot," in *Modernity and Mass Culture*, ed. James Naremore and Patrick Brantlinger (Bloomington: Indiana University Press, 1991), 45. See also Antonio Gramsci, "Americanism and Fordism," in *Selections from the Prison Notebooks*, ed. and trans. Quintin Hoare and Geoffrey Nowell Smith (New York: International, 1971).

39. Alice Kessler-Harris, *Out to Work: A History of Wage-Earning Women in the United States* (Oxford: Oxford University Press, 1982), 259.

40. Kessler-Harris 259–61.

41. Kessler-Harris 256. She cites Norman Cousins, "Will Women Lose Their Jobs?" *Current History and Forum* 41 (September 1939): 14.
42. For a summary of these measures, see Kessler-Harris 256–61.
43. Lewis 375.
44. Lewis 377–78. Class dynamics often were complicated as a result. Despite depicting herself as a worker, later in this passage Susan Hale complains of Reno's "social disorder," where "the garage assistant may be the best golfer at the country club, where you play roulette beside the woman who shampoos your hair, where you gossip with the hotel chambermaid who is also getting a divorce" (378).
45. Lewis 387.
46. Parmer 93.
47. Terry Smith, *Making the Modern: Industry, Art and Design in America* (Chicago: University of Chicago Press, 1993), 57.
48. Lillard 341.
49. In "The Truth about Reno" (n.p., n.d.), 24. Divorce-era tourism pamphlet courtesy of the Nevada Historical Society.
50. Carmen 66.
51. Carmen 128.
52. Reproduced with permission from the Judge Bartlett Papers, Special Collections, University of Nevada-Reno Library.
53. Gramsci 302, 297.
54. Gramsci 297–98.
55. Gramsci 306.
56. Gramsci 304, 296.
57. The War Department shut the houses down in 1942. The photo pictured in figure 12.5 was taken shortly after the Stockade closed.
58. For a more detailed account of the history of the Mann Act, see David J. Langum, *Crossing over the Line: Legislating Morality and the Mann Act* (Chicago: University of Chicago Press, 1994).
59. Lewis 371, and "Letters from a Richmond Wife in Reno."
60. Reprinted by permission of Special Collections Department, University of Nevada-Reno.
61. See Mary McCarthy, "Cruel and Barbarous Treatment," in *The Company She Keeps* (1942; New York: Harcourt Brace Jovanovich, 1970), 3.
62. U. E. Harding, *Roads to Reno* (Grand Rapids: Zondervan, 1943), Courtesy of Nevada Historical Society, 25.
63. Michel Foucault, *Discipline and Punish: The Birth of the Prison,* trans. Alan Sheridan (New York: Vintage, 1979), 242. In distinguishing the prison from the nineteenth-century work mill, Foucault actually adopts the managerial model underlying Fordist industrialism. The prisoners of Reno are Fordist laborers as well as detainees. And as we will see, they are the Reno machine's products and cogs. It is not surprising that a metaphor of imprisonment also

underlies many divorce narratives in which divorcées became their own (re)makers.

64. See Lillard 372.
65. Hamlin 129.
66. Stuart Ewen describes this phenomenon in *All Consuming Images: The Politics of Style in Contemporary Culture* (New York: Basic Books, 1988), 244. See especially Ewen's chapter "Form Follows Waste," 233–58.
67. Carmen 130.
68. Carmen 98.
69. Marian Sims, *Call It Freedom* (Philadelphia: J. B. Lippincott, 1937), 14.
70. Hamlin 193.
71. Hamlin 18.
72. Hamlin 61.
73. Rupert Hughes, *No One Man* (New York: Harper and Bros., 1931), 208.
74. Miller 50.
75. Miller 107.
76. "Letters from a Richmond Wife."
77. Carmen 91.
78. Carmen 5.
79. "Letters from a Richmond Wife" 51.
80. Johnsen 19–39.
81. Theodore Roosevelt, "The Strenuous Life," in *The Call of the Wild (1900–1916),* ed. Roderick Nash (New York: George Braziller, 1970), 80.
82. See Peter J. Schmitt, *Back to Nature: The Arcadian Myth in Urban America* (New York: Oxford University Press, 1969). See also Roderick Nash, *The Nervous Generation: American Thought, 1917–1930* (Chicago: Rand McNally, 1970).
83. Lewis 380.
84. Lillard 342.
85. I refer, of course, to those laid out by Claude Lévi-Strauss in *Elementary Structures of Kinship* (Boston: Beacon Press, 1969), and famously critiqued by Gayle Rubin in "The Traffic in Women: Notes Towards a Political Economy of Sex," in *Toward an Anthropology of Women,* ed. Rayna Reiter (New York: Monthly Review Press, 1975), 157–210.
86. Carmen 149.
87. Carmen 149.
88. Carmen 113. Not coincidentally, Ray's dog is named Sappho.
89. I refer to the unscripted alternative sexual economy that is possible whenever "the goods get together," to borrow from Luce Irigaray. See Luce Irigaray, *Speculum of the Other Woman,* trans. Gillian C. Gill (Ithaca: Cornell University Press, 1985). See also Judith Butler, *Gender Trouble: Feminism and the Subversion of Identity* (New York: Routledge, 1990), 41.
90. Carmen 186.

91. Carmen 201.
92. Carmen 150.
93. Carmen 241.
94. Mary Pechinksi, "The Landscape of Memory," in *Drawing Building Text*, ed. Andrea Kahn (New York: Princeton Architectural Press, 1991), 129.
95. See Ellen Wiley Todd, "Art, the 'New Woman,' and Consumer Culture: Kenneth Hayes Miller and Reginald Marsh on Fourteenth Street, 1920–40," in *Gender and American History since 1890*, ed. Barbara Melosh (London: Routledge, 1993), 127–54.
96. See especially Rita Felski, *The Gender of Modernity* (Cambridge: Harvard University Press, 1995), 61–90.
97. In *The Women* that threat is embodied by the indomitable and seductive perfume clerk, Crystal Allen (Joan Crawford).
98. Parmer 30.
99. Doreen Massey, Luce Irigaray, Edward Casey, Elizabeth Grosz, and others point out that place is a gendered and bodily event. As Casey writes, responding to Irigaray, woman becomes "place *as such*, at once physical and metaphysical—without the opportunity to be a sexually specific body/locus that is neither mere 'thing' nor exalted essence" (327). See also Luce Irigaray, "Place, Interval: A Reading of Aristotle, *Physics IV*," in *An Ethics of Sexual Difference*, trans. C. Burke and G. C. Gill (Ithaca: Cornell University Press, 1993). See also Elizabeth Grosz, *Space, Time, and Perversion* (New York: Routledge, 1995).
100. See Judith Butler, "Imitation and Gender Insubordination," in *Inside/Out: Lesbian Theories, Gay Theories* (New York: Routledge, 1991), 13–31.
101. Carmen 37.

POLITICS AND LABOR IN POETRY OF THE FIN DE SIÈCLE AND BEYOND

FRAGMENTS OF AN UNWRITABLE HISTORY

Cary Nelson

For much of this century we have known that poetry is a palimpsest, that it is layered with earlier poems, with the memory of earlier poems and with echoes of poems forgotten that speak through us now unawares. Both the institutions that promote poetry and the multiple audiences for poetry are palimpsests as well—layered with traces of what is treasured and reviled, commemorated and rejected, witnessed and repressed. The space of the contemporary is also a space of memory; it is shaped in part by what we are willing to remember and capable of remembering. Some traces of the poetic past can live again and others it seems cannot, though our own time is never the ultimate test of a poem's viability. There are no ultimate tests; there are only continuing contexts, new openings and foreclosures of opportunity. The privileged status of the present is an illusion, the fool's gold of cultural pride. It will pass.

Yet in the social spaces in which we do live there are contemporary opportunities that are available to us and us alone. The future cannot seize them; only we can. There are, we all know, multiple spaces and multiple audiences. The bookstore audience, the subway audience, the café audience, the classroom audience, the factory audience; all these and other audiences overlap and articulate their own palimpsests, but they are not identical.

This essay takes up not only neglected or forgotten poems but also marginalized audiences for poetry. The essay has a subtitle: "Fragments of an Unwritable History." I mean that invocation of incapacitation to cut several ways: the history I want to narrate is as yet unwritable because we do not have ready to hand either the full range of modern poetic texts taking up the issues of work and its exploitation or the distinctive and ephemeral way the poetry was published and used at various moments by distinct audiences. Furthermore, and equally important, we have not yet widely recognized who the "we" are who would be writing this history. In other words, neither our disciplinary history in relation to remembering and forgetting labor poetry and its rich cultural life nor our present relation to exploited labor is sufficiently present to mind for such a history to be undertaken. This is thus paradoxically (and perhaps necessarily) at once a moment of incapacitation and a moment of opportunity. In presenting these telling fragments of such a history, then, I must also try to position such a hypothetical historiography in its proper contemporaneity. If this seems a little oblique and abstract, that is my intention. I want to withhold clarity on that issue until its proper moment, at the end of what I have to say.

Let me begin, then, with an exceptional text and a notable moment of literary history. The text is the one American poem of protest against abusive working conditions almost universally remembered, remembered not only by literature professors but also, for many years, by the general public. For decades every high school student read it and some still do. The poem, of course, is Edwin Markham's 1899 poem "The Man with the Hoe," first published that January in the *San Francisco Examiner* and soon reprinted in newspaper after newspaper across the country. It was one of several protest poems Markham published and not the only one to receive wide circulation, but its status is nonetheless exceptional. It became one of the anthems of the American labor movement, though in some ways, as I shall show, an atypical one. It also provoked a genuine national debate about its meaning and implications, one of the few times in our history a poem was the subject of such wide discussion and controversy over its proper interpretation. It was admired, attacked, imitated, and satirized repeatedly; it was reprinted in numerous special editions and pamphlets. People argued over its meaning with a dedication usually reserved for specialists. And it is, as it happens, unquestionably the perfect poem to have played the role it played in American culture then and since. One reader wrote to the *Examiner* (March 11, 1899) worried that the poem would lead to "thousands of misguided country youth flocking to our cities," while another a week earlier had castigated it as "the dreamy note of the inaccurate thinker stirred to sentimental sorrow by the appearance of wrong, too careless or unable to distinguish aright the cause of the trouble."

The poem is an explicit response to an oil painting by the French artist Jean-François Millet, one of several paintings on contemporary agricultural working-class subjects Millet produced at the middle of the nineteenth century. It depicts a roughshod farmer or agricultural worker, probably exhausted and certainly leaning forward on his hoe in a flat scrub landscape as yet untamed and unplowed. Just when Markham first saw the painting or a reproduction of it is unclear; he gave conflicting accounts during the course of his life.[1] In any case, in one of the many glorious ironies surrounding this text and its dissemination and reception, it is worth noting that the painting was first brought to San Francisco, across the bay from Markham's Oakland home, in 1891, by Mrs. William H. Crocker, the wife of the heir to a fortune amassed by one of California's railroad barons. In fact, Charles Crocker had been inspired virtually to enslave Chinese laborers to help build the transcontinental railroad. Millet's painting had provoked something of a scandal when it was first exhibited in Paris; the artist was accused of being both an anarchist and a socialist. But within a few decades its sentiments seemed acceptable to a wealthy San Francisco patron of the arts. She presumably did not see her family's economic history reflected in the overburdened laborer who fills the central third of the canvas.

While the painting was the decisive stimulus for the poem, Markham also clearly had in mind the great American labor struggles of the preceding decades, notably the coal strikes of the 1860s and 1870s, the rail strikes of the 1870s, 1880s, and 1890s, and such historic events as the Haymarket massacre of 1886 and the Homestead, Pennsylvania, strike of steel and iron workers in 1892. The poem is effective in marshaling moral outrage and linking it to literariness on workers' behalf. Its indictment of the ravages wrought by those in power was decisive for its time, in part because Markham treated exploitation as a violation of God's will. The poem is equally effective in issuing a broad revolutionary warning to capitalists and politicians.

"The Man with the Hoe" also crystallizes a hundred years of American labor protest poetry and song and finally takes much of its message to a broad national audience. Markham no doubt knew some of that tradition, at least John Greenleaf Whittier's 1850 *Songs of Labor and Other Poems* if perhaps not more ephemeral texts like John McIlvaine's 1799 broadside poem "Address to the Journeymen Cordwainers L. B. of Philadelphia": "Cordwainers! Arouse! The time has come / When our rights should be fully protected."[2] But the tradition in America had long been persistently dual: professional writers taking up labor issues and agitating in verse for decent wages and working conditions and working people themselves producing their own rousing songs and poems. Philip Foner's marvelous 1975 *American Labor Songs of the Nineteenth Century* is the most comprehensive collection.[3] Indeed we cannot really know whether Millet's man with the hoe is too crushed to speak or has in fact stepped forward to tell us his story.

For Markham, however, the question is settled. "Stolid and stunned, a brother to the ox," the laborer does not utter a word. His presence is riveting but altogether determined by his victimhood. He has no culture of his own. We see "the emptiness of ages in his face." The laborer's imaged form speaks volumes, but he himself is mute. Despite the fact that the subaltern in this case had repeatedly spoken, Markham retroactively declares him unable to speak. The history of indigenous labor protest and song is forgotten and Markham instead speaks on behalf of mute suffering. It is the poem's address that raises the possibility "this dumb Terror shall reply to God, / After the silence of the centuries." The relentless othering of the worker persists throughout the poem despite Markham's evident outrage at his exploitation. It is that consistent othering of the worker—"Who loosened and let down this brutal jaw? . . . Whose breath blew out the light within this brain"—that made the poem widely acceptable at the time and indeed earned it partial acceptance within the dominant culture's literary canon for so long. As a mute object of sympathy, the worker has no role in establishing the meaning of his suffering.

The impulse to dehumanize or infantilize victims, to deny the existence of their alternative cultures, was hardly new. Americans had done it with Native Americans and with their African American slaves. Nor was awareness of the risks of a racial othering and dehumanization unknown. It is one of the themes of abolitionist poetry and it surfaces again in turn-of-the-century poetry protesting the slaughter by American troops of the people of the Philippines, poems contemporary with Markham's.[4] But the appeal of such power relationships leads us repeatedly to reenact them. In Markham's case, ironically, the implicit reaffirmation of such hierarchies helped give the poem remarkable cultural warrant.

Given the poem's huge and instant success it is not surprising that the *Examiner* should want to commemorate its pride in being the first place to publish it. So that same year (1899) the San Francisco paper reinvented the poem as an elaborately illustrated supplement to its Sunday edition. It is by far the most memorable reprinting of "The Man with the Hoe." Already oddly positioned within William Randolph Hearst's sometimes melodramatic newspaper, the poem has its inner tensions further exacerbated by the *Examiner's* richly contradictory fin-de-siècle presentation. Notoriously imperialist, the paper was also by turns sensationalist and antagonistic toward the barons of monopoly capitalism. Markham, wholly in sympathy with the plight of exploited workers, was nonetheless uneasy with organized labor and its aggressive and collective agency from below. All this, curiously, is enhanced by the poem's new incarnation.

The poem is printed on a large sheet of heavy paper about twenty-two inches wide. This broadside in turn had a series of images printed on its reverse side before it was folded in half so as to make the poem into a folder with a front and back cover. Unashamed of stylistic contradiction or cheerfully eclectic, the accompanying images mix elements of a Victorian scrapbook with art nouveau and Edwardian book illustration. An oval portrait of Markham, framed in laurel leaves, shares the cover with an engraving after the central figure in Millet's painting. On the back cover a skeletal grim reaper rides a horse of the apocalypse down a road past poplar trees straining against the wind. Ringing the blade of his scythe is a crown that once perhaps sat on a head of state. Above the image two lines heralding a future of radical change and retribution are quoted from Markham: "When whirlwinds of rebellion shake the world? How will it be with Kingdoms and with Kings."

Inside, the poem is presented in two floral frames on opposite sides of the sheet. On the lower left, a bat-winged figure, part satyr and part serpent, lies vanquished, his ill-gotten crown beside him on the ground. To his left another snake, this one itself satanically crowned, coils itself around the tripod of science and a book of the law, showing us how culture can be allied with the forces of repression but also potentially evoking a populist anti-intellectualism. Above all this, hovering in midair, is the agent of their undoing: a goddess of liberty wielding a flaming sword and a wreath of laurel. On her shoulders an adoring eagle is perched to serve as her wings. Below her the river of life, above her the clouds, sweep in harmonious brush strokes toward a redeemed destiny.

Nowhere in the illustration are there factory owners or workers to be seen. Indeed the illustration interprets the poem as a symbolic confrontation between abstract, mythological forces. Human agency is imaged out of it. If this presentation underlines the poem's high cultural ambitions, then, it also underwrites its relevance to eternal values rather than immediate (and potentially threatening) historical contexts. It is a version of the poem, needless to say, that the English profession would find more suitable, a properly transcendentalizing interpretation of the poem's idealizations. In a way, it is the version of the poem that generations of high school teachers have found fittingly literary. Contemporary

struggles, inequities at arm's distance, are not the concern of this sort of literariness, which awaits a paradise to be regained in the fullness of time but accessible now in unsullied aestheticism.

It was different, very different, among the poets struggling for union representation, a living wage, an eight-hour day. But poems had their use in those struggles too, and some were written or treasured in the midst of them. When the IWW published a commemorative volume recounting the union's history, *Twenty Five Years of Industrial Unionism* (1930), it was a poem, Covington Hall's "La Belle Sansculotte," that the union chose for a frontispiece. Unlike Markham in "The Man with the Hoe," Hall makes his female figure the spirit of class revolution, the spirit expressing the need to overthrow the masters and the spirit guaranteeing the triumph of revolutionary values. Over and over again it was poetry the union movement chose to represent its core values most succinctly and to suggest their long historical reach. Consider another fragment of literary history, this one distributed twenty-four years after Markham's "Man with the Hoe."

The year is 1923, the city Chicago. A national hub for rail transportation, Chicago's commercial and political significance is not in question. Nor is its status as a center of union activity in doubt. But the rail unions were hampered by multiple and divided representation. Hence the amalgamation movement.

In February a mass meeting is planned to galvanize the effort. To build

FIG. 13.2. A 1923 poem card advertising a union organizing meeting and promoting attendance with "St. Peter and the Scab." Author's collection.

St. Peter and the Scab

St. Peter stood guard at the golden gate
With solemn mien and air sedate,
When up at the top of the golden stair
A shrouded figure ascended there,
Applied for admission. He came and stood
Before St. Peter, so great and good,
In hope the City of Peace to win,
And asked St. Peter to let him in.

St. Peter said with a gleam in his eye,
"Who is tending this gate, sir, you or I?
I've heard of you and your gift of gab;
You are what is known on earth as a scab."
Thereupon he arose in his stature tall
And pressed a button upon the wall,
And said to the imp who answered the bell:
"Escort this fellow around to Hell."

"Tell Satan to give him a seat alone
On a red-hot griddle up near the throne;
But stay, e'en the Devil can't stand the smell
Of a cooking scab on a griddle in Hell.
It would cause a revolt, a strike, I know,
If I sent you down to the imps below.
Go back to your masters on earth and tell
That they don't even want a scab in Hell."
[Over]

UNION PRESS 483 ◀━▶ 2003 N. California Ave.

CARY NELSON

attendance a small purple card, just over three by five inches, is printed and distributed to members and interested parties. The card in question had its day— Sunday, February 25, 1923, to be precise—and then most copies were presumably disposed of or lost. This is in any case the only copy I have seen.

A number of things are interesting about the card, including the presence of William Z. Foster as a speaker, Foster in the days when he was not only a national labor leader but also a secret member of the American Communist Party, a party he would later head. The speakers' names appear on one side of the card, along with the time and place of the meeting and other pertinent information. The other side of the card may be somewhat of a surprise to those more familiar with recent union history. It is occupied by a poem, an irreverent, upbeat, cheeky poem about strike breakers, "scabs," and their status in this life and hereafter. Some would call it doggerel, and, if that is the case, the text displays no internal evidence of anticipatory embarrassment at that designation. The poem, which draws on a tradition of literary encounters with St. Peter, is, as it were, altogether enthusiastic about being what it is:

ST. PETER AND THE SCAB

St. Peter stood guard at the golden gate
With solemn mien and air sedate,
When up at the top of the golden stair
A shrouded figure ascended there,
Applied for admission. He came and stood
Before St. Peter, so great and good,
In hope the City of Peace to win,
And asked St. Peter to let him in.

St. Peter said with a gleam in his eye,
"Who is tending this gate, sir, you or I?
I've heard of you and your gift of gab;
You are what is known on earth as a scab."
Thereupon he arose in his stature tall
And pressed a button upon the wall,
And said to the imp who answered the bell:
"Escort this fellow around to Hell."

"Tell Satan to give him a seat alone
On a red-hot griddle up near the throne;
But stay, e'en the Devil can't stand the smell
Of a cooking scab on a griddle in Hell.

It would cause a revolt, a strike, I know,
If I sent you down to the imps below.
Go back to your masters on earth and tell
That they don't even want a scab in Hell."

The poem is published without an author's name because it voices collective rather than uniquely held or subjective values. Its authorship, in effect, is transferrable; it is offered to its readers and they are offered its site of enunciation. Read it aloud, stand with those whose history its sentiments evoke, and it becomes your poem. And if it is your poem, surely you will want to come to the meeting where many of the poem's other readers or authors will gather together. If you feel hailed by the poem, you should feel hailed by the amalgamation movement. And you can feel pride and pleasure in answering the call. The meeting, indeed, is the place where the poem will be read aloud, not necessarily in a literal performance of its words but in a material enactment of its attendant politics and values.

We know, of course, as the people who printed this combination poem card and meeting notice also no doubt knew, that the IWW's *Songs of the Workers* was among its most effective recruiting devices. Following a series of poems cards, the pamphlet *Songs of the Workers* was first published in 1909; it gave new words to familiar tunes and thereby extended general political and economic meaning to workers' individual experiences and drew them to collective action.

At times of crisis or mass action, the IWW continued to print poem cards, such as the poem card "Political Prisoners," which dates from the 1921–22 amnesty campaign that followed the infamous Red Scare after World War I, when most of the IWW's leaders and many of its members were in prison. Both the poem and the illustration are by one of those prisoners, Eugene Barnett, who was framed and convicted after American Legion members stormed an IWW hall in Centralia, Washington, in 1919. It was the IWW victims, not the lawless legion members, who were punished. One IWW member was castrated and lynched, while seven others (including Barnett) received long prison sentences in April 1920. Barnett, who was born in 1891 and later became an ardent member of both the United Mine Workers and the IWW, served over eleven years of a twenty-five- to forty-year sentence. He wrote the poem and drew the illustration while in prison, and it was distributed anonymously to symbolize all those imprisoned unjustly and build support for their release. Issuing it anonymously also reinforced the IWW's determination not to file individual pleas for clemency; they sought freedom for all political prisoners, though Barnett was in fact released when his wife was dying of cancer. The illustration for "Political Prisoners," which was later collected in Barnett's 1940

FIG. 13.3. Eugene Barnett's 1921 poem card. Author's collection.

pamphlet *Nature's Woodland Bowers,* shows the American eagle itself behind bars, and the text describes the same fundamental betrayal of principle:

> Hail! the American eagle,
> Emblem of men once free,
> Languishing now in prison
> In its own loved country.
> Though its heart is broken,

Its spirit is defiant still;
Though prisons break its body
They cannot break its will.

It is not just members of a movement but the basic spirit of democracy that has been imprisoned. The poetic soul of the country—its very will to freedom—is now imperiled. There was an audience of IWW members, families, and sympathizers ready for this message. When the card could get through the mails, carried in the very belly of a corrupt federal system, it could reach out to recruit a still wider audience.

"St. Peter and the Scab," then, issued not long after Barnett's poem card, invokes and extends a tradition in the American labor movement in which poems and songs help workers interpret and articulate their lives and draw them toward solidarity with their peers. Over several decades, the labor movement used poetry not only to build or unify membership but also to educate workers and to restate core beliefs and values. Poetry was the ongoing discourse of pride in the labor movement's universal common sense. It elevated that common sense to a principle of identity and solidarity.

The repeated use of poetry in this way also had effects in other domains. Certainly it helped define more broadly the social uses to which poetry could be put. It thus made poetry "available" to other groups and constituencies that might successfully use poems to build solidarity among existing members and reach out to new ones. If we want to know what poetry meant to audiences in the 1890s, or the 1920s, we need to preserve and have access to objects like these.[5] For they supplement our inevitable speculation about the inherent meanings of texts with evidence of their socially constructed and contingent meaning, with the actual use to which poems were put. Now incredibly rare, all these cards and broadsides make contributions to the historical meaning of the genre. If we want to know what poetry meant in 1923, in other words, we should not let the poem card of "St Peter and the Scab" be swept aside in the wake of the issue of the *Dial* containing T. S. Eliot's *The Waste Land,* published but one year earlier.

Although "St. Peter and the Scab" has no lack of irony, it is not quite the sort of irony English professors have historically valued. And the poem is nothing if not unambiguous about its cultural stance and who its friends and enemies are, despite the fact that the scab serves both as a figure for the devil in disguise and a disguise even the devil would reject. The poem, as one might expect, has left no trace in academic literary history. But it is an interesting example of how poetry was used at a certain moment in time and within a certain tradition.

Let me offer a still more specialized example. If both "The Man with the

Union Poem

By J. P. Thompson

You cannot be a Union Man,
  No matter how you try,
Unless you think in terms of "We,"
  Instead of terms of "I."

Labor Speaks

By Unknown Worker

I built your ships and your railroads,
  And worked in your factories and mines;
I built the good roads that you ride on,
  And crushed your ripe grapes into wine.

I built the fine house that you live in,
  And gathered the grain for your bread;
I worked late at nights on your garments,
  And printed the fine books that your read.

I linked two great oceans together,
  And spanned your rivers with steel,
I built your towering skyscrapers,
  And also your automobile.

Wherever there is progress you will find me,
  For the world without me could not live,
And yet you seek to destroy me
  With the meagre pittance you give.

I am master of field and of factories,
  I am mighty and you are but few,
So, no longer will I bow into submission,
  I am Labor and I ask for my due.

ISSUED BY THE

Vancouver Branch

of the

Industrial
Workers of the World

VANCOUVER, B. C.

Price **5** Cents

FIG. 13.4. A poem card from Rudolph Blum's scrapbook (1916). Author's collection.

Hoe" and "St. Peter and the Scab" were public uses of poetry, my next example is partly a more private one, specifically a nine-by-eleven-and-a-half-inch scrapbook kept between 1916 and 1918. It was compiled in Pittsburgh, Pennsylvania, most likely by one Rudolph Blum, who was twenty years old in 1916. I purchased it from a rare book dealer in Massachusetts for $125 in 1994. The dealer had found it in another bookshop in a box of mixed materials from various sources.

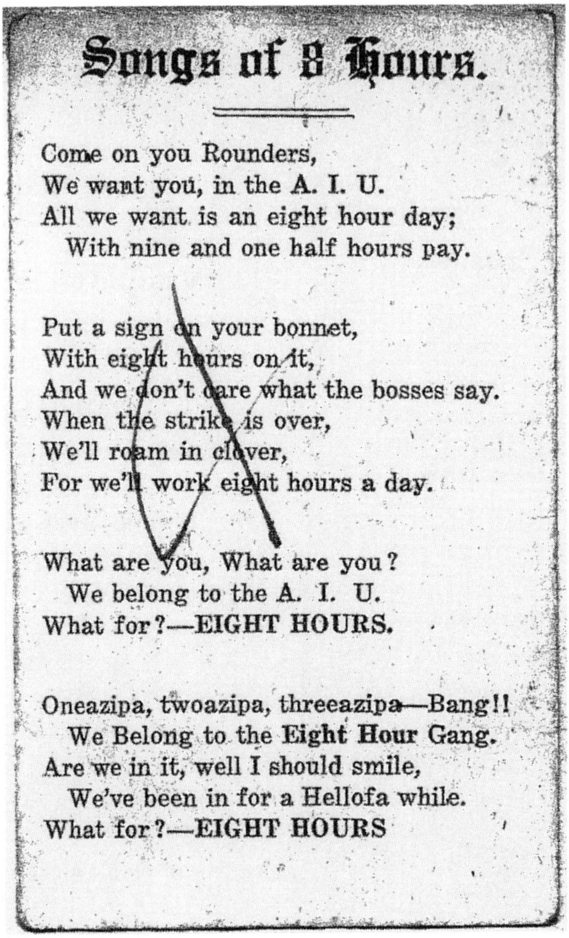

FIG. 13.5. A poem card from Blum's scrapbook. Author's collection.

Following a fragmentary handwritten table of contents listing some of the items to follow and a holograph page reflecting on the realities of modern labor ("To one who has worked amid the crashing din and terrific heat of the steel mills or the tomb like dark and silence of the coal mines. . . . We might well term the modern industrial plants as 'penal institutions' where the working class is serving a life sentence"), the rest of the scrapbook is effectively divided in two halves. The first half includes news clippings, union broadsides, and personal notes, along with the smallest poem card I have yet seen, "Songs of 8 Hours," about four by two and a half inches with four tiny stanzas printed on it .

Remember that at the beginning of that decade, in 1910, 75 percent of

American workers put in a twelve-hour day and nearly a third labored seven days a week. The campaign for the eight-hour day was one of the rallying points for union activity, and this little poem card was one of its organizing devices, small enough to be concealed in the palm of your hand and passed secretly from hand to hand as workers greeted one another at a factory. It was a talisman for utopian yearnings embedded in the struggle for basic rights and sane practices in the workplace:

> Put a sign on your bonnet,
> With eight hours on it,
> And we don't care what the bosses say.
> When the strike is over,
> We'll roam in clover,
> For we'll work eight hours a day.

But I am getting ahead of my story. The second half of the scrapbook is something like a compendium of values, loyalties, and interests. It gathers together the collector's core beliefs and social concerns, and it does so in the form of a fairly substantial personal poetry anthology. Sixty-two poems are clipped from newspapers and three are present in typescript, along with eight assorted editorials, news stories, and prose parables. Like the news stories, notices, and handwritten notes of the first half of the scrapbook, the poems are layered on top of one another in overlapping sequence like the scales of a fish. And the pages are machine pleated, perhaps to facilitate this overlapping technique. The pleated and layered physical form of the scrapbook is not unusual for the period. One can find similar scrapbooks collecting cards or invitations. Blum, then, is reinvigorating a commonplace domestic form with political energy.

The scrapbook is framed temporally by two events in Rudolph Blum's life, both arrests for political activity, the first in 1916, the second in 1918. In April and May of 1916 a strike at the Westinghouse steelworks was on the verge of spreading to other plants in Pittsburgh. The possibility of a general city-wide strike was on everyone's mind. Rudolph Blum, county secretary of the Socialist Party and an IWW sympathizer, was one of the leaders of a march that went from plant to plant to build solidarity. On May 1, steel workers at Braddock rose up to demand an eight-hour day as well, and the following day the march arrived from the city's east. It was met by gunfire from the steel trust guards and when the resulting chaos passed, three workers were dead and forty wounded. Three strike leaders, including Blum, were arrested and charged not only with inciting to riot but also, incredibly, as accessories to murder. It was a judicial scene to be repeated in Centralia three years later. In this case only the first

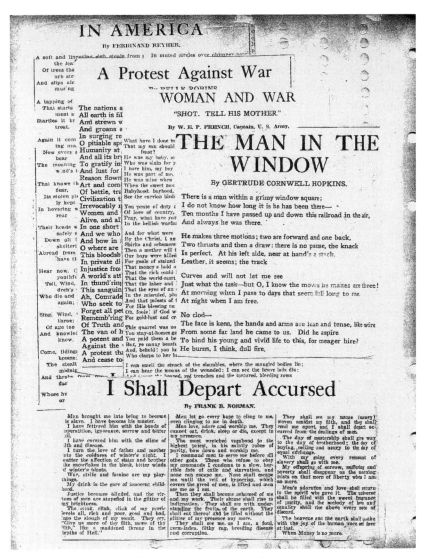

FIG. 13.6. A layered page from Blum's scrapbook. Author's collection.

charge held, and Blum was sentenced to eighteen months in Pittsburgh's notorious county jail. On his release he proceeded to agitate against United States participation in World War I. That brought him to the attention of the Justice Department. An August 1918 newspaper clipping in the scrapbook describes Rudolph and his older brother John, now twenty-two and twenty-four years old respectively, as Austrians and reports that they are being held in the Northside police station as "dangerous alien enemies."

The two arrests—for union organizing and antiwar activism—hang over the poems as well. For the poems are mostly prolabor or antiwar. They thus gather together and articulate the paired ideals underlying Blum's politics and his social activism. Both halves of the book, then, are autobiographical, the first focused on events, the second on values. Some writers with surviving reputations are included here, represented by Edwin Markham's "Man's Right to Work," Carl Sandburg's "Murmurings in a Field Hospital," Louis Ginsberg's "Marching," a portion of a Whitman poem, and reprints of Thomas Carlyle's "What Is War?" and Sir Thomas Moore's "Modern Moloch." Edgar Guest's "Made in America," with its confidence in a workplace where "no slavery darkens the scene," is buried, sardonically, under other poems. But the mostly forgotten poets of the IWW and of the feminist antiwar movement—Estelle Kobrin, Jane Burr, Helen Parsons, Daisy Gill, Meta Stern, Katherine Meserole, Miriam Teichner, and others—are more heavily represented.[6]

Belle Robins in "A Protest against War" urges "the workers of all lands take heed / And cease to slay each other for their masters' greed." Henry Tichenor in "This Night of Death Where Demons Dwell" calls on "comrades of the warring lands" to join hands and "make this the masters' last damned war." Clement Wood in "To Labor" urges workers to "rouse from this mad obedience." S. A. De Witt, represented here with several poems, in "At Last" heralds the moment when "the ghetto ghosts, the outlawed of the earth," will "unite to set the whole world free." Finally, Donald Crocker in "The I.W.W." praises these "sons of the sansculottes" who return "blow for blow" to "the civilization that has cast them out," and two poets eulogize the murdered IWW leader Frank Little. The poems were all public, of course, as most or all were printed in newspapers at the time, from *Women's Sphere* to the *New York Call.* But their use here—to reinforce and deepen Blum's beliefs, whether as aids to reflection, goads to action, or figures for a political community under assault—is more personal and tells us, by implication, something of what such poetry may have meant to modern men and women in the labor movement of the teens.

Blum's scrapbook is thus a model for a way of reading and a record of a certain sort of activist literary memory. Things done and things believed are yoked together, rhymed, in the conceptual agency granted one reader by the poems he collected. He does not simply read serially but rather reads to gather together texts appropriate to a coherently constructed identity. The presence of the poems in radical newspapers of course suggests that other readers used poems the way Blum did whether or not they kept scrapbooks. Thus Blum's scrapbook comes to us as the record of an audience for poetry at the center of the great labor struggles in the early part of the century.

A decade later, with the stock market crash of 1929 and the ensuing Great Depression, the lines between part-time working-class poets and professional writers became increasingly blurred. Newspapers and journals sought out worker poets, and many poets who might have had white-collar jobs found themselves unemployed, doing manual labor, or deeply involved in labor activism. Already sporadically in place for decades, a dialogue—a kind of call-and-response chorus of voices—between professional and unprofessional labor poets began to increase and diversify. They published in some of the same venues, echoed themes and images in one another's work, worked together on cultural and political projects, and soon constituted a collective cultural presence and force. When Edwin Rolfe in 1931 opened his poem "Credo" with lines defining the necessities of collective action, "To welcome multitudes—the miracle of deeds / performed in unison—the mind must first renounce the fiction of the self," he was echoing the poet whose succinct, complementary credo was distributed by the Wobblies on that dark red poem card. It is J. P. Thompson's "Union Poem," only four lines long:

> You cannot be a Union Man,
>   No matter how you try,
> Unless you think in terms of "We,"
>   Instead of terms of "I."

Within only a few years the links between these traditions were so well established they could be commemorated as a key feature of the progressive landscape. Thus when Local 89 of the International Ladies Garment Workers Union, the Italian Dressmakers' Union, met in 1934 in New York at a dinner to celebrate its fifteenth anniversary, they issued a 250-page, red felt–covered, gold-embossed book to mark the occasion. It included greetings from Norman Thomas and Albert Einstein and essays on labor history. Poems, both in Italian and English, also played a major role in the book, and some were beautifully illustrated in color, including two by one of the local's founders, Arturo Giovannitti. Framed on a murder charge during the 1912 Lawrence strike, Giovannitti was one of the legendary figures of the American labor movement. A special color plate honors him at the book's close, and his poems "Te Deum of Labor" and "When the Great Day Came" are given special prominence.

It is the second of these, written in 1934, that I want to comment on briefly, in part because it takes up somewhat the same gendered dichotomy represented in the illustrations for Markham's "Man with the Hoe." "When the Great Day

O THEE *whose rule of sweat and strife*
Is like the sun's impassive course,
Eternal principle of life,
Instinct and will, idea and force,

Essence of each created thing,
Breath of all things that are to be,
God Labor, what we cannot sing
Let our hands do in praise of thee.

Thy law is just, thy burthen light,
Thy grace the sole reward we ask,
To serve thee is a freeman's right,
To obey thee a lordly task,

For all are godlike who fulfill
Thy least desire, thy hardest rule,
And, brain or hand, obey thy will
Through an old thought with a new tool.

Thine everlasting toil combines
All that is good and true and fair:
The sooty demons in the mines,
The grim archangels in the air,

And those who wreath thy brow with roses
Or rear thy towers have but one goal;
Damnation or apotheosis,
Thou art the measure of our soul.

The winds blow forth thy fierce commands
And lo! the swift tides ebb and flow,
Thou smilest and on barren lands
The flowers bloom, the harvests grow;

FIG. 13.7. The first page of Arturo Giovanitti's poem "Te Deum of Labor," from a 1934 union anniversary dinner. Author's collection.

Came" has the long-line incantatory quality of many of Giovannitti's most successful poems. Part biblical, part Whitmanesque, it is also strikingly feminist and antiracist. It begins, in imitation of the opening of Genesis, as a creation poem, but it is actually about the creation of human culture and its ruling divisions. Deeds, he writes, were symbolically assigned a male gender, ideals a female one, and deeds, often free of redeeming values, have ruled the day ever since.

Only when these dichotomies are overturned, when "she who is twirling the spindle and swaying the loom shall go forth into the fields," when "he who warms his hairy hands in the entrails of his foe shall croon a lullaby and rock a cradle at dusk" will we see "the Ideal triumph and the Deed become her manservant forever." It will happen, he argues, when workers take matters into their own hands, when they answer in action the feminized call to principle. "She stands," he concludes,

> In the noonday of the world, upon the ramparts of time,
> Calling, calling, calling,
> Calling to the white man and the yellow man and the black man with the
>   wild shouts of her mouth
> To rise and stand up together,
> To rise and stand up together against nature and destiny,
> To rise and stand up together in one holy fraternity,
> To rise and conquer the earth
> With labor and love and mirth,
> One race, one tongue, one birth,
> One dream of eternity.

Fragments of a nearly forgotten tradition, these pieces of material history help show us that literariness has been historically entwined with real labor struggles. Those relations are, among other things, part of the proper focus of a more comprehensive literary historiography. Yet I cannot help but think that the exclusion of labor struggles from our sense of what is properly poetic is neither accidental nor without real consequences. As we now move decisively into an era when higher education depends more and more heavily on exploited labor, we are often not only blind to the working conditions and rewards of graduate assistants, unemployed Ph.D.'s, and part-time teachers; some tenured faculty are also outraged that their higher pursuits should be interrupted by unseemly complaints from below. "Graduate students," one English professor at Yale sarcastically remarked recently, "have apparently decided to call themselves workers." Contempt for workers might be less easily mustered if we had sustained our awareness of their place in literary history, if we remembered that literariness had served labor throughout our history.

As it is, the discipline's repression of the memory of labor poetry now facilitates the exploitation of untenurable, underpaid, underemployed, or unemployable academic workers. It was not planned that way, since these memories faded in the boom times of the immediate decades following the Second World War. But the repression of these cultural memories was part of the general encapsulation and depoliticization of the academy that took place under Mc-Carthyism. Now one of its consequences is our inability even to recognize let alone confront the social impact of our own employment practices. We have been confronted repeatedly with supposed academic leaders who have collectively shown less articulate empathy toward exploited part-time or unemployed Ph.D.'s than the average American shows toward a stray dog. The impoverished literary history we have constructed and honored is hardly the only reason for that display of ignorance and insensitivity, but it has helped make it possible. Yet as often happens, an increasingly exploitive work environment—sham apprenticeship programs for graduate students, subminimum wages for part-time faculty—has opened a moment of opportunity in which we can recognize the historical basis of our present blindness. This essay occupies such a moment of opportunity. It is time simultaneously to transform our memory of the past and our actions in the present.

NOTES

1. For an account of how the poem came to be written and a summary of contemporary reactions to it, see Lois Rather, *The Man with the Hoe* (Oakland: Rather Press, 1977).

2. "Address to the Journeymen Cordwainers L. B. of Philadelphia," composed of fourteen four-line stanzas, is reproduced in Philip S. Foner, *American Labor Songs of the Nineteenth Century* (Urbana: University of Illinois Press, 1975), 12.

3. For contemporary poems about work, see Peter Oresick and Nicholas Coles, eds., *Working Classics: Poems on Industrial Life* (Urbana: University of Illinois Press, 1990); and Nicholas Coles and Peter Oresick, *For a Living: The Poetry of Work* (Urbana: University of Illinois Press, 1995).

4. For analyses of political poems about the war in the Philippines, see Aaron Kramer, *The Prophetic Tradition in American Poetry, 1835–1900* (Rutherford: Fairleigh Dickinson University Press, 1968); and Cary Nelson, "Modern Poems We Have Wanted to Forget," *Cultural Studies* 6, no. 2 (May 1992): 170–97.

5. What would a specialized library collection look like that might contain the objects I describe in this essay, and what else might be there? The poem card might appear in a labor collection; indeed, the major IWW collection at Wayne State University has several poem cards, though fewer than I have in my living room. So too might the quite wonderful American poetry broadside collection at Brown University, though as it happens its representation of labor poetry broadsides is rather weak. Disciplinary encouragement to collect either the poem cards or the scrapbook I describe below would not

likely be forthcoming. Few labor historians see labor poetry as more than illustrative local color. The overwhelming majority of English professors would consider these poems worthless; indeed, I read several to colleagues, who looked at me either blankly or anxiously. But even if your typical English professor thought such poems worth preserving, he or she would likely think of them as texts. If the poem on the poem card appeared in a newspaper, the newspaper is all you would need. The poem card would simply be a duplication. The scrapbook would be equally irrelevant. If the primary issue is the meaning supposedly inhering in the texts, then the uses people and institutions made of them are unimportant.

Cultural studies suggests instead that we should be interested in the relational nature of meaning and in how meaning was materially realized in actual practices. There is no other way to come to know a historical period. These objects, cards, and scrapbook certainly give us material uses of poetry; moreover, they suggest relations with other discursive practices while by no means fully exemplifying them. In both cases, then, an appropriate collection would include not only diverse material on the labor movements surrounding the card and the scrapbook but also other elements of the subcultures and historical moments they embody. In the case of the antiwar poetry in the scrapbook, it would be hard to imagine anything from the period not relevant. Certainly the proper context for the study of these antiwar poems would include all other prowar and antiwar contemporary discourses. But anything that could help us construct the time, the context, and related institutional and individual practices is worthy of collection.

Given the disciplinary reluctance to see the past this way, it may well be that librarians on their own are better suited to this sort of collecting, though only if they can break out of the constraints that disciplines impose. In any case, the aim, then, is for libraries to develop in-depth collections around particular cultural milieus. For a labor collection I'd want personal and institutional archives, books and ephemera, oral histories, statistical records, film, literature, music, and the graphic arts. I'd want anything and everything that gave meaning to work in a given time. That, I believe, is the direction in which recent cultural theory points us, though few librarians are altogether ready for the mixed museum, junk shop, and library that would result. It certainly means that texts alone, while a library's primary concern, cannot be the only objects of a library's acquisitiveness.

6. See Mark Van Wienen's fine chapter on American World War I antiwar poetry in his *Poets and Partisans* (New York: Cambridge University Press, 1997).

CONTRIBUTORS

MARIA DAMON teaches poetry and poetics at the University of Minnesota. She is the author of *The Dark End of the Street: Margins in American Vanguard Poetry* and with Miekal And, coauthor of *Literature Nation,* a poetic hypertext. She is a member of the National Writers Union.

WALTER KALAIDJIAN teaches in the English Department of Emory University and is the author of *Understanding Theodore Roethke, Languages of Liberation: The Social Text in Contemporary American Poetry,* and *American Culture between the Wars: Revisionary Modernism and Postmodern Critique.* He is completing a new book on modern American poetry, trauma, and extreme experience.

WALTER K. LEW has taught Asian American and Korean literatures at Brown, Cornell, and Columbia Universities. Presently in the doctoral program of UCLA's East Asian Languages and Cultures Department, his forthcoming books include *Kŏri: The Beacon Press Anthology of Korean American Fiction* (coedited with Heinz Insu Fenkl), *Crazy Melon and Chinese Apple: The Poems of Frances Chung*, and a volume of his own poetry and intermedia texts. Lew has edited the poetry anthology, *Premonitions: The Kaya Anthology of New Asian North American Poetry*, and his *Excerpts from: ΔIKTH DIKTE, for DICTEE* is on the work of Theresa Hak Kyung Cha. Lew has been awarded fellowships by the National Endowment for the Arts, New York State Council on the Arts, and Association for Asian Studies, and his multimedia performance pieces have been staged at international film festivals.

JANET LYON is an associate professor of English at Pennsylvania State University and the author of *Manifestoes: Provocations of the Modern*. She is currently at work on a book, *The Perfect Hostess: Salons and Modernity*.

WILLIAM J. MAXWELL is an associate professor of English and Criticism and Interpretive Theory at the University of Illinois at Urbana-Champaign, where he teaches modern American and African-American literature. In 1999, he published *New Negro, Old Left: African-American Writing and Communism between the Wars*. Currently, he is working on an edition of the collected poems of Claude McKay.

CARY NELSON is Jubilee Professor of Liberal Arts and Sciences at the University of Illinois at Urbana-Champaign. His most recent books are *Academic Keywords: A Devil's Dictionary for Higher Education*, *Anthology of Modern American Poetry*, and *Revolutionary Memory: Recovering the Poetry of the American Left*.

DAVID G. NICHOLLS is Chair of the Department of American Culture and Literature at Bilkent University in Turkey, where he also teaches in the Program in Cultures, Civilizations, and Ideas. He has held Rockefeller, Mellon, and Fulbright Fellowships. He is the author of *Conjuring the Folk: Forms of Modernity in African America* and is coeditor of *The Penguin New Writing in India*.

PAULA RABINOWITZ is a professor of English at the University of Minnesota, where she teaches courses on film, feminism, and modern American culture. She is currently a senior fellow at Oregon State University Center for the Humanities, and has been a resident scholar at the Rockefeller Foundation in Bellagio, Italy, and Fulbright professor of American Studies at Terza Universita degli Studi di Roma. She is the coeditor, with Charlotte Nekola, of *Writing Red: An Anthology of American Women Writers, 1930–1940,* and the author of *Labor and Desire: Women's Revolutionary Fiction in Depression America* and *They Must Be Represented: The Politics of Documentary.* She is completing two books, *Frida, Miss O'Keeffe and M.E.: Painting, Feminism and the Marketing of Nationalism,* and *Black and White and Noir: Pulping Twentieth-Century American Politics.*

DANIEL ROSENBERG is an assistant professor of History in the Robert D. Clark Honors College at the University of Oregon. His work concerns the history of language and epistemology since the Enlightenment. He is a past fellow at both the University of California Humanities Research Institute and the Center for Critical Analysis of Contemporary Culture at Rutgers University. He is currently at work on a book entitled *Senses of the Past: Language, Epistemology, and the Problem of Origins in the Enlightenment.*

MARLON B. ROSS is a professor of English and in the Center for Afroamerican and African Studies at the University of Michigan, Ann Arbor. He has published work in eighteenth- and nineteenth-century British literature, twentieth-century African American literature and culture, literary historiography, gender and queer theory, and gay and lesbian studies.

JANI SCANDURA is an assistant professor of English at the University of Minnesota, where she teaches modern and postmodern literatures and film, cultural studies, and theory. She is currently completing a book, *Down in the Dumps: Place, Modernity, and the American Depression,* and is at work on new project that investigates the interplay between sound, modernity, popular culture, and political praxis.

KATHLEEN STEWART teaches anthropology and cultural studies at the University of Texas, Austin. She is the author of *A Space on the Side of the Road: Cultural Poetics in an "Other" America* and various articles on the U.S. political imaginary, including work on conspiracy theory, the aesthetics of everyday life, the impact of late capitalism on practices, sensibilities, and affects, and questions of desire, risk and banality. She is currently completing a book, *The Private Life of Public Culture,* which is based on multi-sited fieldwork in Las Vegas, Orange County, Texas, and New England.

MICHAEL THURSTON is an assistant professor of English at Smith College. He is the author of *Making Something Happen: American Political Poetry between the World Wars.* He is currently at work on a book on twentieth-century lyric poetry as an ethical practice.

JULIA A. WALKER is an assistant professor of English at the University of Illinois at Urbana-Champaign where she specializes in modern drama. She received her Ph.D. from Duke University and has taught at the College of William and Mary. Currently, she is writing a book entitled *Bodies, Voices, Words: Modernism and the American Stage,* and has written articles on contemporary performance theory, nineteenth-century acting, and the early plays of Eugene O'Neill.

INDEX

Haunting, 1, 3–4, 7, 15n. 22, 22, 83; of America, by submerged native peoples, 211; in post-genocidal poetics, 117–19; as traces of mass murder, 110; transitions between the virtual and the actual, 25. *See also* Body, absent; Dreams; Folk, spectral; Folk song, as collective haunting; History and memory; Incorporation; Memory; Mourning; Phantom; Poetry; Repression; Trauma; Unconscious

Hayashi Tatsuo, 179

Hearst, William Randolph, 9, 272

Heine, Heinrich, 136

Hemingway, Ernest, 108, 110; in Smyrna, 110–11

Herskovitz, Melville, 134, 140–41, 145, 147, 148

Hiroshima, 4

History, 81; art as, 210; in *Cane*, 169n. 16; and feminist archaeology, 195, 196; and feminist identity, 196; homosexual, revisionism in, 215n. 32; and modernism, 4; philosophy of, 17n. 56; and progress, 238–41. *See also* History and memory; Intellectual history; Literary history; Social science; *and specific nations and nationalities*

History and memory, 82, 268–69; 286–87; forgetting, 111–16, 127–28; slavery's shadow in Harlem Renaissance, 232–34. *See also* Memory; Poetry; Repression; Trauma

Hitchcock, Alfred, 87, 200

Hitler, Adolf, 112, 199

Hollywood, and modernism, 4. *See also* Celebrity(ies); Film; Mass culture; Media; Popular culture

Holocaust, 4, 13n. 15, 82, 111, 112, 115–16, 119, 120, 122, 143. *See also* Genocide

Homosexuality, in Reno, 258

Hoover, Herbert, and Hoover Dam, 99n. 1

Hoover Dam, 81, 84–106; and propaganda, 98; as symbol, 101n. 19

Horkheimer, Max, 9, 206, 207

Huggins, Nathan, 221

Hughes, Langston, 224, 228, 229, 233

Humanitarianism: *See* Globalization

Hunt, Violet, London salon of, 34

Hurston, Zora Neale, 141, 228, 229, 233

Huston, John, 263–64n. 26

Hutcheon, Linda, 14n. 18

Hutchinson, George, 221–22

Huyssen, Andreas, 9, 14n. 19, 262–63n. 21

Hybridity/hybridization, 230–233; colonization as planting, 179; and cultures East and West, 178–84. *See also* Assimilation; Grafting; Language; Nativism

Hydropathes, the, 36

Icon/legend. *See* Celebrity(ies)

Idealism. *See* Progress

Identity. *See* Assimilation; Ethnicity; Feminism, and national identity; Grafting; Hybridity/hybridization; Immigration; Migration; Nationalism; Nativism; New Negro; New Woman

"If We Must Die" (McKay), 227–29

Im Hwa, 179

Immigration, 7, 8, 16n. 45; as transplantation, 178–82. *See also* Americanization; Assimilation; Legislation

Immigration Act of 1924, 187n. 24

Imperialism, 192, 224; British, 261n. 4; cultural, of the U.S., 200; Japanese, 179, 188n. 40, 188–89n. 43, 189n. 47; and Markham, 272–73; of *San Francisco Examiner*, 272–73

Incohérents, the, 36

Incorporation, 19, 83, 210; and American history, 6; in crisis of substantiation, 132n. 55; cultural, 82; as distinct from hybridization, 6; as distinct from introjection, 6–7; and forgetting, 6; and haunting, 7; of history and place, by Carr, Kahlo, and O'Keeffe, 211; and image, 3; and melancholy, 7; and modernity, 6; and mourning, 6–7, 13n. 13; and repression, 7; and trauma, 118–19, 128; and utterances, 131n. 42. *See also* Body; Dreams; Fantasy;

Haunting; History and memory; Melancholia; Memory; Modernism; Modernity; Mourning; Phantom; Poetry; Repression; Trauma

Incorporation, industrial, 9. *See also* Capital/capitalism; Progress

Industry, 9. *See also* Capital/capitalism

Insanity. *See* Madness

Institute of Turkish Studies, 115

Intellectual history: and genocide, 112; Jewish, 134–150; and modernism, 107–8; and modernization, in China, Japan, Korea, 178–82. *See also* Literary criticism

Interdependency, hemispheric. *See* Globalization

International Ladies Garment Workers Union, 284

Internationalism, African American, 222. *See also* Globalization

Internet. *See* World Wide Web

Invisibility. *See* History and memory; Repression

Irigaray, Luce, 266n. 89, 267n. 99

IWW (International Workers of the World), 74, 273, 276, 281, 283, 284; *Songs of the Workers*, 276

Jameson, Fredric, 14n. 19, 76

Japan, 16n. 45, 177, 179, 188n. 40, 188–89n. 43, 189n. 47. *See also* Imperialism; Nationalism

Jazz, 31, 32, 34, 36, 37, 38, 192. *See also* Black culture; Blues; Folk song; Music

Jewishness, 133–50; and language, 136, 143–46; Stein's attitude toward her own, 134, 142, 143–46; universalized by Freud, 148; and womanishness, 138, 142–46. *See also* Genocide; Holocaust; Language, Nazism; Race; Racism

Jews, 7, 37, 83; prejudice towards in U.S., 113; and scapegoating, 122

Jim Crow, 20, 48–49, 53, 61, 161

Johnson, Jack, 64

Johnson, James P., 229

Johnson, James Weldon, 228

Jones, Florence Embry, 34

Joplin, Janice, 215n. 32

Journalism. *See* Newspapers; Popular culture

Joyce, James, 136

Judaism, relation to Christianity, 137–38

Justice. *See* Legislation

Kahlo, Frida, 192–218; autobiography of, 204

Kalaidjian, Walter, 14n. 15

Kallen, Horace, 8–9

Kang, Younghill, 84, 171–90; *East Goes West: The Making of an Oriental Yankee*, 172–76, 178, 180

Kemal, Mustafa, 113

Kennedy, John F., 1, 3, 11n. 2

Kennedy, John Jr., 1, 3, 11nn. 1, 2, 13n. 12

Kessler, Harry, 32, 40

Kim, Elaine H., 173, 175, 176, 180, 187–88n. 23

Kirby, Jack Temple, 153, 158

Kitchen Mechanic's Revue, A (Razaf), 229–33

Kobrin, Estelle, 283

Korea, 171–90

Korean Americans, and representation of Korea in Kang's work, 176–78

Kracauer, Siegfried, 25

Kramer, Hilton, 213n. 1

Kusami, Yayo, 216–17n. 50

Kwangju Student Uprising of November 1929, 177–78

Labor, 223; African American, 232, 233; and African American art, 231–32; and alienation, 192; and the Harlem Renaissance, 229; history, resources, not adequately collected, 287–88n. 5; gendered divisions and migration, 192; practices in 1910, 280–81; *See also* Gender; Labor; Labor movement; Legislation; Race and labor; Unemployment; Women and labor; Workers

Labor movement: American, 192, 229, 269–86; poetry of, 192, 286–87. *See also* Labor

LaCapra, Dominick, 13n. 15
Landscape: of desire, of maternal, erotic space, in painting of Carr, Kahlo, and O'Keeffe, 206; in self-portraits of Kahlo, 198, 201; Southern, 155–58, 164, 166–67. *See* Feminism, and national identity; Geography
Lane, William "Juba," 40
Langer, William L., 114
Language: abstraction in poetry avoids threatening realities, 272–73; as commodity, 145; in *East Goes West* (Kang), 175–76, 180–84, 190n. 57; hybridity in Kang's cross-cultural expression, 182–84; of New Negro militancy, 227–28; and social categories, 142; Stein's practice as Jewish (adrift), 135, 142–48; in Toomer's *Cane*, 151–70; Yiddish, as homeland in itself, 142–43. *See also* Autobiography; Expressive culture movement; Folk song; Jewishness, and language; Literary criticism; Literary history; Poetry; Speech; Technology, as universal language exemplified in Hoover Dam; Writing
Lash, Scott, 15n. 21
Las Vegas, 263n. 22; and Hoover Dam, 88, 96, 98, 105–6n. 60
Latour, Bruno, 22
Lawrence, D. H., 210
Lawrence, 1912 strike in, 284
Legislation: and Armenian genocide, 113–16, 125; Equal Rights Amendment advocated by O'Keeffe, 201; Federal Economy Act (1932), 24; Immigration Act of 1924, 187n. 24; Mann Act of 1910, limiting women's mobility to prevent "white slavery," 251, 265n. 58; in Nevada, regarding divorce, 243, 261n. 2
Lenin, V. I., 216n. 48, 231
Lesbianism. *See* Homosexuality, in Reno; Reno, Nevada; Sexuality
Letterman, David, 211
Lévi-Strauss, Claude, 266n. 85
Lewis, David Levering, 221, 235n. 11
Lewis, Grace Hegger, *Half a Loaf* as

roman à clef of, 244, 246, 247, 257, 265n. 44
Lewis, Sinclair, 242, 244, 264n. 35
Liang Quichao, 178–79, 188n. 40, 188–89n. 43; social Darwinism of, 178
Libeled Lady (film), 264n. 26
Life, 199, 203
Lifton, Robert Jay, 112, 115–16
Lincoln, Abraham, 222
Literary criticism, 9–10, 20; of Kang's work, 180, 187–88n. 23; marginalizing of *East Goes West*, 175–77
Literary history, 9–10, 196; and activist literary memory, 283–84; African American, 219–37; antiperformative bias in, 69; Brer Rabbit tradition, 225–26; and drama, 76; of Korea, contributions by Kang, 177–78; and labor, 268–88; and literary memory, 268–69, 286–87; and material history, 284, 286, 287–88n. 5; and Razaf, 226–34. *See also* Intellectual history
Literature. *See* Autobiography; Language; Intellectual history; Literary history; Poetry; Writing
Little, Frank, 283
Livesey, Dorothy, 196, 197
Locke, Alain, 59, 192; as anthologizer of *The New Negro*, 224, 225, 229, 231, 234
Lombroso, Cesare, 136, 139
London, Jack, 210
Lowry, Heath, 115
Luce, Henry, 9, 199
Lynching, 49–50, 161, 165, 170n. 34. *See also* Jim Crow; Race, riots is America, as viewed by a Korean immigrant; Racism
Lyotard, Jean-François, 14nn. 16, 17

Madagascar, 222–23
Madness, 39–40; in Breton's *Nadja*, 46n. 33; Jewish and otherwise, 139–40; as the fate of independent women, 255. *See also* Melancholia; Trauma
Madonna, 193, 206, 212
Maisie Goes to Reno (film), 263n. 26

Perkins, Maxwell, 84, 173–75, 181, 182, 183
Pétain, Henri Philippe, 134
Pfister, Joel, 76
Phantom, 13n. 9; as agent of unconscious content, 116–20; as exorcism, 130n. 38; public, Armenian genocide as, 128; and trauma, 116–20. *See also* Dreams; Fantasy; Folk song, as collective haunting; Folk, spectral; Haunting; Incorporation; Mourning
Photography: of Hoover Dam, and its symbolism, 105n. 57; of landscape, 198, 208
Picasso, Pablo, 206
Pickens, William, 20, 50–64
Pickford, Mary, 243
Place. *See* Body, place as; Geography; Landscape
Pluralism. *See* Nationalism
Poetry, 70–72, 78–79n. 11, 82; card, as talisman, 281; ephemerality of, 269–86; and history, 119; and labor, 192; of labor movement, 269–86; of Claude McKay, 228; New Negro, 219–37; political, 270–71, 278, 283; and trauma, 117–20, 123–28. *See also* Feminism; Folk song; Haunting; Incorporation; Language; Mourning; Performance, of labor poetry; Razak, Andy; Repression
Pogrom. *See* Genocide; Trauma
Popular culture, 39; absorbing art, 199; and high culture, 14n. 19; and literary criticism, 10; and mass consumption/mass production of art, 206; Reno narratives and films, 242–44. *See* Blues; Culture; Folk song; Folktale; Jazz; Media; Music; Poetry
Porter, Cole, 232
Porter, Katherine Anne, 242
Postmodernism, 4, 12n. 5, 14nn. 16, 17, 18, 19, 15n. 29; emergence of, imbricated with modernism, 108; and genocide, 116; and modernity, 4, 13n. 15, 14nn. 16, 17, 18, 19, 20, 15nn. 20, 21, 22, 29

Pound, Ezra, 44n. 18, 108–9
Power: corporate, 9; and gender, 55; and Hoover Dam, 87, 88, 90, 98; and machines, 25; and race, 55; in Reno, 248; rivers compared to dams, 103n. 39
Presley, Elvis, and Hoover Dam, 88, 101–2
Primitivism: 30–33, 37–40, 45n. 20; of the dancing of Josephine Baker, 30, 32, 33, 36, 40; and modernism, 30, 36. *See also* Dance; Performance
Print media. *See* Media; Newspapers
Prison/imprisonment: 276; divorce factory as, 265–66n. 63; of Kang, 177, 276; of labor activist, 281–82; political, its effect, 278
Production. *See* Capital/capitalism; Economics; Industry; Mass production; Reproduction, mechanical
Progress, 239, 240–42; African American, 49, 51–55; Chinese tradition seen as incapable of, by Lian Qichao, 178–79; as collective opposition to racism, 184; genocide as underside of, 108; and Jewishness, 143–45; and liberalism, 137–38; and modernity, 6; re-viewed by Gertrude Stein, 195; and trains, 25. *See also* Modernism; Modernity; Modernization
Progressive Era, and masculinity, 55
Proletariat, of Harlem, in its renaissance, 233. *See also* Labor; Workers
Prostitution, legal, in Reno, 251. *See also* Reno, Nevada; Women and labor
Pullman porters, 61–62

Quat'z'Arts, Les, 36
Queer: male colonists in Reno seen as, 258; resonance with Gertrude Stein, 133. *See also* Homosexuality, in Reno

Race, 48–64, 84; and Josephine Baker, 37, 38; and dance of Baker, 42, 43; and geography of Jews, 147; Jews as not constituting a, 146; in Paris, 37, 46n. 31; riots, in America, as viewed by Korean immigrant, 184; and social science, 139–41; and U.S. modernism, 30. *See also* Ethnicity; Masculinity

Race and labor, 52, 54, 56–67, 82, 192, 225; at Hoover Dam, 96. *See also* Labor; Workers

Racialism, 19, 31, 33, 37, 41, 42; and Josephine Baker, 36, 37; and colonialism, 40; defined, 31; in France, 31. *See also* Race

Racial trespassing, 49, 52, 58, 61–63

Racism: against Asian Americans, 174, 181; countered by music, 233; defined, 31; in France, 31; and genocidal imperialism, 140; at Hoover Dam, 96, 99; literary, antiracist protests against, 219–37; philosophical, 154; shocking to immigrants to America, 175, 183–84; of Tin Pan Alley, 223; urban, 164; in the U.S., 29. *See also* African American(s); Armenian people; Asian Americans; Assimilation; Ethnicity; Genocide; Genocide, Armenian; Holocaust; Jews; Lynching; Other/Othering/otherness; Nationalism; Nazism; Turkey

Radio City Music Hall, 204, 216n. 48

Railroad, 20, 49, 61; camp as a leveler, 56. *See also* Trains

Randolph, A. Philip, 223

Ransom, John Crowe ("Criticism, Inc."), 9–10

Raper, Arthur, 156–57, 161, 166

Razaf, Andy, 192, 219–37; "Black and Blue," 219–20; at the *Crusader*, 224; *Hot Chocolates*, 220; jazz/blues songs by, 223; poetry of, published, 223; socialism of, and the Harlem Renaissance, 220–34

Razafkeriefo, Andreamentania (Malagasy name of Razaf), 222

Red Scare, and imprisonment of most IWW leaders, 276

Red Summer, 221, 227

Reno (film), 263n. 26

Reno, Nevada, 192, 238–67. *See also* Body, place as; Divorce; Geography; New Woman

Representation: linguistic, and trauma, 112, 116, 126; and masks/masquerading of blacks, 220, 227; and masks of whiteface form, 227; and trauma, 82; utterances exceeding, 125, 126

Repression, 4, 6, 7; and academia, 286–87; of Communism as precondition of Harlem Renaissance, 221; and genocide, 107–32; literary representation of, 110, 111, 112; as modernism's definitive response to trauma, 111; modernity's post-traumatic stance, 111, 112; and poetry, 118–19, 123–28; and repetition, 112. *See also* Haunting; History and memory; Incorporation; Memory; Mourning; Phantom; Poetry; Trauma; Unconscious

Reproduction, biological, 158–61, 163; and divorce, 254–56; and song, 152, 163–64; and South, 156, 163

Reproduction, mechanical: and alienation of mass production, 207; and art, 194, 196; and the cult of the trademark, 207; of images, 205. *See also* Industry; Media; Photography

Revenant. *See* Haunting; Phantom

Revisionism. *See* History and memory; Memory; Repression

Revue. *See* Performance; Theater

Revue nègre, La, 29–30, 32, 33, 38–39

Rhee, Syngman, 178

Rich, Adrienne, 195–96; 205, 208, 209, 210

Richmond Times, 256

Rivera, Diego, 196, 197, 198, 201, 203, 204, 216n. 48

Rivera, Lupe, 206; memoir of Freda Kahlo, 206

Robeson, Paul, 223

Robins, Belle, 283

Rockefeller, John D., 216n. 48

Rockefeller Center, 204, 216n. 4

Rolfe, Edwin, 284

Roman à clef. See Lewis, Grace Hegger, *Half a Loaf* as roman a clef of

Roosevelt, Franklin Delano, and Hoover Dam, 91, 99n. 1

Roosevelt, Theodore, 16n. 45, 256
Rose, Phyllis, 37, 38, 39
Ross, Edward A., 7–8
Rubenstein, Charlotte Streifer, 213n. 1
Rubin, Gayle, 266n. 85
Rukeyser, Muriel, 125, 197
Rule, Jane, 263–64n. 26
Rural. *See* South, the

Salis, Rodolphe, 37
Salons, 20, 34, 35, 36, 39; compared to
 cabarets, 36; as European bourgeois
 tradition, 34, 35; and the Harlem Re-
 naissance, 45n. 22
Sandburg, Carl, 283
Sanford, John, 210, 217n. 64
San Francisco Examiner, 269–73
Santayana, George, 70, 71, 72
Santner, Eric, 13n. 15
Sarraut, Albert, 44n. 19
Savagery. *See* Primitivism
Scapegoating. *See* Ethnicity; Nationalism;
 Other/othering/otherness
Schnitzler, Arthur, 139
Schultz, Dutch, 220
Science. *See* Economics; Social science;
 Technology
Segalen, Victor, 33
Seton, Mary, 196
Sex: and alienation, 205; and artistic
 identity, 203; incompatibility and di-
 vorce, 244; and race, 63–64. *See also*
 Gender; Prostitution; Sexuality;
 Women
Sexism. *See* Feminism; Gender; New
 Woman; Patriarchy; Women and labor
Sexuality, 20, 137, 138, 139, 142, 145;
 African American, 64; and art, 232; of
 Josephine Baker, 46n. 33; female desire
 seen as deadly outside marriage, 258; of
 O'Keeffe, in photographs, 202; and
 U.S. modernism, 30. *See also* Gender;
 Homosexuality, in Reno; Prostitution;
 Reno, Nevada; Sex; Women's sexuality
Shakespeare, William, 70
Shapiro, Miriam, 211
Shew, William D., 248–49

Shuffle Along, 31
Silencing. *See* Genocide, silencing of;
 Repression
Sinatra, Frank, 223
Singer, Barry, 220
Slavery, 166; African American historical
 burden, 224; white, 251
Slaves/slavery: legacy of, 152; and utopian
 politics of transfiguration, 232
Smalls's Paradise, 229, 233
Smith, Bessie, 223
Smith, Patti, 195, 205, 213
Smith, Roger W., 116
Smith, Susan Harris, 69
Social Darwinism of Liang Quichao, 178
Socialism, 192, 200, 201; and African
 Americans, 255. *See also* Black bolshe-
 vism; Communist Party;
 Marxism/Marxists
Social science: genocidal implications of,
 140; and Judaism, 134–50; as a term,
 136. *See also* Anthropology
Sommer, Doris, 215n. 15
Song. *See* Folk song; Music; Poetry
South, the, 82–83; hope of renewal, 166;
 rural, 152–70
Soviet Union, 192
Space. *See* Geography
Speech, 20; African American, 227–28;
 and alienation, 74; and Americaniza-
 tion, 8; and expression, 71; and the
 Hoover Dam, 86–91, 96–98; and tech-
 nology, 68–69. *See also* Expressive cul-
 ture movement; Language
Spurr, David, 44n. 19
Stalin, Joseph, 141
Standard Oil, 113
State. *See also* Genocide, Armenian;
 Genocide, state-administered
Stein, Gertrude, 5, 35, 82, 94, 133–50,
 193, 195, 205; salon of, 34, 39;
 *Painted Lace, and Other Pieces,
 1914–1937*, 134, 141–42, 145–48
Stern, Meta, 283
Stewart, Susan, 203
Stieglitz, Alfred, 197, 198, 199, 202, 203,
 204, 205, 208

INDEX

Vietnam Unknown Soldier, as gesture toward modernism, 12n. 5
Vietnam Veterans Memorial, 12nn. 3, 5
Vietnam War, 2, 177; Unknown Soldier of, 1

Walker, A'Lelia, New York salon of, 34
Wallace, Maurice, 42
Waller, Fats, 220, 223
Waller, Jennie Maria, 222–23
Waller, John Louis, 222
War. See Body, absent; Mourning; Trauma; Vietnam War; World War I; World War II
Washington, Booker T., 20, 50–51, 53, 54, 57–60, 227, 228, 233. See also Assimilation, as a goal of black culture, and the Harlem Renaissance; Representation, and masks/masquerading of blacks
Waste. See Trash
Weininger, Otto, 82, 134, 136, 148
Werfel, Franz, 113. See also Forty Days of the Musa Dagh, The (film)
West, American, as counterpoint to the East, 239, 256–58
West, Nathanael, 210
"West cure," 256–61
Westernization. See Americanization; Assimilation; China; Grafting; Hybridity/hybridization; Modernization
Westminster, Statutes of (1931), 199
White, Hayden, 13n. 15, 41
Whitman, Walt, 283
Whittier, John Greenleaf, 270–71
Wigley, Mark, 7
Wigman, Mary, 41
Williams, William Carlos, 125
Wilson, Edmund, 215n. 30
Wilson, Woodrow, 109, 110
Winant, Howard, 44n. 15
Wittgenstein, Ludwig, 136
Wobblies. See IWW (International Workers of the World)
Wolfe, Thomas, 174
Wollen, Peter, 245
Women: American, and the modern "moral gap," 259–60; artists, 194, 215n. 30; and biological reproduction, 161; condemned as anti-progressive, 138, 144; divorced, as trash, 255; divorced, recommodified in Reno, 255; independent, as prostitutes, 254–55; and marriage and divorce, 256, 258; and maternity, 197; and migrant men, 160, 170n. 29; and modernism, 193–218; as place, 267n. 99; in rural South, 158–61; womanish writing, 142, 145–46. See also Divorce; Feminism; Femininity; Gender; Jewishness, and womanishness; Marriage; Painting; Patriarchy; Prostitution, legal, in Reno; Reproduction, biological; Sexuality; Women and labor; Women's sexuality
Women, The (film), 243, 253, 254, 259, Fig. 12.8, 260. See also Brokaw, Clare
Women and labor, 244, 245–46, 251, 260. See also Gender; Labor; Prostitution, legal, in Reno; Women
Women's sexuality, 38, 192. See also Femininity; Feminism; Prostitution, legal, in Reno; Sex; Sexuality; Women
Women's Sphere, 283
Wood, Clement, 283
Woolf, Virginia, 108, 111–12, 196; Mrs. Dalloway, 112–13
Workers, 156–58; in Harlem, 230. See also Labor
Workers/proletariat, in the Harlem Renaissance, 225
World War I, 2, 12n. 6, 31, 108–32; and Gertrude Stein, 145. See also Fifteenth Infantry; Turkey, and World War I
World War II, 2; and Gertrude Stein, 134
World Wide Web: offering of Carr, Kahlo, and O'Keeffe establishes feminist modernism, 212; museums digitized for, 206
Writing: calligraphy, as cultural roots, 181; and meaning, 142–48; and melancholia, 144–45; womanish, 142, 145–46. See also Autobiography; History and memory; Intellectual history;